Beginning

C

Ivor Horton

Wrox Press Ltd.®

Beginning C

Published by Wrox Press Ltd,
Arden House, 1102 Warwick Road, Acocks Green, Birmingham B27 9BH, UK.
Printed in Canada
5 6 7 8 9 TRI 00 99

ISBN 1-861001-142

Trademark Acknowledgements

Credits

Author
Ivor Horton

Editors
Dominic Shakeshaft
Jon Hill

Managing Editor
John Franklin

Technical Reviewers
Claus Laud
Terry Walker
Ian Cargill

Beta Testers
Paul Wilson
Mark Holmes
Gordon Rogers

Cover/Design/Layout
Andrew Guillaume
Graham Butler

Index
Simon Gilks

About the Author

Ivor Horton has taught a wide range of programming languages and has brought computer programming to a wide and varied audience. Ivor believes that programming is easier than it looks to people who haven't tried it, and he enjoys trying to make the subject more approachable for beginners.

Ivor's background is in mathematics. He spent many years teaching at IBM, and ran project teams for large scale applications and installations.

Ivor has lived in France, Germany and England, and has travelled extensively through the USA. Ivor's hobbies include photography, growing exotic plants and trying to follow the latest ideas in modern physics.

Beginning C

Table Of Contents

Beginning

C

Introduction

Welcome to *Beginning C*. With this book you will become a competent C programmer.

My objective in this book is to minimize what, in my judgment, are the three main hurdles the aspiring programmer must face: getting to grips with the jargon that pervades every programming language, understanding the *use* of the language elements (as opposed to what they are), and appreciating how the language is applied in a practical context.

Jargon is an invaluable and virtually indispensable means of communication for the competent amateur as well as the expert professional, so it can't be avoided. My approach is to ensure that the beginner understands what the jargon means and gets comfortable with using it in context. In that way, they can use the documentation that comes along with most programming products more effectively, and can also feel competent to read and learn from the literature that surrounds most programming languages.

Comprehending the syntax and effects of the language elements are obviously essential to learning a language, but I believe illustrating *how* the language features work and *how* they are used are equally important. Rather than just use code fragments, I always try to provide the reader with practical working examples that show the relationship of each language feature to specific problems. These can then be a basis for experimentation, to see at first hand the effects of changing the code in various ways.

The practical context needs to go beyond the mechanics of applying individual language elements. To help the beginner gain the competence and confidence to develop their own applications, I aim to provide them with an insight into how things work in combination and on a larger scale than a simple example with a few lines of code. That's why I've ended each chapter with a real life application of what you've learnt. This takes you through a problem and finds its solution in a C program. The great thing about this is that you'll learn to design real programs and manage real code. During the process, you'll also learn how language features can be applied together.

I think it's important for the beginner to realize three things that are true for most programming languages. Firstly, there *is* a lot to it, but this means there will be a greater sense of satisfaction when you've succeeded. Secondly, it's great fun, so you really will enjoy it. Thirdly, it's a lot easier than you think, so you positively *will* make it.

How to Use This Book

Because I believe in the hands-on approach, you'll be writing your first programs almost immediately. Every chapter has several programs to put the theory into practice, and these examples are key to the book. I advise you to type in as many as possible, since the very act of typing in programs is a tremendous aid to remembering the language elements. When you get a program to work for the first time, particularly when you're trying to solve your own problems, you'll find that the great sense of accomplishment and progress make it all worthwhile.

We'll start off quite gently, but as we begin to gain momentum each chapter will cover quite a lot of ground, so take your time and experiment with your own ideas. Try modifying the programs and see what you can do: that's when it gets really interesting. And don't be afraid to try anything out: if you don't understand how something works, just type in a few variations and see what happens. A good approach is to read each chapter through, to get an idea of its scope, and then go back to work through all the examples.

You might find the end of chapter programs quite hard. Don't worry if it isn't all completely clear on the first try. There are bound to be bits that you find difficult to understand at first, because they often apply what you've learned to quite complicated problems. And if you really get stuck, all the end of chapter programs are designed so that you can skip them, carry on with the next chapter, and come back to them later. You can even go through the book to the end without worrying about them. The point of these programs is that they're a useful resource for you - even when you've finished the book.

Who is This Book For?

Beginning C is designed to teach you how to write useful programs as quickly and as easily as possible. This is the tutorial for you, if:

- You're a newcomer to programming, and you want to plunge straight in to the C language - learning about programming and writing C programs right from the start.

- You've done a little bit of programming before, so you understand the concepts behind it - maybe you've used BASIC or PASCAL. Now you're keen to learn C and develop your programming skills further.

This book does not assume any previous programming knowledge on your part, but it does move quickly and easily from the basics to the real meat of the subject. By the end of *Beginning C*, you'll have a thorough grounding in programming the C language.

What You Need To Use This Book

To use this book, you'll need a computer with a C compiler installed, so you can run the examples. There are plenty of C compilers on the market to choose from, and some shareware versions are available over the Internet. Most C++ compilers available today will also compile C, and if you have a version of Microsoft's Visual C++ compiler, then the examples in this book can be compiled as console applications.

More importantly, however, to get the most out of this book you need a willingness to learn, the desire to succeed, and the determination to master the C programming language. You might believe that doing all this is going to be difficult, but I think you'll be surprised by how much you can achieve. I'll help you to start experimenting on you own and to become a successful programmer.

Conventions Used

We use a number of different styles of text and layout in the book to help differentiate between the different kinds of information. Here are examples of the styles we use and an explanation of what they mean.

> *These boxes hold important, not-to-be forgotten, mission critical details which are directly relevant to the surrounding text.*

Background information, asides and references appear in text like this.

- **Important Words** are in a bold type font.
- Words that appear on the screen, such as menu options, are a similar font to the one used on screen, for example, the File menu.
- Keys that you press on the keyboard, like *Ctrl* and *Enter*, are in italics.
- All filenames are in this style: **videos.mdb**.
- Function names look like this: **printf()**.
- We'll be using different types of 'brackets' in the program code. The difference is very important and they are not interchangeable. We will refer to the symbols ( ) as parentheses, the symbols { } as braces and the symbols [ ] as square brackets.
- Code which is new, important or relevant to the current discussion will be presented like this:

```
void main()
{
    cout << "Beginning C";
}
```

whereas code you've seen before, or which has little to do with the matter at hand, looks like this:

```
void main()
{
    cout << "Beginning C";
}
```

Tell Us What You Think

We've tried to make this book as accurate and enjoyable for you as possible, but what really matters is what the book actually does for you. Please let us know your views, whether positive or negative, either by returning the reply card in the back of the book or by contacting us at Wrox Press using either of the following methods:

e-mail:	**feedback@wrox.com**
Internet:	**http://www.wrox.com/**
	http://www.wrox.co.uk/

Source Code and Keeping Up-to-date

We try to keep the prices of our books reasonable, so instead of providing disks, we make the source code for our books available on our web sites:

http://www.wrox.com/

http://www.wrox.co.uk/

We've done everything we can to ensure your download is as fast as possible. The code is also available via FTP:

ftp://ftp.wrox.com

ftp://ftp.wrox.co.uk

If you don't have access to the Internet, then we can provide a disk for a nominal fee to cover postage and packing.

Errata & Updates

We've made every effort to make sure there are no errors in the text or the code. However, to err is human and as such we recognize the need to keep you, the reader, informed of any mistakes as they're spotted and amended.

While you're visiting our web site, please make use of our *Errata* page that's dedicated to fixing any small errors in the book, or offering new ways around a problem and its solution. Errata sheets are available for all our books - please download them, or take part in the continuous improvement of our tutorials and upload a 'fix' or pointer.

For those without access to the net, if you've got a specific problem you can call us on **1-800 USE WROX**. Alternatively, send a letter to:

Wrox Press Inc.,	Wrox Press Ltd,
1512 North Fremont,	30, Lincoln Road,
Suite 103,	Olton,
Chicago	Birmingham,
IL 60622	B27 6PA
USA	UK

Programming in C

C is a powerful and compact computer language that allows you to specify exactly what you want your computer to do. You're in charge: you create a program, which is just a set of instructions, and your computer will obey it.

Programming in C isn't difficult, as you're about to find out. I'm going to teach you all the fundamentals of C programming in an enjoyable and easy-to-understand way, and by the end of even this first chapter, you'll have written your first few C programs. It's as easy as that!

In this chapter you'll learn:

▶ How to create C programs

▶ How C programs are organized

▶ How to write your own program to display text on the screen

Creating C Programs

There are four fundamental stages, or processes, in the creation of any C program. These stages are: **Editing**, **Compiling**, **Linking**, and **Executing** the program. You'll soon know all these processes like the back of your hand (you'll be doing them so easily and so often) but first, let's consider what each process is, and how it contributes to the creation of a C program.

Editing

This is the process of creating and editing C **source code** - the name given to the program instructions you write.

Most C compilers come with a specific editor that can provide a lot of assistance in managing your programs. In fact, they often provide a complete environment for writing, managing, developing and testing your programs. This is sometimes called an **Integrated Development Environment**, or IDE.

You can also use other editors to create your source files, but they must store the code as ASCII text. In general, if you have a compiler system with an editor included then it will provide a lot of features that make it easier to write and organize your source code. There will usually be automatic facilities for laying out the program text appropriately, and color highlighting for important language elements - which not only makes your code more readable, but also provides a clear indicator when you make errors in keying in such elements.

Compiling

The compiler converts your source code into language your computer can understand, and detects and reports errors in the conversion process. The input to this stage is the file you produced during your editing, which is usually referred to as a **source file**.

The compiler can detect a wide range of errors that are due to invalid or unrecognized program code, as well as structural errors, where, for example, part of a program can never be executed. The output from the compiler is known as **object code** and is stored in files called **object files**, which usually have names with the extension **.obj**. The compiler can detect several different kinds of errors during the translation process, and most of these will prevent the object file from being created.

> *In UNIX, object files have the extension* **.o**.

The result of a successful compilation is a file with the same name that you used for the source file, but with the **.obj** extension.

Linking

The linker combines the various files generated by the compiler, adds required code modules from **program libraries** supplied as part of C, and welds everything into an executable whole. The linker can also detect and report errors, for example, if part of your program is missing, or a nonexistent library component is referenced.

> *Program libraries support and extend the C language by providing code to carry out operations that aren't part of the language. For example, libraries can contain code for calculating a square root, comparing two characters or obtaining date and time information.*

In practice, if your program is of any significant size, it will consist of several separate source code files, which can then be linked together. A large program may be difficult to write in one go. By breaking it up into a number of smaller source files, you can make the development of the program a whole lot easier. The source files can be compiled separately, which makes eliminating the simple typographical errors a bit easier. Furthermore, the whole program can usually be developed incrementally. Each source file will have its own file name, and the set of source files that make up the program will usually be integrated under a **project name**, which is used to refer to the whole program.

A successful linking stage will produce an executable file. In a Microsoft Windows environment, this executable file will have a **.exe** extension; in UNIX, there will be no such extension, but the file will be of an executable type. A failure at the linking stage means that, once again, you must go back and edit your source code.

Execution

The execution stage is where you run your program, having completed all the previous processes successfully. Unfortunately, this stage can also generate a wide variety of error conditions, ranging from producing the wrong output, through to sitting there and doing nothing, perhaps crashing your computer for good measure. In all cases, it's back to the editing process to check your source code.

Now for the good news: this is the stage where, at last, you get to see your computer doing exactly what you told it to do!

The processes of editing, compiling, linking, and execution are essentially the same for developing programs in any environment and with any compiled language. The following diagram summarizes how you would typically pass through each of these processes as you create your own C programs.

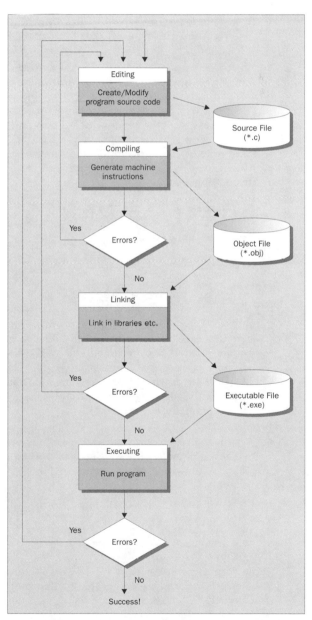

Creating Your First Program

It's time to create our first program. Let's step through the processes of creating a simple C program, from entering the program itself through to executing that program. Don't worry if what you type doesn't mean anything to you at this stage - I'll explain everything as we go along.

Try It Out - An Example C Program

1 Run your editor and type in the following program exactly as written below. Be careful to use the punctuation exactly as you see here.

If you're working in UNIX then the most common text editor is the **vi** editor. Alternately, you might prefer to use the **emacs** editor.

From a PC, you could use a word processor, such as Word or WordPerfect, although these aren't very suitable for producing program code. Word processors have no special facilities to help you edit code, and they normally create a lot of hidden formatting that could cause havoc during compilation. However, if a word processor is your only option, then there's usually an option to save a file as ASCII text without any of this troublesome formatting information.

```
/* Example 1.1 Your Very First C Program - Displaying Hello World */

#include <stdio.h>

void main()
{
   printf("Hello world");
}
```

The brackets used on the fourth and last lines are braces - the curly ones: **{}**, not the square ones **[]** or the round ones **()** - it really does matter. To make it clear what we're talking about, throughout the book, I'll refer to the curly brackets **{}** as braces, the square brackets **[]** as square brackets, and the round brackets **()** as parentheses. Also, make sure you put the slashes the right way (**/**), as later we will be using the backslash (****) as well. Don't forget the semicolon (**;**).

2 When you've entered the source code above, save the program as **hello.c**. You can use whatever name you like instead of **hello**, but the extension must be **.c**. This extension name is the common convention when you write C programs. The extension identifies the contents of the file as C source code. Most compilers will expect the source file to have the extension **.c**, and if it doesn't, the compiler may refuse to process it.

3 Now you're ready to compile your program. Exactly how you do this will depend upon which compiler you're using.

If your C compiler allows you to work in an Integrated Development Environment (IDE) then you should easily be able to find your way to a <u>C</u>ompile menu, from where you can select the <u>C</u>ompile option.

If you're working in UNIX then the standard command to compile your C programs will be **cc**; you can use it like this:

cc -c myprog.c

where **myprog.c** is the program you want to compile. If you omit the **-c** flag then your program will automatically be linked as well. If you're using the GNU compiler then you should type

gcc -c myprog.c

The result of a successful compilation will be an object file.

Most C compilers will have a standard compile option, whether it's from the command line (such as **cc myprog.c**) or a menu option from within an IDE (where you'll find a Compile menu option).

4 Next, we link all the pieces of program, adding in code from the standard libraries that your program needs to execute. Once again, the precise way to do this will depend upon which compiler system you're using.

In UNIX, the modules that are to be linked together are given together with the **cc** command. For example,

cc myprog.c mod1.c mod2.o

These three modules will be linked together. Notice that the last module, here, has the extension **.o**. This is because it has previously been compiled: the **.o** extension tells the compiler that the module is waiting to be linked - and doesn't need to be compiled again. The output of this stage is a file called **a.out**, which you should then rename to something more meaningful.

An alternative form to this is:

cc -o myprog myprog.c mod.c mod2.o

which will compile and link the module **myprog.c** and create an executable file called **myprog** (defined straight after the **-o** flag).

Many C compilers also have a Build option, which will compile and link your program in one step. This option will usually be found, within an IDE, in the Compile menu; alternatively, it may have a menu of its own.

5 Finally, we can execute our program. If everything worked without producing any error messages, then you've done it!

In UNIX and DOS, to execute a program you just enter the name of the file that has been compiled and linked. In Windows, you can use Explorer to locate the **.exe** file of your program, and double-click it.

In most IDEs, you'll find an appropriate menu command that allows you to Run or Execute your compiled program. This option may have a menu of its own, or you may find it under the Compile menu option.

> *If you're working in an IDE, you may need to use the* Window *menu to change to an* Output *window, where the results of your program execution can be seen.*

This is your first program, and you should see the following message on the screen:

```
Hello   world
```

Editing Your First Program

You could try altering the same program to display something else on the screen. For example, if you're a cosmologist, you might want to try editing the program to read like this:

```
/* Example 1.2 Your Second C Program - Saying Hello to the Universe */

#include<stdio.h>

void main()
{
    printf("Hello Universe!");
}
```

You can try recompiling the program, re-linking it, and running it again once you have altered the source. With a following wind, and a bit of luck, you've now edited your first program. You've written a program using the editor, edited it, and then compiled, linked and executed it.

Dealing With Errors

To err is human, and while computers don't generally make mistakes themselves, they're actually very good at indicating where we've slipped up. Sooner or later your compiler is going to present you with a list (and sometimes a list that's longer than you want) of the mistakes that are in your source code. When this happens, you must return to the editing stage, find where the incorrect code is, and change it.

Let's step through an example of this, by creating an error in our source code. Edit our second program example, removing the semicolon (**;**) at the end of the line with **"Hello Universe!"** in it, as shown here:

```
/* Example 1.2 Your Second C Program - Saying Hello to the Universe */

#include<stdio.h>

void main()
{
    printf("Hello Universe!")
}
```

If you now try to compile this program, you'll see an error message that will vary slightly, depending on which compiler you're using. A typical error message is shown below:

```
Syntax error : missing ';' before '}'
HELLO.C - 1 error(s), 0 warning(s)
```

Here, the compiler is able to determine precisely what the error is, and where: there really should be a semicolon at the end of that **Hello Universe** line! As you start writing your own programs, you'll probably get lots of errors in compilation that are caused by simple punctuation mistakes. It's so easy to forget a comma or a bracket, or just to hit the wrong key. Don't worry about this: lots of experienced programmers make exactly the same mistakes - even after years of practice.

One of the great things about compiler errors is that just one mistake can result in a whole stream of abuse from your compiler - as it throws you a multitude of different things that it doesn't like. Keep a cool head: after considering the messages carefully, the basic approach is to go back and edit your source code to fix what you can, and have another go at compiling. With luck, you'll get fewer errors next time around.

To correct our example program, just go back to your editor and re-enter the semicolon. Recompile, check for any other errors, and your program is fit to be run again.

Dissecting a Simple Program

Now that you've written and compiled your first program, let's go through a very similar one and see what the individual lines of code do.

Try It Out - Another C Program

Have a look at this program:

```c
/* Example 1.3 Another Simple C Program - Displaying Great Quotations */

#include <stdio.h>

void main()
{
    printf("Beware the Ides of March!");
}
```

You can probably see that this is virtually identical to our first program. Even so, you could do with the practice, so use your editor to enter this example, and see what happens when you compile and run it. If you type it in accurately, compile it and run it, you should get the following output:

```
Beware the Ides of March!
```

13

Comments

Look at the first line.

```
/* Example 1.3 Another Simple C Program - Displaying Great Quotations */
```

This isn't actually part of the program code, in that it isn't telling the computer to do anything. It's simply a **comment**, and it's there to remind you what the program does - so you don't have to wade through the code (and your memory) to remember. Anything between **/*** and ***/** is treated as a comment. Your compiler will simply ignore anything that's a comment and go on to the next real bit of code.

You should try to get into the habit of documenting your programs, using comments as you go along. Your programs will, of course, work without comments - but when you write longer programs you may not remember what they do or how they work. Put in enough comments to ensure that, in a month from now, you (and any another programmer) can understand the aim of the program and how it works.

Comments don't have to be in a line of their own: they just have to be enclosed between **/*** and ***/**. Let's add some more comments to the program:

```
/* Example 1.3 Another Simple C Program - Displaying Great Quotations */

#include <stdio.h>        /* This is a preprocessor directive    */

void main()               /* This identifies the function main() */
{                         /* This marks the beginning of main()  */

   /* This line displays a quotation */
   printf("Beware the Ides of March!");

}                         /* This marks the end of main() */
```

You can see that using comments can be a very useful way of explaining, in English, what's going on in the program. You can place comments wherever you want in your programs, and you can use them to explain the general objectives of the code as well as the specifics of how the code works. You can also use comments to identify the author of the code and to assert your copyright if you wish.

Pre-Processor Directives

Look at the line:

```
#include <stdio.h>        /* This is a preprocessor directive */
```

This is not strictly part of the executable program, but it is essential in this case - in fact, the program won't work without it. The symbol **#** indicates this is a **pre-processor directive**, which is an instruction to your compiler to do something before compiling the source code. The program that handles these directives is called a preprocessor because it does some processing before the compilation process starts. There are quite a few pre-processor directives, and they are usually placed at the beginning of the program source file.

In this case, the compiler is instructed to 'include' in our program the file **stdio.h**. This file is called a **header file**, because it's usually included at the head of a program. It defines information about functions provided by a standard C library. It will contain C source code and other preprocessor directives. In this case, as we're using the **printf()** function from the standard library, we have to include the **stdio.h** header file. This is because **stdio.h** contains the information that the compiler needs in order to understand what **printf()** means. We'll be using other C header files later in the book.

> *It's common practice to write the header file names in the **#include** directive as lower-case*

Every C compiler that conforms to the ANSI standard for the language will have a set of standard header files supplied with it. Header files primarily contain definitions relating to standard library functions that are available with C. Although all ISO standard C compilers will support the same set of standard library functions, and will have the same set of standard header files available, there may be extra library functions provided with a particular compiler that may not be available with other compilers.

All header files have file names with the extension **.h**. The header file **stdio.h** contains declarations for the standard input and output functions available. Including this file into our program allows us to use the function **printf()**, which occurs a few lines later in our program.

Defining the main() Function

The next four statements define the function **main()**:

```
void main()            /* This identifies the function main() */
{                      /* This marks the beginning of main()   */

    /* This line displays a quotation */
    printf("Beware the Ides of March!");

}                      /* This marks the end of main() */
```

Every C program consists of one or more functions, and every C program must contain a function called **main()** - the reason being that your program will always start execution from the beginning of this function. So imagine that you've created, compiled and linked a file called **progname.exe**. When you execute this program, it causes the function **main()** to be called immediately.

The first line of the definition for the function **main()** is:

```
void main()            /* This identifies the function main() */
```

This defines the start of the function **main()**. Notice that there is *no* semicolon at the end of the line.

The first line identifying this as the function **main()** has the keyword **void** at the beginning. This defines the type of value to be returned by the function. In this case, it signifies that the function **main()** returns no value.

There are circumstances when you would want to return something from **main()** to the operating system - an error code, for example. In those situations, a keyword other than **void** would be used - which we'll cover in a later chapter.

The parentheses that immediately follow the **main()** function enclose a definition of what information is to be transferred to **main()** when it starts executing. In our example, however, you can see that there's no information of this type. Later, we'll see how information is transferred to **main()** and to other functions in a program. In general, however, the function **main()** can call other functions which, in turn, may call further functions - and so on - and for every function that's called, we have the opportunity to pass some information to it within the parentheses that come after its name.

Keywords

In C, a **keyword** is a word with special significance, so you shouldn't use keywords for any other purposes in your program. For this reason, keywords are also referred to as reserved words. In our example, **void** is a keyword. There is a whole set of keywords in C, and we'll become familiar with most of them as we cover more material. You'll find a complete list of C keywords in Appendix C.

The Body of the Function

The general structure of the function **main()** is illustrated here.

The **function body** is the bit between the opening and closing braces following the line where the function name appears. The function body contains all the statements that define what the function does.

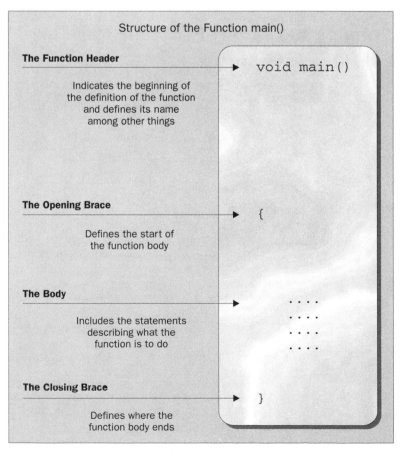

Structure of the Function main()

The Function Header

Indicates the beginning of the definition of the function and defines its name among other things

void main()

The Opening Brace

Defines the start of the function body

{

The Body

Includes the statements describing what the function is to do

. . . .
. . . .
. . . .
. . . .

The Closing Brace

Defines where the function body ends

}

A very simple function body consisting of just one statement is:

```
{                        /* This marks the beginning of main() */

    /* This line displays a quotation */
    printf("Beware the Ides of March!");

}                        /* This marks the end of main() */
```

Every function must have a body, although it can be empty and just consist of the two braces without any statements between them. In this case the function will do nothing.

You may wonder where the use is for a function that does nothing. Actually, this can be very useful when you're developing a program that will have loads of functions. You can declare the set of (empty) functions that you think you'll need to write to solve the problem in hand, which should give you an idea of the programming that needs to be done, and then gradually create the program code for each function. This technique helps you to build your program in a logical and gradual manner.

> *You can see that I've aligned the braces one below the other. I've done this to make it clear where the block of statements that they enclose starts and finishes. Statements between braces are usually indented by two or three spaces - so that the braces stand out. This is good style, as the statements within a block can be readily identified.*

Outputting Information

The body of our function **main()** only includes one statement, which calls the **printf()** function:

```
    /* This line displays a quotation */
    printf("Beware the Ides of March!");
```

As I've said, **printf()** is a standard library function, and it outputs information to the display screen based on what's contained between the parentheses immediately following the function name. In our case, the call to the function displays a simple piece of Shakespearean advice. Notice that this line *does* end with a semicolon.

Arguments

Items enclosed between the parentheses following a function name, as we have with the **printf()** function, are called **arguments.**

If you don't like the quotation we have as an argument, you could display something else by simply including your own choice of words, within quotes, inside parentheses. For instance, you might prefer a line from Macbeth:

```
    printf("Out, damned Spot! Out I say!");
```

Try using this in the example. When you've modified the source code, you need to compile and link the program again before executing it.

> As with all executable statements in C (as opposed to function definitions or pre-processor directives), our **printf()** line must have a semicolon at the end. As we've seen, a very common error, particularly when you first start programming in C, is to forget the semicolon.

Control Characters

We could alter our program to display two sentences on separate lines. Try typing in the following code:

```
/* Example 1.4 Another Simple C Program - Displaying Great Quotations */

#include <stdio.h>

void main()
{
   printf("\nMy formula for success?\nRise early, work late, strike
                                                        oil.");
}
```

The output looks like this:

```
My formula for success?
Rise early, work late, strike oil.
```

Look at the **printf()** statement. After the first sentence we've inserted the characters **\n**. The combination **\n** actually represents a single character.

The backslash (\) is of special significance here. The character immediately following a backslash is always interpreted as a control character. In this case, it's **n** for newline, but there are plenty more. If you wanted to display a backslash itself you'd simply use two backslashes, thus: ****. Similarly, if we actually wanted to display quotes, we could use **\"**. The point about these characters is that it would be impossible to include them in the program directly without confusing the compiler.

Type in the following program:

```
/* Example 1.5 Another Simple C Program - Displaying Great Quotations */

#include <stdio.h>

void main()
{
   printf("\n\"It is a wise father that knows his own child.\"
                                                   Shakespeare");
}
```

The output displays the text:

```
"It is a wise father that knows his own child."  Shakespeare
```

You can use control characters to add a beep to your code to signal something interesting or important. Enter and run the following program:

```
/* Example 1.6 A Simple C Program - Important */

#include <stdio.h>

void main()
{
    printf("\nBe careful!!\a");
}
```

The output of this program is sound and vision. Listen closely, and you should hear the beep through the speaker in your computer.

```
Be careful!!
```

The combination of \ plus another character is referred to as an **escape sequence**. The next table shows a summary of escape sequences that you can use.

Escape Sequence	Action
\n	Insert a newline character
\t	Inserts a horizontal tab
\a	Makes a beep
\"	Inserts a double quote (")
\'	Inserts a single quote (')
\\	Inserts a backslash (\)
\b	Inserts a backspace character

Try displaying different lines of text on the screen and alter the spacing within that text. You can put words on different lines, using **\n**, and you can use **\t** to space the text. You'll get lots more practice with these as we progress through the book.

Developing Programs in C

The process of developing programs in C may not be evident if you've never written a program before. However, it's very similar to plenty of other situations in life where, at the beginning, it just isn't clear how we're going to achieve our objective. Normally, we start with an idea of what we want to achieve - but this needs to be translated into a more precise specification of what we want. Once we've reached this more precise specification, we can work out the series of steps that lead to our final objective. So having an idea that we want to build a house just isn't enough. We need to know what kind of house we want, how large it's going to be, what kinds of materials we have, and where we actually want to build it. This kind of detailed planning is also necessary when we want to write a program.

Let's go through the basic steps that we need to follow when we're writing a program. The house analogy is a useful one, so we'll work with it for a while.

Understanding the Problem

The first step is to get a clear idea of what we want to do. It would be lunacy to start building our house before we'd established what facilities it should provide - how many bedrooms, how many bathrooms, how big it's going to be, and so on. All these things affect the cost of the house in terms of materials and the work involved in building it. Generally, it'll come down to a compromise that best meets our needs within the constraints of the money, the manpower and the time that's available for us to complete the project.

It's the same with developing a program of any size. Even for a relatively straightforward problem, we need to know what kind of input to expect, how the input is to be processed, and what kind of output is required - and how it's going to look. The input could be entered with the keyboard, but it might also involve data from a disk file, or information obtained over a telephone line or a network. The output could simply be displayed on the screen, or it could be printed; perhaps it might involve updating a data file on disk. For more complex programs, we would need to look at plenty more aspects of what the program is going to do. A clear definition of the problem that our program is going to solve is an absolutely essential part of understanding the resources and effort that are going to be needed for the creation of a finished product. Considering these details also forces us to establish whether our project is actually feasible or not.

Detailed Design

To get our house built, we need detailed plans. These plans enable the construction workers to do their job, describing in detail how the house goes together - all the dimensions, the materials to use, and so on. We'll also need a plan of what's to be done and when. We'll want the foundations dug before the walls are built, so the plan must involve a breaking up of the work into sensible units to be performed in a logical sequence.

It's the same with our program. We must specify the logic of the processes that our program needs to perform. These processes will need to be divided up into convenient chunks that are relatively self-contained. If we treat a large program as one huge process, the chances are that we'll never get it to work.

Implementation

From the detailed design of our house, the work can start. Each group of construction workers will need to complete their part of the project at the right time. Each stage will need to be inspected - to check that it's been done properly, before the next stage begins. Omitting these checks could easily result in the whole house collapsing.

Of course, if our program is large, we'll write our source code one unit at a time. As one part is completed we can write the code for the next. Each part will be based on the detailed design specifications, and we'll check out that each piece works, as far as we can, before proceeding to the next. In this way, we'll gradually progress to a fully working program that does everything we intended.

Testing

The house is complete, but there are a lot of things that need to be tested: the drainage, the water and electricity supplies, the heating and so on. Any one of these can result in problems that the contractors need to go back and fix. This is sometimes an iterative process, where problems with one aspect of the house can be the cause of things going wrong somewhere else.

The mechanism with a program is similar. Each of our program modules - the pieces that make up your program - will need to be tested individually. When they don't work properly you need to debug them. Debugging is the process of finding and removing errors in your program. This term is said to originate from the days when finding the errors in a program involved tracing where the information went, and how it was processed, using the circuit diagram for the computer. The story goes that a computer program error was discovered, that was caused by an insect shorting part of the circuit in the computer. The problem was caused by a bug. Subsequently, the term 'bug' was used to refer to any error in a program.

With a simple program, you can often find an error simply by inspecting the code. In general, though, the process of debugging usually involves adding extra program code to produce output that will enable you to check what the sequence of events is, and what intermediate values are produced in a program. With a large program, you'll also need to test the program modules in combination - since, although the individual modules may work, there's no guarantee that they'll work together! The jargon for this phase of program development is 'integration testing'.

Functions and Modular Programming

The word **function** has appeared a few times so far in this chapter with reference to **main()**, **printf()**, function body and so on. I need to explain a little about what 'function' means. Most programming languages, including C, provide a way of breaking up a program into segments, each of which can be written more or less independently of the others. In C we call these segments **functions**. The program code in the body of one function is completely insulated from that of other functions. A function will have a specific interface to the outside world in terms of how information is transferred to it, and how results generated by the function are transmitted back from it. This interface is specified in the first line of the function, where the function name appears.

The diagram shows a simple example of a program to analyze baseball scores that is composed of four modules.

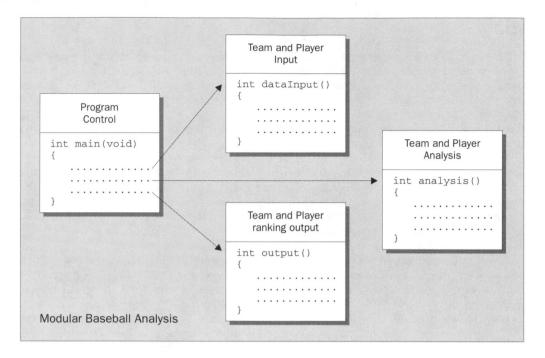

Each of the four modules does a specific, well-defined job. Overall control of the sequence of operations in the program is managed by one module. There is a module to read and check the input data and another module to do the analysis. Once the data is in and analyzed, a fourth module has the task of outputting the team and player rankings.

Breaking a program up into manageable chunks is a very important aspect to programming, so let's go over the reasons for segmenting a program.

▶ Dividing the program into a number of separate functions allows each function to be written and tested separately. This greatly simplifies the process of getting the total program to work.

▶ Several separate functions are easier to handle and to understand than one huge function.

▶ Libraries are just sets of functions that people tend to use all the time. As they've been pre-written and pre-tested, you know they'll work - so you can use them without worrying about their code details. This will accelerate your program development, by allowing you to concentrate on your own code, and is a fundamental part of the philosophy of C. The richness of the libraries greatly amplifies the power of the language.

▶ You can accumulate your own libraries of functions that are applicable to the sort of programs that you're interested in. If you find yourself writing a particular function frequently, you can write a generalized version of it to suit your needs - and build this into your own library. Then, whenever you need to use that particular function, you can simply use your library version.

► In the development of very large programs, which can vary from a few thousand to millions of lines of code, development can be undertaken by teams of programmers - each team working with a defined subgroup of the functions that make up the whole program.

We'll be covering C functions in greater detail in Chapter 8. Because the structure of a C program is inherently functional, you've already met one of the standard library functions in our earliest examples - the function **printf()**.

Try It Out - Exercising What We Know

Let's now look at an example that puts into practice what we've learned so far. First, have a look at it and see whether you can understand what it does without running it. Then type it in, compile, link and run it - and see what happens.

```
/* Example 1.7 A longer program  */

/* Include the header file for input and output */
#include <stdio.h>

void main()

{
   printf("Hi there!\n\n\nThis program is a bit");
   printf(" longer than the others.");
   printf("\nBut really it's only more text.\n\n\n\a\a");
   printf("Hey, wait a minute!! What was that???\n\n");
   printf("\t1.\tA bird?\n");
   printf("\t2.\tA plane?\n");
   printf("\t3.\tA control character?\n");
   printf("\n\t\t\b\bAnd how will this look when it prints out?\n\n");
}
```

The output will be:

```
Hi there!


This program is a bit longer than the others.
But really it's only more text.


Hey, wait a minute!! What was that???

1.     A bird?
2.     A plane?
3.     A control character?

           And how will this look when it prints out?
```

How It Works

The program looks a little bit more complicated, largely because the text strings between parentheses include a lot of escape sequences. Each text string is bounded by a pair of double quotation marks. However, the program is just a succession of calls to the **printf()** function, and demonstrates that output to the screen is controlled by what you pass to the **printf()** function. Let's look at this program in detail.

We've included the **stdio.h** file through the pre-processor directive:

```
/* Include the header file for input and output */
#include <stdio.h>
```

You can see that this is a pre-processor directive because it begins with **#**. The **stdio.h** file provides the definitions we need to be able to use the **printf()** function.

We then define the start of the function **main()** and specify that it doesn't return a value with the line:

```
void main()
```

The opening brace on the next line indicates that the body of the function follows:

```
{
```

The next statement calls the standard library function **printf()** to output Hi there! to your display screen, followed by 2 blank lines and the words This program is a bit.

```
printf("Hi there!\n\n\nThis program is a bit");
```

The two blank lines are produced by our three **\n** escape sequences. Each of these starts a new line when the characters are written to the display. The first ends the line containing Hi there!, and the next two produce the two empty lines. The text This program is a bit appears on the fourth line of output. You can see that this one line of code produces a total of four lines of output on the screen.

The next line of output produced by the next **printf()** starts at the character position immediately following the last character in the previous output. The next statement outputs the text - longer than the others. - with a space as the first character of the text:

```
printf(" longer than the others.");
```

This output will simply continue where the last line left off - following the t in bit. This means that you really do need the space at the beginning of the text, otherwise the computer will display This program is a bitlonger than the others, which is not what you want.

The next statement starts its output on a new line, immediately following the previous line, because of the **\n** at the beginning of the text string between double quotation marks:

```
printf("\nBut really it's only more text.\n\n\n\a\a");
```

It then displays the text and adds 2 empty lines (because of the three **\n** escape sequences) and beeps twice. The next output to the screen will start at the beginning of the line that follows the second empty line produced here.

The next output is produced by the statement:

```
printf("Hey, wait a minute!! What was that???\n\n");
```

This outputs the text, and then leaves one empty line. The next output will be on the line following the empty line.

Each of the next three statements inserts a tab, displays a number, inserts another tab followed by some text, and ends with a new line. This is useful for making your output easier to read.

```
printf("\t1.\tA bird?\n");
printf("\t2.\tA plane?\n");
printf("\t3.\tA control character?\n");
```

This produces three numbered lines of output.

The last statement that produces output adds a new line - so that there'll be an empty line after the previous output. Two tabs are then sent to the display, followed by two backspaces - which moves us back two spaces from the last tab position. Lastly, the text is displayed, and two newline characters are sent to the display.

```
printf("\n\t\t\b\bAnd how will this look when it prints out?\n\n");
```

The closing brace marks the end of the function body.

```
}
```

Common Mistakes

These are a fact of life. When we write a computer program in C, the compiler must convert our source code to machine code, and so there must be some very strict rules governing how we use the language. Leave out a comma where one is expected, or add a semicolon where you shouldn't, and the compiler won't be able to translate your programs into machine code.

You'll be surprised just how easy it is to introduce typographical errors into your program, even after years of practice. If you're lucky, these errors will be picked up when you compile or link your program. If you're really unlucky, they can result in your program apparently working fine, but producing some intermittent erratic behavior. You can end up spending a lot of time tracking these errors down.

Of course, it's not only typographical errors that cause problems. You'll often find that your detailed implementation is just not right. Where you're dealing with complicated decisions in your program, it's easy to get the logic wrong. Your program may be quite accurate from a language point of view, and it may compile and run without a problem - but it won't produce the right answers. These kinds of errors can be the most difficult to find.

Points to Remember

Let's leave **printf()** options for the moment. They can get a bit heavy in large doses, although we'll return to them many times throughout this book. It would be a good idea to summarize what we've gleaned from our first program. We can do this by looking at the overview of the important points in the following diagram:

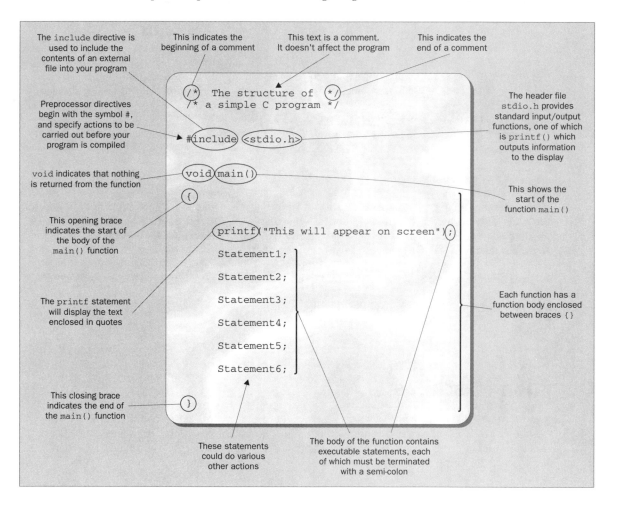

The include directive is used to include the contents of an external file into your program

This indicates the beginning of a comment

This text is a comment. It doesn't affect the program

This indicates the end of a comment

Preprocessor directives begin with the symbol #, and specify actions to be carried out before your program is compiled

The header file stdio.h provides standard input/output functions, one of which is printf() which outputs information to the display

void indicates that nothing is returned from the function

This shows the start of the function main()

This opening brace indicates the start of the body of the main() function

The printf statement will display the text enclosed in quotes

Each function has a function body enclosed between braces {}

This closing brace indicates the end of the main() function

These statements could do various other actions

The body of the function contains executable statements, each of which must be terminated with a semi-colon

```
/*  The structure of  */
/*  a simple C program */

#include <stdio.h>

void main()
{

    printf("This will appear on screen");

    Statement1;

    Statement2;

    Statement3;

    Statement4;

    Statement5;

    Statement6;

}
```

Summary

You've reached the end of the first chapter, and we've already written a few programs in C. We've covered quite a lot of ground, but at a fairly gentle pace. The aim of the chapter was to introduce a few basic ideas rather than teach you a lot about the C programming language. You should be confident about editing, compiling and running your programs. You probably only have a vague idea about how to construct a C program, but don't worry. It'll be a lot easier when you've learnt a bit more about C and written some programs with a bit more meat to them.

You're probably a bit fed up with the **printf()** function - all it does, so far, is display what you type between the parentheses. Well, in the next chapter we're going to move on to more complicated things, actually enabling us to manipulate information and get some rather more interesting results. And by the way, the **printf()** function does a whole lot more that just display text strings - as you will see.

First Steps In Programming

By now you're probably eager to create programs that allow your computer to really interact with the outside world. That is, after all, one of the main attractions of computers. You don't just want programs that work as a glorified typewriter, displaying fixed information that you included in the program code - and indeed, there's a whole world of programming that goes beyond that.

Ideally, you want to be able to enter data from the keyboard and have the program squirrel it away somewhere. This would make the program much more versatile. Your program would be able to access and manipulate this data, and it would be able to work with different data each time you executed it. This whole idea of inputting information that varies each time you run a program is key to the whole enterprise of programming. An item of data that varies in a program is, not altogether surprisingly, called a **variable** - and this is what we're going to look at in this chapter.

This is quite a long chapter, and we'll be covering a lot of ground. However, by the time you reach the end, you'll be able to write some really useful programs.

In this chapter you'll learn:

> How memory is used and what variables are

> How you can calculate in C

> What different types of variables there are, and what you use them for

> What casting is and when you need to use it

> How to write a program that calculates the height of a tree - any tree

Memory in your Computer

First we'll look at how the computer stores the data that is processed in your program. To understand this, you need to know a little bit about memory in your computer, so before we go into our first program we'll have a quick tour of your computer's memory.

The instructions that make up your program, and the data that it acts upon, have to be stored somewhere while your computer is executing that program. When your program is running, this storage place is the machine's memory. It's also referred to as **main memory**, or the Random Access Memory (**RAM**) of the machine.

Your computer also contains another kind of memory called Read Only Memory (**ROM**). As its name suggests, you can't change ROM: you can only read its contents or have your machine execute instructions contained within it. The information contained in ROM was put there when the machine was manufactured. This information is mainly programs that control the operation of the various devices attached to your computer, such as the display, the hard disk drive, the keyboard, and the floppy disk drive. On a PC, these programs are called the Basic Input Output System (**BIOS**) of your computer. We won't need to refer to the BIOS in detail in this book. The interesting memory for our purposes is RAM: this is where your programs and data are stored when they execute. So let's understand a bit more about it.

You can think of the random access memory of your computer as an ordered sequence of boxes. Each of these boxes is in one of two states, either the box is full - when it represents 1, or the box is empty - when it represents 0. Therefore, each box represents one binary digit - either 0 or 1. The computer sometimes thinks of these in terms of **true** and **false**: 1 is true and 0 is false. Each of these boxes is called a **bit** - which is a contraction of **b**inary dig**it**.

> *If you can't remember or have never learned about binary numbers, and you want to find out a little bit more, you'll find more detail in Appendix A. However, you needn't worry about these details if they don't appeal to you. The important point here is that the computer can only deal with 1s and 0s - it can't deal with decimal numbers directly. All the data that your program works with - including the program instructions themselves, will consist of binary numbers internally.*

For convenience, the boxes or bits in your computer are grouped into sets of 8, and each set of eight bits is called a **byte**. To allow us to refer to the contents of a particular byte, we label each byte with a number, starting from 0 for the first byte, 1 for the second byte, and going up to whatever number of bytes you have in your computer's memory. This label for a byte is called its **address**. Thus each byte will have an address that's different to that of all the other bytes in memory. Just as a street address identifies a particular house uniquely, the address of a byte references that byte in your computer's memory uniquely.

To summarize: we have our memory building blocks (called bits) that are in groups of eight (called bytes). A bit can only be either 1 or 0.

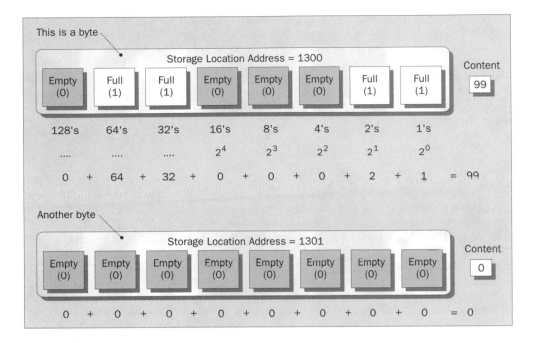

Memory is often expressed in terms of so many kilobytes, megabytes, or even gigabytes. Here's what these words mean:

1 kilobyte (or 1K bytes) is 1024 bytes
1 megabyte (or 1M bytes) is 1024 kilobytes, which is 1,048,576 bytes
1 gigabyte (or 1G bytes) is 1024 megabytes, which is 1,073,741,824 bytes

You might be wondering why we don't work with easier numbers, like one thousand, one million, etc. The reason is this: there are 1024 numbers from 0 to 1023, and 1023 happens to be 10 bits in binary: 11 1111 1111, which is a very convenient binary value. So while one thousand is a very convenient decimal value, it's actually rather inconvenient in a binary machine – it's 1111101000, which is not exactly neat and tidy. The kilobyte (1024 bytes) is therefore defined in a manner that's convenient for your computer, rather than for you. Similarly, for a megabyte, we need 20 bits; and for a gigabyte, we need 30 bits. One point of confusion can arise here, particularly with disk drive capacities. Disk drive manufacturers often refer to a disk as having a capacity of 537 megabytes or 1.2 gigabytes, where they really mean 537 million bytes and 1.2 billion bytes. Of course, 537 million bytes is only 512 megabytes.

Now we know a bit about bytes, let's see how we can use this memory in our programs.

What is a Variable?

A variable is a specific piece of memory in your computer, which is one or more contiguous bytes. Every variable has a name, and you can use that name to refer to that place in memory - and actually store some data there.

Let's start with a program that displays your salary using the **printf()** function that we saw in Chapter 1. If we assume your salary is $10,000 then we can already write that program very easily:

```
/* Example 2.1 What is a Variable? */
#include <stdio.h>

void main()
{
   printf("My salary is $10000");
}
```

I'm sure you don't need any more explanation about how this program works: it's almost identical to those we developed in Chapter 1. So how can we modify this program to allow us to customize the message depending on a value stored in memory? There are, as ever, several ways of doing this. What they all have in common though, is that they use a variable.

In this case, we could allocate a piece of memory that we could call, say, **salary**, and store the value **10000** in it. When you wanted to display your salary, you could use the name we've given to the variable, which is **salary**, and the value stored in it (**10000**) would be displayed. Wherever you use a variable name in a program, the computer accesses the value that's stored there. You can access a variable however many times you need to in your program. And when your salary changes, you can simply change the value stored in the variable **salary** and the whole program will carry on working with the new value. Of course, all these values will be stored as binary numbers inside the computer.

You can have as many variables as you like in a program. The value that each variable contains, at any point during the execution of that program, is determined by the instructions contained in your program. The value of a variable isn't fixed, and it can change as many times as you need it to throughout a program.

Number Variables

There are a several different kinds of variable, and each type of variable is used for storing different kinds of data. We'll start by looking at variables that you can use to store numbers. There are actually several different ways in which you can store numbers in your program, but we'll start with the simplest.

Integer Variables

Let's start with **integer variables**. An integer is any whole number without a decimal point. Examples of integers are:

1
10,999,000,000
-1

You'll recognize these values as integers, but what I've written here isn't quite correct as far as your program's concerned. We can't include commas in an integer, so the second value would actually be written in a program as 10999000000.

Examples of numbers that are *not* integers are:

1.234
999.9
-0.0005

Before we discuss variables in great detail (and believe me, there is a lot of detail!) we'll see a simple variable in action in a program - just so that you can get a feel for how they're used.

Try It Out - Using a Variable

Let's go back to your salary. Have a go at writing the previous program using a variable:

```
/* Example 2.2 Using a variable  */
#include <stdio.h>

void main()
{
  int salary;              /* Declare a variable called salary          */

  salary = 10000;          /* A simple arithmetic assignment statement */

  printf("My salary is %d.", salary);

}
```

You can type in this example, and compile, link and execute it. You'll get the following output:

```
My salary is 10000.
```

How It Works

The first three lines are exactly the same as in all our previous programs. Let's look at the new stuff.

The statement that identifies the memory that we're using to store your salary is:

```
  int salary;              /* Declare a variable called salary          */
```

This is called a **variable declaration** because it declares the name of the variable. The name, in this program, is **salary**.

> *Notice that the variable declaration ends with a semicolon. If you omit it then you'll generate an error.*

The variable declaration also specifies the type of data that the variable will store. We've used the keyword **int** to specify that the variable, **salary**, will be used to store an **int**eger value. The keyword **int** precedes the name of the variable. As you'll see later, declarations for variables that store other kinds of data will consist of another data type keyword followed by a variable name in a similar manner.

> *Remember, keywords are special C words that mean something specific to the compiler. You must not use them as variable names or your compiler will get confused.*

The next statement is:

```
salary = 10000;
```

This is a simple **arithmetic assignment statement**. It takes the value to the right of the equals sign and stores it in the variable on the left of the equals sign. Here we are declaring that the variable **salary** will have the value of **10000**. We're storing the value on the right (**10000**) in the variable on the left (**salary**). The **=** symbol is called the **assignment operator**, because it assigns the value on the right to the variable on the left.

We then have the familiar **printf()** statement - but it's a little different to how we've seen it in action before:

```
printf("My salary is %d.", salary);
```

There are now two **arguments** inside the parentheses, separated by a comma. An argument is an item of data that's passed to a function. In this program statement, the two arguments to the **printf()** function are:

- Argument 1: a **control string,** so called because it controls how the output specified by the following argument (or arguments) is to be presented. This is the character string between the double quotes.

- Argument 2: the variable **salary**. How this variable will be displayed is determined by the first argument - the control string.

The control string is fairly similar to our previous example, in that it contains some text to be displayed. However, if you look carefully, you'll see **%d** embedded in it. This is called a **conversion specifier** for our variable.

> *Conversion specifiers always start with a % character. Since the % sign in a control string always indicates a conversion specifier, if you want to output a % character you must use the sequence %%. If you just write the % character in a control string, the **printf()** function will presume that it signals the start of a conversion specifier.*

Conversion specifiers determine how variables are displayed on the screen. In this case, we have used a **d**, which is a **d**ecimal specifier that applies to integer values (whole numbers). It just means that the second argument, **salary**, will be interpreted and output as a decimal (base 10) number.

Try It Out - Using More Variables

Let's try a slightly longer example:

```
/* Example 2.3 Using more variables */
#include <stdio.h>

void main()
{
   int brothers;              /* Declare a variable called brothers */
   int brides;                /* and a variable called brides       */

   brothers = 7;              /* Store 7 in the variable brothers   */
   brides = 7;                /* Store 7 in the variable brides      */

   /* Display some output */
   printf("%d brides for %d brothers", brides, brothers);
}
```

If you run this program you should get the following output:

```
7 brides for 7 brothers
```

How It Works

This program works in a very similar way to our previous example. We first declare two variables, **brides** and **brothers**, with the statements:

```
   int brothers;              /* Declare a variable called brothers */
   int brides;                /* and a variable called brides       */
```

Both of these variables are declared as type **int**. Notice that they've been declared separately. Each line ends with a semicolon, which means that they are separate statements. Because they are both the same type, we could have saved a line of code and declared them together like this:

```
   int brothers, brides;
```

When you declare several variables in one statement, the variable names following the data type are separated by commas, and the whole line ends with a semicolon. This can be a convenient format, although there is a downside, which is that it isn't so obvious what each variable is for - because you can't add individual comments to describe each variable.

The next two statements initialize both variables with the value 7:

```
   brothers = 7;              /* Store 7 in the variable brothers   */
   brides = 7;                /* Store 7 in the variable brides      */
```

In the next statement, we have a control string that will display a line of text. Within this text, the **%d** conversion specifiers will be replaced by the values currently stored in the variables indicated by the second and third arguments to the **printf()** function call - in this case, **brides** and **brothers**:

```
   printf("%d brides for %d brothers", brides, brothers);
```

The conversion specifiers are replaced in order, so the value of **brides** corresponds to the first specifier, and the value of **brothers** corresponds to the second. This would be clearer if we changed the statements that set the values of the variables to:

```
brothers = 8;              /* Store 8 in the variable brothers   */
brides = 4;                /* Store 4 in the variable brides     */
```

In this somewhat dubious scenario, the **printf()** statement would show clearly which variable corresponded to which conversion specifier, since the output would be:

```
4 brides for 8 brothers
```

Naming Variables

The name we give to a variable, conveniently referred to as a **variable name**, can be defined with some flexibility. A variable name is a string of one or more letters and digits, but a name must begin with at least one letter (incidentally, the underscore character counts as a letter). Examples of good variable names are:

```
Radius
diameter
Auntie_May
Knotted_Wool
D666
```

A variable name cannot include any other characters. **8_Ball** and **6_pack** are not legal, because they begin with numbers. Neither is **Hash!** nor **Mary-Lou**. This last example is a common mistake. **Mary_Lou** would be quite acceptable (remember not to leave any gaps though-**Mary Lou** would specify two variable names). Don't use the underscore as the first letter of your variable, as this could clash with a system variable used in the standard library - and create mayhem. Variables starting with one or two underscore characters are often used in the header files. For example, **_This** and **_That** are best avoided.

Although you can call variables whatever you want, within the above constraints, it's worth calling them something that gives you a clue to what they contain. A variable named **x** that stores your salary may be confusing: far better to call it **salary** and leave no one in any doubt.

> *The number of characters permitted in a variable name will depend upon your compiler. Up to 31 characters are generally supported, so you can use names up to this length without any problems. I suggest you don't make your variable names longer than this, as they become cumbersome - and some compilers will just truncate names that are too long.*

Another very important point to remember when naming your variables is that C is case-sensitive, which means that capitals and small letters are completely different. Try changing the **printf()** statement so that one of the variable names starts with a capital letter, as follows:

```
/* Example 2.3 Using more variables */
#include <stdio.h>
```

```
void main()
{
   int brothers;              /* Declare a variable called brothers */
   int brides;                /* and a variable called brides       */

   brothers = 7;              /* Store 7 in the variable brothers   */
   brides = 7;                /* Store 7 in the variable brides      */

   /* Display some output */
   printf("%d brides for %d brothers", Brides, brothers);
}
```

You'll get an error when you try to compile this version of the program. C thinks that the two variables **brides** and **Brides** are different, so it doesn't understand what **Brides** refers to. This is a common error. As I have said before, punctuation and spelling mistakes are two of the main causes of trivial errors, although this doesn't make them any less annoying.

Using Variables

You now know how to name and declare your variables; but, so far, this hasn't been much more useful than anything we learned in Chapter 1. Let's try another program. This time we'll use the values in the variables before we produce the output.

Try It Out - Doing a Simple Calculation

This program does a simple calculation using the values of the variables:

```
/* Example 2.4 Simple calculations */
#include <stdio.h>

void main()
{
   int Total_Pets;                  /* The total number of pets     */
   int Cats;                        /* The number of cats as pets   */
   int Dogs;                        /* The number of dogs as pets   */
   int Ponies;                      /* The number of ponies as pets */
   int Others;                      /* The number of other pets     */

   /* Set the number of each kind of pet */
   Cats = 2;
   Dogs = 1;
   Ponies = 1;
   Others = 46;

   /* Calculate the total number of pets */
   Total_Pets = Cats + Dogs + Ponies + Others;

   printf("We have %d pets in total", Total_Pets);/* Output the result */
}
```

How It Works

First of all, look at how the statements in the program body are indented. All the statements between the braces are indented by the same amount. This makes it clear that all these statements belong together. We'll discuss program layout in more detail a little later, but for now, try to organize the programs the way that you see them here - indenting a group of statements that lie between an opening and closing brace by the same amount. It makes your programs much easier to read.

We begin our code by defining five variables of type **int**:

```
int Total_Pets;      /* The total number of pets      */
int Cats;            /* The number of cats as pets    */
int Dogs;            /* The number of dogs as pets    */
int Ponies;          /* The number of ponies as pets */
int Others;          /* The number of other pets      */
```

Since each of these variables will be used to store a count of a number of animals, they're definitely going to be whole numbers. As you can see, they're all declared as type **int**. We could declare them all on one line in a single statement, but by keeping them on separate lines we can add comments explaining what each variable is for. Note that we could have declared all five variables in a single statement, and included the comments, as follows:

```
int Total_Pets,      /* The total number of pets      */
  Cats,              /* The number of cats as pets    */
  Dogs,              /* The number of dogs as pets    */
  Ponies,            /* The number of ponies as pets */
  Others;            /* The number of other pets      */
```

All we've done here is spread one statement over several lines so that we can add the comments in an orderly fashion. Notice that there are commas separating each of the variable names. This is essentially the same as the statement,

```
int Total_Pets, Cats, Dogs, Ponies, Others;
```

but with a comment after each comma and after the semicolon. You can spread C statements over as many lines as you want. The semicolon determines the end of the statement, not the end of the line.

OK, back to the program. The variables are given specific values in these four assignment statements:

```
Cats = 2;
Dogs = 1;
Ponies = 1;
Others = 46;
```

Notice that the variable **Total_Pets** doesn't have an explicit value set. It will get its value as a result of the calculation using the other variables:

```
/* Calculate the total number of pets */
Total_Pets = Cats + Dogs + Ponies + Others;
```

In this arithmetic statement, we calculate the sum of all our pets on the right of the assignment operator by adding the values of each of the variables together. This total value is then stored in the variable, **Total_Pets**, on the left of the assignment operator. The new value replaces any old value that was stored in the variable **Total_Pets**. If **Total_Pets** already had a value assigned (suppose that we initialized it to 25), this value would be overwritten by the new calculation.

The **printf()** statement shows the result of the calculation by displaying the value of **Total_Pets** on the screen:

```
printf("We have %d pets in total", Total_Pets);
```

Try changing the numbers of some of the types of animals, or maybe add some more of your own. Remember to declare them, initialize their value, and include them in the **Total_Pets** statement.

Initializing Variables

In the previous example, we declared each variable with a statement such as:

```
int Cats;                        /* The number of cats as pets   */
```

We then used the statement:

```
Cats = 2;
```

to set the value of the variable **Cats** to 2. So what was the value before this statement was executed? Well, it could be anything. The first statement creates the variable called **Cats**, but its value will be whatever was left in memory from the last program that used this bit of memory. The assignment statement set the value to 2, but it would be much better to initialize the variable when we declared it. We can do this with the following statement:

```
int Cats=2;                      /* The number of cats as pets   */
```

This statement declares the variable **Cats** as type **int**, and sets its initial value to 2. Initializing variables as you declare them is, in general, a good idea. It avoids any doubt about what their initial values are, and if the program doesn't work as it should, it can help you track down the errors.

> *Avoiding spurious values for variables at the outset can also minimize the chances of your computer crashing (that is, hanging up, or removing the proverbial ball) when things do go wrong. From now on, we'll always initialize variables in our examples, even if it's just to 0.*

Arithmetic Statements

The previous program was the first one that really *did* something. It was very simple, just adding a few numbers, but it *was* a significant step forward. This was an elementary example of using an arithmetic statement to perform a calculation. Let's now look at some more sophisticated calculations that you can do.

Basic Arithmetic Operations

In C, an arithmetic statement is of the form:

```
Variable_Name = Arithmetic Expression;
```

The arithmetic expression on the right of the **=** sign specifies a calculation, using values stored in variables, and/or explicit numbers, that are combined using arithmetic operators such as add (**+**), subtract (**-**), multiply (*****), and divide (**/**). There are also other operators, as we shall see.

In the previous example the arithmetic statement was:

```
Total_Pets = Cats + Dogs + Ponies + Others;
```

The effect of this statement is to calculate the value of the arithmetic expression to the right of the **=**, and store that value in the variable specified on the left-hand side. In C, the **=** symbol is an active thing. It doesn't just specify that the two sides are equal, as it does in mathematics. It actively stores the value resulting from the expression on the right, in the variable on the left. This means that you could have:

```
Total_Pets = Total_Pets + 2;
```

This would be ridiculous as a mathematical equation, but in programming it's fine. Let's look at it in context. Imagine we'd rewritten the last part of the program to include the above statement. Here is a fragment of the program, as it would appear with the statement added:

```
Total_Pets = Cats + Dogs + Ponies + Others;    /* Value stored is 50 */
Total_Pets = Total_Pets + 2;                    /* Value stored is 52 */
printf("The total number of pets is: %d", Total_Pets);
```

The value of **Total_Pets** can change depending on what you do to it. By the end of the first line of the fragment, **Total_Pets** contains the value 50. Then, in the second line, we add 2 to that value. The final total that will be displayed is therefore 52.

> *In arithmetic operations, you always work out the expression on right hand side of the = sign first, and store the result in the variable on the left-hand side. The new value replaces the value that was previously contained in the variable to the left of the assignment operator.*

Anything that results in a numeric value is known as an **arithmetic expression.** The following are all arithmetic expressions:

```
3
1+2
Total_Pets
```

After these have been evaluated, they all produce a single numeric value. In a moment, we'll take a closer look at how an expression is made up, and we'll see the rules governing its evaluation. First, though, we'll try some simple examples using the basic arithmetic operators that we have at our disposal. These operators are:

Action	Operator
Addition	+
Subtraction	-
Multiplication	*
Division	/
Modulus	%

In case you haven't come across the modulus operator before, it just calculates the remainder after dividing one integer by another; so 12%5 would produce 2, because 12 divided by 5 leaves a remainder of 2. We'll look at this in more detail shortly. All these operators work as you'd expect - with the exception of division, which has a slight aberration from the norm when applied to integers, as we shall see. Since we've already looked at an example of addition, we'll try subtraction next.

Try It Out - Subtraction

Let's get back to programming and look at a food-based program that demonstrates subtraction:

```
/* Example 2.5 Calculation with cookies */
#include <stdio.h>

void main()
{
   int cookies = 5;

   cookies = cookies - 2;    /* Subtract 2 from the value of cookies  */

   printf("\nI've eaten 2 cookies.  There are %d cookies left", cookies);

   cookies = cookies - 3;    /* Subtract 3 from the value of cookies */

   printf("\nI've eaten the rest.  Now there are %d cookies left\n",
                                               cookies);
}
```

This program produces the following output:

```
I've eaten 2 cookies.  There are 3 cookies left
I've eaten the rest.  Now there are 0 cookies left
```

How It Works

Let's see what is happening in this program. First, an integer variable, **cookies**, is declared and assigned an initial value of **5**:

```
   int cookies = 5;
```

The subtraction operator is used to subtract **2** from the value of **cookies**:

```
cookies = cookies - 2;      /* Subtract 2 from the value of cookies  */
```

The result of the subtraction, 3, is stored back in the variable **cookies**. The **printf()** statement displays the number of cookies that are left after two have been eaten:

```
printf("\nI've eaten 2 cookies.  There are %d cookies left", cookies);
```

The value stored in **cookies** is displayed using the conversion specifier, **%d**, for integer values. The value of **cookies** will replace the **%d** in the output string. The string will be displayed starting on a new line because of the **\n** at the beginning. The next statement subtracts **3** from the current value of **cookies**:

```
cookies = cookies - 3;      /* Subtract 3 from the value of cookies */
```

Since the value of **cookies** immediately before executing this statement was only 3, when **3** is subtracted 0 are left, which is displayed by the final **printf()**:

```
printf("\nI've eaten the rest. Now there are %d cookies left\n",
                                                          cookies);
```

Easy, isn't it? Let's finish our tour of the arithmetic operators with a quick look at multiplication and division.

Try It Out - Multiplication and Division

Multiplication and division are used in exactly the same way, as you'd expect. This example is very simple, but it's a good demonstration of how division and multiplication work.

Suppose we have a jar of 42 cookies and a group of 7 children. We will share out the cookies equally among the children and work out how many each child has. Then we will get 2 more cookies for each child and work out how many cookies there are in total.

```
/* Example 2.6 cookies and kids */
#include <stdio.h>

void main()
{
    int cookies = 42;                   /* Number of cookies in the jar */
    int children = 7;                   /* Number of children           */
    int cookies_per_child = 0;          /* Number of cookies per child  */

    /* Calculate how many cookies each child gets
                                  when they are divided up */

    /* Number of cookies per child */
    cookies_per_child = cookies / children;

    printf("\nYou have %d children and %d cookies", children, cookies);
    printf("\nGive each child %d cookies.", cookies_per_child);
```

```
    /* Give each child two more cookies */
    cookies_per_child = cookies_per_child + 2;

    printf("\nThe children want more cookies, so you buy 2 more for
                                                            each.");
    printf("\nNow each child has %d cookies.", cookies_per_child);

    /* Calculate the total number of
                           cookies distributed among the children */
    cookies = cookies_per_child * children;

    printf("\nThere are now %d cookies in total\n", cookies);
}
```

When you run this program you'll get the this output:

```
You have 7 children and 42 cookies.
Give each child 6 cookies.
The children want more cookies, so you buy 2 more for each.
Now each child has 8 cookies.
There are now 56 cookies in total.
```

How It Works

Let's go through this, step by step. Three integer variables, **cookies**, **children** and **cookies_per_child** are declared and initialized with the statements:

```
int cookies = 42;          /* Number of cookies in the jar */
int children = 7;          /* Number of children           */
int cookies_per_child = 0; /* Number of cookies per child  */
```

The number of cookies is divided by the number of children by using the division operator **/** to produce the number of cookies given to each child:

```
/* Number of cookies per child */
cookies_per_child = cookies / children;
```

The next two statements output what's happening, including the value stored in **cookies_per_child**:

```
printf("\nYou have %d children and %d cookies", children, cookies);
printf("\nGive each child %d cookies.", cookies_per_child);
```

Next the value of **cookies_per_child** is increased by 2 to simulate giving two extra cookies to each child:

```
/* Give each child two more cookies */
cookies_per_child = cookies_per_child + 2;
```

43

The number of cookies that each child now has is then displayed:

```
    printf("\nThe children want more cookies, so you buy 2 more for
                                                      each.");
    printf("\nNow each child has %d cookies.", cookies_per_child);
```

Notice that we're still using the same variable, **cookies_per_child**. The original value has been replaced by a new value, which in this case is the old value plus 2. The variable name is the same - it's only the value that has changed. Whenever you use this variable from now on, it will always have this new value (unless, of course, you do another calculation and replace it with a newer value).

Lastly, the multiplication operator, *, is used to multiply the new number of cookies per child by the number of children to find out the new total number of cookies. This new value of **cookies** is then printed out:

```
    /* Calculate the total number of
                    cookies distributed among the children */
    cookies = cookies_per_child * children;

    printf("\nThere are now %d cookies in total\n", cookies);
```

Here, the variable **cookies** has also had a new value stored in it - so, of course, the old value is lost.

More on Division with Integers

In the previous example, when we divided the number of cookies, 42, by the number of children, 7, the result was exact. Of course, this is not always the case. When you perform division with integers, you always get a whole number as a result - and if there's a remainder, it's ignored. The next example will illustrate this point.

```
/* Example 2.7 dividing integer numbers */
#include <stdio.h>

void main()
{
   int cookies = 15;
   int children = 6;
   int each = 0;

   each = cookies/children;
   printf("%d divided by %d = %d", cookies, children, each);
}
```

When you run this program you will get the following output:

```
15 divided by 6 = 2
```

The result is 2, and the remainder, 3, has been thrown away. This effect can be quite useful. There are lots of situations where you only want the result of a calculation to be a whole number.

Usually, you only deal in whole numbers of people, for example. If you need to divide a group of people into teams of 5, then you want a whole number of teams. Four and two fifths teams is not very useful.

However, there are lots of circumstances where you will want a more precise division, with a decimal result. To get an accurate result, we need to use another kind of variable - one that stores numbers in a different form. The type of variable we need is called a **floating point variable.** We'll come on to these very shortly.

If you're dividing one integer by another and you want to know what the remainder is, the modulus operator can help.

Try It Out - The Modulus Operator

The final operator on our list is the modulus operator, **%**. This is only applicable to integer values. The other operators, as we'll see, can be applied to other types of numeric values. The modulus operator produces the amount that's left over after we have divided one integer by another. For example, the modulus of 14/3 is 2. (14 divided by 3 is 4, with 2 remainder.)

Let's go back to our theme of cookies and children, as it illustrates the modulus operator very well. Let's suppose that we have 5 children and we want to divide 10 cookies and 12 apples between them.

```
/*Example 2.8 cookies, kids and apples */
#include <stdio.h>
void main()
{
   int cookies = 10;        /* Number of cookies          */
   int apples = 12;         /* Number of apples           */
   int children = 5;        /* Number of children         */
   int cookies_left = 0;    /* Number of cookies left over */
   int apples_left = 0;     /* Number of apples left over  */

   /* Calculate how many cookies remain */
   cookies_left = cookies % children;

   printf("\nDistribute the cookies and apples equally between the
                                                  kids.");
   printf("\nEach child gets %d cookies.", cookies/children);
   printf("\nThere are %d cookies left.", cookies_left);

   /* Calculate how many apples are left */
   apples_left = apples % children;

   printf("\nEach child gets %d apples.", apples/children);
   printf("\nThere are %d apples left.\n", apples_left);
}
```

This program produces the following output:

```
Distribute the cookies and apples equally between the kids.
Each child gets 2 cookies.
There are 0 cookies left.
Each child gets 2 apples.
There are 2 apples left.
```

How It Works

We'll go through what's happening. First, we declare five variables that we need in the calculation, and set initial values for them:

```
int cookies = 10;       /* Number of cookies           */
int apples = 12;        /* Number of apples            */
int children = 5;       /* Number of children          */
int cookies_left = 0;   /* Number of cookies left over */
int apples_left = 0;    /* Number of apples left over  */
```

We'll use the last two variables that we've declared here to store calculated values: the number of cookies and the number of apples that are left over when they've been divided equally among the children.

We calculate the number of cookies left over, after dividing what we have among the children, with this statement:

```
/* Calculate how many cookies remain */
cookies_left = cookies % children;
```

The expression **cookies % children** produces just the whole number remaining, when the value in the left variable, **cookies**, is divided by the value in the right variable, **children**. If the division is exact, as it is in this case, the remainder is zero - and this is the value that's stored.

We then call the **printf()** function in three successive statements:

```
printf("\nDistribute the cookies and apples equally between the
                                                        kids.");
printf("\nEach child gets %d cookies.", cookies/children);
printf("\nThere are %d cookies left.", cookies_left);
```

The first statement just outputs a message. The second outputs the number of cookies that each child requires. The expression **cookies/children** produces this value. As you can see, we can use an expression as an argument to a function if we wish. The value of the expression is calculated, and the result is passed to the **printf()** function - just the same as if we'd stored the result in a variable and put that as the argument. Of course, if we wanted to use the value elsewhere, we would need to store it in a variable. Here, the result is lost once it has been passed to the function, as it isn't saved anywhere. The third statement outputs the number of cookies left over - 0 in this case.

Then next three statements do exactly the same as the previous four, but for apples instead of cookies:

```
        /* Calculate how many apples are left */
        apples_left = apples % children;

        printf("\nEach child gets %d apples.", apples/children);
        printf("\nThere are %d apples left.\n", apples_left);
```

Here the modulus operator is used again, this time to work out the apple split. The remainder is not zero because 5 does not divide into 12 exactly: the remainder is 2.

Unary Operators

The operators that we've dealt with so far have been **binary operators**. These operators are called **binary** operators because they operate on two data items. For example, multiplication is a binary operator because you multiply one value by another. However, there are some operators which are **unary**, meaning that they only need one item of data, or one value, to operate on. We'll see more examples later, but for now we'll just take a look at the single most common unary operator.

The Unary Minus (-) Operator

You'll find the unary operator very useful in more complicated programs. It makes whatever is positive negative, and vice versa. You might not immediately realize when you would use this, but think about double-entry book keeping. You have $200 in the bank. You record what happens to this money in a book with two columns, one for money that you pay out and another for money that you receive. One column is your expenditure (negative) and the other is your revenue (positive).

You decide to buy a CD for $50 and a $25 book. If all goes well, when you compare the initial value in the bank and subtract the expenditure ($75) you should end up with what's left. The diagram below shows how these entries could typically be recorded in a double-entry system.

	Income	Expenditure	Bank Balance
Check received	$200		$200
CD		$50	$150
Book		$25	$125
Closing Balance	$200	$75	$125

If these numbers were stored in variables, you could enter both the revenue and expenditure as positive values, and only make the number negative when you wanted to calculate how much was left. You could do this by simply placing a minus in front of the variable name.

To output the amount you'd spent as a negative value you could write:

```
int expenditure = 75;
printf("Your balance has changed by %d.", -expenditure);
```

Which would result in:

    Your balance has changed by -75.

The minus sign will remind you that you've spent this money rather than gained it! Note that the expression **-expenditure** does not change the value stored in expenditure - it is still 75. The value of the expression is –75.

Of course, you also use the unary minus operator every time you write a negative number, such as –75 or –1.25.

Variables and Memory

So far, we've only looked at integer variables - without considering how much space they take up in memory. Each time you declare a variable, the computer allocates a space in memory big enough to store that particular type of variable. Every variable of a particular type will always occupy the same amount of memory - the same number of bytes - but different types of variables require different amounts of memory to be allocated.

You saw at the beginning of this chapter how a computer's memory is organized into bytes. Each variable will occupy some number of bytes in memory, so, how many bytes are needed to store an integer? Well, one byte can store an integer value from -128 to +127. This would be enough for the integer values we've seen so far, but what if we wanted to store a count of the average number of stitches in a pair of knee-length socks - one byte wouldn't be anywhere near enough. Consequently, not only do we have variables of different types in C, including integer variables, but we also have several varieties of integer variables to provide for different ranges of integers to be stored.

As we describe each type of variable, we'll show a table containing the range of values that can be stored and the memory the variable will occupy. We'll summarize all these in a complete table of all the variable types at the end of this chapter.

Types of Integer Variables

We have three flavors of integer variables that we can declare. Each type is specified by a different keyword, as shown in the following table.

Keyword	Number of Bytes	Range of Values
int	2 or 4 (depending on your computer)	-32,768 to +32,767 or -2,147,438,648 to 2,147,438,647
short	2	-32,768 to +32,767
long	4	-2,147,438,648 to 2,147,438,647

The table reflects the typical size of each type of integer variable. As you can see, integer variables may occupy two or four bytes - depending on which type you specify.

Variables of type **int** can be either two or 4 bytes, depending on what kind of computer and C which compiler you're using. For example, the statement:

```
int cookies = 0;
```

declares a variable that will occupy two bytes on some machines and 4 bytes on others. On a PC, **int** will often be 2 bytes, and that's what we'll assume throughout this book. This variation may seem a little strange, but the **int** type is intended to correspond to the size of integer that the computer has been designed to deal with most efficiently, and this can vary between different types of machine. Ultimately, it's the compiler that determines what you get. Although at one time the majority of PC compilers created **int** variables as 2 bytes, with more recent C compilers on a PC, variables of type **int** occupy four bytes because all modern processors move data around at least 4 bytes at a time.

> *The sizes of all these types are compiler-dependent, with the restriction that the size of* ***short*** *variables should be less than or equal to those of type* ***int***, *which in turn should be less than or equal to the size of variables of type* ***long***.

If you use the keyword **short** as an alternative to **int** you'll get 2-byte variables. The previous declaration could have been written:

```
short cookies = 0;
```

The keyword **short** is actually an abbreviation for **short int** so you could write:

```
short int cookies = 0;
```

This is exactly the same as the previous statement. When you write just **short** in a variable declaration, the **int** is implied. Most people prefer to use this form: it's perfectly clear and it saves a bit of typing.

If we need integers with a bigger range, to store the number of hamburgers sold by all the McDonalds in Chicago in one day, for instance, we can use the keyword **long**:

```
long Big_Number;
```

This defines an integer variable with a length of 4 bytes, which provides for a range of values from -2,147,438,648 to 2,147,438,647. Instead of **long**, you can write **long int** if you wish, since it amounts to the same thing. The full names of the three types of integer variable we have described here are therefore **short int**, **int**, and **long int**.

Integer Constants

Since we can have different kinds of integer variables, you might expect to have different kinds of integer constants, and you do. If you just write an integer value 100 for example, this will be of type **int**. If you want to make sure it is type **long** you must append an **L**, upper or lower case, to the numeric value. So the integer 100 as a long value is written **100L**. To declare and initialize the variable **Big_Number** we could write:

```
long Big_Number = 10000000L;
```

An integer value will also be **long** if it is outside the range of type **int**. Thus if your compiler implementation uses two bytes to store type **int** values, the values **1000000** and **33000** will be of type **long** by default.

You can also write integer values in hexadecimal form - that is, to base 16. The digits in a hexadecimal number are the equivalent of decimal values 0 to 15, and are represented by 0 through 9 and A though F. Since there needs to be a way to distinguish between 99_{10} and 99_{16}, hexadecimal numbers are written with the prefix **0x** or **0X**. You would therefore write 99_{16} in your program as **0x99**.

Floating Point Values

Floating point variables are used to store floating point numbers. Floating point numbers hold values with a decimal point in them, so you can represent fractional as well as integral values. The following are examples of floating point values:

1.6
0.00008
7655.899

Because of the way floating point numbers are represented, they only hold a fixed number of decimal digits; however, they can represent a very wide range of values - much wider than integer types. Floating point numbers are often expressed as a decimal value multiplied by some power of 10. For example, each of the previous examples of floating point numbers could be expressed as follows:

Value	With an exponent:	Can also be written in C as:
1.6	0.16×10^1	0.16E1
0.00008	0.8×10^{-4}	0.8E-4
7655.899	0.7655899×10^4	0.7655899E4

The center column shows how the numbers in the left column could be represented with an exponent. This is not how you write them in C: it's just an alternative way of representing the same value. The right-hand column shows how the representation in the center columns would be expressed in C. The **E** in each of the numbers is for exponent, and you could equally well use a small letter **e**. Of course, you can write each of these numbers in your program without an exponent, just as they appear in the left hand column - but for very large or very small numbers, the exponent form is very useful. You'd rather write **0.5E-15** than **0.000000000000005**, wouldn't you?

Floating Point Variables

There are three different types of floating point variable, as shown in the following table.

Keyword	Number of Bytes	Range of Values
`float`	4	±3.4E38 (6 digit precision)
`double`	8	±1.7E308 (15 digit precision)
`long double`	10	±1.2E4932 (19 digit precision)

A floating point variable is declared in a very similar way to integer variables:

```
float Radius;
double Biggest;
```

If you need to store numbers with up to 6 digits of accuracy (a range of 10^{-38} to 10^{+38}), then you should use variables of type **float**. Values of type **float** are known as **single precision** floating point numbers. This will occupy 4 bytes in memory, as you can see from the table. Using variables of type **double** will allow you to store **double precision** floating point values. Each variable of type double will occupy 8 bytes in memory, and give you 15 digit precision with a range of 10^{-308} to 10^{+308}. Variables of type **double** suffice for the majority of requirements, but some specialized applications require even more accuracy and range. The **long double** type provides the exception range and precision shown in the table. Note that the range and precision for each type is implementation-dependent, so while the values I've given are typical, they may be different with your C compiler.

To write a constant of type **float** you append an **f** to the number to distinguish it from type **double**. We could have initialized the last two variables with the statements:

```
float Radius = 2.5f;
double Biggest = 123E30;
```

The variable **Radius** has the initial value 2.5, and the variable **Biggest** is initialized to the number that is written 123 followed by thirty zeros. To specify a **long double** value, you need to append an **L** or **l** to the number. For example:

```
long double huge = 1234567.89123L;
```

Division Using Floating Point Values

Let's get back to the sort of division problem we saw earlier. If we write the division operation using variables of type **float** then we'll get an accurate answer, as the example below illustrates:

Try It Out - Division with Floats

```
/* Example 2.9 division with floats */
#include <stdio.h>

void main()
{
   float x = 10.0f;
   float y = 4.0f;
```

```
    float z = 0.0f;

    z = x / y;
    printf("%f divided by %f = %f", x, y, z);
}
```

Which gives this output:

```
10.000000 divided by 4.000000 = 2.500000
```

This result is a bit more accurate than the one we obtained earlier.

How It Works

Note that we've used a new format specifier for float variables in the **printf()** statement.

```
    printf("%f divided by %f = %f", x, y, z);
```

The format specifier **%f** displays the result as a single precision floating point number. Note that the format specifier must correspond to the type of value that you're outputting. If you output a value of type float with the specifier **%d** that's intended for use with integer values, you'll get rubbish. This is because the float value will be interpreted as an integer - which it is not. Similarly, if you use **%f** with a value of an integer type then you'll also get rubbish as output.

Try experimenting with different variable types and different format specifiers. I've included a table in the summary for you to refer to. You can get some strange results, but this is a valuable lesson. If you write a program that runs perfectly well (or seems to) and does some complicated math, the last thing you want to find is that although it gives an answer, it's completely wrong!

> *As a rule, you should only use the floating point types when you need to. If you have to use floating point variables to hold integer values, you can't rely on their values being exact. In floating point, 0.9999999 is as good as 1.0 and, in most instances, it will make no difference. However, if you round it down to an integer, it isn't one at all, it's zero.*

More Complex Expressions

Now we all know that arithmetic can get a lot more complicated than just dividing a couple of numbers. In fact, if that was all we were trying to do then we may as well use paper and pencil. Now that we have the tools of addition, subtraction, multiplication and division at our disposal, we can really start to do some heavy calculations.

For these more complicated calculations, you'll need more control over the sequence of operations when an expression is evaluated. Parentheses provide you with this capability. They can also help to make expressions clearer when they're getting intricate.

Parentheses in Arithmetic Expressions

We can use parentheses in arithmetic expressions, and they work much as you'd expect. Sub-expressions contained within parentheses are evaluated in sequence from the innermost pair of parentheses to the outermost, with the normal rules for operator precedence - where multiplication and division happen before addition or subtraction.

Therefore, the expression:

2*(3+3*(5+4))

evaluates to 60. You start with 5+4 which produces 9. Then you multiply that by 3 which gives 27. Then you add 3 to that total (giving 30) and multiply the whole lot by 2.

You can also insert spaces to separate operands from operators to make your arithmetic statements more readable. If you're not quite sure of how an expression will be evaluated according to the precedence rules, you can always put in some parentheses to make sure it produces the result you want.

Try It Out - Arithmetic in Action

We can now try another program. We can have a go at calculating the circumference and area of a circle from an input value for the radius. You may remember from elementary math the equations to calculate the area and circumference of a circle using π or Pi, (circumference = $2\pi r$ and area = πr^2). If you don't, then don't worry. This isn't a math book, so just look at how the program works.

```
/*Example 2.10 calculations on a circle */
#include <stdio.h>

void main()
{
   float radius = 0.0f;             /* The radius of a circle        */
   float circumference = 0.0f;      /* The circumference of a circle */
   float area = 0.0f;               /* The area of a circle          */
   float Pi = 3.14159f;

   printf("\nInput the radius of a circle:");
   scanf("%f", &radius);                   /* Read the radius entered      */
   circumference = 2.0f*Pi*radius;         /* Calculate the circumference */
   area = Pi*radius*radius;                /* Calculate the area          */
   printf("\nThe circumference is %f", circumference);
   printf("\nThe area is %f", area);
}
```

How It Works

Up to the first **printf()** the program looks much the same as those we've seen before.

```
   float radius = 0.0f;             /* The radius of a circle        */
   float circumference = 0.0f;      /* The circumference of a circle */
   float area = 0.0f;               /* The area of a circle          */
   float Pi = 3.14159f;
```

We declare and initialize four variables, and **Pi** has its usual value. The next statement outputs a prompt for input from the keyboard:

```
   printf("\nInput the radius of a circle:");
```

In the next statement, which deals with the input of the radius of the circle, we've used a new standard library function, the **scanf()** function:

```
    scanf("%f", &radius);                /* Read the radius entered     */
```

scanf() is another function that requires **stdio.h** to be included. This function handles input from the keyboard. In effect it takes what you enter through the keyboard and interprets it as specified by the first argument, which is a control string between the quotes (in this case **%f** for a value of type **float**). It stores the result in the variable **radius** that's specified as the second argument. The first argument is a control string similar to the one we used with the **printf()** function, except that it controls input rather than output.

You've probably noticed something new here - the **&** preceding the variable name **radius**. This is called the **address of** operator, and it's needed to make the **scanf()** function work. For the moment, we won't go into any more detailed explanation on the **address of** operator. If you don't quite understand, just believe it for the moment and we'll see more on this, particularly in Chapter 11. The only thing to remember is to use the **address of** operator (the **&** sign) before a variable when you're using the **scanf()** function, and not to use it when you use the **printf()** function.

> *If you're really curious about the **address of** operator… it's used to pass the address of the variable **radius** in the memory to the function **scanf()**. This is essential, since **scanf()** is going to store the input value there.*
>
> *In the case of the **printf()** statements lower down, there's no **&** preceding the variable names, so the actual value that the variable contains is transferred to the function. This makes sense, because we want the function to simply output that value - it doesn't need the address, since it isn't going to change the value.*

Next, we have two statements that calculate the results we're interested in:

```
    circumference = 2.0f*Pi*radius;      /* Calculate the circumference */
    area = Pi*radius*radius;             /* Calculate the area          */
```

The first statement computes the circumference of a circle, using the value that was input for the radius; the second statement calculates the area. Note that, if you forget the **f** in **2.0f**, you'll probably get a warning message from your compiler. This is because without the **f**, the value is of type **double**, and you would be mixing different types in the same expression. We will see more about this later.

The next two statements output the values we've calculated:

```
    printf("\nThe circumference is %f", circumference);
    printf("\nThe area is %f", area);
```

These two **printf()** statements output the values of the variables **circumference** and **area**, using the format specifier **%f**. As we've already seen, in both statements the format control string contains text to be displayed, as well as a format specifier for the variable to be output.

If you compile and run this program, you should get output similar to this:

```
Input the radius of a circle: 5
The circumference is 31.415901
The area is 78.539749
```

Of course, you can run this and enter whatever values you want for the radius. You could experiment with different forms of floating point input here, and you could try entering something like **1E1**, for example.

Try It Out - What Are You Worth?

We can look at a similar example that's a little more personal. Let's return to our earlier discussion of your salary, and take it a bit further to see what you're really worth.

```c
/* Example 2.11 Work out your wage */
#include <stdio.h>

void main()
{
   float salary = 0.0f;            /* Annual salary                      */
   float rate_per_hour = 0.0f;     /* Average rate per hour              */
   float rate_per_second = 0.0f;   /* Average rate per second            */
   float hours= 0.0f;              /* Average hours worked per week      */
   float weeks = 0.0f;             /* Number of weeks worked in the year */

   printf("\nEnter your annual salary: ");
   scanf("%f", &salary);

   printf("Enter the number of weeks you work per year: ");
   scanf("%f", &weeks);

   printf("Enter the number of hours you usually work per week: ");
   scanf("%f", &hours);

   /* Calculate the average rate per hour and per second */
   rate_per_hour = salary / (hours * weeks);
   rate_per_second = rate_per_hour / 3600.f;

   printf("\nYou earn $%.2f.\nThis is $%.2f per hour and $%f per
                   second.", salary, rate_per_hour, rate_per_second);
   printf("\nAsk for a rise tomorrow!\n");
}
```

By now you probably know what the output from this will be, but the format specifiers for the output variables in the **printf()** statement are a little different. Here is the output:

```
Enter your annual salary: 20000
Enter the number of weeks you work per year: 52
Enter the number of hours you usually work per week: 40
```

```
You earn $20000.00.
This is $9.62 per hour and $0.002671 per second.
Ask for a rise tomorrow!
```

How It Works

First we declare all the variables we need:

```
float salary = 0.0f;            /* Annual salary                       */
float rate_per_hour = 0.0f;     /* Average rate per hour               */
float rate_per_second = 0.0f;   /* Average rate per second             */
float hours= 0.0f;              /* Average hours worked per week       */
float weeks = 0.0f;             /* Number of weeks worked in the year */
```

All the variables are declared as type **float** to enable us to display the hourly rate and rate per second as decimal values. Decimal values are unlikely to be whole integers.

Next, we get the input data we need from the keyboard:

```
printf("\nEnter your annual salary: ");
scanf("%f", &salary);

printf("Enter the number of weeks you work per year: ");
scanf("%f", &weeks);

printf("Enter the number of hours you usually work per week: ");
scanf("%f", &hours);
```

There is a prompt for each of the values required, produced by the three statements calling the **printf()** function. The values for the salary, the number of weeks worked in a year, and the number of hours worked in a week, are all read as **float** values using the **%f** specifier. The values read are stored in the variables **salary**, **weeks**, and **hours** respectively.

The results are calculated by these statements:

```
/* Calculate the average rate per hour and per second */
rate_per_hour = salary / (hours * weeks);
rate_per_second = rate_per_hour / 3600.f;
```

We get the rate per hour by dividing the salary by the total number of hours worked in a year. We then get the rate per second by dividing the rate per hour by 3600 - the number of seconds in an hour. Note how we've written 3600 here, as **3600.f**. Because it has a decimal point, this value is automatically a floating point value, and because of the **f** at the end, it is a value of type **float**. If you omit the **f** then the value will be of type **double**. This will work OK, but you'll get a warning message from the compiler, because all the other values are of type **float**. We'll see more about mixing different types of values in an expression later on.

The output is produced by the last two statements:

```
printf("\nYou earn $%.2f.\nThis is $%.2f per hour and $%f per
                second.", salary, rate_per_hour, rate_per_second);
printf("\nAsk for a rise tomorrow!\n");
```

These final **printf()** statements are the interesting part. They're straightforward enough, except that the first two conversion specifiers have a number in the middle: **%.2f**. The **.2** indicates that you're only interested in the result to 2 decimal places. It has the effect of rounding the result to two decimal places. Therefore, with the values entered as above, the salary is output as **20000.00** and the rate per hour as **9.62**. For the rate per second, we need to leave it as a normal float; otherwise, we won't get as far as the actual figure - unless, of course, you earn an obscene amount that we don't want to know about.

Defining Constants

We've taken the example of calculating the circumference and area of a circle. Although we've defined **Pi** as a variable it is, really, a constant value that we don't want to change.

We actually have a couple of choices when handling **Pi**. The value of π is a set number - always. Therefore, we can define **Pi** as a symbol that's to be replaced in the program by its value. It isn't a variable at all, but more a sort of alias. Alternatively, we can define it as a variable having a fixed value. You can use whichever method you prefer.

Try It Out - Defining a Constant

Let's look at the first alternative, treating **PI** as an alias for its value:

```
/* Example 2.12 More circles */
#include <stdio.h>
#define PI 3.14159f

void main()
{
   float radius = 0.0f;
   float circumference = 0.0f;
   float area = 0.0f;

   printf("Input the radius of a circle:");
   scanf("%f", &radius);
   circumference = 2.0f*PI*radius;
   area = PI*radius*radius;
   printf("\nThe circumference is %f", circumference);
   printf("\nThe area is %f", area);
}
```

How It Works

After the comment and the **#include** directive for the header file, we have a pre-processor directive:

```
#define PI 3.14159f
```

We have now defined **PI** as a symbol that represents **3.14159f**. We've used **PI** rather than **Pi** as it's common convention in C to write identifiers that appear in a **#define** statement in capital letters. Wherever we reference **PI** within an expression in the program, the pre-processor will substitute the value we've specified for it in the **#define** directive. All the substitutions will be made before compiling the program. When the program is ready to be compiled, it will no longer contain references to **PI**, as all occurrences will have been replaced by the numeric value specified in the **#define** directive. This all happens internally while your program is processed. Your source program will not be changed: it will still contain the symbol **PI**.

Try It Out – Defining a Variable with a Fixed Value

We can now try the approach that involves defining a variable with a value that is fixed. And while we're here, we can add another finesse to shorten the program:

```
/* Example 2.13 Circles again but shorter */

#include <stdio.h>

void main()
{
   float radius = 0.0f;          /* The radius of a circle        */
   const float Pi = 3.14159f;    /* Defines the value of Pi as fixed */

   printf("Input the radius of a circle:");
   scanf("%f", &radius);

   printf("\nThe circumference is %f", 2.0f*Pi*radius);
   printf("\nThe area is %f", Pi*radius*radius);
}
```

How It Works

Following the declaration for the variable **radius**, we have the statement:

```
   const float Pi = 3.14159f;    /* Defines the value of Pi as fixed */
```

This declares the variable **Pi** and defines a value for it; **Pi** is still a variable here, but the initial value we've given it can't be changed. The **const** modifier achieves this effect. It can be applied to any statement declaring a variable of any type to fix the value of that variable. Of course, the value must appear in the declaration in the same way as shown here - following an **=** sign after the variable name. The compiler will check your code for attempts to change variables that you've declared as **const**, and if it discovers that you attempt to change a **const** variable then it will complain. There are ways to trick the compiler to change **const** variables, but this defeats the whole point of using **const** in the first place.

The following two statements produce the output from the program:

```
   printf("\nThe circumference is %f", 2.0f*Pi*radius);
   printf("\nThe area is %f", Pi*radius*radius);
```

In this example, we've done away with the variables storing the circumference and area of the circle. The expressions for these now appear as arguments in the **printf()** statements where they are evaluated, and their values are passed directly to the function.

In general, when passing a value to a function, the value can be the result of evaluating an expression - rather than the value of a particular variable. The compiler will actually create a temporary variable to hold the value, which is subsequently discarded. This is fine, as long as we don't want to use these values elsewhere!

Choosing the Correct Type for the Job

In C you have to be careful when doing calculations as to the type of variable that you're using. If you use the wrong type then you may find that errors creep into your programs that can be hard to detect. This is best shown with an example.

Try It Out - The Right Types of Variables

Here's a great example of how things can go horribly off course if you use the wrong type of variable:

```
/* Example 2.14 Choosing the correct type for the job  1*/
#include <stdio.h>
#define  REVENUE_PER_150 4.5f

void main()
{
    short JanSold = 23500;        /* Stock sold in January      */
    short FebSold = 19300;        /* Stock sold in February     */
    short MarSold = 21600;        /* Stock sold in March        */
    float  RevQuarter = 0.0f;     /* Sales revenue for the quarter */

    /* Calculate quarterly total     */
    short QuarterSold = JanSold+FebSold+MarSold;

    /* Output monthly sales and total for the quarter */
    printf("\nStock sold in\n Jan: %d\n Feb: %d\n Mar:%d",
            JanSold,FebSold,MarSold);

    printf("\nTotal stock sold in first quarter: %d",QuarterSold);

    /* Calculate the total revenue for the quarter and output it */
    RevQuarter = QuarterSold/150*REVENUE_PER_150;
    printf("\nSales revenue this quarter is:$%.2f\n",RevQuarter);
}
```

These are fairly simple calculations, and you can see that the total stock sold in the quarter should be 64400. This is just the sum of each of the monthly totals, but if you run the program then the output you get is this:

```
Stock sold in
 Jan: 23500
 Feb: 19300
 Mar: 21600
Total stock sold in first quarter: -1136
Sales revenue this quarter is :$-31.50
```

Obviously all is not right here. It doesn't take a genius, or an accountant, to tell you that adding 3 big, positive numbers together shouldn't give a negative result!

How It Works - The Problem

Let's consider what's happening in the program. We have two pre-processor directives at the outset:

```
#include <stdio.h>
#define  REVENUE_PER_150 4.5f
```

The **include** statement adds the contents of the **stdio.h** header file to our program which allows us to use **printf()**. We then define a constant, **REVENUE_PER_150** that we'll use when calculating the revenue for the quarter. Because it's defined as **4.5f** the value will be of type **float**.

Next, we declare four variables and assign initial values to them.

```
short JanSold = 23500;        /* Stock sold in January       */
short FebSold = 19300;        /* Stock sold in February      */
short MarSold = 21600;        /* Stock sold in March         */
float  RevQuarter = 0.0f;     /* Sales revenue for the quarter */
```

The first three variables are of type **short**, which is quite adequate to store the initial value. The **RevQuarter** variable is of type **float** because we want two decimal places for the quarterly revenue.

The next statement declares the variable **QuarterSold** and stores the sum of the sales for each of the months:

```
/* Calculate quarterly total    */
short QuarterSold = JanSold+FebSold+MarSold;
```

The error that has occurred is in the declaration of the **QuarterSold** variable. We've declared it to be of type **short** and given it the initial value of the sum of the 3 monthly figures. We know that their sum is 64400 and that the program outputs a negative number. The error must therefore be in this assignment statement.

The problem arises because we've tried to store a number that's too large for type **short**. If you remember, the maximum value that a **short** variable can hold is 32,767. The computer cannot interpret the value of **QuarterSold** correctly, and happens to give a negative result. The solution to our problem is to use a **long** integer that will allow us to store much larger numbers.

Solving the Problem

Try changing the program and running it again. We only need to change two lines in the body of the function **main()**. The new improved program is as follows:

```
/* Example 2.15 Choosing the correct type for the job  2 */
#include <stdio.h>
#define  REVENUE_PER_150 4.5f
```

```
void main()
{
    short JanSold = 23500;        /* Stock sold in January      */
    short FebSold = 19300;        /* Stock sold in February     */
    short MarSold = 21600;        /* Stock sold in March        */
    float  RevQuarter = 0.0f;     /* Sales revenue for the quarter */

    /* Calculate quarterly total */
    long QuarterSold = JanSold+FebSold+MarSold;

    /* Output monthly sales and total for the quarter */
    printf("Stock sold in\n Jan: %d\n Feb: %d\n Mar: %d\n",
           JanSold,FebSold,MarSold);

    printf("Total stock sold in first quarter: %ld\n",QuarterSold);

    /* Calculate the total revenue for the quarter and output it */
    RevQuarter = QuarterSold/150*REVENUE_PER_150;
    printf("Sales revenue this quarter is:$%.2f\n",RevQuarter);
}
```

When you run this program the output is more satisfactory:

```
Stock sold in
 Jan: 23500
 Feb: 19300
 Mar: 21600
Total stock sold in first quarter: 64400
Sales revenue this quarter is :$1930.50
```

The stock sold in the quarter is correct, and we have a reasonable result for revenue. Notice that we used **%ld** to output the total stock sold. This is to tell the compiler that it is to use a **long** conversion for the output of this value. Just to check the program, calculate the result of the revenue with a calculator.

The result you should get is, in fact, $1932.00. Somewhere, we've lost a dollar and a half! Not such a great amount, but try saying that to an accountant! We need to find the lost $1.50. Consider what's happening when we calculate the value for revenue in the program.

```
RevQuarter = QuarterSold / 150 * REVENUE_PER_150;
```

Here, we're assigning a value to **RevQuarter**. The value is the result of the expression on the right of the **=** sign. The result of the expression will be calculated, step by step, according to the precedence rules we've already looked at in this chapter. Here we have quite a simple expression that is calculated from left to right, as division and multiplication have the same priority. Let's work through it:

QuarterSold/150 is calculated as 64400/150, which should produce the result 429.333.

This is where our problem arises. **QuarterSold** is an integer and so the computer truncates the result of the division to an integer, ignoring the .333. This means that when the next part of the calculation is evaluated the result will be slightly out.

429*REVENUE_PER_150 is calculated as 429 * 4.5 which is 1930.50

We now know where the error has occurred, but what can we do about it? We could change all of our variables to floating point types, but that would defeat the object of using integers in the first place. The numbers entered really are integers so we'd like to store them as such. Is there an easy solution to this? The answer is - Yes. In C you have the ability to convert a value of one type to another type. This process is called is called **casting**.

Type Casting in Arithmetic Expressions

Let's look at the expression to calculate the quarterly revenue.

```
RevQuarter = QuarterSold/150*REVENUE_PER_150;
```

We know that this has to be amended so that the expression is calculated in floating point form. If we cast the value of **QuarterSold** to type **float**, then the expression will be evaluated as floating point and our problem will be solved. To do this, we place the type that we want to cast the variable to in parentheses before the variable. The statement to calculate the result correctly will thus be:

```
RevQuarter = (float)QuarterSold/150*REVENUE_PER_150;
```

We'll do this in the third version of our program:

```c
/* Example 2.16 Choosing the correct type for the job  3 */
#include <stdio.h>
#define  REVENUE_PER_150 4.5f

void main()
{
    short JanSold = 23500;          /* Stock sold in January      */
    short FebSold = 19300;          /* Stock sold in February     */
    short MarSold = 21600;          /* Stock sold in March        */
    float  RevQuarter = 0.0f;       /* Sales revenue for the quarter */

    /* Calculate quarterly total */
    long QuarterSold = JanSold+FebSold+MarSold;

    /* Output monthly sales and total for the quarter */
    printf("Stock sold in\n Jan: %d\n Feb: %d\n Mar: %d\n",
            JanSold,FebSold,MarSold);

    printf("Total stock sold in first quarter: %ld\n",QuarterSold);

    /* Calculate the total revenue for the quarter and output it */
    RevQuarter = (float)QuarterSold / 150 * REVENUE_PER_150;
    printf("Sales revenue this quarter is:$%.2f\n",RevQuarter);
}
```

The output from this new improved program is:

```
Stock sold in
 Jan: 23500
 Feb: 19300
 Mar: 21600
 Total stock sold in first quarter: 64400
 Sales revenue this quarter is :$1932.00
```

This is exactly what we require. We're using the right type of variables in the right place. We are also ensuring we don't use integer arithmetic when we want to keep the fractional part of the result of a division.

Automatic Casting

Look at the result of the second version of the program again.

```
 Sales revenue this quarter is :$1930.50
```

Even without the explicit cast statement in the expression, the result in the output was in floating point form already, even though it was still wrong. This is because the compiler automatically casts variables when it's dealing with expressions that contain variables of different types. For each pair of variables of a different type that are involved in an operation, the compiler automatically casts the variable that is of a type with a more limited range to the type of the other variable. So, referring back to the expression to calculate revenue:

QuarterSold / 150 * REVENUE_PER_150

This was evaluated as:

64400 (**int**) / 150 (**int**) which equals 429 (**int**)
Then 429 (**int** cast to **float**) is multiplied by 4.5 (**float**) giving 1930.5 (**float**)

Casting applies when a binary operator applies to two values of different types. With the first operation, the numbers are both of type **int**, so the result is an **int**. With the second operation, the first value is type **int** and the second value is type **float**. Type **int** is more limited in its range than type **float**, so the **int** value is therefore automatically cast to type **float**. Whenever there's a mixture of types in one arithmetic expression, C will use certain rules to convert some of them to enable the expression to be evaluated. Let's have a look at some of these conversion rules now.

Conversion Rules in Casting

An arithmetic operation involving two values can only be performed if the values are of the same type. For each operation in an expression that involves two different types, your compiler will promote the variable with the type that has the more restricted range of values to be the same type as the other variable. The order of types in this context is **long double** highest, then **double**, then **float**, followed by **long**, then **int**, and finally the lowest, **char**. You haven't seen type **char** yet, but we'll be looking at it in a moment.

Let's look at these conversion rules in practice. If we declare three variables, **A** as **double** and **B** and **C** as **long**, we can see how the following expression is worked out.

```
A + B - C
```

Here, we first evaluate **A + B**. **A** is **double** and **B** is **long**, so **B** will be cast to **double** and the result will be **double**. To subtract **C** from this result, **C** is first cast to **double** and we end up with the final result as **double**.

Casts in Assignment Statements

You can also cause an implicit cast by assigning the value of a variable of one type to another. This can cause values to be changed. For instance, if you assign a **float** or **double** value to a variable of type **int** or **long**, the fractional part of the **float** or **double** will be lost - and just the integer part will be stored.

For example, after executing the following code fragment:

```
int number = 0;
float decimal = 2.5f;
number = decimal;
```

the value of **number** will be 2. Because we've assigned the value of **decimal** (2.5) to an **int** variable, **number**, the **.5** at the end will be lost and only the **2** will be stored. Notice how we've used a specifier **f** at the end of **2.5f**. We have seen this used before: it indicates to the compiler that this variable is a single precision floating point variable - of type **float**. Just to remind you, any constant you define with a decimal point is floating point and will be double precision floating point by default. If you don't want it to be double precision then you need to append the **f**.

Note that the assignment statement:

```
number = decimal;
```

will normally result in a warning from the compiler, since in this case it's able to recognize the potential for losing information.

More Numeric Data Types

To complete the set, we should now examine the remaining numeric data types that we haven't yet discussed. The first is one that we mentioned above: type **char**, which can store a character, but which is nevertheless an integer type.

The Character Type

Values of type **char** occupy the least amount of memory of all the data types. They require just one byte, as indicated below.

Keyword	Number of Bytes	Range of Values
Char	1	-128 to +127 or 0 to 255 (unsigned)

A **char** variable can hold any single character; for example, you could store any one of the following:

```
'P'
'p'
'C'
'?'
```

It can be any lower or uppercase letter, and it doesn't have to be alphanumeric. Here are two examples of **char** variable declarations:

```
char first = 'A';
char last = 'Z';
```

Note the way in which the initializing character value is enclosed within single quotes, not double quotes. Double quotes are used to define a string of characters, which is rather different. The single quotes indicate we're defining a single character to be stored in a single byte. You may be wondering why we're including type **char** as a numeric data type when it holds letters. Well, it's quite logical: variables of type **char** can actually hold numeric values. More than that, you can consider a value stored in a variable of type **char** as an integer or as a character, depending on whatever's most convenient to you.

An example of a **char** variable holding a numeric value is:

```
char character = 74;
```

A **char** variable can have any numeric value from -128 to +127 since it occupies a single byte. It has a sort of dual personality: you can interpret it as a character or as an integer.

Try It Out - Character Building

If you're wondering how on earth the computer knows whether it's dealing with a character or an integer, let's look at an example that should make it clear. Here, you'll meet the conversion specifier again, which tells the computer whether to output a character or an integer.

```
/* Example 2.17 Characters and numbers */
#include <stdio.h>

void main()
{
   char first_example = 'T';
   char second_example = 20;

   printf("\nThe first example as a letter looks like this - %c",
             first_example);
```

```
    printf("\nThe first example as a number looks like this - %d",
            first_example);
    printf("\nThe second example as a letter looks like this - %c",
            second_example);
    printf("\nThe second example as a number looks like this - %d\n",
            second_example);
}
```

The output from this program is the following:

```
The first example as a letter looks like this - T
The first example as a number looks like this - 84
The second example as a letter looks like this - ¶
The second example as a number looks like this - 20
```

How It Works

The program starts off by declaring two variables of type **char**:

```
char first_example = 'T';
char second_example = 20;
```

One is initialized with a letter and the other with a number. The next four statements output each of the variables in two ways:

```
printf("\nThe first example as a letter looks like this - %c",
        first_example);
printf("\nThe first example as a number looks like this - %d",
        first_example);
printf("\nThe second example as a letter looks like this - %c",
        second_example);
printf("\nThe second example as a number looks like this - %d\n",
        second_example);
```

The **%c** conversion specifier interprets the contents of the variable as a single character, and the **%d** specifier interprets it as an integer. The numeric values that are output are the codes for the corresponding characters. These will be ASCII codes in most instances, and that's what we'll assume in this book.

> *Not all computers use the ASCII character set, so you may get different values than those show above. If you do, don't worry: the reason C uses the notation 'character' is to get around this problem. So 'A' represents a capital A, no matter which character coding system the program is compiled on, and no matter what number it is internally stored as.*

ASCII stands for American Standard Code for Information Interchange, and it's pronounced 'as-key', with a soft s. Have a look at Appendix B for the full ASCII table.

Try using different numbers and letters in the program. See what results you get.

Try It Out - Using char

Let's look at another example of how variables of type **char** can be used in practice:

```c
/* Example 2.18 Using char  */
#include <stdio.h>

void main()
{
   char first = 'A';
   char second = 'B';
   char last = 'Z';

   char number = 40;

   char ex1 = first + 2;       /* Add 2 to 'A'        */
   char ex2 = second - 1;      /* Subtract 1 from 'B' */
   char ex3 = last + 2;        /* Add 2 to 'Z'        */

   printf("\nCharacter values      %c   %c   %c", ex1, ex2, ex3);
   printf("\nNumerical equivalents %d  %d  %d", ex1, ex2, ex3);
   printf("\nThe number %d is the same as the character %c", number,
number);
}
```

If you run the program you should get the following output:

```
Character values         C  A  \
Numerical equivalents   67 65 92
The number 40 is the same as the character (
```

How It Works

This program shows the equivalence between numbers and ASCII characters. It also demonstrates how we can happily perform arithmetic with **char** variables that we've initialized with characters. The first three statements in the body of **main()** are:

```c
char first = 'A';
char second = 'B';
char last = 'Z';
```

These initialize the variables **first**, **second**, and **last**, to the character values you see. The numerical value of these variables will be the ASCII codes for the respective characters. Because we can treat them as numeric, as well as characters, we can perform arithmetic operations with them.

The next statement initializes a variable of type **char** with an integer value:

```c
char number = 40;
```

The initializing value must be within the range of values that a one-byte variable can store - so it must be between –128 and 127. Of course, we can interpret the contents of the variable as a character. In this case, it will be the character that has the ASCII code value 40, which happens to be a left parenthesis.

The next three statements declare three more variables of type **char**:

```
      char ex1 = first + 2;       /* Add 2 to 'A'       */
      char ex2 = second - 1;      /* Subtract 1 from 'B' */
      char ex3 = last + 2;        /* Add 2 to 'Z'       */
```

These statements create new values and therefore new characters from the variables **first**, **second** and **last**; the results of these expressions are stored in the variables, **ex1**, **ex2**, and **ex3**.

The next two statements output the three variables, **ex1**, **ex2**, and **ex3**, in two different ways:

```
      printf("\nCharacter values       %c   %c   %c", ex1, ex2, ex3);
      printf("\nNumerical equivalents %d  %d  %d", ex1, ex2, ex3);
```

The first statement interprets the values stored as characters by using the **%c** conversion specifier, and the second statement outputs the same variables again, but this time interprets the values as integers. The two lines of output show the three characters with their ASCII codes one line below.

The last line outputs the variable, **number**, as a character and as an integer:

```
      printf("\nThe number %d is the same as the character %c", number,
      number);
```

To output the variable twice, we just write it twice - as the second and third arguments to the **printf()** function. It is output first as an integer value, and then as a character.

This ability to perform arithmetic with characters can be very useful. For instance, to convert from upper case to lower case you simply add the result of **'a'-'A'** (which is 32 for ASCII) to the upper case character; and to achieve the reverse, just subtract **'a'-'A'**. You can see how this works if you have a look at the decimal ASCII values for the alphabetic characters in Appendix B.

Unsigned Integers - Using Positive Integers

If you're sure you're dealing with just positive integers, there is a way of increasing the maximum value that you can use. The **unsigned** modifier can be used with all of the basic integer types we've covered, to define types that are only positive integers. This allows us to handle integers roughly twice as large as we otherwise might. The **unsigned** modifier is used as follows:

```
      unsigned char a_value;        /* Can be from 0 to +255         */
      unsigned int number;          /* Can be from 0 to +65,535      */
      unsigned long big_number;     /* Can be from 0 to 4,294,967,295 */
```

You must be absolutely sure that you only need positive values if you want to use these. Unsigned variables can't assume negative values at all.

When you want to specify an integer value as unsigned, you append the letter **U**, as upper or lower case, to the numeric value. For example, you could write:

```
number = 25U;
```

This sets the unsigned variable, **number**, of type **int**, to 25.

If you want to define a value that's of type **unsigned long**, you need a **U** and an **L** as a suffix to the numeric value. Both letters can be in upper or lower case. For example:

```
big_number = 100000000UL;
```

which stores the value 100000000 in the variable **big_number**.

To output an unsigned integer, you use the format specifier **%u**. For example, we could output the value of the unsigned integer variable, called **number**, with the statement:

```
printf("The value of number is %u", number);
```

We've now covered all the numeric data types in C, so here's the complete table that I promised you:

Variable Type	Keyword	Number of Bytes	Range of Values
Character	**char**	1	-128 to +127 or 0 to 255
Unsigned Character	**unsigned char**	1	0 to 255
Integer	**int**	2 or 4	-32,768 to +32,767 or -2,147,438,648 to 2,147,438,647
Unsigned Integer	**unsigned int**	2 or 4	0 to 65,535 or 0 to 4,294,967,295
Integer	**short**	2	-32,768 to +32,767
Unsigned Integer	**unsigned short**	2	0 to 65,535
Integer	**long**	4	-2,147,438,648 to 2,147,438,647
Unsigned Integer	**unsigned long**	4	0 to 4,294,967,295
Floating Point	**float**	4	±3.4E38(6 digits)
Floating Point	**double**	8	±1.7E308(15 digits)
Floating Point	**long double**	10	±1.2E4932 (19 digits)

The op= Form of Assignment

Sometimes, C provides you with shortcuts. Here, we're going to discuss one such shortcut. Let's consider the following line of code:

```
number = number + 10;
```

This sort of assignment, where you're incrementing a variable by some amount, comes up very often - so there's a shorthand version:

```
number += 10;
```

The important bit is the **+=** operator after the variable name. This statement has exactly the same effect as the previous one and it saves a bit of typing. It's actually one of a family of operators that can be expressed as the **op=** family where **op** can be any of the arithmetic operators:

```
+   -   *   /   %
```

It can also be a few others that we haven't covered yet. These are:

```
<<   >>   &   ^   |
```

However, we'll defer our discussion of these to Chapter 3. The **op=** set of operators always work in the same way. If we have a statement of the form:

```
lhs op= rhs;
```

then the effect is the same as a statement of the form:

```
lhs = lhs op (rhs);
```

Note the parentheses around the **rhs** expression. This means that **op** applies to the entire **rhs** expression, whatever it is. So just to reinforce our understanding of this, we'll look at some examples. The statement:

```
variable *= 12;
```

is the same as:

```
variable = variable * 12;
```

We now have two different ways of incrementing an integer variable by 1. Both of the following statements achieve the same result:

```
Count = Count +1;
Count += 1;
```

We'll learn about yet another way in the next chapter. This amazing level of choice tends to make it virtually impossible for indecisive individuals to write programs in C.

Because the **op** in **op=** applies to all of the **rhs** expression, the statement:

```
a /= b+1;
```

is the same as:

```
a = a/(b+1);
```

Our computational facilities have been rather constrained so far. We've only been able to use a very basic set of arithmetic operators. We can get more power to our calculating elbow using standard library facilities but, for the moment, we'll stick with what we've got. Rest assured that we will come to the others later.

Designing a Program

Now it's time for our end of chapter real-life example. It would be a great idea to try out some of our numeric types in a new program. I'll take you through the whole process as if we were writing a program from scratch. This covers getting the problem, analyzing it, preparing a solution, writing the program and, of course, running it. This teaches you the real art of programming, beyond just the theory.

The Problem

The height of trees is very interesting to many people. For one thing, if a tree is being cut down, knowing its height tells you how far away *safe* is. Our problem is to find out the height of a tree without using a very long ladder. For this, we'll need the help of a friend of yours - preferably a short friend. The tree we're measuring needs to be taller than both you and your friend.

The Analysis

Let's start by naming the tall person (you) Lofty and the shorter person (your friend) Shorty. If you're vertically challenged, the roles can be reversed. For more accurate results the tall person should be significantly taller than the short person. So that you can get an idea of what we're trying to do in this program, consider the following diagram.

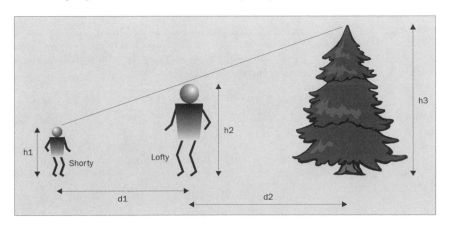

Finding the height of the tree is actually quite simple. We can get the height of the tree, h_3, if we know the other dimensions shown in the illustration: h_1 and h_2 - which are the heights of Shorty and Lofty; and d_1 and d_2 - which are the distances between Lofty and Shorty, and from Lofty to the tree, respectively. We can use the technique of similar triangles to work out the height of the tree. We can see this better by showing it in a simplified diagram.

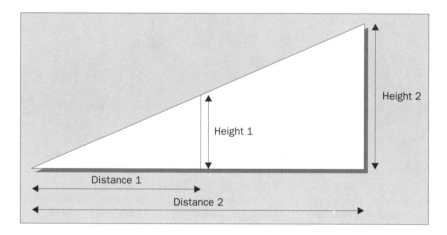

Here, because the triangles are similar, **height1** divided by **distance1** is equal to **height2** divided by **distance2**. Using this relationship, we can get the height of the tree from the height of Shorty and Lofty, and the distances to the tree, as shown below.

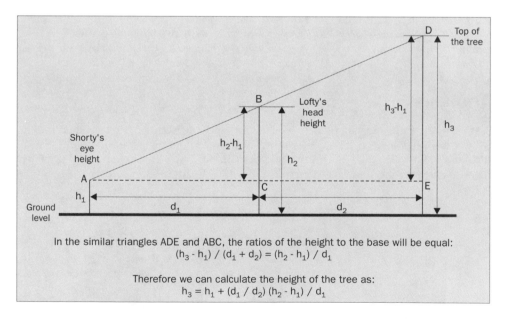

In the similar triangles ADE and ABC, the ratios of the height to the base will be equal:
$$(h_3 - h_1) / (d_1 + d_2) = (h_2 - h_1) / d_1$$

Therefore we can calculate the height of the tree as:
$$h_3 = h_1 + (d_1 / d_2) (h_2 - h_1) / d_1$$

The triangles ADE and ABC are the same as those shown in the previous diagram. Using the fact that the triangles are similar, we can calculate the height of the tree as shown in the bottom equation in the diagram.

This means that we can calculate the height of the tree in our program from four values:

▶ The distance between Shorty and Lofty, d_1 in the diagram. We'll use a variable **shorty_to_lofty** to store this value.

▶ The distance between Lofty and the tree, d_2 in the diagram. We'll use a variable **lofty_to_tree** to store this value.

▶ The height of Lofty to the top of his head, h_2 in the diagram. We'll use a variable **lofty** to store this value.

▶ The height of Shorty, but only up to the eyes, h_1 in the diagram. We'll use a variable **shorty** to store this value.

We can then plug these values into the equation for the height of the tree.

Our first task is to get these four values into the computer. We can then use our ratios to find out the height of the tree, and finally output the answer. The steps are:

1 Input the values we need.

2 Calculate the height of the tree using the equation in the diagram.

3 Display the answer.

The Solution

1 So, our first step is to get the values that we need to work out the height of the tree. This means that we have to include the **stdio.h** header file, since we need to use both **printf()** and **scanf()**. We then have to decide what variables we need to store these values in. After that, we can use **printf()** to ask the questions and **scanf()** to get the values.

We'll first get Lofty's height as a number of whole feet, and then a number of inches - prompting for each value as we go along. We'll then convert this into just inches, as this makes Lofty's height easier to work with. We'll do the same thing for Shorty's height (but only up to his eyes), and finally the same for the distance between them. For the distance to the tree, we'll only use whole feet, since this will be accurate enough - and again we'll convert the distance to inches. So here goes with the first part of the program:

```
/*Example 2.19  Calculating the height of trees*/
#include <stdio.h>

void main()
{
    long shorty = 0;          /* Shorty's height in inches            */
    long lofty = 0;           /* Lofty's height in inches             */
    long feet = 0;            /* A whole number of feet               */
    long inches = 0;          /* A whole number of inches             */
    long shorty_to_lofty = 0;/* Distance from shorty to lofty in inches */
    long lofty_to_tree = 0;/* Distance from lofty to the tree in inches */
```

```
      /* Get lofty's height */
      printf("Enter Lofty's height to the top
                              of his/her head, feet first: ");
      scanf("%ld", &feet);
      printf("             ...and then inches: ");
      scanf("%ld", &inches);
      lofty = feet * 12 + inches;

      /* Get Shorty's height up to his/her eyes */
      printf("Enter Shorty's height up to his/her eyes, feet first: ");
      scanf("%ld", &feet);
      printf("                        ... and then inches: ");
      scanf("%ld", &inches);
      shorty = feet * 12 + inches;

      /* Get the distance from Shorty to Lofty */
      printf("Now enter the distance between
                              Shorty and Lofty, feet first: ");
      scanf("%ld", &feet);
      printf("
                                      ... and then inches: ");
      scanf("%ld", &inches);
      shorty_to_lofty = feet * 12 + inches;

      /* Get the distance from Lofty to the tree */
      printf("Finally enter the distance
                              to the tree to the nearest foot: ");
      scanf("%ld", &feet);
      lofty_to_tree = feet * 12;

      /* The code to calculate the height of the tree will go here */

      /* The code to display the result will go here             */
}
```

Notice how we've spaced the program code out to make it easier to read. You don't have to do it this way, but if you decide to change the program next year, it'll be a great help if you can see how the program works by how it's laid out. You should always add comments to your programs to help with this. It's particularly important to at least make clear what the variables are used for, and to document the basic logic of the program. Note that we have added a couple of extra variables, feet and inches, to store the initial input. We then convert the input to inches and store it in the appropriate variable.

2   Now that we have all the data we need, we can calculate the height of the tree. All we need to do is implement the equation for the tree height in terms of our variables. We'll also declare a variable to store the height of the tree.

You need to add the code that's shown here as shaded:

```
/*Example 2.19   Calculating the height of trees*/
#include <stdio.h>

void main()
{
   long shorty = 0;         /* Shorty's height in inches                 */
   long lofty = 0;          /* Lofty's height in inches                  */
   long feet = 0;           /* A whole number of feet                    */
   long inches = 0;         /* A whole number of inches                  */
   long shorty_to_lofty = 0;/* Distance from shorty to lofty in inches */
   long lofty_to_tree = 0;/* Distance from lofty to the tree in inches */
   long tree_height = 0;   /* Height of the tree in inches              */

   /* Get lofty's height */
   printf("Enter Lofty's height to the
                                    top of his/her head, feet first: ");
   scanf("%ld", &feet);
   printf("
                                              ...and then inches: ");
   scanf("%ld", &inches);
   lofty = feet * 12 + inches;

   /* Get Shorty's height up to his/her eyes */
   printf("Enter Shorty's height up to his/her eyes, feet first: ");
   scanf("%ld", &feet);
   printf("                        ... and then inches: ");
   scanf("%ld", &inches);
   shorty = feet * 12 + inches;

   /* Get the distance from Shorty to Lofty */
   printf("Now enter the distance between
                                    Shorty and Lofty, feet first: ");
   scanf("%ld", &feet);
   printf("
                                          ... and then inches: ");
   scanf("%ld", &inches);
   shorty_to_lofty = feet * 12 + inches;

   /* Get the distance from Lofty to the tree */
   printf("Finally enter the distance to
                                    the tree to the nearest foot: ");
   scanf("%ld", &feet);
   lofty_to_tree = feet * 12;

   /* Calculate the height of the tree in inches */
   tree_height = shorty + (shorty_to_lofty + lofty_to_tree) *
                 (lofty-shorty)/shorty_to_lofty;

   /* The code to display the result will go here */
}
```

That was very straightforward. The statement to calculate the height is essentially the same as the equation in the diagram.

3 Finally, we need to print the answer. To do this we'll convert **tree_height**, which is in inches, back into feet and inches:

```c
/*Example 2.19  Calculating the height of trees*/
#include <stdio.h>

void main()
{
   long shorty = 0;        /* Shorty's height in inches            */
   long lofty = 0;         /* Lofty's height in inches             */
   long feet = 0;          /* A whole number of feet               */
   long inches = 0;        /* A whole number of inches             */
   long shorty_to_lofty = 0;/* Distance from shorty to lofty in inches */
   long lofty_to_tree = 0;/* Distance from lofty to the tree in inches */
   long tree_height = 0;   /* Height of the tree in inches         */

   /* Get lofty's height */
   printf("Enter Lofty's height to the top
                                 of his/her head, feet first: ");
   scanf("%ld", &feet);
   printf("
                                              ...and then inches: ");
   scanf("%ld", &inches);
   lofty = feet * 12 + inches;

   /* Get Shorty's height up to his/her eyes */
   printf("Enter Shorty's height up to his/her eyes, feet first: ");
   scanf("%ld", &feet);
   printf("                              ... and then inches: ");
   scanf("%ld", &inches);
   shorty = feet * 12 + inches;

   /* Get the distance from Shorty to Lofty */
   printf("Now enter the distance between
                                 Shorty and Lofty, feet first: ");
   scanf("%ld", &feet);
   printf("
                                 ... and then inches: ");
   scanf("%ld", &inches);
   shorty_to_lofty = feet * 12 + inches;

   /* Get the distance from Lofty to the tree */
   printf("Finally enter the distance to the
                                 tree to the nearest foot: ");
   scanf("%ld", &feet);
   lofty_to_tree = feet * 12;

   /* Calculate the height of the tree in inches */
   tree_height = shorty + (shorty_to_lofty + lofty_to_tree)*
                 (lofty-shorty)/shorty_to_lofty;
```

```
        /* Display the result in feet and inches */
        printf("The height of the tree is %ld feet and %ld inches.",
                               tree_height / 12, tree_height % 12);
}
```

And there we have it. The output from the program looks something like this:

```
Enter Lofty's height, feet first: 6
              ...and then inches: 2
Enter Shorty's height up to their eyes, feet first: 4
                         ... and then inches: 6
Now enter the distance between Shorty and Lofty, feet first: 5
                              ... and then inches: 0
Finally enter the distance to the tree to the nearest foot: 20
The height of the tree is 12 feet and 10 inches.
```

Summary

This chapter has covered a huge amount of ground. It was pretty tough, but to write good programs you need to understand the fundamentals. You won't remember it all first time round, but you can always look back over it if you need to. Armed with this knowledge, we can really make use of the power of C.

By now, you know how a C program is structured, and you should be fairly comfortable with any kind of arithmetic calculation. You should also be able to choose variable types to suit the job in hand. Aside from arithmetic we have added quite a bit of input and output capability to our knowledge. You're now at ease with inputting values into variables via **scanf()**. You can output text messages, and character and numeric variables to the screen.

As a final summary, let's recap the variable types and the format specifiers we've used so far. You can look back at the next page to remind yourself, as we continue through the book. Not bad for the first two chapters, is it?

In the next chapter we shall start looking at how we can control the program by making decisions depending on the values we enter. As you can probably imagine, this is key to creating interesting and professional programs.

Variable Type	Keyword	Number of Bytes	Range of Values
Character	**char**	1	-128 to +127 or 0 to 255
Unsigned Character	**unsigned char**	1	0 to 255
Integer	**int**	2 or 4	-32,768 to +32,767 or -2,147,438,648 to 2,147,438,647
Unsigned Integer	**unsigned int**	2 or 4	0 to 65,535 or 0 to 4,294,967,295
Integer	**short**	2	-32,768 to +32,767
Unsigned Integer	**unsigned short**	2	0 to 65,535

Table Continued on Following Page

Variable Type	Keyword	Number of Bytes	Range of Values
Integer	**long**	4	-2,147,438,648 to 2,147,438,647
Unsigned Integer	**unsigned long**	4	0 to 4,294,967,295
Floating Point	**float**	4	±3.4E38(6 digits)
Floating Point	**double**	8	±1.7E308(15 digits)
Floating Point	**long double**	10	±1.2E4932 (19 digits)

Format Specifier	Purpose
%c	Character value
%d	Signed decimal integer
%ld	Long signed decimal integer
%u	Unsigned decimal integer
%f	Single precision floating point number

Making Decisions

In the last chapter you learned how to do calculations in your programs. In this chapter, we'll take great leaps forward in the range of programs we can write and the flexibility we can build into them. We'll add one of the most powerful programming tools - the ability to compare variables with other variables and constants, and based on the outcome, choose to execute one set of statements or another.

What this means is that we'll be able to control the sequence in which statements are executed in a program. Up until now, all the statements in our programs have been executed strictly in sequence. In this chapter we're going to change all that.

In this chapter you'll learn:

- How to make decisions based on arithmetic comparisons
- What logical operators are - and how you can use them
- More about reading data from the keyboard
- How you can write a program that can be used as a calculator

The Decision-Making Process

We'll start with the essentials of decision-making in a program. Decision-making in a program is concerned with choosing to execute one set of program statements rather than another. In everyday life you do this kind of thing all the time. Each time you wake up you have to decide whether it's a good idea to go to work. You may go through these questions:

```
Do I feel well?      If the answer is no, stay in bed.
                     If the answer is yes, go to work.
```

You could rewrite this as:

```
If I feel well, I will go to work.
Otherwise, I will stay in bed.
```

That was a straightforward decision. Later, as you're having breakfast, you notice it's raining, so you think:

> If it's raining as hard as it did yesterday, I will take the bus. If it's raining harder than yesterday, I will drive to work. Otherwise, I will risk it and walk.

This is a more complex decision process. It's a decision based on several levels in the amount of rain falling, and can have any of three different results.

As the day goes on, you're presented with more of these decisions. Without them you'd be stuck with only one course of action. Until now, in this book, you've had exactly the same problem with your programs. All the programs will run a straight course to a defined end, without making any decisions. This is a severe constraint on what our programs can do, and one that we'll relieve now. First, let's set up some basic building blocks of knowledge that will enable us to do this.

Arithmetic Comparisons

To make a decision, we need a mechanism for comparing things. This involves some new operators. Since we're dealing with numbers, comparing numerical values is basic to decision making. We have three fundamental operators:

`<`	**is less than**
`==`	**is equal to**
`>`	**is greater than**

> *The 'equal to' operator has **two** successive equal signs (==). You'll almost certainly use one equals sign on occasions by mistake. This will cause considerable confusion until you spot the problem.*
>
> *Look at the difference. If you type **my_weight = your_weight** it's an assignment that puts the value from the variable **your_weight** into the variable **my_weight**. If you type the expression **my_weight == your_weight** then you're comparing the two values: you're asking **whether** they're exactly the same - not making them the same.*

Logical Expressions

Have a look at these examples:

        5 < 4   1 == 2   5 > 4

These expressions are called logical expressions, and each of them can result in just one of two values: either true or false. The value true is represented by 1, or more generally by any positive integer; false is represented by 0. The first expression is false since 5 is patently not less than 4. The second expression is also false since 1 is not equal to 2. The third expression is true since 5 is greater than 4.

The Basic if Statement

Now we have some logical operators, we need a statement allowing us to make a decision. The simplest available to us is the **if** statement. If we wanted to compare our weights, and print a different sentence depending on the result, we could write the body of a program as:

```
if( your_weight > my_weight)
  printf("You are fatter than me.\n");

if(your_weight < my_weight)
  printf("I am fatter than you.\n");

if(your_weight == my_weight)
  printf("We are exactly the same weight.\n");
```

Let's go through this and see how it works. The first **if** tests whether the value in **your_weight** is greater than the value in **my_weight**. The expression for the comparison appears between the parentheses that immediately follow the keyword **if**. If the result of the comparison is true, then the statement immediately after the **if** will be executed. This just outputs the message:

```
You are fatter than me.
```

Execution will then continue with the next **if**. What if the expression between the parentheses in the first **if** is false? In this case, the statement immediately following the **if** will be skipped, so the message won't be displayed. It will only be displayed if **your_weight** is greater than **my_weight**.

> *Note how the statement following the* **if** *is indented. This is to show that it is dependent on the result of the* **if** *test.*

The second **if** works in essentially the same way. If the expression between parentheses after the keyword **if** is true, then the following statement will be executed to output the message:

```
I am fatter than you.
```

This will be the case if **your_weight** is less than **my_weight**. If this isn't so, the statement will be skipped and the message won't be displayed. The third **if** is again the same. The effect of these statements is to print one message that will depend on whether **your_weight** is greater than, less than, or equal to **my_weight**. Only one message will be displayed because only one of these can be true.

The general form or **syntax** of the **if** statement is as follows:

```
if(expression)
  Statement1;

Next_statement;
```

Notice that the expression that forms the test (the **if**) is enclosed in parentheses, and that there is no semicolon at the end of the first line. This is because both the line with the **if** keyword, and the following line, are tied together. The second line could be written following straight on from the first, like this:

```
if(expression) Statement1;
```

but for the sake of clarity, people tend to put **Statement1** on a new line.

The **expression** in parentheses can be any expression giving a result of true or false. If the expression is true, then **Statement1** is executed, after which the program continues with **Next_statement**. If the expression is false then **Statement1** is skipped and execution continues immediately with **Next_statement**. This is illustrated in the figure.

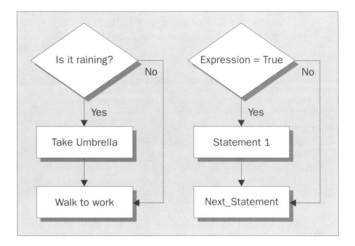

We could have used the basic **if** statement to add some politically incorrect comments in our program at the end of the previous chapter - which calculated the height of a tree. For example, we could have added the following code just after we'd calculated the height of the shortest person:

```
if(Shorty < 36)
   printf("\nMy, you really are on the short side, aren't you?");
```

Here, we've used the **if** statement just to add a gratuitously offensive remark should the individual be less than 36 inches tall.

Try It Out - Checking Conditions

Let's see the **if** statement in action. This program gets the user to enter a number between 1 and 10 and then tells them how big that number is.

```
/* Example 3.1 A simple example of the if statement */
#include <stdio.h>

void main()
{
   int number = 0;
   printf("\nEnter an integer between 1 and 10: ");
   scanf("%d",&number);
```

```
    if (number > 5)
      printf("You entered %d which is greater than 5", number);

    if (number < 6)
      printf("You entered %d which is less than 6", number);
  }
```

Sample output from this program would be:

```
Enter an integer between 1 and 10: 7
You entered 7 which is greater than 5
```

or:

```
Enter an integer between 1 and 10: 3
You entered 3 which is less than 6
```

How It Works

As usual, we include a comment to remind us what the program does. We include the **stdio.h** header file to allow us to use the **printf()** statement. We then have the beginning of the **main()** function of the program. This function doesn't return a value - as indicated by the keyword **void**.

```
/* Example 3.1 A simple example of the if statement*/
#include <stdio.h>

void main()
{
```

In the next three statements, we get the input:

```
    int number = 0;
    printf("\nEnter an integer between 1 and 10: \n");
    scanf("%d",&number);
```

We declare an integer variable called **number** that we initialize to zero, and then we prompt the user to enter a number between 1 and 10. This value is then read using the **scanf()** function and stored in the variable **number**.

The next statement is an **if**:

```
    if (number > 5)
      printf("You entered %d which is greater than 5", number);
```

We compare the value in **number** with the value 5. If **number** is greater than 5 then we execute the next statement, which displays a message, and we go to the next part of the program. If it isn't, the **printf()** is simply skipped. We've used the **%d** conversion specifier to repeat the number the user typed in.

85

We then have another **if** statement:

```
if (number < 6)
  printf("You entered %d which is less than 6", number);
```

This compares the value entered with 6 and, if it's smaller, we execute the next statement to display a message. Otherwise, the **printf()** is skipped and the program ends. In all cases, only one of the two possible messages will be displayed - because the number will always be less than 6 or greater than 5.

The **if** statement enables you to be selective about what input you accept, and what you finally do with it. For instance, if you have a variable and you want to have its value specifically limited at some point, even though higher values may arise somehow in the program, you could write:

```
if( x > 90)
  x = 90;
```

This would ensure that if anyone entered a value of **x** that was larger than 90, your program would automatically change it to 90. This would be invaluable if you had a program that could only specifically deal with values within a range. You could also check whether a value was lower than a given number and, if not, set it to that number. In this way you could be sure that the value was within the given range.

Extending the if Statement - if else

The **if** statement can be extended with a small addition that gives us a lot more flexibility. Imagine it rained a little yesterday. We could write:

```
If the rain today is worse than the rain yesterday I will take my
umbrella

Else I will take my jacket

Then I will go to work
```

The syntax of the **if else** statement is:

```
if(expression)
  Statement1;
else
  Statement2;

Next_statement;
```

Here, we have an either-or situation. You will always execute either **Statement1** or **Statement2** - depending on whether **expression** is true or false:

▶ If **expression** is true, **Statement1** is executed and the program continues with **Next_statement**.

▶ If **expression** is false then **Statement2** following the **else** keyword is executed, and the program continues with **Next_statement**.

The sequence of operations involved here is shown in the next figure.

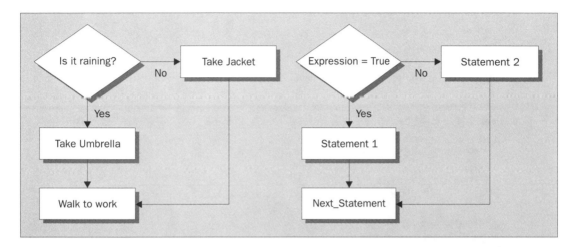

Try It Out - Using if to Analyze Numbers

We can now use our **if else** in a simple example. We can let the user enter a number and then check to see whether the number they input is odd or even. We know that all even numbers are divisible by 2 with no remainder. This means we can decide if a number is even or not by using the modulus operator to produce the remainder after division by 2. If the result is zero, we have an even number.

```c
/* Example 3.2 Using ifs to analyze numbers */
#include <stdio.h>

void main()
{
   long Test = 0;        /* Stores the integer to be checked */

   /* Prompt message */
   printf("Enter an integer less than two million:");

   /* Read the input */
   scanf(" %ld", &Test);

   /* Test for odd or even by checking the remainder
                           after dividing by 2   */
   if( Test % 2L == 0)
     printf("\nThe number %ld is even", Test);  /* Result is even */
   else
     printf("\nThe number %ld is odd", Test);   /* Result is odd  */
}
```

Typical output from this program would be:

```
Enter an integer less than two million: 242424
The number 242424 is even

Enter an integer less than two million: 242425
The number 242425 is odd
```

How It Works

Let's look at what's going on here. We first declare a **long** variable called **Test** and initialize it to 0:

```
long Test = 0;        /* Stores the integer to be checked */
```

Next, we prompt the user to enter some input:

```
/* Prompt message */
printf("Enter an integer less than two million:");

/* Read the input */
scanf(" %ld", &Test);
```

The user inputs a number and it is stored in the variable. Notice that we've used **%ld** as the specifier for reading in the value to be tested. This ensures the compiler reads it as a **long** integer.

```
/* Test for odd or even by checking the remainder
                                      after dividing by 2   */
if( Test % 2L == 0)
  printf("\nThe number %ld is even", Test);  /* Result is even */
else
  printf("\nThe number %ld is odd", Test);   /* Result is odd  */
```

This is the part we're really interested in. What's going on in the **if** expression? The expression **Test %2L == 0** first calculates the remainder resulting from dividing the number entered by the user (stored in **Test**) by 2 (this is the action of the modulus operator, **%**). The result is tested for equality with zero. The **L** is there to specify that the number 2 is a long integer. Notice that we're using two equals signs (**==**). Try it with one equals sign and you get an error.

> *Remember, you use == when you are asking **whether** two variables are exactly the same. You use = when you're storing a value in a variable.*

An even number will have a zero remainder after division by 2, and so the expression will be true. So, if the number is even then the first statement is executed - and it prints the appropriate message. If the number is odd then the remainder will be 1 after division by 2, so the statement after the **else** will be executed. It then prints a different (but appropriate) message. Without the **else** statement option, we would have had to use two **if** statements: one to test for even, the other to test for odd - which is what we did in the previous program.

We could rewrite the expression to be tested in the **if** a little more simply, if we rearrange the whole **if else** statement:

```
if( Test%2L)
   printf("\nThe number %ld is odd", Test);   /* Result is odd  */
else
   printf("\nThe number %ld is even", Test);  /* Result is even */
```

Here, we don't bother to compare the remainder with zero, and we've reversed the **if** and **else** statements. If the number is odd, the expression **Test%2L** will have the value 1, which represents true, so the statement after the **if** will be executed. If the number is even then **Test%2L** will have the value 0, which is false, so the number after the **else** is executed. This is a little simpler, but probably not clearer. Whatever its pros and cons, you'll often meet this sort of construct in **if** statements.

Using Blocks of Code in if Statements

We can also replace **Statement1**, or **Statement2**, or even both, by a block of statements enclosed between braces **{}**. This means that we can supply many instructions to the computer after making a check of an expression, simply by placing these instructions together between braces.

This could be represented in a real life situation as below:

```
If the weather is sunny
I will walk to the park, eat a picnic and walk home

else
I will stay in, watch football and drink beer
```

The syntax for this is as follows:

```
if(expression)
{
  StatementA1;
  StatementA2;
  ...
}
else
{
  StatementB1;
  StatementB2;
  ...
}
Next_statement;
```

All the statements that are in a block between the braces following an **if** statement will be executed if **expression** is true. If **expression** is false, all the statements between the braces following the **else** will be executed. In either case, execution continues with **Next_statement**.

> *Have a look at the indentation. The braces are not indented, but the statements between the braces are. This makes it clear that all the statements between an opening and a closing brace belong together.*

Nested if Statements

It's also possible to have **if**s within **if**s. These are called nested **if**s. For example:

```
if the weather is good I will go out in the yard
    and if it's cool enough I will sit in the sun
    else I will sit in the shade
else I will stay indoors
I will then drink some lemonade.
```

This corresponds to:

```
if (expression1)
{
    StatementA;
    if (expression2)
        StatementB;
    else
        StatementC;
}
else
    StatementD;
Statement E;
```

Here, the second **if** is only checked if the first **if** is true. The braces enclosing **StatementA** and the second **if** are necessary to make both of these statements a part of what's executed when **expression1** is true. Note how the **else** is aligned with the **if** it belongs to. The logic of this is illustrated in the following figure:

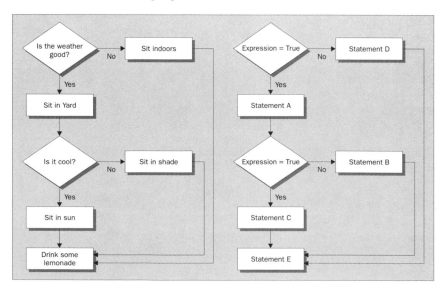

Try It Out - Analyzing Numbers Some More

We can now exercise our **if** skills with a couple more examples. Let's take our previous example a bit further. The program tests to see whether you enter an odd or an even number. We can extend this so that if the number is even, we then test to see whether half that number is also even!

```c
/* Example 3.3 Using nested ifs to analyze numbers further */
#include <stdio.h>

void main()
{
   long Test = 0L;       /* Stores the integer to be checked */

   /* Prompt message */
   printf("Enter an integer less than two billion:");
   /* Read the input */
   scanf(" %ld", &Test);

   /* Test for odd or even by checking the remainder
                                 after dividing by 2 */
   if( Test % 2L == 0L)
   {
     printf("\nThe number %ld is even", Test);

     /* Now check whether half the number is also even */
     if ( (Test/2L) % 2L == 0L)
     {
       printf("\nHalf of %ld is also even", Test);
       printf("\nThat's interesting isn't it?");
     }
   }
   else
     printf("\nThe number %ld is odd", Test);
}
```

The output will look something like this:

```
Enter an integer less than two billion: 20
The number 20 is even
Half of 20 is also even
That's interesting isn't it?
```

or this:

```
Enter an integer less than two billion: 9
The number 9 is odd
```

How It Works

This is only marginally more complicated than the previous example. Let's look at the new bits.

```
if( Test % 2L == 0L)
{
  printf("\nThe number %ld is even", Test);

  /* Now check whether half the number is also even */
  if ( (Test/2L) % 2L == 0L)
  {
    printf("\nHalf of %ld is also even", Test);
    printf("\nThat's interesting isn't it?");
  }
}
else
  printf("\nThe number %ld is odd", Test);
```

Here, we have a block of statements that's executed if the value entered is even. The first statement is the same as in the previous program; the second statement is another **if**. This prints a second comment if half the value entered is also even. This is called a nested **if**.

Notice that the first statement is an **if-else**, whereas the nested **if** is a plain **if**. This is fine, but it means that if the number is even but half of that number is odd, you only display:

```
Enter an integer less than two billion: 10
The number 10 is even
```

Try adding a line to make the second **if** an **if-else** that prints **"Half of %ld is odd"**. The answer comes just before the next heading.

> *You can nest **if**s anywhere inside another **if**, but I don't recommend this as a technique that you should use extensively - otherwise your program is likely to end up being very hard to follow.*
>
> *There are a couple of extra parentheses in the nested **if** expressions (**Test/2L**). These are not strictly necessary, but it helps to make it clear what's going on. Making programs easier to follow is the essence of good programming style.*

The answer to my question above would be to insert:

```
else
  printf("\nHalf of %ld is odd", Test);
```

after the second **if**'s closing brace.

Some Additional Comparison Operators

We can now add a few more numerical comparison operators that we can use in **if** statements. Three additional operators make up the complete set:

>=	is greater than or equal to
<=	is less than or equal to
!=	is not equal to

These are fairly self explanatory, but let's consider some examples anyway - starting with a few arithmetic examples:

```
6 >= 5        5 <= 5        4 <= 5        4 != 5        10 != 10
```

These are all true, except for the last one which is false, since 10 most definitely *is* equal to 10. These operators also can be applied to characters, as well. If you remember, character types also have a numeric value associated with them. The ASCII table in Appendix B gives you a full listing of all the standard characters and their numeric equivalents. Just to remind you for the next few examples, the table below is an extract from Appendix B.

Character	ASCII Code - Decimal
A	65
B	66
P	80
Q	81
Z	90
b	98

A **char** value may be expressed either as an integer between -128 and +127 or as a keyboard character between quotes, such as 'A'. Here are a few examples:

```
'Z' >= 'A'        'Q' <= 'P'        'B' <= 'b'        'B' != 66
```

With the ASCII values of the characters in mind, the first expression is true, since **'Z'** which has the code value 90 comes after **'A'** with the code value of 65. The second is false, as **'Q'** does not come before **'P'**. The third is true. This is because, in ASCII code, lower-case letters are 32 higher than their upper-case equivalents. The last is false. The value **66** is indeed the decimal ASCII representation for the character **'B'**.

Try It Out - Converting Upper-Case to Lower-Case

Let's exercise our new logical operators in an example. Here, we have a program that will convert any capital letter that's entered to a small letter.

```c
/* Example 3.4 Converting upper-case to lower-case */
#include <stdio.h>

void main()
{
   char letter = 0;     /* Stores a character */

   /* Prompt for input */
   printf("\nEnter an upper-case letter:");
   /* Read a character */
   scanf("%c", &letter);
```

```
                /* Check that the the input is a capital letter */
          if(letter >= 'A')        /* Is is A or greater?   */
            if (letter <= 'Z')    /* and is it Z or lower? */
            {          /* It is upper case */
              /* Convert from upper to lower case */
              letter = letter - 'A'+ 'a';
              printf("\nYou entered an upper-case %c", letter);
            }
            else           /* It is not an upper case letter */
              printf("\nTry using the shift key, Bud! I want a capital
                                                        letter.");
          }
```

Sample output from this program might be:

```
Enter an upper-case letter:G
You entered an upper-case g
```

or:

```
Enter an upper-case letter:s
Try using the shift key, Bud! I want a capital letter.
```

How It Works

In the first three statements, we declare a variable of type **char** called **letter**, we prompt the user to input a capital letter, and we store the character entered in the variable **letter**:

```
    char letter = 0;     /* Stores a character */

    /* Prompt for input */
    printf("\nEnter an upper-case letter:");
    /* Read a character */
    scanf("%c", &letter);
```

If a capital letter was entered, the character in letter must be between **'A'** and **'Z'**, so the next **if** checks if the character is greater than or equal to **'A'**:

```
    if (letter >= 'A')
```

If the expression is true, we continue with the nested **if** that tests whether **letter** is less than or equal to **'Z'**:

```
    if (letter <= 'Z')
```

If this expression is true then we convert the character to lower-case and output a message - by executing the block of statements following the **if**:

```
    {          /* It is upper case */
      /* Convert from upper to lower case */
      letter = letter - 'A'+ 'a';
      printf("\nYou entered an upper-case %c", letter);
    }
```

To convert to lower case, we subtract the ASCII code for **'A'** from **letter**, and add the ASCII code for **'a'**. If **letter** contained **'A'**, subtracting **'A'** would produce 0, and adding **'a'** would result in **'a'**. If **letter** contained **'B'**, subtracting **'A'** would produce 1, and adding **'a'** would result in **'b'**. You can see this conversion works for any upper case letter. Note that although this works fine for ASCII, there are coding systems where this won't work, because the letters don't have a contiguous sequence of codes. If you want to be sure that the conversion works for any code, you must use the standard library function **tolower()**, which converts the character passed as an argument to lower case. To use this function, you need to include the header file **ctype.h** in your program.

If the expression **letter <= 'Z'** is false we go straight to the statement following **else** and display a different message:

```
    else          /* It is not an upper case letter */
      printf("\nTry using the shift key, Bud! I want a capital
                                            letter.");
```

There's something wrong though. What if the character that was entered was less than **'A'**? There's no **else** clause for the first **if** - so the program just ends without outputting anything. To deal with this, we must add another **else** clause at the end of the program. The complete nested **if** would then become:

```
    if(letter >= 'A')           /* Is is A or greater?        */
      if (letter <= 'Z')        /* and is it Z or lower?      */
      {                         /* It is upper case           */
        letter = letter - 'A '+ 'a';/* Convert from upper to lower case */
        printf("\nYou entered an upper-case %c", letter);
      }
      else                      /* It is not an upper case letter   */
        printf("\nTry using the shift key, Bud!
                                I want a capital letter.");
    else
      printf("You didn't enter a capital letter");
```

Now we always get a message. Note the indentation to show which **else** belongs to which **if**. The indentation doesn't determine what belongs to what. It just provides a visual cue. An **else** always belongs to the **if** that immediately precedes it that is not already spoken for by another **else**.

We used a nested **if** statement to check for two conditions in the above example but, as you can imagine, this could get very confusing when you've got lots of different criteria that you need to check for. The good news is that C has thought of this - and allows you to use logical operators to simplify the situation.

Logical Operations

Sometimes it just isn't enough to perform a single test for a decision. You may want to combine two or more checks on values and, if they are all true, then perform a certain action. Or you may want to perform a calculation if one or more of a set of conditions are true.

For example, you may only want to go to work if you're feeling well *and* it's a weekday. Just because you feel great doesn't mean you want to go in on a Saturday. Alternatively, you could say that you'll stay at home if you feel ill *or* if it's a weekend. These are exactly the sort of circumstances for which the logical operators were intended.

The AND Operator &&

We can look, first, at the logical AND operator, `&&`, which is called a **binary operator**, because it operates on 2 items of data. The AND operator combines two logical expressions; that is, two expressions that have a value true or false. The expression:

```
Test1 && Test2
```

has the value true if both expressions `Test1` and `Test2` are true. If either one is false, the overall result is false. The obvious place to use the `&&` operator is in an `if` expression. Let's take an example:

```
if( age > 12 && age < 20 )
  printf("You are officially a teenager.");
```

The `printf()` statement will only be executed if `age` has a value between 13 and 19 inclusive. Naturally, you can use more than one of these logical operators in an expression:

```
if( age > 12 && age < 20 && savings > 5000 )
  printf("You are a rich teenager.");
```

All three conditions must be true for the `printf()` to be executed. That is, the `printf()` will only be executed if the value of **age** is between 13 and 19 inclusive, and the value of **savings** is greater than 5000.

The OR Operator ||

The situation where you want to check for any of two or more conditions being true is covered by the logical OR operator, `||`. An example of using this operator is:

```
if( A < 10 || B > C || C > 50 )
  printf("At least one of the conditions is True.");
```

The `printf()` will only be executed if *at least* one of the three conditions, **A<10**, **B>C**, **C<50**, is true.

We can also use the logical operators in combination, as in the following code fragment:

```
if ((age > 12 && age <20) || savings>5000)
  printf ("Either you're a teenager, or you're rich, or possibly both.");
```

The `printf()` statement will be executed if the value of **age** is between 12 and 20, or the value of **savings** is greater than 5000, or both. As you can see, when you start to use more operators things can get confusing.

The NOT Operator !

Last but not least is the logical NOT operator, represented by **!**. The **!** operator is a unary operator, because it applies to just one operand. The logical NOT operator reverses the value of a logical expression: true becomes false, and false becomes true. Suppose we have two variables, **a** and **b,** with the values 5 and 2 respectively; then the expression **a>b** is true. If we use our logical NOT operator, the expression **!(a>b)** is false. I recommend that you avoid using this operator as far as possible: it tends to result in code that becomes difficult to follow. As an illustration, we can rewrite the previous example as:

```
if ((!(age >= 12) && !( age >= 20)) || !(savings <= 5000))
{
  printf("\nYou're either not a teenager and rich ");
  printf("or not rich and a teenager,\n");
  printf("or neither not a teenager nor not rich.");
}
```

As you can see, it becomes incredibly difficult to unravel the nots!

Try It Out - A Better Way to Convert Letters

You'll remember that earlier in this chapter we had a program to enter an upper-case character. We used a nested **if** to ensure that the input was of the correct type, and then we printed the small letter equivalent - or a remark indicating that the input was of the wrong type.

We can now see that all this was completely unnecessary, since we can do it like this:

```
/* Example 3.5   Testing letters the easy way */
#include <stdio.h>
void main()
{
   char Letter =0;        /* Stores an input character */

   /* Prompt for input          */
   printf("\nEnter an upper case letter:");
   /* Read the input character  */
   scanf(" %c", &Letter);

   /* Verify upper case letter  */
   if ((Letter >= 'A') && (Letter <= 'Z'))
   {
     /* Convert to lower case      */
     Letter = Letter + 'a'-'A';
     printf("\nYou entered an upper-case %c.", Letter);
   }
   else
     printf("\nTry using the shift key, Bud! I want a capital letter.");
}
```

How It Works

The output is similar, but not exactly the same as the original program. In the corrected version of the program, we generated a different message when the input was less than `'A'`. This version is rather better though. Compare the mechanism to test the input in the two programs and you'll see how much neater our second solution is. This is the original version:

```
if (letter >= 'A')
   if (letter <= 'Z')
```

This is the new version:

```
/* Verify upper case letter   */
if ((Letter >= 'A') && (letter <= 'Z'))
```

Rather than having confusing nested **if** statements, here we have checked that the character entered is greater than `'A'` *and* less than `'Z'` in one statement. Notice that we've put extra parentheses around the two expressions to be checked. They aren't really needed in this case, but they don't hurt, and they leave you or any other programmers in no doubt as to the order of execution.

The Conditional Operator

There's another statement that you can use to test data, but it doesn't alter the sequence of execution depending on the result of the test. Instead, it produces a different value.

This type of operator is called the **ternary operator** or the **conditional operator**. This sounds as though it has some relationship with an aquatic bird, perhaps reminiscent of the old, rather cruel saying 'leave no tern unstoned'. It has nothing at all to do with this. It is sometimes called the ternary operator because it involves three arguments simultaneously. We've seen unary operators, binary operators, and now a ternary operator. The general representation of a ternary operator looks like this:

```
condition ? result1 : result2
```

Notice the use of punctuation. There is a question mark after the test **condition**. The two possible results follow, and are separated by a colon. This produces the value **result1** if **condition** has the value true, or the value **result2** if **condition** produces the value false. We can use this in a statement such as:

```
x = y>7 ? 25 : 50;
```

Executing this statement will result in **x** having the value **25** if **y** is greater than 7, or the value **50** otherwise. This is a nice shorthand way of writing:

```
if( y>7 )
   x = 25;
else
   x = 50;
```

This enables you to express some things very economically. An expression for the minimum of two variables can be written very simply using the conditional operator. We could write an expression that compared our salaries and obtained the greater of the two, like this:

```
YourSalary > MySalary ? YourSalary : MySalary
```

Try It Out - Using the Conditional Operator

This salary business could translate into a short example:

```c
/* Example 3.6 Who has the bigger salary? */
#include <stdio.h>

void main()
{
   int MySalary=0;          /* Stores my salary    */
   int YourSalary=0;        /* Stores your salary */

   /* Get your salary */
   printf("\nEnter your salary: ");
   scanf("%d", &YourSalary);

   /* Get my salary */
   printf("Enter my salary: ");
   scanf("%d", &MySalary);

   /* Ouput the larger salary */
   printf ("\nThe person that earns the most earns $%d\n",
                   MySalary > YourSalary ? MySalary : YourSalary);
}
```

Some typical output from the program would be:

```
Enter your salary: 10000
Enter my salary: 15000

The person that earns the most earns $15000
```

This is a simple application of the conditional operator. Similarly, the expression to calculate which is the lower salary would be:

```
YourSalary < MySalary ? YourSalary : MySalary
```

You could also calculate the lower salary using the expression:

```
YourSalary > MySalary ? MySalary : YourSalary
```

In spite of its odd appearance, you'll see the conditional operator crop up quite frequently in C programs. A very handy application of this operator, that you'll see in examples in this book and elsewhere, is to vary the contents of a message or prompt depending on the value of an expression. For example, if you wanted to display a message indicating the number of pets that a person has, and you want the message to change between singular and plural, then you could write:

```
printf("You have %d pet%s.", Pets, Pets == 1 ? "" : "s" );
```

The **%s** specifier is used when you want to output a string. If **Pets** is equal to 1 an empty string will be output in place of the **%s**, otherwise **"s"** will be output. Thus, if **Pets** has the value 1, the statement will output the message:

```
You have 1 pet.
```

However, if the variable **Pets** is 5 then you'll get this output:

```
You have 5 pets.
```

You can use this mechanism to vary an output message depending on the value of an expression in many different ways: '**she**' instead of '**he**', '**wrong**' instead of '**right**', and so on. We'll see this in action later in the chapter.

Operator Precedence - Who Goes First?

With all the parentheses we've used in the examples in this chapter, now is a good time to come back to **operator precedence**. Operator precedence determines the sequence in which operators in an expression are executed. We have the logical operators **&&, ==, !=**, and **||** plus the comparison operators and the arithmetic operators. When we have more than one operator in an expression, how do we know which ones are used first? This order of precedence can affect the result of an expression very substantially.

For example, suppose we are to process job applications, and we want to only accept applicants who are 25 or older and have graduated from Harvard or Yale. The age condition we can represent by this conditional expression:

```
Age >= 25
```

and we can represent graduation by the variables **Yale** and **Harvard**, which may be true or false. Now we can write the condition as:

```
Age >= 25 && Harvard || Yale
```

Unfortunately, this will result in howls of protest - since we will now accept Yale graduates who are under 25. In fact, this statement will accept Yale graduates of any age. But if you're from Harvard, you must be 25 or over to be accepted! Because of operator precedence, this expression is effectively:

```
( Age >= 25 && Harvard ) || Yale
```

So we take anybody at all from Yale. I'm sure those wearing a Y front sweat shirt will claim that this is as it should be, but what we really meant was:

```
Age >= 25 && ( Harvard || Yale )
```

Let's have a look at a table that shows the order of precedence for the operators we have seen:

Operators	Associativity
( )	left to right
! ~ unary+ unary-	right to left
Type casts such as **(int)** or **(double)**	right to left
* / %	left to right
Binary+ binary-	left to right
<< >>	left to right
< <= > >=	left to right
== !=	left to right
&	left to right
^	left to right
|	left to right
&&	left to right
||	left to right
?: (conditional operator)	left to right
= op= (e.g. += -= etc.)	right to left

You haven't met the **++** and **--** operators yet, but you will in Chapter 4. You'll see the operators **~**, **<<**, **>>**, **&**, **^**, and **|**, later in this chapter.

The operators are shown here with the highest precedence operators (that is, those to be executed first) at the top. All the operators that appear in the same row in the table are of equal precedence. The sequence of execution for operators of equal precedence is determined by their **associativity**, which determines whether they are selected from left to right or from right to left. Naturally, parentheses come at the very top of the list of operators, since they are used to override the natural priorities defined.

As you can see, all the comparison operators are below the binary arithmetic operators, and the binary logical operators are below the comparison operators. As a result, arithmetic is done first, then comparisons, and then logical combinations. Assignments come last in this list, so they are only performed once everything else has been completed. The ternary operator squeezes in just above assignment operators.

Note that the **!** operator is highest, apart from parentheses. As a result, the parentheses around logical expressions are often essential.

Try It Out - Using Logical Operators without Confusion

Look at the following example. We want a program that will take applicant interviews for a large pharmaceutical corporation. The program should offer interviews to applicants who meet certain educational specifications (can you guess where the company's Chief Executive studied?).

```
/* Example 3.7 Confused recruiting policy  */
#include <stdio.h>

void main()
{
   int age = 0;         /* Age of the applicant                    */
   int college = 0;   /* Code for college attended               */
   int subject = 0;   /* Code for subject studied                */
   int interview = 0;/* Flag for interview 1 for accept, 0 for reject */

   /* Get data on the applicant */
   printf("\nWhat college? 1 for Harvard, 2 for Yale, 3 for other: ");
   scanf("%d",&college);
   printf("\nWhat subject? 1 for Chemistry, 2 for economics,"
                                             " 3 for other: ");
   scanf("%d", &subject);
   printf("\nHow old is the applicant? ");
   scanf("%d",&age);

   /* Check out the applicant */
   if((age>25 && subject==1) && (college==3 || college==1))
     interview =1;
   if(college==2 &&subject ==1)
     interview =1;
   if(college==1 && subject==2 && !(age>28))
     interview =1;
   if(college==2 && (subject==2 || subject==3) && age>25)
     interview =1;

   /* Output decision for interview */
   if(interview)
     printf("\n\nGive 'em an interview");
   else
     printf("\n\nReject 'em");
}
```

Output from this program should be something like this:

```
What college? 1 for Harvard, 2 for Yale, 3 for other: 2
What subject? 1 for Chemistry, 2 for Economics, 3 for other: 1
How old is the applicant? 24

Give 'em an interview
```

How It Works

The program works in a fairly straightforward way. The only slight complication is with the number of operators and **if** statements to check a candidate out:

```
if((age>25 && subject==1) && (college==3 || college==1))
  interview =1;
if(college==2 &&subject ==1)
  interview =1;
```

```
    if(college==1 && subject==2 && !(age>28))
       interview = 1;
    if(college==2 && (subject==2 || subject==3) && age>25)
       interview =1;
```

The actual recruiting policy used to produce the program is:

> 1) Graduates over 25 who studied chemistry and who are not from Yale

> 2) Graduates from Yale who studied chemistry

> 3) Graduates from Harvard who studied economics and are not older than 28

> 4) Graduates from Yale who are over 25 and who didn't study chemistry

The final **if** statement tells us whether to invite the applicant for an interview or not; it uses the variable **interview**:

```
    if(interview)
       printf("\n\nGive 'em an interview");
    else
       printf("\n\nReject 'em");
```

The variable **interview** is initialized to zero, but if any of the criteria are met then we assigned the value 1 to it. The **if** expression is just the variable interview, so the expression is false when **interview** is 0 and true when **interview** has any non-zero value.

This could be a lot simpler though. Let's look at the conditions that result in an interview. We can specify each of these with an expression:

1) Graduates over 25 who studied chemistry and who are not from Yale.	`age>25&&college!=2`
2) Graduates from Yale who studied chemistry.	`college==2 && subject==1`
3) Graduates from Harvard who studied economics and are not older than 28.	`college==1 && subject==2 && age<=28`
4) Graduates from Yale who are over 25 and who didn't study chemistry.	`college==2 && age>25 subject!=1`

The variable **interview** should be set to 1 if any of these four conditions is true; so we can now combine them using the || operator to set the value of the variable **interview**:

```
  interview = (age>25&&college!=2)||( college==2 && subject==1)||
              (college==1 && subject==2 && age<=28)||
              (college==2 && age>25 subject!=1);
```

Now we don't need the **if** statements to check the conditions at all. We just store the logical value, 1 or 0, which arises from combining these test expressions. If fact, you could dispense with the variable **interview** altogether, by just putting the combine expression for the checks into the last **if**:

```
if((age>25&&college!=2)||( college==2 && subject==1)||
        (college==1 && subject==2 && age<=28)||
        (college==2 && age>25 subject!=1))
  printf("\n\nGive 'em an interview");
else
  printf("\n\nReject 'em");
```

Multiple Choice Questions

You may be wondering how we handle the situation where you have to check a lot of different conditions. It would be very tiresome to write pages and pages of **if** statements. Well, there is a simple solution - provided in the form of the **switch** statement.

The switch Statement

This last of the testing statements, the **switch** statement, is probably the most fun to use. While it is, perhaps, something of an anomaly in programming, it's analogous to picking a winner in a horse race - or any other race for that matter. You have a fixed number of choices, and some condition that allows you to make a selection. For betting on a horse, the most common selection mechanism is a pin; but in C we have to be a little more precise.

Imagine there were 3 horses in a race - numbered 1, 2 and 3. Suppose number 3 wins the race and number 2 comes second. We could use the **switch** statement as follows:

```
switch (YourChoice)
{
   case 3:
     printf("Congratulations! You win!");
     break;
   case 2:
     printf("Almost won - second place. Better luck next time.");
     break;
   default:
     printf("Too bad, you lose.");
}
```

This is just to give you a feel for how the **switch** statement works. The value of the expression in parentheses following the keyword **switch**, which is **YourChoice** in this case, determines which of the statements between braces will be executed. If the value matches the value specified after one of the **case** keywords, then the following statements will be executed. If **YourChoice** has the value 2, for example, then this message will be displayed:

```
Almost won - second place. Better luck next time.
```

The effect of the **break** statement following the **printf()** is to skip over the other statements within that block, and continue with whatever statement follows the closing brace. If **YourChoice** has a value that doesn't correspond to any of the cases, the statement following the **default** keyword is executed - so you simply get the default message. For any number of horses in the race you could leave the above code exactly as it is. Anything other than 3 or 2 will always result in the default. Both **default** and **break** are keywords in C.

The general way of describing the **switch** statement is:

```
switch (integer_expression)
{
  case constant_expression_1:
    statements_1;
    break;
    . . . .
  case constant_expression_n:
    statements_n;
    break;
  default:
    statements;
}
```

The test is based on the value of **integer_expression**. If that value corresponds to one of the **case** values defined by the associated **constant_expression_n**, then the statements following that **case** value are executed. If the value of **integer_expression** differs from every one of the **case** values, then the statements following **default** are executed.

You can leave out **default** keyword and its associated statements. If none of the **case** values match, then nothing happens. Notice, however, that all of the **case** values for the associated **constant_expression** must be different. If they aren't, and you try to compile the program, then you'll get an error message. The **break** statement jumps to the statement after the closing brace.

Notice the punctuation and formatting. There's no semicolon at the end of the first **switch** expression. The body of the statement is enclosed within braces (curly brackets). The **constant_expression** is followed by a colon, and each subsequent statement ends with a semicolon, as usual.

Let's look at the **switch** statement in action with an example.

Try It Out - Picking a Lucky Number

This example assumes that we're operating a lottery where there are three winning numbers. Participants are required to guess a winning number, and our **switch** statement is designed to end the suspense and tell them about any valuable prizes they may have won:

```
/* Example 3.8 Lucky Lotteries    */
#include <stdio.h>

void main()
{
    int choice = 0;   /* The number chosen */

    /* Get the choice input */
    printf("\nPick a number between 1 and 10 and you may win a prize! ");
    scanf("%d",&choice);
```

```
      /* Check for an invalid selection */
    if((choice>10) || (choice <1))
      choice = 11;    /* Selects invalid choice message */

    switch(choice)
    {
      case 7:
        printf("\nCongratulations!");
        printf("\nYou win the collected works of Amos Gruntfuttock.");
        break;        /* Jumps to the end of the block */

      case 2:
        printf("\nYou win the folding thermometer-pen-watch-umbrella.");
        break;        /* Jumps to the end of the block */

      case 8:
        printf("\nYou win the lifetime supply of aspirin tablets.");
        break;        /* Jumps to the end of the block */

      case 11:
        printf("\nTry between 1 and 10. You wasted your guess.");
                    /* No break - so continue with the next statement */

      default:
        printf("\nSorry, you lose.\n");
    }
 }
```

Typical output of this program would be:

```
Pick a number between 1 and 10 and you may win a prize! 3
Sorry, you lose.
```

or:

```
Pick a number between 1 and 10 and you may win a prize! 7
Congratulations!
You win the collected works of Amos Gruntfuttock.
```

or, if you enter an invalid number:

```
Pick a number between 1 and 10 and you may win a prize! 92
Try between 1 and 10. You wasted your guess.
Sorry, you lose.
```

How It Works

We do the usual sort of thing to start with. We declare an integer variable **choice**. Then we ask the user to enter a number between 1 and 10 and store the value they type in **choice**.

```
    int choice = 0;   /* The number chosen */

    /* Get the choice input */
    printf("\nPick a number between 1 and 10 and you may win a prize! ");
    scanf("%d",&choice);
```

Before we do anything else, we check that the user has really entered a number between 1 and 10:

```
    /* Check for an invalid selection */
    if((choice>10) || (choice <1))
        choice = 11;   /* Selects invalid choice message */
```

If the value is anything else, we automatically change it to 11. We don't have to do this, but to ensure the user is advised of their mistake, we set the variable **choice** to 11 - which produces the error message generated by the **printf()** for that case value.

Next, we have the switch statement that will select from the cases between the braces that follow, depending on the value of **choice**:

```
    switch(choice)
    {
      ...
    }
```

If **choice** has the value 7, the **case** corresponding to that value will be executed:

```
    case 7:
      printf("\nCongratulations!");
      printf("\nYou win the collected works of Amos Gruntfuttock.");
      break;        /* Jumps to the end of the block */
```

The two **printf()** calls are executed, and the **break** will jump to the statement following the closing brace for the block (which ends the program, in this case, since there isn't one).

The same goes for the next two cases:

```
    case 2:
      printf("\nYou win the folding thermometer-pen-watch-umbrella.");
          break;   /* Jumps to the end of the block */

    case 8:
      printf("\nYou win the lifetime supply of aspirin tablets.");
      break;        /* Jumps to the end of the block */
```

These will correspond to values for the variable **choice** of 2 or 8.

The next case is a little different:

```
    case 11:
      printf("\nTry between 1 and 10, you wasted your guess.");
                   /* No break - so continue with the next statement */
```

There's no **break** statement, so execution continues with the **printf()** for the **default** case after displaying the message. The upshot of this is that we get both lines of output if **choice** has been set to 11. This is entirely appropriate in this case; but usually, you'll want to put a **break** statement at the end of each case. Remove the **break** statements from the program, and try entering 7 to see why. You'll get all the output messages.

The **default** case is:

```
default:
   printf("\nSorry, you lose.\n");
```

This will be selected if the value of **choice** does not correspond to any of the other case values.

Although it isn't strictly necessary, many programmers always put a **break** statement after the **default** case statements - or whichever is the last **case** in the **switch**. This provides for the possibility of adding further **case** statements to the **switch**. The **case** statements can be in any order in a **switch**, and **default** does not have to be the last.

Try It Out - Yes or No

To illustrate another use for the **switch** statement let us suppose we have a **char** variable, **letter**, which we expect to have the value **'y'** or **'Y'** for one action, and **'n'** or **'N'** for another. We can do this using the **switch** statement in the following program. On its own it may be fairly useless, but you've probably encountered many situations where a program has asked just this question and then performed some action as a result (saving a file for example).

```c
/* Example 3.9 Testing cases */
#include <stdio.h>

void main()
{
   char letter = 0; /* Stores an input character */
   printf("Enter Y or N: ");
   scanf(" %c", &letter);

   switch (letter)
   {
     case 'y': case 'Y':
       printf("\nYou responded in the affirmative.");
       break;

     case 'n': case 'N':
       printf("\nYou responded in the negative.");
       break;

     default:
       printf("\nYou did not respond correctly...");
       break;
   }
}
```

Typical output from this would be:

```
Enter Y or N: y
You responded in the affirmative.
```

How It Works

When we declaring the variable **letter** as a character, we also take the opportunity to initialize it to zero. We then ask the user to type something in and store that value as usual.

```
char letter = 0; /* Stores an input character */

printf("Enter Y or N: ");
scanf(" %c", &letter);
```

The **switch** statement uses the character stored in **letter** to select a case:

```
switch ( letter )
{
   ...
}
```

The first case in the **switch** provides for the possibility of the user entering an upper-case or a lower-case letter Y:

```
case 'y': case 'Y':
  printf("\nYou responded in the affirmative.");
  break;
```

Both values, **'y'** and **'Y'** will result in the same **printf()** being executed. In general, you can put as many cases together like this as you want. Notice the punctuation for this. The two cases are combined, and each has a terminating colon after the case value.

The negative input is handled in a similar way:

```
case 'n': case 'N':
  printf("\nYou responded in the negative.");
  break;
```

If the character entered does not correspond with any of the case values, the **default** case is selected:

```
default:
  printf("\nYou did not respond correctly...");
  break;
```

Note the **break** statement after the **printf()** statements for the default case, as well as the legal **case** values. As before, this causes execution to break off at that point, and continue after the end of the **switch** statement. Again, without it you'd get the statements for succeeding cases executed and, unless there's a **break** statement preceding the valid cases, you'd get the following statement (or statements), including the **default** statement, executed as well.

109

The goto Statement

The **if** statement has provided us with the ability to choose one or another block of statements, depending on a test. This is a powerful tool that enables us to alter the naturally sequential nature of a program. We no longer have to go from A to B to C to D. We can go to A and then decide whether to skip B and C and go straight to D.

The **goto** statement, on the other hand, is a blunt instrument. It directs the flow of statements to change *unconditionally* - do not pass go, do not collect $200. When your program hits a **goto** it does just that. It goes to the place you send it, without checking any values or asking the user whether that was really what they wanted.

I'm only going to mention the **goto** statement very briefly, because it is not as great as it might at first seem. The problem with **goto** statements is that they seem too easy. This might sound perverse, but the important word is *seem*. It feels so simple that one can be tempted into using it all over the place, where it would be better to use a different statement. This can result in heavily tangled code.

To use the **goto**, the position to be moved to is defined by a **statement label** at that point. A statement label is defined in exactly the same way as a variable name, which is a sequence of letters and digits, the first of which must be a letter. Like other statements, the **goto** ends with a semicolon:

```
goto there;
```

The destination must have the same label as appears in the **goto** statement, which is **there** in this case. The label is written preceding the statement it applies to, with a colon separating the label from the rest of the statement. For example:

```
there: x=10; /* A labelled statement */
```

The **goto** statement can be used in conjunction with an **if** statement. For example:

```
    ....
if (Dice == 6)
    goto Waldorf;
else
    goto Jail;  /* Go to the statement labelled Jail */

Waldorf:
    Comfort = high;
    ....
Jail:           /* The label itself. Program control is sent here */
    Comfort = low;
    ....
```

We roll the dice. If we get 6 then we go to the **Waldorf**; otherwise, we go to **Jail**. This might seem perfectly fine, but, at the very least, it is confusing. To understand the sequence of execution you need to hunt for the destination labels. Imagine your code was littered with **goto**s. It would be very difficult to follow, and perhaps even more difficult to fix, when things go wrong. So it's best to avoid the **goto** where possible - in theory this is always the case, but there are one or two instances where it's a useful option.

Bitwise Operators

Before we come to the big example for the chapter, let's look at a group of operators that look a bit like the logical operators we saw earlier, but in fact are quite different. These are called the bitwise operators, because they operate on the bits in integer values. There are six bitwise operators:

   &   Bitwise AND operator

   | Bitwise OR operator

   ^   Bitwise Exclusive OR operator (EOR)

   ~   Bitwise NOT operator, also called the **1's complement operator**

   >>   Shift right operator

   <<   Shift left operator

All of these only operate on integer types. The **~** operator is a unary operator - it applies to one operand, and the others are binary operators.

The bitwise AND operator, **&**, combines the corresponding bits of its operands in such a way that if both bits are 1, the resulting bit is 1; otherwise the resulting bit is 0. Suppose we declare the following variables:

```
int x = 13;
int y = 6;
int z = x&y;     /* AND the bits of x and y */
```

After the third statement, **z** will have the value 4 (binary 100). This is because the corresponding bits in **x** and **y** are combined as follows:

x	0	0	0	0	1	1	0	1
Y	0	0	0	0	0	1	1	0
x&y	0	0	0	0	0	1	0	0

Obviously the variables would have more bits than I've shown here, but they would all be zero. With the values shown, only in the case of the third bit from the right in the two variables, **x** and **y**, are both bits 1, so this is the only case where the result is 1.

> *A word of caution - it's important not to get the bitwise operators and the logical operators muddled. The expression **x&y** will produce quite different results from **x&&y** in general. Try it out and see.*

The bitwise OR operator, **|**, results in 1 if either or both of the corresponding bits are 1; otherwise the result is 0. Let's look at a specific example. If we combined the same two values using the **|** operator in a statement such as:

```
int z = x|y;     /* OR the bits of x and y */
```

the result would be:

x	0	0	0	0	1	1	0	1
y	0	0	0	0	0	1	1	0
x|y	0	0	0	0	1	1	1	1

The value stored in **z** would therefore be 15 (binary 1111).

The bitwise exclusive OR, ^, produces a 1 if both bits are different, and 0 if they are the same. Again, using the same initial values, the statement:

```
int z = x^y;        /*Exclusive OR the bits of x and y */
```

would result in **z** containing the value 11 (binary 1011), because the bits combine as follows:

x	0	0	0	0	1	1	0	1
y	0	0	0	0	0	1	1	0
x^y	0	0	0	0	1	0	1	1

The unary operator, ~, flips the bits of its operand, so 1 becomes 0 and 0 becomes 1. If we apply this operator to **x** with the value 13 as before, and we write:

```
int z = ~x;        /*Store 1's complement of x */
```

Then **z** will have the value -14. The bits are set as follows:

x	0	0	0	0	1	1	0	1
~x	1	1	1	1	0	0	1	0

The value 11110010 is -14 in 2's complement representation of negative integers. If you're not familiar with 2's complement form, and you want to find out about it, I've described it in Appendix A.

The shift operators shift the bits in the left operand by the number of positions specified by the right operand. You could specify a shift left operation with the following statements:

```
int value = 12;
int shiftcount = 3;                 /* Number of positions to be shifted */
int result = value << shiftcount;/* Shift left shiftcount positions    */
```

The variable **result** will contain the value 96. The binary number in **value** is 00001100. The bits are shifted to the left 3 positions, and zeros introduced on the right, so the value of **value << shiftcount**, as a binary number, will be 01100000.

The right shift operator moves the bits to the right, but it's a little more complicated than left shift. For **unsigned** values, the bits that are introduced on the left (in the vacated positions as the bits are shifted right) are filled with zeros.

Let's see how this works in practice. Suppose we declare a variable:

```
unsigned int value = 65372U;
```

As a binary value in a two byte variable, this is:

$$1111 \quad 1111 \quad 0101 \quad 1100$$

Suppose we now execute the statement:

```
unsigned int result = value >> 2;   /* Shift right two bits */
```

The bits in **value** will be shifted two places to the right, introducing zeros at the left hand end, and the value stored in **result**. In binary this will be:

$$0011 \quad 1111 \quad 1101 \quad 0111$$

which is the decimal value 16343.

For signed values that are negative, where the leftmost bit will be 1, it depends on your system. In most cases, the sign bit is propagated, so the bits introduced are 1 bits - but it may be that zeros are introduced in this case. Let's see how this affects the result.

Suppose we define a variable with the statement:

```
int newValue = -164;
```

This happens to be the same bit pattern as the unsigned value - remember that this is the 2's complement representation of the value:

$$1111 \quad 1111 \quad 0101 \quad 1100$$

If we now execute the statement:

```
int newResult = newValue >> 2;       /* Shift right two bits */
```

If, as is usually the case, the sign bit is propagated, 1's will be inserted on the left as the bits are shifted to the right, so **newResult** will end up as:

$$1111 \quad 1111 \quad 1101 \quad 0111$$

This is the decimal value -41, which is what you might expect since it amounts to -164/4. If the sign bit is not propagated, however, as can occur on some computers, the value in **newResult** will be:

$$0011 \quad 1111 \quad 1101 \quad 0111$$

So shifting right two bits in this case has changed the value -164 to +16343, perhaps a rather unexpected result.

The op= use of Bitwise Operators

You can use all of the binary bitwise operators in the **op=** form of assignment. The exception is the operator, ~, which is a unary operator. As you saw in the previous chapter, a statement of the form:

```
lhs op= rhs;
```

is equivalent to the statement:

```
lhs = lhs op (rhs);
```

This means that if you write:

```
value <<= 4;
```

the effect is to shift the contents of the integer variable, **value**, left 4 bit positions. It is exactly the same as:

```
value = value << 4;
```

You can do the same kind of thing with the other binary operators. For example you could write the statement:

```
value &= 0xFF;
```

where **value** is an integer variable. This is equivalent to:

```
value = value & 0xFF;
```

The effect is to keep the rightmost 8 bits in value as whatever they are, and to set all the others to zero.

Using Bitwise Operators

The bitwise operators look interesting in an academic kind of way, but what use are they? They don't come up in everyday programs, but in some areas they become very useful. One major use of the bitwise AND, **&**, and the bitwise OR, **|**, is in operations to test and set individual bits in an integer variable. With this capability, we can use individual bits to store data which involves one of two choices. For example, we could use a single integer variable to store several characteristics of a person. We could store whether they were male or female with one bit, and use three other bits to specify whether they could speak French, German or Italian. We might use anther bit to record whether their salary was $50,000 or more. So in just 4 bits we have a substantial set of data recorded. Let's see how this would work out.

The fact that we only get a 1 bit when both of the bits being combined are 1 means that we can use the **&** operator to select out a part of an integer variable, or even just a single bit. We first define a value, usually called a **mask**, that we use to select the bit or bits that we want. It will contain 1 bits for the positions we want to keep and 0 bits for the positions we want to discard. We can then AND this mask with the value that we want to select from. Let's look at an example. We can define masks with the following statements:

```
unsigned int male     = 0x1; /* Mask selecting first (rightmost) bit  */
unsigned int french   = 0x2; /* Mask selecting second bit             */
unsigned int german   = 0x4; /* Mask selecting third bit              */
unsigned int italian  = 0x8; /* Mask selecting fourth bit             */
unsigned int payBracket = 0x10;/* Mask selecting fifth bit            */
```

In each case, a 1 bit will indicate that the particular condition is true. These masks in binary each pick out an individual bit, so we could have an **unsigned int** variable, **personalData**, which would store five items of information about a person. If the first bit is 1 the person is male, and if the first bit is 0, the person is female. If the second bit is 1 then the person speaks French, and if it is zero they don't - and so on for all five bits at the right hand end of the data value.

We could therefore test the variable, **personalData**, for a German speaker, with the statement:

```
if(personalData & german)
   /* Do something because they speak German */
```

The expression **personalData & german** will be positive - that is, true - if the bit corresponding to the mask, **german**, is 1; otherwise it will be zero.

Of course, there is nothing to prevent us from combining several expressions involving masks to select individual bits with the logical operators. We could test whether someone was a female who spoke French or Italian with the statement:

```
if(!(personalData & male) && ((personalData & french) ||
    (personalData & italian)))
   /* We have a French or Italian speaking female */
```

As you can see, it's easy enough to test individual bits or combinations of bits. The only other thing we need to understand is how to set individual bits. The OR operator swings into action here.

We can use the OR operator set individual bits in a variable using the same mask that we use to test the bits. If we want to set the variable **personalData** to record a person as speaking French, we can do it with this statement:

```
personalData |= french;  /* Set second bit to 1 */
```

The second bit from the right in **personalData** will be set to 1, and all the other bits will remain as they were. Because of the way the | operator works, we can set multiple bits in a single statement:

```
personalData |= french|german|male;
```

This sets the bits to record a French and German speaking male. If the variable **personalData** previously recorded that the person spoke Italian, that bit would still be set, so the OR operator is additive. If a bit was already set it will stay set.

What about resetting a bit? Suppose we wanted to change the male bit to female. This amounts to resetting a 1 bit to 0, and it requires the use of the ! operator with the bitwise AND:

115

```
    personalData &= !male;    /* Reset male to female */
```

This works because **!male** will have a 0 bit set for the bit that indicates male, and all the other bits as 1. Thus the bit corresponding to male will be set to 0 - 0 ANDed with anything is 0, and all the other bits will be as they were. If another bit is 1 then **1&1** will still be 1. If another bit is 0 then **0&1** will still be 0.

We've used the example of using bits to record specific items of personal data. If you want to program a PC using the Windows API, individual bits are often used to record the status of various window parameters.

Try It Out – Using Bitwise Operators

Let's exercise some of the bitwise operators in a slightly different example, but using the same principles that we have discussed. This example will illustrate how you can use a mask to select multiple bits from a variable. We'll write a program that sets a value in a variable, and then uses the bitwise operators to reverse the sequence of hexadecimal digits. Here's the code:

```
/* Example 3.10 Exercising bitwise operators */
#include <stdio.h>

void main()
{
   unsigned int original = 0xABC;
   unsigned int result = 0;
   unsigned int mask = 0xF;                /* Rightmost four bits */

   printf("\n original = %X", original);

   /* Insert FIRST digit in result */

   /* Put right 4 bits from original in result */
   result |= original&mask;

   /* Get SECOND digit */

   /* Shift original right four positions     */
   original >>= 4;

   /* Make room for next digit                */
   result <<= 4;

   /* Put right 4 bits from original in result */
   result |= original&mask;

   /* Get THIRD digit */
   /* Shift original right four positions     */
   original >>= 4;

   /* Make room for next digit                */
   result <<= 4;
```

```
      /* Put right 4 bits from original in result */
      result |= original&mask;

      printf("\t result = %X\n", result);
   }
```

This will produce the output:

```
   original = ABC  result = CBA
```

How It Works

This uses the idea of masking that we just discussed. The rightmost hexadecimal digit in **original** is obtained by ANDing the value with **mask** in the expression **original&mask**. This sets all the other hexadecimal digits to zero. Since the value of mask as a binary number is:

0000   0000   0000   1111

you can see that only the first four bits on the right are kept. Any of these four bits that is 1 will stay as 1, and any that are 0 will stay as 0. All the other bits will be 0 since 0 ANDed with anything is 0.

Once we've selected the rightmost four bits, we then store the result with the statement:

```
      /* Put right 4 bits from original in result */
      result |= original&mask;
```

The content of **result** is ORed with the hexadecimal digit that's produced by the expression on the right hand side.

To get at the second digit in **original**, we need to move it to where the first digit was. We do this by shifting original right by four bit positions:

```
      /* Shift original right four positions      */
      original >>= 4;
```

The first digit is shifted out and is lost.

To make room for the next digit from **original**, we shift the contents of **result** left by four bit positions, with the statement:

```
      /* Make room for next digit                 */
      result <<= 4;
```

Now we want to insert the second digit from **original**, which is now in the first digit position, into **result**. We do this with the statement:

```
      /* Put right 4 bits from original in result */
      result |= original&mask;
```

To get the third digit we just repeat the process. Clearly you could repeat this for as many digits as you want.

Designing a Program

You've reached the end of Chapter 3 successfully, and now we'll apply what we've learnt by building a useful program.

The Problem

The problem I'm setting is to write a simple calculator that can add, subtract, multiply, divide, and find the modulus of two numbers.

The Analysis

All the math involved is simple, but the processing of the input adds a little complication. We need to make checks on the input to make sure that the user hasn't asked the computer to do the impossible. We'll allow the user to input the calculation in one go. For example:

```
34.87 + 5
```

or

```
9 * 6.5
```

So the steps to writing this program are:

1 Get the user input for the calculation that they want the computer to perform

2 Check that input to make sure that it's understandable

3 Perform the calculation and display the result

The Solution

1 Getting the user input is quite easy. We'll be using **printf()** and **scanf()**, so we need the **stdio.h** header file. The only new thing we'll do is in the way we get the input. As I said earlier, rather than asking the user for each number individually, and then asking for the operation to be performed, we'll get the user to type it in more naturally. We can do this because of the way **scanf()** works, but we'll discuss that after you've seen the first part of the program. Let's kick off the program with the code to read the input:

```
/*Example 3.11 A calculator*/
#include <stdio.h>

void main()
{
```

```
    double number1 = 0.0;    /* First operand value a decimal number  */
    double number2 = 0.0;    /* Second operand value a decimal number */
    char operation = 0;      /* Operation - must be +, -, *, /, or %  */

    printf("\nEnter the calculation\n");
    scanf("%lf %c %lf", &number1, &operation, &number2);

    /* Plus the rest of the code for the program */
}
```

scanf() is fairly clever when it comes to reading data. You don't actually need to enter each input data item on a separate line. All that's required is some whitespace between each item of input. (Whitespace is created by pressing *Space*, *Tab* or *Enter.*)

2 Next, we must check to make sure that the input is correct. The most obvious check to perform is that the operation to be performed is valid. We've already decided that the valid operations are: **+**, **-**, **/**, ***** and **%**, so we need to check that the operation is one of these.

We also need to check the second number to see if it's zero if the operation is either **/** or **%.** If the right operand is **0**, then these operations are invalid. We could do all the above checks using **if** statements, but there's a far better way of doing this with a **switch** statement.

```
/*Example 3.11 A calculator*/
#include <stdio.h>

void main()
{
    double number1 = 0.0;    /* First operand value a decimal number  */
    double number2 = 0.0;    /* Second operand value a decimal number */
    char operation = 0;      /* Operation - must be +, -, *, /, or %  */

    printf("\nEnter the calculation\n");
    scanf("%lf %c %lf", &number1, &operation, &number2);

    /* Code to check the input goes here */
    switch(operation)
    {
      case '+':                /* No checks necessary for add           */
        break;

      case '-':                /* No checks necessary for subtract      */
        break;

      case '*':                /* No checks necessary for multiply      */
        break;

      case '/':
        if(number2 == 0)       /* Check second operand for zero         */
          printf("\n\n\aDivision by zero error!\n");
          break;
```

```
            case '%':
              if((long)number2 == 0)      /*  Check second operand for zero  */
                printf("\n\n\aDivision by zero error!\n");
                break;

            default:                 /* Operation is invalid if we get to here */
              printf("\n\n\aIllegal operation!\n");
          }

      /* Plus the rest of the code for the program */
    }
```

Because we are casting the second operand to an integer when the operator is **%**, it isn't sufficient to just check the second operand against zero: we must check that **number2** doesn't have a value that will result in zero when it's cast to type **long**.

3 So now we've checked the input, we can calculate what the answer is. We have a choice here. We could calculate each result in the **switch** and store it to be output after the **switch**; or we could simply output the result for each case. Let's go for the latter approach. The code we need to add is:

```
/*Example 3.11 A calculator*/
#include <stdio.h>

void main()
{
    double number1 = 0.0;   /* First operand value a decimal number  */
    double number2 = 0.0;   /* Second operand value a decimal number */
    char operation = 0;     /* Operation - must be +, -, *, /, or %  */

    printf("\nEnter the calculation\n");
    scanf("%lf %c %lf", &number1, &operation, &number2);

    /* Code to check the input goes here */
    switch(operation)
    {
      case '+':             /* No checks necessary for add       */
        printf("= %lf\n", number1 + number2);
        break;

      case '-':             /* No checks necessary for subtract */
        printf("= %lf\n", number1 - number2);
        break;

      case '*':             /* No checks necessary for multiply */
        printf("= %lf\n", number1 * number2);
        break;

      case '/':
        if(number2 == 0)     /* Check second operand for zero     */
          printf("\n\n\aDivision by zero error!\n");
```

```
          else
            printf("= %lf\n", number1 / number2);
          break;

      case '%':                /* Check second operand for zero    */
        if((long)number2 == 0)
          printf("\n\n\aDivision by zero error!\n");
        else
          printf("= %ld\n", (long)number1 % (long)number2);
          break;

      default:                 /* Operation is invalid if we get to here */
        printf("\n\n\aIllegal operation!\n");
    }
  }
```

Notice how we cast the two numbers from **double** to **long** when we calculate the modulus. This is because **%** only works with integers in C. All that's left is to try it out! Don't forget the spaces between the operands and the operator. You'll get an error message if you don't include these spaces. Here's some typical output:

```
Enter the calculation
56 * 75
= 4200.000000
```

Here's another sample:

```
Enter the calculation
7 % 0

Division by zero error!
```

Summary

This chapter has ended with quite a complicated example. In the first 2 chapters, we really just looked at the groundwork for C programs. We could do some reasonably useful things, but we couldn't control the program once it had started. In this chapter, we start to feel the power of the language.

You've learned how to compare variables and then use **if**, **if-else** and **switch** statements to affect the outcome. You also know how to use logical operators to combine comparisons between your variables. You should understand a lot more, now, about making decisions and taking different paths through your program code.

In the next chapter, you'll learn how to write even more powerful programs: programs that can repeat instructions over and over again. By the end of Chapter 4, you'll think your calculator is small fry.

Loops

In the last chapter we learned how to compare items and base our decisions on the result. We were able to choose how the computer reacted based on the input to a program.

We ended the chapter with a promise of even greater things. You're probably starting to get a feel for the power of C programming, but perhaps feeling frustrated by the fact that you're still restricted in what you can do. In the lottery example in the last chapter, it would have been nice to allow the user to get another try. Having to restart the calculator program for each calculation was a bit tedious, too. You could have fixed this using the **goto** statement, but now I'll introduce you to a much better way to program this sort of task.

In this chapter, I'll show you how to repeat a block of statements - using something called a **loop**. Here's what you'll be learning about:

▶ How you can repeat a statement, or a block of statements, as many times as you want

▶ How you can repeat a statement, or a block of statements, until a particular condition is fulfilled

▶ How you use the **for**, **while** and **do-while** loops

▶ What the increment and decrement operators do, and how you can use them

▶ How you can write a program that plays a Simple Simon game

Loops

The programming mechanism that executes a series of instructions repeatedly a given number of times, or until a particular condition is fulfilled, is called a **loop**.

The loop is a fundamental programming tool, along with the ability to compare items. Once you can compare items and repeat actions, you can combine them to control how many times a block of statements is executed. For example, you can keep performing a particular action until two items that you are comparing are the same. Once they *are* the same, you can go on to perform a different action.

In the lottery example, you could give the user exactly 3 guesses - in other words, let them continue to guess, until a variable called **number_of_guesses**, for instance, equals 3. Alternatively, you could set up a specific number (zero for example) so that when the user types it in, the program ends. The user will then be able to continue entering guesses as long as he or she wants. When they've had enough, they just need to type in zero.

The way a typical loop works is illustrated in the figure.

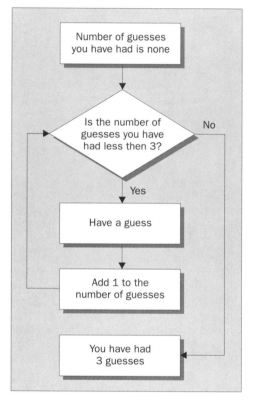

More often than not, you'll find that you want to apply the same calculation to different sets of data values. Without loops, you'd need to write out the instructions to be performed as many times as there were sets of data values to be processed - which isn't very satisfactory. A loop allows you to use the same program code for any number of sets of data to be entered.

Before we discuss the various types of loops available to us in C, I'll briefly mention two operators that you'll encounter frequently in C programs: the increment and decrement operators. These operators are often used with loops, which is why we'll discuss them here. We'll start with the briefest of introductions to the increment and decrement operators. Then I'll throw us straight into an example of how we can use them in the context of a loop. Once we're comfortable with how loops work, we'll actually come back to the increment and decrement operators to investigate some of their idiosyncrasies. By then, you'll be a confident exponent of loops, and you'll be ready to use them in your own programs.

The Increment and Decrement Operators - A Quick Tour

The **increment operator** (**++**) and the **decrement operator** (**--**) are used to increment or decrement the value of the integer variable that they apply to. You can think of them as meaning 'plus one' and 'minus one' for the time being. So if you have an integer variable number, with the value 6, you can increment it with the statement:

```
++number;   /* Increase the value by 1 */
```

So, after executing this statement, number will contain the value 7. Similarly, you could decrease the value of **number** by one with the statement:

```
--number;   /* Decrease the value by 1 */
```

These operators are a real asset once you get used to them, especially when you're writing loops. Don't be misled though. The two examples we've seen may make them look trivial, but there's more to these operators than is apparent at first sight - as we shall discover a little later in this chapter.

Right now, let's get back to our main discussion and take a look at the simplest form of loop, the **for** loop. There are other types of loop, **while** and **do-while**, that are similar to the **for** loop. We'll give the **for** loop a larger slice of our time, however, because once you've cracked this one, the others will be easy.

The for Loop

The **for** loop used in its basic form enables you to execute a block of statements a given number of times. Let's suppose we want to display the numbers from 1 to 10. Instead of writing ten **printf()** statements, we could write this:

```
int count = 0;
for(count = 1 ; count <= 10 ; ++count)
  printf("\n%d", count);
```

The **for** loop operation is controlled by the contents of the parentheses that follow the keyword **for**. The action that we want to occur each time the loop repeats is the statement, or block of statements, that's placed between the braces that immediately follow the parentheses. In our case, this is just the call to the **printf()** function; but it could be a whole block of code enclosed between braces.

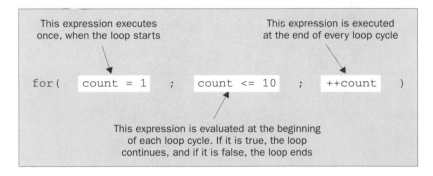

There are three expressions that control the loop, which appear between the parentheses, and are separated by semicolons. The effect of each of these is shown in the diagram, but we'll now take a much closer look at exactly what's going on.

▶ The first expression is executed only once, when the loop starts. In our code fragment, the first expression initializes a variable, **count,** to 1. This is the expression **count = 1**.

▶ The second expression must be a logical expression and, in our case, it's **count <= 10**. The second expression is evaluated before each loop iteration, and if it is true, the loop continues. Remember that false is a zero value, and any non-zero value is true. When the expression is false, the loop ends, and execution of the program continues with the first statement following the loop block or loop statement. Our loop will end when **count** reaches 11.

▶ The third expression, **++count** in our case, is executed at the end of each iteration. Here, we use the increment operator to add 1 to the value of **count**. As a result, on the first iteration, **count** will be 1; so the **printf()** will output 1, and on the second iteration the **printf()** will output the value 2. This will continue until the value 10 has been displayed. At the start of the next iteration, **count** will be 11, and since the second control expression will be false, the loop will end.

Notice the punctuation. The **for** loop parameters are contained within parentheses, and each expression is separated from the next by a semicolon. You can omit any of the control expressions, but if you do, you must still include the semicolon. For example, you could declare and initialize the variable **count** to 1 outside the loop:

```
int count = 1;
```

Then you wouldn't need to specify the first control expression, and the **for** loop could look like this:

```
for( ; count <= 10 ; ++count)
  printf("\n%d", count);
```

As a trivial example we could make this into a real program simply by adding a few lines:

```
/*Example 4.1 List ten integers */
#include <stdio.h>

void main()
{
   int count = 1;
   for( ; count <= 10 ; ++count)
     printf("\n%d", count);
   printf("\nWe have finished.");
}
```

This will list the numbers from 1 to 10 on separate lines and then output the message:

```
We have finished.
```

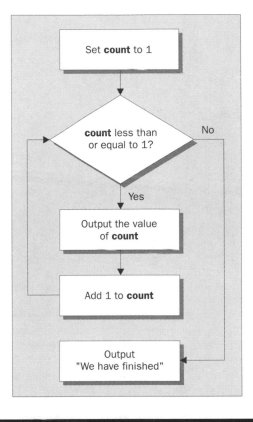

We can illustrate the logic of this with a flow chart.

In this example, it's easy to see what the variable **count** starts out as, so this code is quite OK. In general though, unless the variable controlling the loop is initialized very close to the loop statement itself, it's better to initialize it in the first control expression. That way, there's less potential for error.

Let's try a slightly different example.

Try It Out - Drawing a Box

Consider a situation where you want to draw a box on the screen using ***** characters. We could just use the **printf()** statement lots of times, but the typing would be exhausting. We can use a **for** loop to draw a box much more easily. Let's try it.

```
/* Example 4.2 Drawing a box */
#include <stdio.h>

void main()
{
   int count = 0;
   printf("\n**************");      /* Draw the top of the box    */

   for(count = 1 ; count <= 8 ; ++count)
     printf("\n*           *");   /* Draw the sides of the box  */

   printf("\n**************\n");   /* Draw the bottom of the box */
}
```

127

No prizes for guessing, but the output from this program looks like this:

```
* * * * * * * * * * * * * *
*                        *
*                        *
*                        *
*                        *
*                        *
*                        *
*                        *
*                        *
* * * * * * * * * * * * * *
```

How It Works

The program itself is really very simple. The first statement declares the variable **count**:

```
int count = 0;
```

The first **printf()** statement is then used to output the top of the box to the screen:

```
printf("\n**************");      /* Draw the top of the box   */
```

The next statement is our **for** loop:

```
for(count = 1 ; count <= 8 ; ++count)
    printf("\n*            *");   /* Draw the sides of the box */
```

This repeats the **printf()** statement 8 times to output the sides of our box. You probably understand this, but let's look again at how it works and pick up a bit more jargon. The loop control is:

```
for(count = 1 ; count <= 8 ; ++count )
```

The operation of the loop is controlled by the three expressions that appear between the parentheses following the keyword, **for**.

```
count = 1
```

This initializes the **loop control variable**, or **loop counter**, which in this case is the integer variable, **count**, which we set to 1. We could have used other types of variables for this, but integers are convenient for the job. The next expression is:

```
count <= 8
```

This is the **continuation condition** for the loop. This is checked *before* each loop iteration, to see whether the loop should continue. If the expression is true, the loop continues. If it is false, the loop ends and execution continues with the statement following the loop. In our example, the loop continues as long as the variable **count** is less than or equal 8. The last expression is:

```
++count
```

This statement increments the loop counter at the end of each loop iteration. The loop statement that outputs the sides of the box will therefore be executed 8 times. After the eighth iteration, **count** will be incremented to 9 and the continuation condition will be false - so the loop will end.

Program execution will then continue by executing the statement:

```
printf("\n**************\n");     /* Draw the bottom of the box */
```

This prints the bottom of the box on the screen.

> *Whenever you find yourself repeating something more than a couple of times it's worth considering a loop. They will usually save you time and memory.*

The general pattern of the **for** loop is:

```
for(starting_condition; continuation_condition ; action_per_iteration)
   Statement;

Next_statement;
```

The statement to be repeated is represented by **Statement**. In general, this could equally well be a block of statements enclosed between a pair of braces.

The **starting_condition** usually (but not always) sets an initial value to a loop control variable. The loop control variable is typically, but not necessarily, a counter of some kind that tracks how often you go round the loop.

The **continuation_condition** is a logical expression evaluating to true or false. This determines whether the loop should continue to be executed or not. As long as this condition has the value true, the loop continues. It typically checks the value of the loop control variable - but any logical expression can be placed here, as long as you know what you're doing.

As we've already seen, the **continuation_condition** is tested at the beginning of the loop rather than the end. This obviously makes it possible to have a **for** loop whose statements are not executed at all if the **continuation_condition** starts out as false.

The **action_per_iteration** is executed at the end of each loop iteration, and is usually (but again not necessarily) an increment of the loop control variable. At each iteration of the loop, the statement or block of statements immediately following the **for** statement is executed. The loop is terminated, and execution continues with **Next_statement**, as soon as the **continuation_condition** is false.

The Increment and Decrement Operators

Now we've seen an increment operator in action, let's delve a little deeper and find out what else these increment and decrement operators can do. They're both unary operators, which means they are only used with one argument. We know they're used to increment (increase) or decrement (decrease) a value stored in a variable of one of the integer types.

The Increment Operator

Let's start with the increment operator. This takes the form **++** and adds 1 to the variable it acts on. For example, assuming our variables are of type **int**, the following three statements all have exactly the same effect:

```
count = count + 1;
count += 1;
++count;
```

Each statement increments the variable **count** by 1. The last form is clearly the most concise.

Thus, if we declared a variable **count** and initialized it to 1:

```
int count = 1;
```

and then we repeated the following statement 6 times in a loop:

```
++count;
```

by the end of the loop, **count** would have a value of 7. Each time you execute **++count** you add one more to the value stored in the variable. At the outset, **count** has the value 1 stored in it. After the first cycle, **count** would equal 2. Then, before the second iteration starts, **count** is equal to 2; and after the second iteration, **count** would equal 3, and so on up to 7.

You can also use the increment operator in an expression. The action of this operator in an expression is to increment the value of the variable, then use the incremented value in the expression. For example, suppose **count** has the value 5, and we execute the statement:

```
total = ++count + 6;
```

This results in the variable **count** being incremented to 6, and the variable **total** being assigned the value 12. The one statement modifies two variables. The variable **count**, with the value 5, has 1 added to it making 6, and then 6 is added to this value to produce 12 for the expression on the right hand side of the assignment operator. This value is stored in **total**.

Prefixing and Postfixing the Increment Operator

So far, we've written the operator, **++**, in front of the variable to which it applies. This is called the **prefix form**. It can also be written *after* the variable to which it applies, and this is referred to as the **postfix form**. In this case, the effect is slightly different from the prefix form when it is used in an expression. If you write **count++** in an expression, the incrementing of the variable **count** occurs *after* its value has been used. This sounds more complicated than it is. Let's look at the earlier example:

```
total = 6 + count++;
```

With the same initial value of 5 for **count**, **total** is assigned the value 11. This is because the initial value of **count** is used to evaluate the expression (6+5). The incrementing by 1 (the **++**) is only applied to the variable **count** after the expression has been evaluated.

The statement above is therefore equivalent to these two statements:

```
total = 6 + count;
++count;
```

Note, however, that when you use the increment operator in a statement by itself (as in the second statement above, which increments **count**), it doesn't matter whether you write the prefix or the postfix version of the operator. They both have the same effect.

Where we have an expression such as **a++ + b**, or worse, **a+++b**, it is less than obvious what is meant to happen, or what the compiler will achieve. They are actually the same, but in the second case you might really have meant **a + ++b** which is different - since it evaluates to one more than the other two expressions.

For example, if **a = 10** and **b = 5** then in the statement:

```
x = a++ + b;
```

x will have the value 15 (from 10 + 5) because **a** is incremented after the expression is evaluated. The next time you use the variable **a**, however, it will have the value 11.

On the other hand, if you execute the following statement, with the same initial values for **a** and **b**:

```
y = a + ++b;
```

y will have the value 16 (from 10 + 6) because **b** is incremented before the statement is evaluated.

It's a good idea to use parentheses in all these cases to make sure there's no confusion. So you should write these statements as:

```
x = (a++) + b;
y = a + (++b);
```

The Decrement Operator

The decrement operator works in much the same way. This takes the form **--** and subtracts 1 from the variable it acts on. It's used in exactly the same way as **++**. For example, assuming the variables are of type **int**, the following three statements all have exactly the same effect:

```
count = count - 1;
count -= 1;
--count;
```

They each decrement the variable **count** by 1. For example if **count** has the value 10, then the statement:

```
total = --count + 6;
```

results in the variable **total** being assigned the value 15 (from 9+6).

The variable **count**, with the initial value of 10, has 1 subtracted from it so that its value is 9. Then 6 added to the new value making the value of the expression on the right of the assignment operator 15.

Exactly the same rules that we discussed in relation to the increment operator apply to the decrement operator. For example, if **count** has the initial value 5, then the statement:

```
total = --count + 6;
```

results in **total** having the value 10 (from 4+6) assigned, whereas:

```
total = 6 + count-- ;
```

sets the value of **total** to 11 (from 6+5). Both operators are usually applied to integers, but we shall also see, in later chapters, how they can be applied to certain other data types in C.

The for Loop Revisited

Now we understand a bit more about **++** and **--** let's get on with another example that uses a loop.

Try It Out - Summing Numbers

This is a more useful and interesting program than drawing a box with asterisks (unless what you really needed was, of course, a box drawn with asterisks). Have you ever wanted to know what all the house numbers in your street totaled? Here, we're going to read in an integer value, and then use a **for** loop to sum all the integers from 1 to the value entered.

```c
/*  Example 4.3 Sum the integers from 1 to a user-specified number */
#include <stdio.h>

void main()
{
   long sum = 0L; /* Stores the sum of the integers       */
   int count = 0; /* The number of integers to be summed */
   int i = 0;      /* The loop counter                    */

   /* Read the number of integers to be summed */
   printf("\nEnter the number of integers you want to sum: ");
   scanf(" %d", &count);

   /* Sum integers from 1 to count */
   for(i = 1 ; i <= count ; i++)
     sum += i;

   printf("\nTotal of the first %d numbers is %ld\n", count, sum);
}
```

The typical output you should get from this program is:

```
Enter the number of integers you want to sum: 10

Total of the first 10 integers is 55
```

How It Works

We start by declaring and initializing three variables:

```
long sum = 0L; /* Stores the sum of the integers     */
int count = 0; /* The number of integers to be summed */
int i = 0;     /* The loop counter                    */
```

We'll use **sum** to hold the final value of our calculations. We declare it as type **long** to allow the maximum total we can deal with to be as large an integer as possible. The variable **count** will store the integer that's entered as the number of integers to be summed, and we'll use this value to control the number of iterations in the **for** loop. The variable **i** is the loop counter.

We deal with the input by means of the following statements:

```
printf("\nEnter the number of integers you want to sum: ");
scanf(" %d", &count);
```

After the prompt, we read in the integer to define the sum required. So if the user enters 4, for instance, then the program will compute the sum of 1, 2, 3 and 4.

The sum is calculated in the loop:

```
for(i = 1 ; i <= count ; i++)
   sum += i;
```

The loop variable **i** is initialized to 1 by the starting condition in the **for** loop. On each iteration, the value of **i** is added to **sum**, and then **i** is incremented, so the values 1, 2, 3, and so on up to the value stored in **count**, will be added to **sum**. The loop ends when the value of **i** exceeds the value of **count**.

As I've hinted, with the occasional 'not necessarily' in my description of how the **for** loop is controlled, you have a lot of flexibility about what you can use as control expressions. The next program demonstrates how this flexibility might be applied to shortening the previous example slightly.

Try It Out - The Flexible for

```
/* Example 4.4 Summing integers - compact version */
#include <stdio.h>

void main()
{
   long sum = 0L; /* Stores the sum of the integers     */
   int count = 0; /* The number of integers to be summed */
   int i = 0;     /* The loop counter                    */
```

```
      /* Read the number of integers to be summed */
      printf("\nEnter the number of integers you want to sum: ");
      scanf(" %d", &count);

      /* Sum integers from 1 to count */
      for (i = 1 ; i<= count ; sum += i++ );

      printf("\nTotal of the first %d numbers is %ld\n", count, sum);
}
```

Typical output would be:

```
    Enter the number of integers you want to sum: 6

    Total of the first 6 numbers is 21
```

How It Works

This will execute exactly the same as the previous program. The only difference is that we have placed the summing operation in the third control expression for the loop:

```
    for (i = 1 ; i<= count ; sum += i++ );
```

The loop statement is empty: it's just the semicolon after the closing parenthesis. This expression adds the value of **i** to **sum**, and then increments **i** ready for the next iteration. It works this way because we've used the postfix form of the increment operator. If you use the prefix form here then you'll get the wrong answer, because the total in **sum** will include the number **count+1** from the first iteration of the loop, instead of just **count**.

Modifying the Loop Variable

Of course, we aren't limited to incrementing the loop control variable by 1. We can change it by any value, positive or negative. We could have summed the first n integers backwards if we wished, as in the following example:

```
/* Example 4.5 Summing integers backwards */
#include <stdio.h>
void main()
{
  long sum = 0L;   /* Stores the sum of the integers     */
  int count = 0;   /* The number of integers to be summed */
  int i = 0;       /* The loop counter                   */

  /* Read the number of integers to be summed */
  printf("\nEnter the number of integers you want to sum: ");
  scanf(" %d", &count);

  /* Sum integers from count to 1 */
  for (i = count ; i >= 1 ; sum += i-- );

  printf("\nTotal of the first %d numbers is %ld\n", count, sum);
}
```

This produces the same output as the previous example. The only change is in the loop control expressions. The loop counter is initialized to **count**, rather than to 1, and it is *decremented* on each iteration. The effect is to add the values **count**, **count-1**, **count-2**, and so on down to 1. Again, if you used the prefix form then the answer would be wrong, because you would start with adding **count-1** instead of just **count**.

Just to keep any mathematically inclined readers happy, I should mention that it's quite unnecessary to use a loop to sum the first *n* integers. A tidy little formula:

```
n*(n+1)/2
```

will do the trick much more efficiently. However, it wouldn't teach you much about loops, would it?

A for Loop with No Parameters

As I've already mentioned, we have no obligation to put any parameters in the **for** loop statement at all. The minimal **for** loop looks like this:

```
for ( ;; )
  statement;
```

Here, as previously, **statement** could also be a block of statements enclosed between braces. Since the condition for continuing the loop is absent, as is the initial condition and the loop increment, the loop will continue indefinitely. As a result, unless you want your computer to be indefinitely doing nothing, **statement** must contain the means of exiting from the loop - as in the next example.

Try It Out - A Minimal for Loop

This example will compute the average of an arbitrary number of values:

```
/* Example 4.6 The almost indefinite loop - computing an average */
#include <stdio.h>

void main()
{
   char Test = 'N';   /* Records yes or no to continue the loop */
   float total = 0.0; /* Total of values entered               */
   float value = 0.0; /* Value entered                          */
   int count = 0;     /* Number of values entered               */

   printf("\nThis program calculates the average of"
                                 " any number of values.");

   for( ;; )    /* Infinite loop */
   {
     printf ("\nEnter a value: ");   /* Prompt for the next value */
     scanf(" %f", &value);           /* Read the next value       */
     total += value;                 /* Add value to total        */
     ++count;                        /* Increment count of values */
```

```
      /* check for more input */
    printf("Do you want to enter another value? (Y or N): ");
    scanf(" %c", &Test );     /* Read response Y or N */

    if( Test == 'N' || Test == 'n' ) /* look for any sign of no */
      break;                         /* Exit from the loop      */
  }
  /* output the average */
  printf ("\nThe average is %f\n", total/count );
}
```

Typical output from this program is:

```
This program calculates the average of any number of values.
Enter a value: 2.5
Do you want to enter another value? (Y or N): y

Enter a value: 3.5
Do you want to enter another value? (Y or N): y

Enter a value: 6.0
Do you want to enter another value? (Y or N): n

The average is 4.000000
```

How It Works

The general logic of the program is illustrated below.

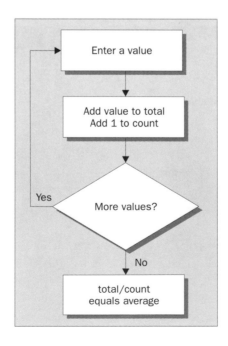

We've set up the loop to continue indefinitely, since the **for** loop has no end condition specified - or indeed any loop control expressions:

```
for( ;; )    /* Infinite loop */
```

Therefore, so far as the loop control is concerned, the block of statements enclosed between the braces will be repeated indefinitely.

We display a prompt and read an input value in the loop with these statements:

```
printf ("\nEnter a value: ");   /* Prompt for the next value */
scanf(" %f", &value);           /* Read the next value       */
```

Next, we add the value entered to our variable **total**:

```
total += value;                 /* Add value to total        */
```

We then increment the count of the number of values:

```
++count;                        /* Increment count of values */
```

Having read a value and added it to the total, we check with the user to see whether more input is to be entered:

```
/* check for more input */
printf("Do you want to enter another value? (Y or N): ");
scanf(" %c", &Test );    /* Read response Y or N */
```

This prompts for either **'Y'** or **'N'** to be entered. The character entered is checked in the **if** statement:

```
if( Test == 'N' || Test == 'n' ) /* look for any sign of no */
   break;                        /* Exit from the loop       */
```

If you enter a character **N**, or **n**, to indicate that you've finished entering data, the **break** statement will be executed. We've seen the **break** statement before, in the context of the **switch** statement. The effect here is similar. Executing **break** within a loop has the effect of jumping out of the loop, so that execution continues with the statement following the closing brace for the loop block. This is the statement:

```
printf ("\nThe average is %f\n", total/count );
```

This calculates the average of the values entered by dividing the value in **total** by the count of the number of values. The result is then displayed.

Loops in Action - Limiting Your Input

You can use a **for** loop to limit the amount of input from the user. We can write a simple program to demonstrate how this can work. The program will implement a guessing game.

Try It Out - A Guessing Game

This program is going to get the user to guess the number that the program has picked as the lucky number. It uses one **for** loop and plenty of **if** statements. I've also thrown in a conditional operator, just to check you haven't forgotten how to use it!

```c
/*  Example 4.7  A Guessing Game */
#include <stdio.h>

void main()
{
   long chosen = 15; /* The lucky number            */
   int guess = 0;    /* Stores a guess              */
   int count = 3;    /* The maximum number of tries */

   printf("\nThis is a guessing game.");
   printf("\nI have chosen a number between 1 and 20"
                                    " which you must guess.\n");

   for( ; count>0 ; --count)
   {
     printf("\nYou have %d tr%s left.", count,
                             count == 1 ? "y" : "ies");
     printf("\nEnter a guess: "); /* Prompt for a guess  */
     scanf("%d", &guess);         /* Read in a guess     */

     /* Check for a correct guess */
     if (guess == chosen)
     {
       printf("\nYou guessed it!");
       return;  /* End the program */
     }

     /* Check for an invalid guess */
     if(guess<1 || guess > 20)
       printf("I said between 1 and 20.\n ");
     else
       printf("Sorry. %d is wrong.\n", guess);
   }
   printf("\nYou have had three tries and failed."
                        " The number was %ld\n", chosen);
}
```

Some sample output would be:

```
This is a guessing game.
I have chosen a number between 1 and 20 which you must guess.

You have 3 tries left.
Enter a guess: 5
Sorry. 5 is wrong.
```

```
You have 2 tries left.
Enter a guess: 18
Sorry. 18 is wrong.

You have 1 try left.
Enter a guess: 7
Sorry. 7 is wrong.

You have had three tries and failed. The number was 15
```

How It Works

We first declare and initialize three variables of type **int**: **chosen**, **guess** and **count**:

```
long chosen = 15;  /* The lucky number          */
int guess = 0;     /* Stores a guess            */
int count = 3;     /* The maximum number of tries */
```

These are to store, respectively, the number that's to be guessed, the number that is the user's guess, and the number of guesses they are permitted. Notice that we've created a variable to store the chosen number. We could just have used the number 15 in the program, but doing it this way makes it much easier to alter the value of the number that the user must guess.

We provide the user with an initial explanation of the program:

```
printf("\nThis is a guessing game.");
printf("\nI have chosen a number between 1 and 20"
                                " which you must guess.\n");
```

The number of guesses that can be entered is controlled by the loop:

```
for( ; count>0 ; --count)
{
   ...
}
```

All the operational details of the game are within this loop, which will repeat **count** times.

There's a prompt for a guess to be entered, and the guess itself is read by these statements:

```
printf("\nYou have %d tr%s left.", count,
                          count == 1 ? "y" : "ies");
printf("\nEnter a guess: "); /* Prompt for a guess  */
scanf("%d", &guess);         /* Read in a guess     */
```

The first **printf()** looks a little complicated, but all it does is insert **"y"** after **"tr"** in the output when **count** is 1, and **"ies"** after **"tr"** in the output in all other cases. We must, after all, get our plurals right.

After reading a guess, using **scanf()**, we check whether it's correct with these statements:

```
/* Check for a correct guess */
if (guess == chosen)
{
  printf("\nYou guessed it!");
  return;  /* End the program */
}
```

If the guess is correct, we display a suitable message and execute the **return** statement. The **return** statement ends the function **main()** and so the program ends. We'll see more about the **return** statement when we discuss functions in greater detail in Chapter 8.

We can only reach the last check in the loop if you didn't guess correctly:

```
/* Check for an invalid guess */
if(guess<1 || guess > 20)
  printf("I said between 1 and 20.\n ");
else
  printf("Sorry. %d is wrong.\n", guess);
```

This group of statements tests whether the value you entered is within the prescribed limits. If it isn't, a message is displayed reminding you of the limits. If it was a valid guess, a message is displayed telling you it was incorrect.

The loop ends after three iterations and thus three guesses. The statement after the loop is:

```
printf("\nYou have had three tries and failed."
                  " The number was %ld\n", chosen);
```

This will only be executed if all three guesses were wrong. It displays an appropriate message, revealing the number to be guessed; then the program ends.

This program is designed so that you can easily change the value of the variable **chosen** and have endless fun. Well, endless fun for a short while anyway.

The while Loop

That's enough of the **for** loop. Now that we've seen several examples of **for** loops, let's look at a different kind of loop: the **while** loop. With a **while** loop, the mechanism for repeating a set of statements allows execution to continue for as long as a specified logical expression is true. In English, this could be represented like this:

```
While this condition is true

        Keep on doing this;
```

Alternatively:

```
While you are hungry

        Eat sandwiches
```

This means that you ask yourself 'Am I hungry?' If the answer is yes then you eat a sandwich and then ask yourself 'Am I still hungry?' You keep eating sandwiches until the answer is no, at which point you go on to do something else - drink some coffee maybe.

The syntax for this is:

```
while( expression )
   Statement1;

   Statement2;
```

As always, **statement1** could be a block of statements. The logic of the **while** loop is shown in the next diagram.

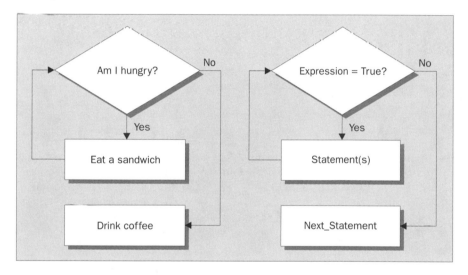

Just like the **for** loop, the condition for continuation of the **while** loop is tested at the start, so that if **expression** starts out false, none of the loop statements will be executed. If you answer the first question 'No, I'm not hungry' then you don't get to eat any sandwiches at all, moving straight on to the whole coffee issue.

Try It Out - Using the while Loop

This looks fairly straightforward, so let's go straight into that old favorite, summing house numbers:

```
/*  Example 4.8 While programming and summing integers */
#include <stdio.h>

void main()
{
    long sum = 0L; /* The sum of the integers            */
    int i = 1;     /* Indexes through the integers        */
    int count = 0; /* The count of integers to be summed */
```

```
      /* Get the count of the number of integers to sum */
      printf("\nEnter the number of integers you want to sum: ");
      scanf(" %d", &count);

      /* Sum the integers from 1 to count */
      while(i <= count)
         sum += i++;

      printf("Total of the first %d numbers is %ld\n", count, sum);
   }
```

Typical output from this program would be:

```
Enter the number of integers you want to sum: 7
Total of the first 7 numbers is 28
```

How It Works

Well, this works pretty much the same as when we used the **for** loop. The only aspect of this example worth discussing is the **while** loop itself.

```
      while(i <= count)
         sum += i++;
```

It contains a single statement action accumulating **sum**, which continues to be executed with **i** values up to 10. Because we have the postfix increment operator here (the **++** comes after the variable), **i** is incremented *after* its value is used to compute **sum** on each iteration. What the statement really means is:

```
      sum += i;
      ++i;
```

So the value of **sum** is not affected by the increment of **i** until the next loop iteration.

Let's see whether we can explain this, in relatively plain English, so that we are sure we understand what's really happening.

▶ *Entering the while loop*:

When you enter the **while** loop, **i** is 1 and **count** has the value corresponding to whatever you have typed in (let's say 3). When the loop starts, we first check whether **i <= count** is true. In this case, it amounts to **1<=3**, which is true - so we execute the loop statement:

```
      sum += i++;
```

▶ *First time through the while loop*:

First, the value of **i** (which is 1) is added to the variable **sum**. The variable **sum** was equal to 0, and it's now equal to 1. The variable **i** is then incremented after the value to be stored in **sum** has been calculated, because we've used the postfix increment operator.

So **i** now has the value 2 and we return to the beginning of the loop. We now check the **while** expression and see whether the value in **i** is still less than or equal to **count**. Since **i** is now 2, which is indeed less than 3, we execute the loop statement again.

▶ *Second time through the while loop*:

In the second loop iteration, we add the new value of **i** (which is now 2) to the old value of **sum** (which is 1) and store the result in **sum**. The variable **sum** now equals 3. We add 1 to **i** so **i** now has the value 3, and we go back to the beginning of the loop to check whether the control expression is still true.

▶ *Third time through the while loop*:

At this point **i** is equal to **count** so we can still continue the loop. We add the new value of **i** (which is 3) to the old value of **sum** (which is also 3) and store the result in **sum**, which now has the value 6. We add 1 to **i**, so **i** now has the value 4, and we go back to check the loop expression once more.

▶ *Last time through the while loop*:

Now **i** which has the value 4 is greater than **count**, which has the value 3, so the expression **i <= count** is false - and we leave the loop.

This example has used the increment operator as postfix. How could we change the program above to use **++** as a prefixed operator? Have a go, and see whether you can work it out. The answer is given below.

Try It Out - Using ++ as a Prefix Operator

The obvious bit of code that will change will be the **while** loop:

```
sum += ++i;
```

Try just changing this. If you run the program now you get the wrong answer:

```
Enter the number of integers you want to sum: 3
Total of the first 3 numbers is 9
```

This is because the **++** operator is adding 1 to the value of **i** *before* it stores the value in **sum**. The variable **i** starts at 1 and is increased to 2 on the first iteration, whereupon that value is added to **sum**.

To make the first loop iteration work correctly, we need to start **i** off as 0. This means that the first increment would make the value of **i** 1, which is what we want. So we must change the declaration of **i** to:

```
int i = 0;
```

However, the program still doesn't work properly, because it carries on doing the calculation until the value in **i** is greater than **count**; so we get one more iteration than we need. The alteration we need to fix this is to change the control expression so that the loop continues while **i** is less than but not equal to count:

```
    while(i < count)
```

Now our program will produce the correct answer. This example should help you really understand postfixing and prefixing these operators.

Nested Loops

Sometimes you may want to place one loop inside another. For each house in a street you might want to count the number of occupants. You step from house to house, and for each house, you count the number of occupants. Going through all the houses could be an outer loop, and for each iteration of the outer loop you would have an inner loop that counted the occupants.

The simplest way to understand how a nested loop works is to look at a simple example.

Try It Out - Using Nested Loops

To demonstrate a nested loop, we'll use a simple example based on our summing integers program. We produce the sums of all integers, step-by-step, up to the value entered. For every house, we are producing the sum of all the numbers - from the first house up to the current house. If you look at the program output it will become clearer.

```c
/* Example 4.9 Sums of integers step-by-step   */
#include <stdio.h>

void main()
{
   long sum = 0L; /* Stores the sum of integers      */
   int i = 1;      /* Outer loop control variable     */
   int j = 1;      /* Inner loop control variable     */
   int count = 0; /* Number of sums to be calculated */

   /* Prompt for, and read the input count */
   printf("\nEnter the number of integers you want to sum: ");
   scanf(" %d", &count);

   for( i = 1 ; i <= count ; i++ )
   {
     sum = 0L;   /* Initialize sum for the inner loop */

     /* Calculate sum of integers from 1 to i */
     for(j = 1 ; j <= i ; j++ )
       sum += j;

     printf("\n%d\t%ld", i, sum); /* Output sum of 1 to i */
   }
}
```

You should see some output like this:

```
Enter the number of integers you want to sum: 5

1               1
2               3
3               6
4               10
5               15
```

As you can see, if you enter 5, then the program calculates the sums of the integers from 1 to 1, from 1 to 2, from 1 to 3, from 1 to 4, and from 1 to 5.

How It Works

The program calculates the sum from 1 to each integer value, for all values from 1 up to the value of **count** that you enter. The important thing to grasp about this nested loop is that the inner loop completes all its iterations *for each iteration* of the outer loop. Thus the outer loop sets up the value of **i** that determines how many times the inner loop will repeat.

```
for( i = 1 ; i <= count ; i++ )
{
  sum = 0L;  /* Initialize sum for the inner loop */

  /* Calculate sum of integers from 1 to i */
  for(j = 1 ; j <= i ; j++ )
    sum += j;

  printf("\n%d\t%ld", i, sum); /* Output sum of 1 to i */
}
```

The outer loop starts off by setting **i** to 1, and the loop is repeated for successive values of **i** up to **count**. For each iteration of the outer loop, and therefore for each value of **i**, **sum** is initialized to zero, the inner loop is executed, and the result displayed by the **printf()** statement. The inner loop accumulates the sum of all the integers from 1 to the current value of **i**:

```
  /* Calculate sum of integers from 1 to i */
  for(j = 1 ; j <= i ; j++ )
    sum += j;
```

Each time the inner loop finishes, the **printf()** to output the value of **sum** is executed. Control then goes back to the beginning of the outer loop for the next iteration.

Look at the output again to see the action of the nested loop. The first loop simply sets the variable **sum** to zero each time round, and the inner loop adds up all the numbers from 1 to the current value of **i**. You could modify the nested loop to use a **while** loop for the inner loop, and to produce output that would show what the program is doing a little more explicitly.

Try It Out – Nesting a while Loop within a for Loop

```c
/* Example 4.10 Sums of integers while loop nested in for loop */
#include <stdio.h>

void main()
{
    long sum = 1L; /* Stores the sum of integers        */
    int i = 1;        /* Outer loop control variable       */
    int j = 1;        /* Inner loop control variable       */
    int count = 0; /* Number of sums to be calculated */

    /* Prompt for, and read the input count */
    printf("\nEnter the number of integers you want to sum: ");
    scanf(" %d", &count);

    for( i = 1 ; i <= count ; i++ )
    {
        sum = 1L; /* Initialize sum for the inner loop */
        j=1;        /* Initialize integer to be added    */
        printf("\n1");

        /* Calculate sum of integers from 1 to i */
        while(j < i)
        {
            sum += ++j;
            printf("+%d", j); /* Output +j - on the same line */
        }
        printf(" = %ld\n", sum); /* Output  = sum */
    }
}
```

This will produce the output:

```
Enter the number of integers you want to sum: 5

1 = 1

1+2 = 3

1+2+3 = 6

1+2+3+4 = 10

1+2+3+4+5 = 15
```

How It Works

The difference is within the outer loop:

```c
for( i = 1 ; i <= count ; i++ )
{
```

```
      sum = 1L; /* Initialize sum for the inner loop */
      j=1;      /* Initialize integer to be added    */
      printf("\n1");

      /* Calculate sum of integers from 1 to i */
      while(j < i)
      {
        sum += ++j;
        printf("+%d", j); /* Output +j - on the same line */
      }
      printf(" = %ld\n", sum); /* Output  = sum */
  }
```

The outer loop control is exactly the same as before. The difference is what occurs during each iteration. The variable **sum** is initialized to 1 within the outer loop, because the **while** loop will add values to **sum** starting with 2. The integer to be added is stored in **j**, which is also initialized to 1. The first **printf()** in the outer loop just goes to a new line and outputs 1, the first integer in the set to be summed. The inner loop adds the integers from 2 up to the value of **i**. For each integer value in **j** that's added to **sum**, the **printf()** in the inner loop outputs **+j** on the same line as the 1 that was output first. Thus the inner loop will output +2, then +3 and so on - for as long as **j** is less than **i**. Of course, for the first iteration of the outer loop, **i** is 1, so the inner loop will not execute at all, because **j<i** (1<1) is false from the beginning.

When the inner loop ends, the **printf()** is executed. This outputs an equals sign followed by the value of **sum**. Control then returns to the beginning of the outer loop for the next iteration.

The do-while Loop

There is a third type of loop, the **do-while** loop. Now you may be thinking, why should we need this when we already have the **for** and the **while** loops? Well, there's actually a very subtle difference between the **do-while** loop and the other two. The test for whether the loop should continue is at the *end* of the loop.

The **while** loop tests at the beginning of the loop. So before any action takes place, we check the expression. Look at this fragment of code:

```
int number = 4;

while(number < 4)
{
  printf("\nNumber = %d", number);
  number++;
}
```

Here, you would never output anything. The control expression **number<4** is false from the start, so the loop block is never executed.

The **do-while** loop, however, always executes at least once. We can see this if we replace the **while** loop, above, with a **do-while** loop - and leave the rest of the statements the same:

```
int number = 4;

do
{
  printf("\nNumber = %d", number);
  number++;
}
while(number < 4);
```

Now when we execute this loop, we get Number = 4 displayed. This is because the expression **number < 4** is only checked at the end of the first iteration of the loop.

The general representation of the **do-while** loop is as follows:

```
do
  Statement;
while (expression);
```

> *Notice the semicolon after the **while** statement in a **do-while** loop. There isn't one in the **while** loop.*

As always, a block of statements between braces can be in place of **Statement**. In a **do-while** loop, if the value of **expression** is true then the loop continues. The loop will only exit when the value of **expression** becomes false. You can see how this works more clearly in the next diagram.

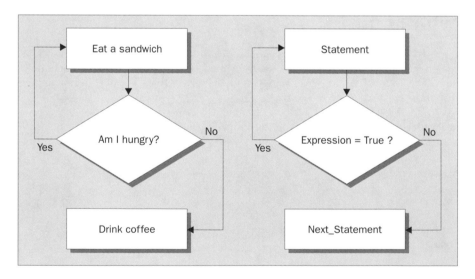

Here, you can see that we eat a sandwich *before* we check whether we're hungry or not. We will always eat at least 1 sandwich.

Try It Out - Using a do while Loop

We can illustrate the **do-while** loop with a little program that reverses the digits of a positive number:

```
/* Example 4.11 Reversing the digits */
#include <stdio.h>
void main()
{
   int number = 0; /* The numbr to be reversed */
   int rebmun = 0; /* The reversed number      */
   int temp = 0;   /* Working storage          */

   /* Get the value to be reversed */
   printf("\nEnter a positive integer: ");
   scanf(" %d", &number);

   temp = number; /* Copy to working storage  */

   /* Reverse the number stored in temp */
   do
   {
     rebmun = 10*rebmun + temp % 10; /* Add the rightmost digit    */
     temp = temp/10;                 /* Remove the rightmost digit */
   } while (temp);                   /* Continue while temp>0      */

   printf ("\nThe number %d reversed is  %d rebmun ehT\n",
                                        number, rebmun );
}
```

The following is a sample of output from this program:

```
Enter a positive integer: 43

The number 43 reversed is 34 rebmun ehT
```

How It Works

The best way to explain what's going on here is to step you through a small example. We'll assume that the number 43 was entered by the user.

After reading the input integer and storing it in the variable **number**, the program copies the value in **number** to the variable **temp**.

```
   int temp = 0;   /* Working storage          */
```

This is necessary, because the process of reversing the digits destroys the original value, and we want to output the original integer along with the reversed version.

The reversal of the digits is done in the **do-while** loop:

```
/* Reverse the number stored in temp */
   do
   {
     rebmun = 10*rebmun + temp % 10; /* Add the rightmost digit   */
     temp = temp/10;                 /* Remove the rightmost digit */
   } while (temp);                    /* Continue while temp>0      */
```

We get the rightmost digit from the value stored in **temp** by using the modulus operator, **%**, to get the remainder after dividing by 10. Since **temp** originally contains 43, **temp%10** will be 3. We assign the value of **10*rebmun + temp%10** to **rebmun**. Initially, the value of the variable **rebmun** is zero, so on the first iteration 3 is stored in **rebmun**.

We've now stored the rightmost digit of our input in **rebmun**, and so we now remove it from **temp** by dividing **temp** by 10. Since **temp** contained 43, **temp/10** will be rounded down to 4.

At the end of the loop the **while(temp)** condition is checked, and since **temp** contains the value 4, it is true. Therefore, we go back to the top of the loop to begin another iteration.

Remember: any positive integer is true. False is represented by zero.

This time, the value stored in **rebmun** will be 10 times **rebmun**, which is 30, plus the remainder when **temp** is divided by 10, which is 4 - so the result is that **rebmun** becomes 34. We again divide **temp** by 10, so it will contain 0. Now when we arrive at the end of the loop iteration, **temp** is 0, which is false, so the loop finishes and we have reversed our number. You can see how this would work with numbers with more digits. An example of the program running with a longer number is:

```
Enter a positive integer: 1234

The number 1234 reversed is 4321 rebmun ehT
```

This form of loop is used relatively rarely, compared with the other two forms. Keep it in the back of your mind though: when you need a loop that always executes at least once, it delivers the goods.

Designing a Program

It's time to try our skills on a bigger programming problem, and to apply some of what you've learned in this chapter and the previous chapters. I'll also introduce a few new standard library functions that you're sure to find useful.

The Problem

The problem we're going to solve is to write a game of Simple Simon. Simple Simon is a memory-test game. The computer displays a sequence of digits on the screen for a short period of time. You then have to memorize them, and when the digits disappear from the screen, you must enter exactly the same sequence of digits. Each time you succeed, you can repeat the process to get a longer list of digits for you to try. The objective is to continue the process for as long as possible.

The Analysis

The program generates a sequence of integers between 0 and 9, and displays them on the screen for one second. The player then has to try to enter the identical sequence of digits. The sequence gradually gets longer until the player gets it wrong. A score is then calculated based on the number of successful tries and the time taken, and the player asked if they would like to play again.

The logic of the program is quite straightforward. We could express it in general terms with this flow chart.

Each box describes an action in the program, and the diamond shapes represent decisions. Let's use the flowchart as a basis for coding the program.

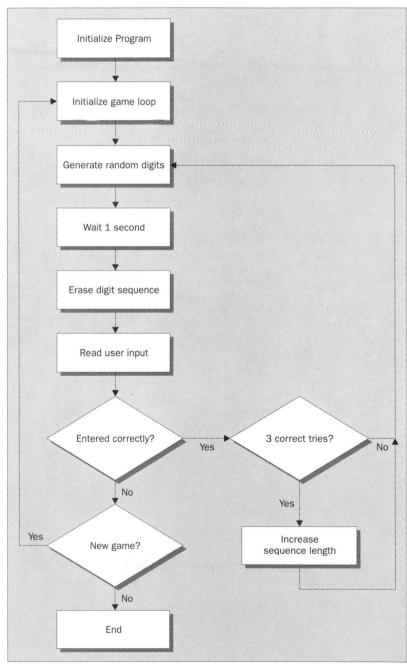

The Solution

1 We can start by putting in the main loop for a game. The player will always want to have at least one game, so the loop check should go at the end of the loop. The **do-while** loop fits the bill very nicely. Our initial program code will be:

```
/*Example 4.12 Simple Simon */
#include <stdio.h>  /* For input and output */

void main()
{
   /* Records if another game is to be played */
   char another_game = 'Y';

   /* Rest of the declarations for the program */

   /* Describe how the game is played */
   printf("\nTo play Simple Simon, ");
   printf("watch the screen for a sequence of digits.");
   printf("\nWatch carefully, as the digits are only displayed"
                                              " for a second! ");
   printf("\nThe computer will remove them, and then prompt you ");
   printf("to enter the same sequence.");
   printf("\nWhen you do, you must put spaces between the digits. \n");
   printf("\nGood Luck!\nPress return to play\n");
   scanf("%c", &another_go);

   /* One outer loop iteration is one game */
   do
   {
     /* Code to play the game */

     /* Output the score when the game is finished */

     /* Check if new game required*/
     printf("\nDo you want to play again (y/n)? ");
     scanf("%c", &another_game);
   }while(another_game == 'y' || another_game == 'Y');
}
```

As long as the player enters **'y'** or **'Y'** at the end of a game, he or she will be able to play again.

Note how we can automatically concatenate two strings in the **printf()** statement:

```
   printf("\nWatch carefully, as the digits are only displayed"
                                              " for a second! ");
```

This is a convenient way of splitting a long string over two or more lines. You just put each piece of the string between its own pair of double quote characters.

2 Next, we can add a declaration for another variable that we'll need in the program, called **correct**, to record whether the entry from the player is correct or not. We can make this of type **int**, but define the symbols **TRUE** and **FALSE** by using **#define** pre-processor directives, and then use these to set the value of **correct**. We'll use this variable to control the loop that plays a single game.

```
/*Example 4.12 Simple Simon */
#include <stdio.h>  /* For input and output         */

#define TRUE  1       /* Defines the symbol TRUE      */
#define FALSE 0       /* Defines the symbol False     */

void main()
{
   /* Records if another game is to be played */
   char another_game = 'Y';

   /* TRUE if correct sequence entered, FALSE otherwise */
   char correct = TRUE;

   /* Rest of the declarations for the program */

   /* Describe how the game is played */
   printf("\nTo play Simple Simon, ");
   printf("watch the screen for a sequence of digits.");
   printf("\nWatch carefully, as the digits are only displayed"
                                        " for a second! ");
   printf("\nThe computer will remove them, and then prompt you ");
   printf("to enter the same sequence.");
   printf("\nWhen you do, you must put spaces between the digits. \n");
   printf("\nGood Luck!\nPress return to play\n");
   scanf("%c", &another_go);

   /* One outer loop iteration is one game */
   do
   {
      /* By default indicates correct sequence entered  */
      correct = TRUE;

      /* Other code to initialize the game */

      /* Inner loop continues as long as sequences are
                               entered correctly */
      while(correct)
      {
         /* Play the game */
      }

      /* Output the score when the game is finished */
```

```
    /* Check if new game required*/
    printf("\nDo you want to play again (y/n)? ");
    scanf("%c", &another_game);
  }while(another_game == 'y' || another_game == 'Y');
}
```

Defining symbols for **TRUE** and **FALSE,** as we've done here, is a very useful mechanism for making a program more readable. Instead of using 1 and 0 in the program for values of **correct**, we have **TRUE** or **FALSE**, which makes it quite clear that we're treating **correct** as a logical variable. Defining symbols in this way is also useful where you may want to change a value in a program that's used many times. By defining a symbol for it at the beginning of the program, using a **#define** directive, you make it possible to change the value throughout the program just by modifying the **#define** directive.

A word of warning: the code will compile as it is, and you should compile it to check it out; but you shouldn't run it yet! As you develop your own programs, you'll want to make sure that the code will at least compile along each step of the way. If you wrote all the program code in one go, then you could end up with hundreds of errors to correct; and as you correct one problem, more may appear. This can be very frustrating. By checking out the program incrementally, you can minimize this - and the problems are easier to manage. This brings us back to our current program. If you run this, then your computer will be completely taken over by the program, because it contains an infinite loop. The reason is the inner **while** loop. The condition for this loop is always true, since the loop doesn't do anything to change the value of **correct**. However, we'll be writing that bit of the program shortly.

3   Now we have a difficult bit to do: generating the sequence of random digits. There are two problems to be tackled here. The first is to actually generate the sequence of random digits. The second is to check the player's input against the computer-generated sequence.

The main difficulty with generating the sequence of digits is that the numbers have to be random. Luckily for us, C comes to the rescue and provides us with a standard function, **rand()**, which returns a random integer each time you call it. We can get a random digit by just getting the remainder after dividing by 10, by using the **%** operator.

The numbers generated by the **rand()** function are **pseudo-random**, which means that the sequence of numbers is generated using a starting seed number, and for a given seed the sequence will always be the same. If we use the function with the default seed value, we'll always get exactly the same sequence, which won't make the game very challenging. However, C provides another standard function **srand()** which we can call to initialize the sequence with a particular seed that's passed as an argument to the function. All we need to do is to figure out how we can generate a different seed each time. Both the **rand()** and **srand()** functions require that you include the **stdlib.h** header file into the program.

Now, let's think about this a bit more. We'll need the sequence of random digits twice: once to display, and the second time to check against the player's input. We have a function, **rand()**, which can produce the same sequence of numbers twice - if the sequence is started each time with the same seed - by calling **srand()**. This means that we don't need to store the sequence of numbers. We can just generate the same sequence twice.

The only problem that remains is choosing the number to use as a seed with **srand()**. This number has to be different each time the program is run, otherwise we'll get the same sequences each time the program is run. Yet again, C is our knight in shining armor, and actually provides us with a function that returns a number that is continuously changing. This number represents the length of time in seconds since January 1st 1970, so you can see that it'll be quite between impossible to get the same sequence of numbers on successive occasions. The function that returns this number is called **time()** and it requires the **time.h** header file. We must specify the argument to **time()** as **NULL**, which is a symbol defined in **stdlib.h**. We'll defer discussing what **NULL** means until Chapter 7.

Now let's add some more code to the program, which will generate the sequence of random digits and check them against what the player enters:

```
/*Example 4.12 Simple Simon */
#include <stdio.h>  /* For input and output      */

#define TRUE  1     /* Defines the symbol TRUE   */
#define FALSE 0     /* Defines the symbol False  */

void main()
{
    /* Records if another game is to be played */
    char another_game = 'Y';

    /* TRUE if correct sequence entered, FALSE otherwise */
    char correct = TRUE;

    /* Number of sequences entered successfully */
    int counter = 0;

    int sequence_length = 0; /* Number of digits in a sequence       */
    int i = 0;               /* Loop counter                         */
    long seed = 0;           /* Seed value for random number sequence */
    int number = 0;          /* Stores an input digit                */

    /* Rest of the declarations for the program */

    /* Describe how the game is played */
    printf("\nTo play Simple Simon, ");
    printf("watch the screen for a sequence of digits.");
    printf("\nWatch carefully, as the digits are only displayed"
                                        " for a second! ");
    printf("\nThe computer will remove them, and then prompt you ");
    printf("to enter the same sequence.");
    printf("\nWhen you do, you must put spaces between the digits. \n");
    printf("\nGood Luck!\nPress return to play\n");
    scanf("%c", &another_go);

    /* One outer loop iteration is one game */
    do
    {
```

```
      /* By default indicates correct sequence entered  */
      correct = TRUE;

         /* Initialize count of number of successful tries */
         counter = 0;

         /* Initial length of a digit sequence is 3          */
         sequence_length = 2;

      /* Other code to initialize the game */

      /* Inner loop continues as long as sequences are
                                  entered correctly */
      while(correct)
      {
         /* On every third successful try,
                             increase the sequence length     */
         sequence_length += counter++%3 == 0;

         /* Set seed to be the number of seconds since Jan 1,1970 */
         seed = time(NULL);

         /* Generate a sequence of numbers and display the number */
         srand((int)seed);       /* Initialize the random sequence */
         for(i = 1; i <= sequence_length; i++)
           printf("%d ", rand() % 10);    /* Output a random digit */

         /* Wait one second */

         /* Now overwrite the digit sequence */

         /* Prompt for the input sequence */

         /* Check the input sequence of digits against the original  */
         srand((int)seed);             /* Restart the random sequence  */
         for(i = 1; i <= sequence_length; i++)
         {
           scanf("%d", &number);       /* Read an input number         */
           if(number != rand() % 10) /* Compare against random digit */
           {
             correct = FALSE;        /* Incorrect entry              */
             break;                  /* No need to check further...  */
           }
         }
   printf("%s\n", correct? "Correct!" : "Wrong!");
      }

      /* Output the score when the game is finished */

      /* Check if new game required*/
      printf("\nDo you want to play again (y/n)? ");
```

```
        scanf("%c", &another_game);
    }while(another_game == 'y' || another_game == 'Y');
}
```

We've declared five new variables that we need to implement the **while** loop that executes as long as the player is successful. Each iteration of this loop displays a sequence that the player must repeat. The variable **counter** records the number of times the player is successful, and **sequence_length** records the current length of a sequence of digits. Although we initialize these when we declare them, we must also initialize their values in the **do-while** loop, as this ensures that the initial conditions for the game are set. The variable **i** is used as a control variable. We also declare a variable, **seed**, of type **long**, that we'll pass as an argument to **srand()** to initialize the random number sequence returned by the function **rand()**. The value for **seed** is obtained in the **while** loop by calling the standard library function **time()**.

At the beginning of the **while** loop, you can see that we increase the value stored in **sequence_length** by adding the value of the expression **counter++%3 == 0** to it.

There are some other things to notice about the code. First is the conversion of **seed** from a **long** to an **int** when we pass it to the **srand()** function. This is because **srand()** requires that we use **int**, but we have the value returned from **time()** stored as type **long**. Since the number of seconds since January 1st, 1970 is in excess of 800,000,000, we need a four byte variable to store it. By casting it to **int**, we're using the low order two bytes of the number - but this should still give us a unique seed for each game. Second, we obtain a digit between 0 and 9 by taking the remainder when we divide the random integer returned by **rand()** by 10. This is not the best way of obtaining random digits in the range 0 to 9, but it's a very easy way.

Outputting the sequence of digits is done in the **for** loop. This just outputs the low order digit of the value returned by **rand()**. We then have some comments indicating the other code we have to add that to delay for one second, and then to erase the sequence from the screen. We then have the code to check the sequence entered by the player. This re-initializes the random number generating process by calling **srand()** with the same seed value that was used at the outset. Each digit entered is compared with the low order digit of the value returned by the function **rand()**. If there is a discrepancy, **correct** is set to **FALSE** so the while loop will end.

Of course, if you try to run this code as it is, the sequence will not be erased, so it is not usable yet. Next, we should add the code to complete the **while** loop.

4 We must now erase the sequence, after a delay of one second. How can we get the program to wait? One way is to use another standard library function. The library function **clock()** returns the time since the program started, in units of clock ticks. The header file **time.h** defines a symbol **CLOCKS_PER_SEC** that is the number of clock ticks in one second. All we have to do is wait until the value returned by the function **clock()** has increased by **CLOCKS_PER_SEC**. We can do this by storing the value returned by the function **clock()** and then check, in a loop, when the value returned by **clock()** is **CLOCKS_PER_SEC** more than the value stored. Then we know one second has passed. With a variable **now** to store the time, the code for the loop would be:

```
for( ;clock() - now < CLOCKS_PER_SEC; );   /* Wait one second */
```

157

We also need to decide how we can erase the sequence of computer generated digits. This is actually quite easy. We can move to the beginning of the line by outputting the escape character `'\r'`, which is carriage return. All we then need to do is output a sufficient number of spaces to overwrite the sequence of digits. Let's fill out the code we need in the **while** loop:

```
/*Example 4.12 Simple Simon */
#include <stdio.h>  /* For input and output     */

#define TRUE  1    /* Defines the symbol TRUE  */
#define FALSE 0    /* Defines the symbol False */

void main()
{
   /* Records if another game is to be played */
   char another_game = 'Y';

   /* TRUE if correct sequence entered, FALSE otherwise */
   char correct = TRUE;

   /* Number of sequences entered successfully        */
   int counter = 0;

   int sequence_length = 0; /* Number of digits in a sequence       */
   int i = 0;               /* Loop counter                         */
   long seed = 0;           /* Seed value for random number sequence */
   int number = 0;          /* Stores an input digit                */

   /* Stores current time - seed for random values */
   long now = 0;

   /* Rest of the declarations for the program */

   /* Describe how the game is played */
   printf("\nTo play Simple Simon, ");
   printf("watch the screen for a sequence of digits.");
   printf("\nWatch carefully, as the digits are only displayed"
                                       " for a second! ");
   printf("\nThe computer will remove them, and then prompt you ");
   printf("to enter the same sequence.");
   printf("\nWhen you do, you must put spaces between the digits. \n");
   printf("\nGood Luck!\nPress return to play\n");
   scanf("%c", &another_go);

   /* One outer loop iteration is one game */
   do
   {
     /* By default indicates correct sequence entered  */
     correct = TRUE;

     /* Initialize count of number of successful tries */
     counter = 0;
```

```
    /* Initial length of a digit sequence is 3        */
    sequence_length = 2;

    /* Other code to initialize the game */

    /* Inner loop continues as long as sequences are
                                      entered correctly */
    while(correct)
    {
       /* On every third successful try,
                                 increase the sequence length */
       sequence_length += counter++%3 == 0;

       /* Set seed to be the number of seconds since Jan 1,1970 */
       seed = time(NULL);

       now = clock();  /* record start time for sequence */

       /* Generate a sequence of numbers and display the number */
       srand((int)seed);        /* Initialize the random sequence */
       for(i = 1; i <= sequence_length; i++)
         printf("%d ", rand() % 10); /* Output a random digit    */

       /* Wait one second */
       for( ;clock() - now < CLOCKS_PER_SEC; );

       /* Now overwrite the digit sequence */
       printf("\r");            /* go to beginning of the line */
       for(i = 1; i <= sequence_length; i++)
         printf("  ");          /* Output two spaces          */

       /* Only output message for the first try */
       if(counter == 1)
         printf("\nNow you enter the sequence  - don't forget"
                                      " the spaces\n");
    else
         printf("\r");   /* Back to the beginning of the line */

       /* Check the input sequence of digits against the original  */
       srand((int)seed);             /* Restart the random sequence  */
       for(i = 1; i <= sequence_length; i++)
       {
         scanf("%d", &number);     /* Read an input number        */
         if(number != rand() % 10) /* Compare against random digit */
         {
           correct = FALSE;        /* Incorrect entry             */
           break;                  /* No need to check further...  */
         }
       }
    printf("%s\n", correct? "Correct!" : "Wrong!");
    }
```

```
        /* Output the score when the game is finished */

        /* Check if new game required*/
        printf("\nDo you want to play again (y/n)? ");
        scanf("%c", &another_game);
    }while(another_game == 'y' || another_game == 'Y');
}
```

We record the time returned by **clock()** before we output the sequence. The **for** loop that's executed when the sequence has been displayed continues until the value returned by **clock()** exceeds the time recorded in **now** by **CLOCKS_PER_SEC**, which of course will be one second.

Since we haven't used a **\n** at any point when we displayed the sequence, we're still on the same line when we complete the output of the sequence. We can go to the start of the line by executing a carriage return without a linefeed, and outputting **"\r"** does just that. We then output two spaces for each digit that was displayed, thus overwriting each of them with blanks. Immediately following that, we have a prompt for the player to enter the sequence that was displayed. We only output this the first time round, otherwise it gets rather tedious. On the second and subsequent tries, we just back up to the beginning of the now blank line, ready for the user's input.

5 All that remains is to generate a score to display, once the player has got a sequence wrong. We'll use the number of sequences completed, and how many seconds it took to complete them, to calculate this score. We can arbitrarily assign 100 points to each digit correctly entered, and divide this by the number of seconds taken for the game. This means the faster you are the higher the score, and the more sequences you enter correctly the higher the score.

Actually, there is also one more problem with this program that we need to see to. If one of the numbers typed by the player is wrong, then the loop exits, and the player is asked if they want to play again. However, if the digit in error is not the last digit, then we could end up with the next digit entered as the answer to Do you want to play again (y/n)? because these digits will still be in the keyboard buffer. What we need to do is remove any information that's still in the keyboard buffer. So there are two problems: first, how to address the keyboard buffer; and secondly, how to clean out the buffer.

> *The keyboard buffer is memory that's used to store input from the keyboard. Our program looks in the keyboard buffer for input rather than getting it directly from the keyboard itself.*

With standard input and output, that is, from the keyboard and to the screen, there are actually two buffers, one for input called **stdin**, and one for output called **stdout**. Now that we know what the buffer is called, how do we remove the information in it? Well, C provides us with a function for clearing out buffers. Although this function tends to be used for files, which I'll cover later in the book, it will actually work for any buffer at all: we simply tell the function which buffer we mean. The function we need is **fflush()**. So to clean out the contents of the input buffer, we simply use:

```
fflush(stdin);
```

as you'll see below. Here's the complete program, which includes calculating the scores and flushing the input buffer:

```c
/*Example 4.12 Simple Simon */
#include <stdio.h>    /* For input and output          */
#include <stdlib.h>   /* For random number generation */
#include <time.h>     /* For time functions            */

#define TRUE  1      /* Defines the symbol TRUE    */
#define FALSE 0      /* Defines the symbol False   */

void main()
{
   /* Records if another game is to be played */
   char another_game = 'Y';

   /* TRUE if correct sequence entered, FALSE otherwise */
   char correct = FALSE;

   /* Number of sequences entered successfully */
   int counter = 0;

   int sequence_length = 0; /* Number of digits in a sequence          */
   int i = 0;               /* Loop counter                            */
   long seed = 0;           /* Seed value for random number sequence */
   int number = 0;          /* Stores an input digit                   */

   /* Stores current time - seed for random values  */
   long now = 0;

   /* Time taken for game in seconds */
   long time_taken = 0;

   /* Describe how the game is played */
   printf("\nTo play Simple Simon, ");
   printf("watch the screen for a sequence of digits.");
   printf("\nWatch carefully, as the digits are only displayed"
                                           " for a second! ");
   printf("\nThe computer will remove them, and then prompt you ");
   printf("to enter the same sequence.");
   printf("\nWhen you do, you must put spaces between the digits. \n");
   printf("\nGood Luck!\nPress return to play\n");
   scanf("%c", &another_game);

   /* One outer loop iteration is one game */
   do
   {
     /* By default indicates correct sequence entered */
     correct = TRUE;

     /* Initialize count of number of successful tries*/
     counter = 0;
```

```c
      /* Initial length of a digit sequence is 3        */
      sequence_length = 2;

      /* Record current time at start of game           */
      time_taken = clock();

    /* Inner loop continues as long as sequences are
       entered correctly */
    while(correct)
    {
      /* On every third successful try,
                         increase the sequence length */
      sequence_length += counter++%3 == 0;

      /* Set seed to be the number of seconds since Jan 1,1970 */
      seed = time(NULL);

      now = clock();    /* record start time for sequence        */

      /* Generate a sequence of numbers and display the number */
      srand((int)seed);       /* Initialize the random sequence */
      for(i = 1; i <= sequence_length; i++)
        printf("%d ", rand() % 10);   /* Output a random digit */

      /* Wait one second */
      for( ;clock() - now < CLOCKS_PER_SEC; );

      /* Now overwrite the digit sequence */
      printf("\r");            /* go to beginning of the line */
      for(i = 1; i <= sequence_length; i++)
        printf("  ");          /* Output two spaces */

      if(counter == 1) /* Only output message for the first try */
        printf("\nNow you enter the sequence  - don't forget"
                                          " the spaces\n");
  else
        printf("\r"); /* Back to the beginning of the line */

      /* Check the input sequence of digits against the original */
      srand((int)seed);       /* Restart the random sequence    */
      for(i = 1; i <= sequence_length; i++)
      {
        scanf("%d", &number);        /* Read an input number        */
        if(number != rand() % 10)  /* Compare against random digit */
        {
          correct = FALSE;  /* Incorrect entry               */
          break;            /* No need to check further... */
        }
      }
printf("%s\n", correct? "Correct!" : "Wrong!");
    }
```

```
      /* Calculate total time to play the game in seconds)*/
      time_taken = (clock() - time_taken) / CLOCKS_PER_SEC;

      /* Output the game score */
      printf("\n\n Your score is %d", --counter * 100 / time_taken);

      fflush(stdin);

   /* Check if new game required*/
   printf("\nDo you want to play again (y/n)? ");
   scanf("%c", &another_game);

  }while(another_game == 'y' || another_game == 'Y');
}
```

The definitions required for the function **fflush()** are in the header file **stdio.h**, for which we already have a **#include** directive. Now we just need to see what happens when we actually play:

```
To play Simple Simon, watch the screen for a sequence of digits.
Watch carefully, as the digits are only displayed for a second!
The computer will remove them, and then prompt you to enter the same
sequence.
When you do, you must put spaces between the digits.

Good Luck!
Press return to play


Now you enter the sequence  - don't forget the spaces
2 1 4
Correct!
8 7 1
Correct!
4 1 6
Correct!
7 9 6 6
Correct!
7 5 4 6
Wrong!


 Your score is 16
Do you want to play again (y/n)? n
```

163

Summary

In this chapter, we've covered all we need to know about repeating actions using loops. With the powerful set of programming tools you've learnt up to now, you should be able to create quite complex programs of your own.

In keeping with this chapter topic, we'll now repeat ourselves and reiterate some of the rules and recommendations we've come across so far.

▶ Before you start programming, work out the logic of the process and computations you want to perform, and write it down - preferably in the form of a flow chart. Try to think of lateral approaches to a problem: there may be a better way than the obvious approach.

▶ Use parentheses to ensure expressions do what you want, and are readily understood.

▶ Comment your programs to explain all aspects of their operation and use. Assume the comments are for the benefit of someone else reading your program with a view to extending or modifying it. Explain the purpose of each variable as you declare it.

▶ Program with readability foremost in your mind. Go for the simple, easy to understand programming style, rather than the flashy, convoluted, and opaque use of the language facilities.

▶ In complicated logical expressions, avoid using the operator, !, as far as you can.

▶ Use indentation to visually indicate the structure of your program.

Prepared with this advice, you can move on to the next chapter with confidence.

Arrays

When we write programs, we often need to store lots of related information about one thing. For example, if you were writing a program for a regular basketball player then you might want to store the scores for a season of games. You could then print out the basketball scores from the different games, or work out an on-going average. Armed with what you've learnt so far, you could write a program that does this using a different variable for each score. However, if there are a lot of games, this won't be very efficient. All your scores are really the same kind of thing. The values are different, but they're all basketball scores. Ideally, you would want to group these values together without having to declare separate variables for each one.

In this chapter, I'll show you how to do just that. I'll then show you how powerful this can be when you write programs that process collections of information like this. These collections are called **arrays**.

In this chapter you'll learn:

> What arrays are

> How to use arrays in your programs

> How memory is used by an array

> What a multidimensional array is

> How to write a program to work out your hat size

> How to write a game of tic-tac-toe

An Introduction to Arrays

The best way to show you what an array is, and how powerful it can be, is to go through an example where we can contrast using an array with not using an array. We'll use an example to show what kinds of problems arise, and then we'll see how an array will solve them. For this example, we'll look at ways in which we can find the average score of the students in a college.

Programs without Arrays

To find the average score of a class of students we'll assume that there are only 10 students in the class (mainly to avoid typing in a lot of numbers). To work out the average of a set of numbers, we add them all together and then divide by how many numbers we have (in this case 10):

```
/* Example 5.1 Averaging ten numbers without storing the numbers */
#include <stdio.h>

void main()
{
   int number = 0;          /* Stores a number              */
   int count = 10;          /* Number of values to be read */
   long sum = 0L;           /* Sum of the numbers           */
   float average = 0.0f;    /* Average of the numbers       */
   int i = 0;               /* Loop counter                 */

   /* Read the ten numbers to be averaged */
   for(i = 0; i < count; i++)
   {
     printf("Enter grade: ");
     scanf("%d", &number);      /* Read a number */
     sum += number;             /* Add it to sum */
   }

   average = (float)sum / count;    /* Calculate the average */

   printf("\nAverage of the ten numbers entered is: %f\n", average);
}
```

If we're only interested in the average then we don't have to remember what the previous grades were. All we're interested in is the sum of them all, which we then divide by **count**, which has the value 10. This simple program uses a single variable, **number**, to store each grade, as it is entered, within the loop. The loop repeats for values of **i** of 0, 1, 2 and so on up to 9; so there are 10 iterations. We've done this sort of thing before, so the program should be clear.

But let's assume that you want to develop this into a longer program where you'll need the values you enter later. Perhaps you might want to print out each person's grade, with the average grade next to it. In the previous program, we only had one variable. Each time you add a grade, the old value is no longer stored - and you can't get it back.

So how do you store the results? One way you can do this is by declaring ten integers to store the grades in; but then you can't use a **for** loop to enter the values. Instead, you have to enter the values individually. This would work, but it's quite tiresome:

```
/* Example 5.2 Averaging ten numbers, storing the numbers the hard way */
#include <stdio.h>

void main()
{
```

```
    int number0 = 0, number1 = 0, number2 = 0, number3 = 0, number4 = 0;
    int number5 = 0, number6 = 0, number7 = 0, number8 = 0, number9 = 0;

    long sum = 0L;           /* Sum of the numbers      */
    float average = 0.0f;    /* Average of the numbers */

    /* Read the ten numbers to be averaged */
    printf("Enter the first five numbers,\n");
    printf("use a space or RETURN between each number.\n");
    scanf("%d%d%d%d%d", &number0, &number1, &number2, &number3, &number4);
    printf("Enter the last five numbers,\n");
    printf("use a space or RETURN between each number.\n");
    scanf("%d%d%d%d%d", &number5, &number6, &number7, &number8, &number9);

    /* Now we have the ten numbers, we can calculate the average */
    sum = number0 + number1+ number2 + number3 + number4+
          number5 + number6 + number7 + number8 + number9;
    average = (float)sum / 10.0f;

    printf("\nAverage of the ten numbers entered is: %f\n", average);
}
```

This is OK for ten students, but what if your class had 30 students, or 100, or 1000? How can you do it then? Well, this is where arrays come in.

What is an Array?

An array is a collection of data items, referred to as **elements**, that are all of the same type. This is an important feature of an array - the elements of individual arrays are all of type **int**, or of type **long**, or whatever. So we can have **int** arrays, **float** arrays, **long** arrays and so on. To declare an array of type **int** in which we can store 10 items of data, we write:

```
long numbers[10];
```

This is very similar to how you would declare a normal variable that contains a single value, except that we have placed a number between square brackets **[]** following the name. This defines how many elements we want to store in our array. The important feature here is that all the data items stored in the array are accessed by the same name; in our case, this is **numbers**.

If we only have one variable name, but are storing 10 values, how do we differentiate between them? Each individual value in the array is referenced and accessed by what is called an **index value**. An index value is an integer that's written after the array name, between square brackets **[]**. Each element in an array has a different index value. The index values in the above array would run from 0 to 9. Therefore, the array elements would be referred to as **numbers[0]**, **numbers[1]**, **numbers[2]** … **numbers[9]**. You can see this in the following figure.

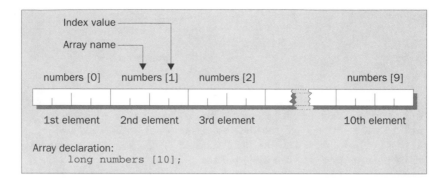

Notice that the index values don't start from 1, they start from 0. In a 10-element array, the last element's index value is 9. This means that to access the fourth value in our array we would type **numbers[3]**.

> *The individual elements of an array have index values starting at zero. This can sometimes cause confusion, at first, because the fifth element of an array (called* **array** *for instance) will have an index of 4 (**array[4]**). Remember that the last element always has an index value of one less than the number of elements. You can think of the index value for an element as the offset from the first element. The first element has an offset of 0; the second element has an offset of 1, and so on.*

To access an individual value in the array **numbers**, we could also place an expression in the square brackets following the array name. The expression would have to result in an integer value that corresponded to one of the possible index values. For example, you could write **numbers[i-2]**. If **i** had the value 3, this would access **numbers[1]**, the second element in the array.

To summarize: there are two ways to access an element of an array. You can use a simple integer to explicitly reference which element you want to access. Alternatively, you can use an integer expression that's evaluated during the execution of the program.

If you use an index value in your program that's outside the legal range for an array, the program won't work properly. After all, who knows what number you'd get if you asked for the score of the 11th student when you only had 10!

Using Arrays

That's a lot of theory, but we still haven't solved our average score problem. Let's put what we've just learnt into practice.

Try It Out - Averages with Arrays

Now that we understand arrays, we can use an array to store all the scores we want to average. This means that all the values will be saved, and we'll be able to re-use them. We can now rewrite the program to average ten scores:

```
/* Example 5.3 Averaging ten numbers, storing the numbers the easy way */
#include <stdio.h>

void main()
{
   int numbers[10];          /* Array storing 10 values     */
   int count = 10;           /* Number of values to be read */
   long sum = 0L;            /* Sum of the numbers          */
   float average = 0.0f;     /* Average of the numbers      */
   int i = 0;                /* Loop counter                */

   printf("\nEnter the 10 numbers:\n");  /* Prompt for the input */

   /* Read the ten numbers to be averaged */
   for(i = 0; i < count; i++)
   {
     printf("%2d> ",i+1);
     scanf("%d", &numbers[i]);        /* Read a number */
     sum += numbers[i];               /* Add it to sum */
   }

   average = (float)sum / count;    /* Calculate the average */

   printf("\nAverage of the ten numbers entered is: %f\n", average);
}
```

The output from the program looks something like this:

```
Enter the ten numbers:
 1> 450
 2> 765
 3> 562
 4> 700
 5> 598
 6> 635
 7> 501
 8> 720
 9> 689
10> 527

Average of the ten numbers entered is: 614.700000
```

How It Works

We start off the program with the ubiquitous **#include** directive for **stdio.h** because we want to use **printf()** and **scanf()**. At the beginning of **main()** we declare an array of ten integers, and then the other variables that we'll need for this example:

```
   int numbers[10];          /* Array storing 10 values     */
   int count = 10;           /* Number of values to be read */
   long sum = 0L;            /* Sum of the numbers          */
   float average = 0.0f;     /* Average of the numbers      */
   int i = 0;                /* Loop counter                */
```

171

We then prompt for the input to be entered with this statement:

```
    printf("\nEnter the 10 numbers:\n");  /* Prompt for the input */
```

Next, we have a loop to read the values and accumulate the sum:

```
    /* Read the ten numbers to be averaged */
    for(i = 0; i < count; i++)
    {
      printf("%2d> ",i+1);
      scanf("%d", &numbers[i]);     /* Read a number */
      sum += numbers[i];            /* Add it to sum */
    }
```

Because the loop counts from 0 to 9, rather than 1 to 10, we can use the loop variable **i**, directly, to reference each of the members of the array. The **printf()** call outputs the current value of **i+1** followed by **>**, so it has the effect you see in the output. By using **%2d** as the format specifier we ensure that each value is output as two digits, so the numbers are aligned. If we'd used **%d** instead, the output for the tenth line would have been out of alignment. I'll introduce you to more modifiers as we go along.

We read each value entered into element **i** of the array using the **scanf()** function; the first value will be stored in **number[0]**, the second number entered will be stored in **number[1]**, and so on up to the tenth value entered, which will be stored in **number[9]**. For each iteration of the loop, the value read is added into **sum**.

When the loop ends, we calculate the average and display it with these statements:

```
    average = (float)sum / count;    /* Calculate the average */

    printf("\nAverage of the ten numbers entered is: %f\n", average);
```

We've calculated the average by dividing the sum by 10. Notice how, in the call to **printf()**, we've told the compiler to convert **sum** (which is defined as **long**) into type **float**. This is to ensure that the division is done using floating point values - so we do not discard any fractional part of the result.

Try It Out - Retrieving the Numbers Stored

This example, in itself, doesn't show how useful the array is, but we can expand it a little to demonstrate one of the advantages. I've only made a minor change to the original program (highlighted below), but now the program displays all the values we typed in. Having the values stored in an array means that we can access those values whenever we want.

```
/* Example 5.4 Reusing the numbers stored */
#include <stdio.h>

void main()
{
    int numbers[10];          /* Array storing 10 values     */
    int count = 10;           /* Number of values to be read */
```

```
      long sum = 0L;                /* Sum of the numbers         */
      float average = 0.0f;    /* Average of the numbers     */
      int i = 0;                    /* Loop counter               */

      printf("\nEnter the 10 numbers:\n");   /* Prompt for the input */

      /* Read the ten numbers to be averaged */
      for(i = 0; i < count; i++)
      {
        printf("%2d> ",i+1);
        scanf("%d", &numbers[i]);        /* Read a number */
        sum += numbers[i];               /* Add it to sum */
      }

      average = (float)sum / count;    /* Calculate the average */

      for(i = 0; i < count; i++)
        printf("\nGrade Number %d was %d", i + 1, numbers[i]);

      printf("\nAverage of the ten numbers entered is: %f\n", average);
    }
```

Typical output would be:

```
    Enter the ten numbers:
     1> 56
     2> 64
     3> 34
     4> 51
     5> 52
     6> 78
     7> 62
     8> 51
     9> 47
    10> 32

    Grade No 1 was 56
    Grade No 2 was 64
    Grade No 3 was 34
    Grade No 4 was 51
    Grade No 5 was 52
    Grade No 6 was 78
    Grade No 7 was 62
    Grade No 8 was 51
    Grade No 9 was 47
    Grade No 10 was 32
    Average of the ten numbers entered is: 52.700000
```

How It Works

I'll just explain the new bits:

```
for(i = 0; i < count; i++)
    printf("\nGrade Number %d was %d", i + 1, number[i]);
```

We've simply added another **for** loop to step through the elements in the array and output each value. We use the loop control variable to produce the sequence number for the value of the number of the element, and to access the corresponding array element. These values obviously correspond to the numbers we typed in.

Before we go any further with these wonderful information containers called arrays, we need to look into how your variables are stored in the computer memory. We also need to understand how an array is different from the variables we've seen up to now.

A Reminder About Memory

Let's quickly recap what we learnt about memory in Chapter 2.

You can think of the memory of your computer as an ordered line of boxes. Each of these boxes is one of two states: either the box is full (let's call this state 1), or the box is empty (this is state 0). Each box is referred to as a **bit**.

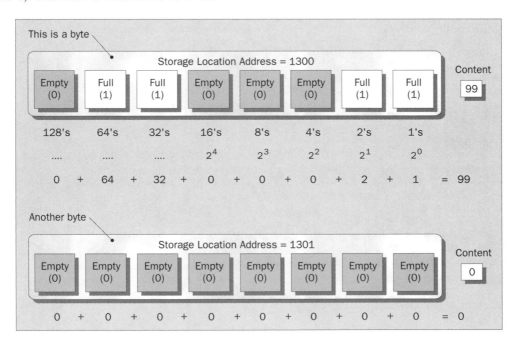

For convenience, we group our boxes into sets of 8 which we call a **byte**. To get to the contents of each byte, it's labeled with a number, starting from 0 for the first byte in memory and going up to whatever number of bytes there are in memory. This label for a byte is called its **address**.

We've already been using the **address of** operator, **&**, extensively with the **scanf()** function. We've been using this as a prefix to the variable name, because the function needs to store data from the user into the variable. The **address of** operator simply gives us the address of the variable - and this then allows us to store information there. The best way to get a feel for the **address of** operator is to use it a bit more, so let's try.

Try It Out - Using the Address of Operator

The variables that you use in your programs all take up a certain amount of memory, measured in bytes; the exact amount of memory is dependent on the type of the variable. Let's try finding the address of some variables of different types with the following program:

```
/* Example 5.5 Using the & operator */
#include<stdio.h>

void main()
{
   /* declare some integer variables */
   long a = 1L;
   long b = 2L;
   long c = 3L;

   /* declare some floating point variables */
   double d = 4.0;
   double e = 5.0;
   double f = 6.0;

   printf("\nThe address of a is: %p  The Address of b is: %p", &a, &b);
   printf("\nThe address of c is: %p", &c);
   printf("\nThe address of d is: %p  The Address of e is: %p", &d, &e);
   printf("\nThe Address of f is: %p\n", &f);
}
```

Output from this program will be something like this:

```
The address of a is: 0064FDF4  The Address of b is: 0064FDF0
The address of c is: 0064FDEC
The address of d is: 0064FDE4  The Address of e is: 0064FDDC
The Address of f is: 0064FDD4
```

Don't be too concerned if the addresses you get are different from these. What you'll get simply depends on what operating system you have and what's running at the time.

How It Works

We declare three variables of type **long** and three of type **double**:

```
   /* declare some integer variables */
   long a = 1L;
   long b = 2L;
   long c = 3L;
```

```
/* declare some floating point variables */
double d = 4.0;
double e = 5.0;
double f = 6.0;
```

We then obtain the addresses of these variables, using the **address of** operator, and output them in the **printf()** function calls:

```
printf("\nThe address of a is: %p  The Address of b is: %p", &a, &b);
printf("\nThe address of c is: %p", &c);
printf("\nThe address of d is: %p  The Address of e is: %p", &d, &e);
printf("\nThe Address of f is: %p\n", &f);
```

The **address of** operator is the **&** that precedes the variables. We've also used another format specifier, **%p**, to output the address of the variables. This format specifier outputs the address in hexadecimal format. Each of the addresses on my computer is eight hexadecimal digits, although on your machine it may be different.

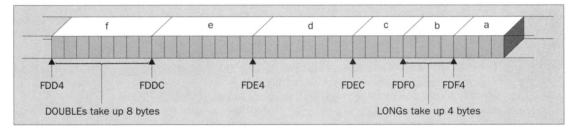

In fact, the interesting part isn't the program itself so much as the output. Look at the addresses that have been displayed. You can see that the value of the address gets steadily lower, in a regular pattern. On my computer, the address of **b** is 4 lower than that of **a**, and **c** is lower than **b** also by 4. You can deduce from this that variables of type **long** occupy four bytes. There's a similar situation with the variables **d**, **e**, and **f**, except that the difference is 8. This demonstrates that 8 bytes are used to store a value of type **double**.

Hexadecimal Number Representation

As a quick summary of binary and hexadecimal numbers, look at the following table that compares values in the different formats. To remind you how the system works, look at the figure after the table.

Decimal	Binary	Hexadecimal	Decimal	Binary	Hexadecimal
0	0000	0	8	1000	8
1	0001	1	9	1001	9
2	0010	2	10	1010	A
3	0011	3	11	1011	B
4	0100	4	12	1100	C
5	0101	5	13	1101	D
6	0110	6	14	1110	E
7	0111	7	15	1111	F

From the table you can see that a 4 digit binary number (from 0000 to 1111) can represent values from 0 to 15 in decimal. This is the same range as for a single hexadecimal digit (0 to F) so each hexadecimal digit defines four bits. Hexadecimal is frequently used when dealing with a numeric value held in a byte of memory, precisely because of this relationship between hexadecimal and binary. Two hexadecimal digits represent one byte.

DECIMAL					BINARY						HEXADECIMAL		
(10*10*10)	(10*10)	10	U		(2*2*2*2)	(2*2*2)	(2*2)	2	U		(16*16)	16	U
1000s	100s	10s	1s		16s	8s	4s	2s	1s		256s	16s	1s
0	0	1	6	=	1	0	0	0	0	=	0	1	0
0	0	2	3	=	1	0	1	1	1	=	0	1	7
0	0	2	8	=	1	1	1	0	0	=	0	1	C

Representing Characters

We've reviewed how numbers are stored in memory, but what about characters and all the other alphabetic information that we wish to hold as computer data? We use computers to store records about people; for example, detailing their names and addresses. For these tasks, numbers alone aren't enough: so what method does the computer provide for characters?

Basically, the answer is none. However, we can store characters by adopting the convention that each character will be represented by a number that we can accommodate in a single byte of memory. So, to represent the letter **'A'**, if we're using ASCII codes, we use the decimal number 65, (or hexadecimal **0x41**). For **'T'** we use the decimal value 84, which is **0x54** in hexadecimal.

There is a code corresponding to each character and symbol that we can use in a program. These include codes for upper and lower case letters, for the characters '0' to '9', and also for various symbols. You shouldn't confuse these characters '0' to '9' with the corresponding integers - the character '9' has the value 57. Also, as we have seen, there are many non-printing characters, such as the newline character, **'\n'**, or the backspace character, **'\b'**.

You'll find the full set of ASCII codes in Appendix B.

Arrays and Addresses

With arrays, the method of addressing individual elements is slightly different from a simple variable. Suppose we have an array called **number**, with the capacity to store 10 values:

```
long number[10];
```

The array name **number** gets you to the right area of memory where your data is stored, and the specific location is found with the index value. As we said earlier, the index value represents an offset from the first element of the array.

When we declare an array, we give the compiler all the information it needs to allocate the memory for the array. We tell it the type of value (which will require a certain number of bytes) and how many there will be (the number of elements). The address of the whole array (the array name) gets you to the first element. An index value specifies how many elements along you have to go to address the element you want. The address of an array element is going to be the address of the first element, plus the index value for the element multiplied by the number of bytes required to store each element - which is dependent on the type.

This figure represents the way that array variables are held in memory.

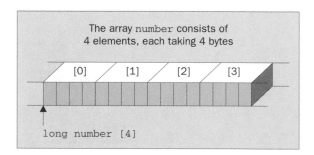

The array number consists of 4 elements, each taking 4 bytes

[0]   [1]   [2]   [3]

long number [4]

We can obtain the address of an array element in a similar fashion to ordinary variables. For an integer variable called **value**, we would use the following statement to print its address:

```
printf("\n%p", &value);
```

To output the address of the third element of an array called **number**, we could write the following:

```
printf("\n%p", &number[2]);
```

Remember that we use the value 2, in the brackets, to reach the third element. Here, we've taken the address of the element with the **address of** operator. If you used the same statement without the **&**, you'd display the actual value stored in the 3rd element of the array, not its address.

Initializing an Array

Of course, you may want to assign initial values for the elements of your array, even if it's only for the sake of safety. To do this, you just specify the list of initial values between braces, and separated by commas, in the declaration. For example:

```
double values[5] = { 1.5, 2.5, 3.5, 4.5, 5.5 };
```

This declares the array, **values**, with 5 elements. The elements are initialized with **values[0]** having the initial value 1.5, **value[1]** having the initial value 2.5, and so on. To initialize the whole array, there should be one value for each element. If there are fewer initializing values than elements, the elements without initializing values will be set to 0. Thus if you write:

```
double values[5] = { 1.5, 2.5, 3.5 };
```

The first three elements will be initialized with the values between braces, and the last two elements will be initialized with zero.

If you put more initializing values than there are array elements, you'll get an error message from the compiler.

178

Finding the Size of an Array

We have a special operator in C that computes the number of bytes that a variable occupies. This is the operator **sizeof**. Of course, **sizeof** is a keyword in C so you can't use it as a variable name. Let's see how it works. If you declare a variable with the statement:

```
double value = 1.0;
```

Then the statement:

```
printf("\nThe size of value is%2d bytes.", sizeof value);
```

will output the line:

```
The size of value is 8 bytes.
```

This is because a variable of type **double** occupies 8 bytes in memory. Of course, you can store the size value you get with **sizeof** if you want:

```
int value_size = sizeof value;
```

The **sizeof** operator works with arrays too. We can declare an array with the statement:

```
double values[5] = { 1.5, 2.5, 3.5, 4.5, 5.5 };
```

Now we can output the number of bytes that the array occupies with the statement:

```
printf("\nThe size of the array, values, is%2d bytes.", sizeof values);
```

This will produce the output:

```
The size of the array, values, is 40 bytes.
```

We can also obtain the number of bytes occupied by a single element of the array with the expression **sizeof values[0]**. This expression will have the value 8. Of course, any legal index value for an element could be used to produce the same result. We can therefore use the **sizeof** to calculate the number of elements in an array:

```
int ElementCount = sizeof values/sizeof values[0];
```

After executing this statement, the variable **ElementCount** will contain the number of elements in the array **values**.

The **sizeof** operator can also be applied to a data type, such as in the expression **sizeof(int)**. Note that the parentheses are mandatory here. We could have written the previous statement to calculate the number of array elements like this:

```
int ElementCount = sizeof values/sizeof(double);
```

This would produce the same result as before, since the array is of type **double** and **sizeof(double)** would have produced the number of bytes occupied by a **double** value. Because there's the risk that you might accidentally use the wrong type, it's probably better to

179

use the first kind statement in practice, where the variable itself is referenced. Although the **sizeof** operator does not require the use of parentheses when applied to a variable, it is common practice to use them anyway - so our earlier example would more typically be written:

```
int ElementCount = sizeof(values)/sizeof(values[0]);
```

Multidimensional Arrays

So far, we've been dealing with arrays with one index value to reference an element. These are called one-dimensional arrays. We aren't limited to just one index dimension for an array. You can declare arrays of two or more dimensions. If you grew carrots in a field in 25 rows of 50 plants, you could use a two-dimensional array to record how big each carrot turned out to be. If you had ten fields of carrots on your farm then you could use a three-dimensional array. One dimension would be for the fields, one dimension for the row in the field, and the third for each particular carrot. Of course, if you had several farms... well, you get the idea. Let's stick to two dimensions for the moment and work our way up. A two-dimensional array can be declared as:

```
float carrots[25][50];
```

This declares an array **carrots** containing 25 rows of 50 floating point elements. Similarly, we can declare another two-dimensional array of floating point numbers with the statement:

```
float numbers[3][5];
```

Like the vegetables in the field, we tend to visualize these as rectangular arrangements, because it's convenient to do so. They are actually stored in memory sequentially by row, as shown in the figure below.

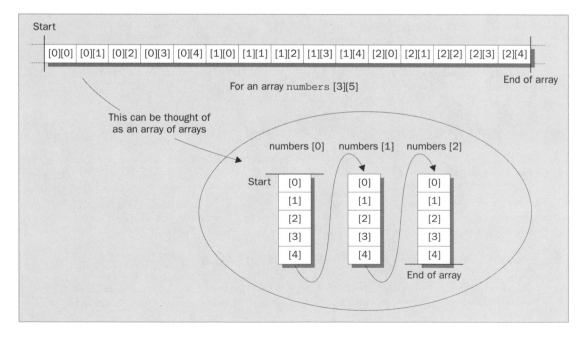

Each element of an array needs a certain number of bytes to store it. To show an array of a different size, the following figure illustrates how the array **numbers[4][10]** of type **float** is stored.

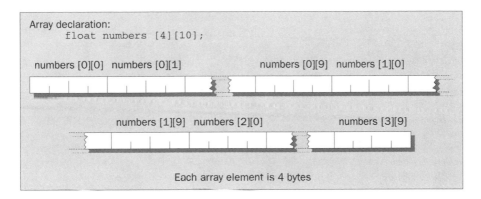

It's easy to see that the rightmost index varies first. You can also envisage a two-dimensional array as one-dimensional, where each element is itself a one-dimensional array. Let's look at the **numbers** array above. The first row of ten numbers of type **float** is held in memory at an address labeled **numbers[0][0]**, and the next ten at **numbers[1][0]**, the next ten at **numbers[2][0]**, and so on. The amount of memory that's allocated to each element is, of course, dependent on the type of variables that the array contains. An array of type **double** will need more memory to store each element than an array of type **float** or type **int**.

Initializing Multidimensional Arrays

Let's first consider a two-dimensional array. The basic structure of the declaration, with initialization, is the same as we have seen before - except that we need to put the initial values for each row between braces **{}**. For example:

```
int numbers[3][4] = {
                     { 10, 20, 30, 40 },    /* Values for first row  */
                     { 15, 25, 35, 45 },    /* Values for second row */
                     { 47, 48, 49, 50 }     /* Values for third row  */
                    };
```

Each set of values for a row is between braces, and the whole lot goes between another pair of braces. The set for each row is separated from the next set by a comma.

If you specify fewer initializing values than there are elements in a row, the remaining elements in a row without values specified will be initialized to zero.

For arrays of three or more dimensions, the process is extended. A three-dimensional array, for example, will have three levels of nested braces, with the inner level containing sets of initializing values for a row. For example:

```
int numbers[2][3][4] = {
                        {                        /* First block of 3 rows  */
                        { 10, 20, 30, 40 },
                        { 15, 25, 35, 45 },
                        { 47, 48, 49, 50 }
                    },
                    {                            /* Second block of 3 rows */
                        { 10, 20, 30, 40 },
                        { 15, 25, 35, 45 },
                        { 47, 48, 49, 50 }
                    }
                };
```

As you can see, the initializing values are between an outer pair of braces which enclose two blocks of three rows, each between braces. Each row is also between braces, so we have three levels of nested braces for a three-dimensional array!

Try It Out - Multidimensional Arrays

Let's move away from vegetables and turn to more practical applications. We could use arrays in a program to help you to work out your hat size (most useful). With this program, you just enter the circumference of your head, in inches, and your hat size will be displayed.

```
/* Example 5.6 Know your hat size - if you dare...  */
#include <stdio.h>
#define TRUE  1
#define FALSE 0

void main()

{
   char Size[3][12] = {         /* Hat sizes as characters */
      {'6', '6', '6', '6', '7', '7', '7', '7', '7', '7', '7', '7'},
      {'1', '5', '3', '7', ' ', '1', '1', '3', '1', '5', '3', '7'},
      {'2', '8', '4', '8', ' ', '8', '4', '8', '2', '8', '4', '8'}
                    };

   int Headsize[12] =           /* Values in 1/8 inches    */
      {164,166,169,172,175,178,181,184,188,191,194,197};

   float Cranium = 0.0;      /* Head circumference in decimal inches */
   int Your_Head = 0;        /* Headsize in whole eighths           */
   int i = 0;                /* Loop counter                        */
   int hat_found = FALSE;    /* Indicates when a hat is found to fit */
   int too_small = FALSE;    /* Indicates headsize is too small     */

   /* Get the circumference of the head */
   printf("\nEnter the circumference of your head above your eyebrows "
       "in inches as a decimal value: ");
   scanf(" %f", &Cranium);
```

```
   /* Convert to whole eighths of an inch */
   Your_Head = (int)(8.0*Cranium);

   /* Search for a hat size */
   for (i = 0 ; i < 12 ; i++)
   {
     /* Find head size in the Headsize array */
     if(Your_Head > Headsize[i])
       continue;

     /* If it is the first element and the head size */
     /* is more than 1/8 smaller then the head is    */
     /* too small for a hat.                         */
     if(( i == 0) && (Your_Head < Headsize[0]-1))
     {
       printf("\nYou are the proverbial pinhead. No hat for"
                                       " you I'm afraid.\n");
       too_small = TRUE;
       break;              /* Exit the loop */
     }

     /* If head size is more than 1/8 smaller than the */
     /* current element in Headsize array, take the    */
     /* next element down as the head size             */
     if( Your_Head < Headsize[i]-1 )
       i--;

     printf("\nYour hat size is %c %c%c%c\n",
             Size[0][i], Size[1][i], (i==4)?' ' : '/', Size[2][i]);
     hat_found = TRUE;
     break; /* Exit the loop */
   }

   /* Check for no hat found and head not too small */
   if (!hat_found && !too_small)
     printf("\nYou, in technical parlance, are a fathead."
                               " No hat for you, I'm afraid.\n");
}
```

Typical output from this program would be:

```
Enter the circumference of your head above your eyebrows in inches as a
decimal value: 22.5
Your hat size is 7 1/4

Enter the circumference of your head above your eyebrows in inches as a
decimal value: 29
You, in technical parlance, are a fathead. No hat for you I'm afraid.
```

183

How It Works

Before we start discussing this example, I should give you a word of caution. Don't use it to assist large football players to determine their hat size unless they're known for their sense of humor.

This example is here to illustrate using arrays rather than programming elegance, so it looks a bit complicated. Let's go through what's happening.

After the **#include** directive for **stdio.h**, we use two pre-processor directives to define the symbols **TRUE** and **FALSE** for use in the program:

```
#define TRUE  1
#define FALSE 0
```

The first declaration in the body of **main()** is:

```
char Size[3][12] = {          /* Hat sizes as characters */
    {'6', '6', '6', '6', '7', '7', '7', '7', '7', '7', '7', '7'},
    {'1', '5', '3', '7', ' ', '1', '1', '3', '1', '5', '3', '7'},
    {'2', '8', '4', '8', ' ', '8', '4', '8', '2', '8', '4', '8'}
                    };
```

This array corresponds to twelve possible hat sizes, each of which is made up of 3 values. For each size we've stored three characters, making it more convenient to output the fractional sizes. The smallest hat size is 6 1/2, so the first three characters corresponding to the first size are in **Size[0][0]**, **Size[1][0]**, and **Size[2][0]**. They contain the characters **'6'**, **'1'**, and **'2'** representing the size 6 1/2. The biggest hat size is 7 7/8 and is stored in **Size[0][11]**, **Size[1][11]**, **Size[2][11]**.

We then declare the array **Headsize**, which provides the reference dimensions in this declaration:

```
int Headsize[12] =           /* Values in 1/8 inches     */
   {164,166,169,172,175,178,181,184,188,191,194,197};
```

The values in the array are all whole eighths of an inch. They correspond to the values in the **Size** array containing the hat sizes. This means that a head size of 164 eighths of an inch (about 20.5 inches) will give a hat size of 6 1/2.

Notice that the head sizes don't run consecutively. We could get a head size of 171, for example, which doesn't fall into a definite hat size. We need to be aware of this later in the program so that we can decide which is the closest hat size for the head size.

After declaring our arrays, we then declare all the variables we are going to need:

```
float Cranium = 0.0;       /* Head circumference in decimal inches */
int Your_Head = 0;         /* Headsize in whole eighths            */
int i = 0;                 /* Loop counter                         */
int hat_found = FALSE;     /* Indicates when a hat is found to fit */
int too_small = FALSE;     /* Indicates headsize is too small      */
```

Notice that **Cranium** is declared as type **float**, but the rest are all type **int**. This becomes important later. We're using the variables **hat_found** and **too_small** as logical values, so we use the symbol **FALSE** to initialize these.

Next, we prompt for your head size to be entered in inches, and the value is stored in the variable **Cranium** (remember it's type **float**, so we can store values that aren't whole numbers):

```
printf("\nEnter the circumference of your head above your eyebrows "
    "in inches as a decimal value: ");
scanf(" %f", &Cranium);
```

The value stored in **Cranium** is then converted into eighths of an inch with this statement:

```
Your_Head = (int)(8.0*Cranium);
```

The value stored in **Your_Head** will then be in the same units as the values stored in the array **Headsize**. Note that we need the cast to **int** here to avoid a warning message from the compiler. The parentheses around the expression **(8.0*Cranium)** are also necessary: without them we would only cast the value **8.0** to **int**, not the whole expression.

We use the value stored in **Your_Head** to find the closest value in the array **Headsize[12]** that is not less than that value:

```
for (i = 0 ; i < 12 ; i++)
{
  /* Find head size in the Headsize array */
  if(Your_Head > Headsize[i])
    continue;
  . . .
}
```

Our process is a simple one, and is carried out in this **for** loop. On each loop iteration we compare your head size with a value stored in the array **Headsize** to find the first value that is less than or equal to your input size. The **if** compares the size you entered with the current **Headsize** element, and as long as **Your_Head** is greater, the **continue** is executed to go to the next iteration.

The **continue** statement is for use in a loop, and of course **continue** is a keyword. In some respects it's similar to the **break** keyword (which we've used before) in that it causes the computer to skip the rest of the statements in the loop. However, unlike the **break** statement, the loop isn't exited. Instead, the loop continues with the next iteration, after incrementing the loop variable **i**, and checking the that the loop condition **i<12** is true.

Once the value in the **i**th element of **Headsize** is greater than **Your_Head**, we should be able find your hat size - so the continue statement is not executed, and we proceed with the rest of the loop iteration.

It's possible that someone could enter a value that was too small for our hats, so we first check for a small head:

```
      /* If it is the first element and the head size */
      /* is more than 1/8 smaller then the head is    */
      /* too small for a hat.                         */
      if(( i == 0) && (Your_Head < Headsize[0]-1))
      {
        printf("\nYou are the proverbial pinhead. No hat for"
                                          " you I'm afraid.\n");
        too_small = TRUE;
        break; /* Exit the loop */
      }
```

This **if** checks whether the value of **Your_Head** happens to be less than the first value in the **Headsize** array. To be precise, it checks whether **Your_Head** is more than 1 eighth of an inch less with the expression **(Your_Head < Headsize[0]-1)**. If so, then we know that the value entered must be smaller than that for the size 6 1/2 (our smallest size), and we output the pinhead message. We also assign the value **TRUE** to **too_small**. We then execute the **break** statement to break out of the loop, because there's no point in checking against any of the larger sizes.

If we didn't exit the loop as a result of the previous **if** statement, we can definitely find a suitable hat size. We first check whether the value in **Your_Head** is more than 1 unit away from the current **Headsize** array element and, if so, we adjust the index value **i** to select the previous element as the size:

```
      if( Your_Head < Headsize[i]-1 )
        i--;
```

You could have achieved the same result with a single statement:

```
      i -= Your_Head < Headsize[i]-1;
```

The logical expression on the right hand side of the assignment will have the value 1 or 0. When it is 1, **i** will be decremented, which is the result we want.

We now use the value of the loop counter, **i**, to select the size of the hat for the given head size. We then set **hat_found** to **TRUE**, and we exit the loop:

```
      printf("\nYour hat size is %c %c%c%c\n",
             Size[0][i], Size[1][i], (i==4)?' ' : '/', Size[2][i]);
      hat_found = TRUE;
      break; /* Exit the loop */
```

As I said, the hat sizes are stored in the array **Size** as characters to simplify the outputting of fractions. The **printf()** here uses the conditional operator to decide when to print a blank and when to print a slash (**/**) for the fractional output value. The fifth element of the **Headsize** array corresponds to a hat size of exactly 7. We don't want it to print 7 /; we just want 7. Therefore, we customize the **printf()** depending on whether element **i** is equal to 4 (remember this is the fifth element, starting your count from zero).

There are three possible situations with the head size that you enter. It may be too small, in which case the output will be dealt with inside the loop. It may be just right for a hat size, in which case the output will be produced as I've just described. The third possibility is that your head is too large for a hat - and this will be dealt with after the loop, since all the elements of **Headsize** must be checked. This situation will result in both **too_small** and **hat_found** having the value **FALSE** after the loop has completed; so we test for this with the statements:

```
if (!hat_found && !too_small)
   printf("\nYou, in technical parlance, are a fathead."
                              " No hat for you, I'm afraid.\n");
```

The **printf()** will only be executed if the size stored in **Your_Head** was greater than all the values in the **Headsize** array.

Remember, when using this program, that if you lie about the size of your head, your hat will not fit. The more mathematically astute, and any hatters reading this book, will appreciate that the hat size is simply the diameter of a notionally circular head. Therefore, if you have the circumference of your head in inches, you can produce your hat size by dividing this value by π.

Designing a Program

Now that we've learnt about arrays, let's see how we can apply them in a bigger problem. Let's have a go at writing another game.

The Problem

The problem we're set is to write a program that allows two people to play tic-tac-toe (or noughts and crosses) on the computer.

The Analysis

Tic-tac-toe is played on a 3-by-3 grid of squares. The two players take it in turns to enter either an X or an O in the grid. The player that first manages to get three of their symbols in a line horizontally, vertically, or diagonally, is the winner. We know how the game works, but how does that translate into designing our program. What we need is:

- **A 3-by-3 grid in which to store the turns of the two players.** That's easy. We can just use a two-dimensional array with three rows of three elements.

- **A way for a square to be selected when a player takes his or her turn.** We can label the nine squares with digits 1 to 9. A player will just need to enter the number of the square to select it.

- **A way to get the two players to take alternate turns**. We can identify the two players as 1 and 2, with Player 1 going first. We can then determine the player number by the number of the turn. On odd-numbered turns it is player 1. On even-numbered turns it's player 2.

- **Some way of specifying where to place the player symbol on the grid, and checking to see if it's a valid selection.** A valid selection is a digit from 1 to 9. If we label the first row of squares with 1, 2, and 3, the second row with 4, 5, and 6, and the third row with 7, 8, and 9, we can calculate a row index and a column index from the square number. If we subtract 1 from the player's choice of square number, the square numbers are effectively 0 through 8:

	Original			Subtract 1	
1	2	3	0	1	2
4	5	6	3	4	5
7	8	9	6	7	8

Then the expression **choice/3** gives the row number, as you can see:

	Original less 1			Divide by 3	
0	1	2	0	0	0
3	4	5	1	1	1
6	7	8	2	2	2

The expression **choice%3** will give the column number:

	Original less 1			Remainder after ÷ 3	
0	1	2	0	1	2
3	4	5	0	1	2
6	7	8	0	1	2

▶ **A method of finding out if one of the players has won.** After each turn, we'll need to check to see if any row, column, or diagonal in the board grid contains identical symbols. If it does, the last player has won.

▶ **A way to detect the end of the game.** Since the board has nine squares, a game consists of up to nine turns. The game ends when a winner is discovered, or after nine turns.

The Solution

1 We can first add the code for the main game loop and the code to display the board:

```
/* Example 5.7 Tic-Tac-Toe */
#include <stdio.h>

void main()
{
   int i = 0;         /* Loop counter              */
   int player = 0;    /* Player number - 1 or 2 */
   int winner = 0;    /* The winning player        */

   char board[3][3] = {         /* The board */
              {'1','2','3'},   /* Initial values are reference numbers */
              {'4','5','6'},   /* used to select a vacant square for   */
              {'7','8','9'}    /* a turn.                              */
                   };
```

```
    /* The main game loop. The game continues for up to 9 turns */
    /* As long as there is no winner                            */
    for( i = 0; i<9 && winner==0; i++)
    {
      /* Display the board */
      printf("\n\n");
      printf(" %c | %c | %c\n", board[0][0], board[0][1], board[0][2]);
      printf("---+---+---\n");
      printf(" %c | %c | %c\n", board[1][0], board[1][1], board[1][2]);
      printf("---+---+---\n");
      printf(" %c | %c | %c\n", board[2][0], board[2][1], board[2][2]);

      player = i%2 + 1; /* Select player */

      /* Code to play the game */
    }
    /* Code to output the result */
}
```

Here, we've declared the following variables: **i**, for the loop variable; **player**, which stores the identifier for the current player, 1 or 2; **winner**, which will contain the identifier for the winning player and the array, **board**, which is of type **char**. The array is of type char because we want to place the symbols **'X'** or **'O'** in the squares. The array is initialized with the characters for the digits that identify the squares. The main game loop continues for as long as the loop condition is true. This will be false if **winner** contains a value other than 0 (which indicates that a winner has been found) or the loop counter is equal to, or greater than 9 (which will be the case when all nine squares on the board have been filled).

When we display the grid in the loop, we use vertical bars and underline characters to delineate the squares. When a player selects a square, the symbol for that player will replace the digit character.

2 Next, we can implement the code for the player to select a square, and to ensure that the square is valid:

```
/* Example 5.7 Tic-Tac-Toe */
#include <stdio.h>

void main()
{
    int i = 0;       /* Loop counter                          */
    int player = 0; /* Player number - 1 or 2                 */
    int winner = 0; /* The winning player                     */
    int choice = 0; /* Square selection number for turn */
    int row = 0;     /* Row index for a square             */
    int column = 0; /* Column index for a square          */

    char board[3][3] = {        /* The board */
             {'1','2','3'},  /* Initial values are reference numbers */
             {'4','5','6'},  /* used to select a vacant square for   */
             {'7','8','9'}   /* a turn.                              */
                     };
```

189

```
/* The main game loop. The game continues for up to 9 turns */
/* As long as there is no winner                            */
for( i = 0; i<9 && winner==0; i++)
{
  /* Display the board */
  printf("\n\n");
  printf(" %c | %c | %c\n", board[0][0], board[0][1], board[0][2]);
  printf("---+---+---\n");
  printf(" %c | %c | %c\n", board[1][0], board[1][1], board[1][2]);
  printf("---+---+---\n");
  printf(" %c | %c | %c\n", board[2][0], board[2][1], board[2][2]);

  player = i%2 + 1; /* Select player    */

  /* Get valid player square selection */
  do
  {
    printf("\nPlayer %d, please enter the number of the square "
           "where you want to place your %c: ",
             player,(player==1)?'X':'O');
    scanf("%d", &choice);

    row = (choice-1)/3;                    /* Get row index of square    */
    column = (choice-1)%3;                 /* Get column index of square */
  }while(choice<1 || choice>9 || board[row][column]>'9');

  /* Insert player symbol */
  board[row][column] = (player == 1) ? 'X' : 'O';

  /* Code to check for a winner */
}
/* Code to output the result */
}
```

We prompt the current player for input in the **do-while** loop and read the square number into the variable **choice,** which we declared as type **int**. We'll use this value to compute the row and column index values in the array; the value therefore needs to be numeric rather than of type **char**. The row and column index values are stored in the integer variables, **row** and **column**, and we compute these values using the expressions we saw earlier. The **do-while** loop condition verifies that the square selected is valid. There are three possible ways that an invalid choice could be made: the integer entered for the square number could be less than the minimum, 1; it could be greater than the maximum, 9; or it could select a square that already contains **'X'** or **'O'**. In the latter case, the contents of the square will have a value greater than the character **'9'**, since the ASCII codes for **'X'** and **'O'** are greater than the ASCII code for **'9'**. If the choice entered fails on any of these conditions, we just repeat the request to select a square.

3 We can add the code to check for a winning line next. This needs to be executed after every turn:

```c
/* Example 5.7 Tic-Tac-Toe */
#include <stdio.h>

void main()
{
   int i = 0;        /* Loop counter                           */
   int player = 0; /* Player number - 1 or 2                 */
   int winner = 0; /* The winning player                     */
   int choice = 0; /* Square selection number for turn       */
   int row = 0;      /* Row index for a square                 */
   int column = 0; /* Column index for a square              */
   int line=0;       /* Row or column index in checking loop */

   char board[3][3] = {        /* The board */
              {'1','2','3'},  /* Initial values are reference numbers */
              {'4','5','6'},  /* used to select a vacant square for   */
              {'7','8','9'}   /* a turn.                              */
                     };

   /* The main game loop. The game continues for up to 9 turns */
   /* As long as there is no winner                            */
   for( i = 0; i<9 && winner==0; i++)
   {
     /* Display the board */
     printf("\n\n");
     printf(" %c | %c | %c\n", board[0][0], board[0][1], board[0][2]);
     printf("---+---+---\n");
     printf(" %c | %c | %c\n", board[1][0], board[1][1], board[1][2]);
     printf("---+---+---\n");
     printf(" %c | %c | %c\n", board[2][0], board[2][1], board[2][2]);

     player = i%2 + 1;               /* Select player     */

     /* Get valid player square selection           */
     do
     {
       printf("\nPlayer %d, please enter the number of the square "
              "where you want to place your %c: ",
               player,(player==1)?'X':'O');
       scanf("%d", &choice);

       row = (choice-1)/3;               /* Get row index of square    */
       column = (choice-1)%3;            /* Get column index of square */
     }while(choice<1 || choice>9 || board[row][column]>'9');

     /* Insert player symbol */
     board[row][column] = (player == 1) ? 'X' : 'O';

     /* Check for a winning line - diagonals first */
     if((board[0][0]==board[1][1] && board[0][0]==board[2][2]) ||
        (board[0][2]==board[1][1] && board[0][2]==board[2][0]))
       winner = player;
```

```
        else
          /* Check rows and columns for a winning line */
          for(line = 0; line <= 2; line++)
            if((board[line][0]==board[line][1] &&
                board[line][0]==board[line][2])||
               (board[0][line]==board[1][line] &&
                board[0][line]==board[2][line]))
              winner = player;
    }
    /* Code to output the result */
}
```

To check for a winning line, we must compare any element in the line with the other two elements. We check both diagonals in the board array with the **if** expression, and if either diagonal has identical symbols in all three elements, we set **winner** to the current player. The current player, identified in **player**, must be the winner since he or she was the last to place a symbol on a square. If neither diagonal has identical symbols we check the rows and the columns in the **else** clause, which is a **for** loop. The **for** loop contains one statement, an **if**. This checks both a row and a column for identical elements, and if either is found, **winner** is set to the current player. Each value of the loop variable, **line**, is used to index a row and a column. Thus the **for** loop will check the row and column corresponding to index value 0, which is the first row and column, then the second row and column, and finally the third row and columns corresponding to **line** having the value 2. Of course, if winner is set to a value here, the main loop condition will be false, so the loop will end and we will continue with the code following the main loop.

4 The final task is to display the grid with the final position, and to display a message for the result. If **winner** is zero, the game is a draw; otherwise **winner** contains the player number of the winner:

```
/* Example 5.7 Tic-Tac-Toe */
#include <stdio.h>

void main()
{
   int i = 0;        /* Loop counter                        */
   int player = 0; /* Player number - 1 or 2               */
   int winner = 0; /* The winning player                   */
   int choice = 0; /* Square selection number for turn    */
   int row = 0;      /* Row index for a square               */
   int column = 0; /* Column index for a square            */
   int line=0;       /* Row or column index in checking loop */

   char board[3][3] = {          /* The board */
               {'1','2','3'},  /* Initial values are reference numbers */
               {'4','5','6'},  /* used to select a vacant square for   */
               {'7','8','9'}   /* a turn.                              */
                      };
```

```
/* The main game loop. The game continues for up to 9 turns */
/* As long as there is no winner                            */
for( i = 0; i<9 && winner==0; i++)
{
  /* Display the board */
  printf("\n\n");
  printf(" %c | %c | %c\n", board[0][0], board[0][1], board[0][2]);
  printf("---+---+---\n");
  printf(" %c | %c | %c\n", board[1][0], board[1][1], board[1][2]);
  printf("---+---+---\n");
  printf(" %c | %c | %c\n", board[2][0], board[2][1], board[2][2]);

  player = i%2 + 1;    /* Select player */

  /* Get valid player square selection */
  do
  {
    printf("\nPlayer %d, please enter the number of the square "
           "where you want to place your %c: ",
           player,(player==1)?'X':'O');
    scanf("%d", &choice);

    row = (choice-1)/3;              /* Get row index of square    */
    column = (choice-1)%3;          /* Get column index of square */
  }while(choice<1 || choice>9 || board[row][column]>'9');

  /* Insert player symbol */
  board[row][column] = (player == 1) ? 'X' : 'O';

  /* Check for a winning line - diagonals first */
  if((board[0][0]==board[1][1] && board[0][0]==board[2][2]) ||
     (board[0][2]==board[1][1] && board[0][2]==board[2][0]))
    winner = player;
  else
    /* Check rows and columns for a winning line */
    for(line = 0; line <= 2; line ++)
      if((board[line][0]==board[line][1] &&
          board[line][0]==board[line][2])||
         (board[0][line]==board[1][line] &&
          board[0][line]==board[2][line]))
        winner = player;
}
/* Game is over so display the final board */
printf("\n\n");
printf(" %c | %c | %c\n", board[0][0], board[0][1], board[0][2]);
printf("---+---+---\n");
printf(" %c | %c | %c\n", board[1][0], board[1][1], board[1][2]);
printf("---+---+---\n");
printf(" %c | %c | %c\n", board[2][0], board[2][1], board[2][2]);
```

```
    /* Display result message */
    if(winner == 0)
      printf("\nHow boring, it is a draw\n");
    else
      printf("\nCongratulations, player %d, YOU ARE THE WINNER!\n",
                                                winner);
  }
```

Typical output from this program and a very bad player number 2 would be:

```
 1 | 2 | 3
---+---+---
 4 | 5 | 6
---+---+---
 7 | 8 | 9

Player 1, please enter your go: 1

 X | 2 | 3
---+---+---
 4 | 5 | 6
---+---+---
 7 | 8 | 9

Player 2, please enter your go: 2

 X | O | 3
---+---+---
 4 | 5 | 6
---+---+---
 7 | 8 | 9

Player 1, please enter your go: 5


 X | O | 3
---+---+---
 4 | X | 6
---+---+---
 7 | 8 | 9

Player 2, please enter your go: 3


 X | O | O
---+---+---
 4 | X | 6
---+---+---
 7 | 8 | 9

Player 1, please enter your go: 9
```

```
X | O | O
---+---+---
4 | X | 6
---+---+---
7 | 8 | X
```

Congratulations, player 1, YOU ARE THE WINNER!

Summary

In this chapter, I've explained what arrays are and how to use them. We've covered a bit more about memory in your computer - to help you understand how your computer works with the information you give it. We've looked at one-dimensional and multi-dimensional arrays, and I've showed you how these work, in practice, by going through the design and implementation of a game of tic-tac-toe.

This chapter has covered some ideas that extend your capability to deal with much more complicated programming problems. Once you start dealing with arrays, particularly multi-dimensional arrays, you're dealing with a lot more information. The possibilities for your programs increase immensely, although you do have to invest more time in planning and designing your programs.

Up until now, we've mainly concentrated on processing numbers. Our examples haven't really dealt with text to any great extent. We're going to put that right in the next chapter, where we're going to be writing programs that can process and analyze strings of characters.

Applications with Strings and Text

In the last chapter you were introduced to arrays, and we saw the benefits of being able to declare an array of numbers in a program. In this chapter, we'll extend our knowledge of arrays to discover the programming power of arrays of characters - which are called **strings**.

As you'll find out, C doesn't provide us with a string data type, as some other languages do. Instead, C uses an array of type **char** to store a string. In this chapter, I'll show you exactly how the standard library functions can help you manipulate strings in your programs. The results, I can promise you, are extremely worthwhile: strings allow us to manipulate text - which is an important element in many programs.

In this chapter you'll learn:

- How you can create string variables
- How to join one or more strings together to form a single string
- How you compare strings
- How to use arrays of strings
- What library functions are available to handle strings, and how you can apply them
- How to write a password protection program

What is a String?

We've already met examples of **string constants** - quite frequently in fact. A string constant is a sequence of characters or symbols between a pair of double quote characters. Anything between a pair of double quotes is interpreted by the compiler as a string, including any special characters and embedded spaces. Every time we've displayed a message using **printf()**, we have defined the message as a string constant. Here are some examples of strings used in this way:

```
printf("This is a string.");
printf("This is quite a long string");
printf("AAA");
```

The string constants are the letters and characters contained between the pairs of double quotes. The characters in a string are stored in successive bytes of memory, with each byte containing a numerical ASCII code representing the corresponding letter, space or other symbol within the string.

Our three example strings are represented in the following figure. The decimal ASCII codes that would be stored in memory are shown below the characters.

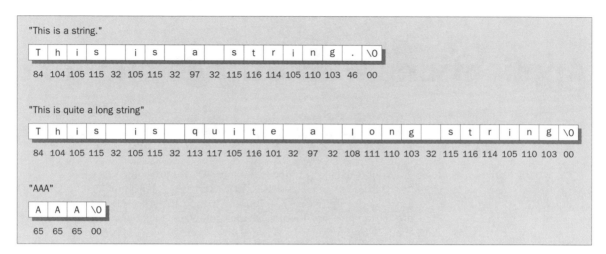

In C, a special character is always added as the last character in the string, to mark where that string ends. This character is known as the **null character** (not to be confused with **NULL**, which we'll come to later), and it has the value zero.

> *The upshot of using the null character to signal the end of a string, in C, is that the length of any string is always one greater than the number of characters in it. This is important, as we'll see later.*

There's nothing to prevent you adding a `\0` character to the end of a string yourself, but if you do, you'll simply end up with two null characters! So let's see how the null character `\0` works with a simple example. Have a look at the following program:

```
/* Example 6.1 Displaying a string */
#include <stdio.h>

void main()
{
   printf("The character \0 is used to terminate a string");
}
```

If we run this program, then the output is:

```
The character
```

Not quite what we planned: only the first part of string has been displayed. The output ends after the first two words because the **printf()** stops printing the string when it reaches the first null character **\0**. Even though there's another **\0** at the end of **string**, it will never be reached.

String and Text Handling Methods

From our discussion of arrays, in the previous chapter, we're already excellently equipped to handling strings and text.

Declaring String Variables

We can use arrays of type **char** to hold strings. This is the simplest form of string variable; we can declare a **char** array variable as:

```
char string[20];
```

This variable can hold up to 19 characters, allowing one for the termination character.

> *Remember that you must declare the array dimension to be at least one character greater than the number of characters that you want to store, since the compiler will automatically add '\0' to the end of the string.*

We can also initialize this string variable with the following declaration:

```
char string[] = "This is a string.";
```

Here, we haven't explicitly defined the array dimension. The compiler will assign a value to the dimension that is just sufficient to hold the initializing string constant. In this case it will be 18 characters, allowing an extra one for the terminating **'\0'**. Each element of the array will contain one character of the string. We could, of course, have put a value for the dimension ourselves - but if the compiler does it, we can be sure that it'll be correct.

We can also initialize just part of a string array:

```
char str[40] = "To be";
```

The compiler will initialize the first five elements, from **str[0]** to **str[4]**, with the characters of the specified string. **str[5]** will contain the null value **'\0'**. Of course, space is allocated for all 40 elements of the array, and they're all available for us to use.

Initializing a **char** array and declaring it as constant is a good way of handling standard messages:

```
const char message[] = "The end of the world is nigh";
```

In this example, because we've declared **message** as a **const**, it's protected from any modification within the program. Any attempt to modify the message will result in an error message from the compiler. Of course, if you do need to be able to change the message, you simply don't specify the array as **const**.

The main disadvantage of using **char** arrays like this is that it can easily lead us to a wastage of memory. This is because **char** arrays are, by definition, of a fixed length - so we must declare these kinds of arrays with their dimension set to accommodate the maximum string length that we need. In most circumstances, our typical string length will be somewhat less than this maximum - but the memory space will have still been reserved. The result is that we end up wasting precious memory.

Since we usually use character arrays to store strings of a *variable* length, it's important for us to be able to ascertain the exact size of these variable length strings. Once we know the length of a string, we can arrange to use just the amount of memory storage that we need - which is a much more efficient method of storing our strings.

Try It Out - Finding Out the Length of a String

In this example, we're going to initialize two strings and then find out how many characters there are in each (excluding the null character):

```
/* Example 6.2 Lengths of strings  */
#include <stdio.h>
void main()
{
   char str1[40] = "To be or not to be";
   char str2[40] = ",that is the question";
   int count = 0;        /* Stores the string length */

   /* Increment count till we reach the string */
   while (str1[count] != '\0')
     count++;           /* terminating character */

   printf("\nThe length of the string \"%s\" is %d characters.",
                                           str1,count);

   count = 0;                    /* Reset to zero for next string    */

   while (str2[count] != '\0')   /* Count characters in second string */
     count++;

   printf("\nThe length of the string \"%s\" is %d characters.",
                                           str2, count);
}
```

The output you will get from this program is:

```
The length of the string "To be or not to be" is 18 characters.
The length of the string ",that is the question" is 21 characters.
```

How it Works

Let's go through it. First, we have some declarations:

```
char str1[40] = "To be or not to be";
char str2[40] = ",that is the question";
int count = 0;        /* Stores the string length */
```

We declare two arrays of type **char**, each initialized with a string of a length considerably less than the length of the array. We also declare and initialize a counter variable called **count** to use in the loops we need in the program.

Next, we set up the first loop - to work out the length of the first string:

```
/* Increment count till we reach the string */
while (str1[count] != '\0')
   count++;          /* terminating character */
```

Using a loop in this way is very common in programming with strings. To find the length, we simply use the **while** loop to keep incrementing a counter until we reach the end of string character. The condition for the continuation of the loop is therefore whether the terminating **'\0'** has been reached. At the end of the loop, the variable **count** will contain the number of characters in the loop, excluding the terminating null.

It would also have been possible to put the incrementing of **count** in the **while** condition with a statement such as this:

```
while (str1[ count++ ] != '\0');
```

However, we would then have to decrement **count** by 1 after the loop had finished, because **count** would have been incremented one more time on the exit from the loop when the **'\0'** is detected. This would be fine if we wanted the string length to include the termination character. However, with the loop as we have it in the example, we come out with the correct value, since **count** is incremented in the loop proper, rather than in the exit condition.

Now we have the length, we display the string with the statement:

```
printf("\nThe length of the string \"%s\" is %d characters.",
                                          str1, count);
```

This also displays the count of the number of characters that the string contains, excluding that terminating null character. Notice that we're using a new conversion specifier, **%s**. This outputs characters from the string until it reaches the terminating null. If there were no terminating character, the **%s** specifier would result in the **printf()** call continuing to output characters until it found one somewhere in memory. In some cases this can mean a lot of output! We're also using the escape character, **'\"'**, to include a double quote in the string. If we didn't precede the double quote character with this backslash, the compiler would think it had reached the end of the string.

Finding the length of the second string, and displaying the result, is performed in exactly the same way as the first string.

Operations with Strings

Now we can display string variables, let's move on to consider how we can actually manipulate strings.

The first thing to appreciate is that we can't use the assignment operator to copy a string in the way we would with **int** or **double** variables. To achieve the equivalent of an arithmetic assignment with a string, the second string must be copied, element by element, to the first string. In fact, performing any operation on string variables is very different from the arithmetic operations we've seen so far. Let's look at some of common operations you might want to perform with strings.

Joining Strings Together

Joining one string on to the end of another is a common requirement. For instance, we might want to assemble a single message from two or more strings. A solid example of this could be when we're processing error messages: these messages could consist of a few basic text strings plus a variety of strings that are appended - to make the message specific to a particular error.

Try It Out - Joining Strings

We could extend the last example to join some strings:

```
/* Example 6.3 Joining strings */
#include <stdio.h>
void main()
{
   char str1[40] = "To be or not to be";
   char str2[40] = ",that is the question";
   int count1 = 0;                   /* Length of str1 */
   int count2 = 0;                   /* Length of str2 */

   /* find the length of the first string */
   /* Increment count till we reach the string */
   while (str1[count1] != '\0')
     count1++;      /* terminating character */

   /* Find the length of the second string */
   /* Count characters in second string      */
   while (str2[count2] != '\0')
     count2++;

   /* Check that we have enough space for both strings  */
   if(sizeof(str1) < count1 + count2 + 1)
     printf("\nYou can't put a quart into a pint pot.");
   else
   {
     /* Copy 2nd string to first  */
     count2 = 0;                      /* Reset index for str2 to 0    */
```

```
        while( str2[count2] != '\0' ) /* Copy up to null from str2    */
          str1[count1++] = str2[count2++];

        str1[count1] = '\0';           /* Make sure we add terminator */
        printf("\n%s", str1 );         /* Output combined string      */
    }
  }
```

Typical output from this program would be:

    To be or not to be, that is the question

How it Works

This program first finds the lengths of the two strings, exactly as before. It then checks that **str1** has enough elements to hold both strings and the terminating null character:

```
      if(sizeof(str1) < count1 + count2 + 1)
        printf("\nYou can't put a quart into a pint pot.");
```

Notice how the **sizeof** operator is used to get the total number of bytes in the array by just using the array name as an argument. This value is the number of characters that the array will hold, since each character occupies one byte.

If we discover that the array is too small to hold the contents of both strings, then we display a message and end the program. It's essential not to attempt to place more characters in the array than it can hold, as this will overwrite some area memory that could contain important data, or even machine instructions. This is likely to crash your program.

We reach the **else** block only if we're sure that both strings will fit in the first array. Here, we reset the variable **count2** to zero and copy the second string to the first array, with these statements:

```
      else
      {
        /* Copy 2nd string to first  */
        count2 = 0;                    /* Reset index for str2 to 0   */

        while( str2[count2] != '\0' ) /* Copy up to null from str2    */
          str1[count1++] = str2[count2++];

        str1[count1] = '\0';           /* Make sure we add terminator */
        printf("\n%s", str1 );         /* Output combined string      */
      }
```

The variable **count1** starts from the value left by the loop that determined the length of the first string, **str1**. This is why we've used two variables to count the string length for the two strings.

Since the array is indexed from 0, the value stored in **count1** will point to the element containing **'\0'** at the end of the first string. So, when we use **count1** to index the array **str1**, we know that we're starting at the end of the message proper, and that we'll overwrite the null character at the end of the first string with the first character of the second string.

We then copy characters from **str2** to **str1** until we find the **'\0'** in **str2**. We still have to add a terminating **'\0'** to **str1**, since it isn't copied from **str2**. The end result of the operation is that we've added the contents of **str2** to the end of **str1**, overwriting the terminating null character for **str1**, and adding a terminating null to the end of the combined string.

We could have replaced the three lines of code above with a more concise method of copying the second string:

```
while ((str1[count1++] = str2[count2++]) != '\0');
```

This would replace the loop we have in the program, as well as the statement to put a **'\0'** at the end of **str1**. This statement would copy the **'\0'** from **str2** to **str1**, since the copying occurs in the loop continuation condition itself. Let's carefully consider what happens at each stage of this **while** statement.

Notice the parentheses around our assignment, highlighted here:

```
while ((str1[count1++] = str2[count2++]) != '\0');
```

Since parentheses have the highest order of precedence, they ensure that the assignment is performed before the result is compared with **'\0'**. The sequence of events is therefore as follows. First, assign the value of **str2[count2]** to **str1[count1]**. Next, increment each of the counters by one, using the postfix form of the **++** operator. Finally, check whether the last character stored in **str1** was **'\0'**. The loop ends after the **'\0'** has been copied to **str1**.

The diagram on the following page illustrates this process in a little more detail. The top box shows the two strings, **str1** and **str2**, that we're processing, and the line of code that contains our **while** statement. **count1** is an index to the end of **str1**, and **count2** is our index within **str2**.

Stage 1, in this diagram, describes how we copy a single character from **str2** to the end of **str1**. Stage 2 details how we then increment the indexes **count1** and **count2** in both strings. Stage 3 then describes our test condition for the **while** statement: if the last character that we copied from **str2** to **str1** was a **'\0'** then exit the loop; otherwise, return to Stage 1, and copy another character etc. When the **while** loop finally exits, all the characters from **str2** will have been appended to **str1**, including the final **'\0'** character.

The actions of
```
while ((str1[count1++] = str2[count2++]) != '\0';
```

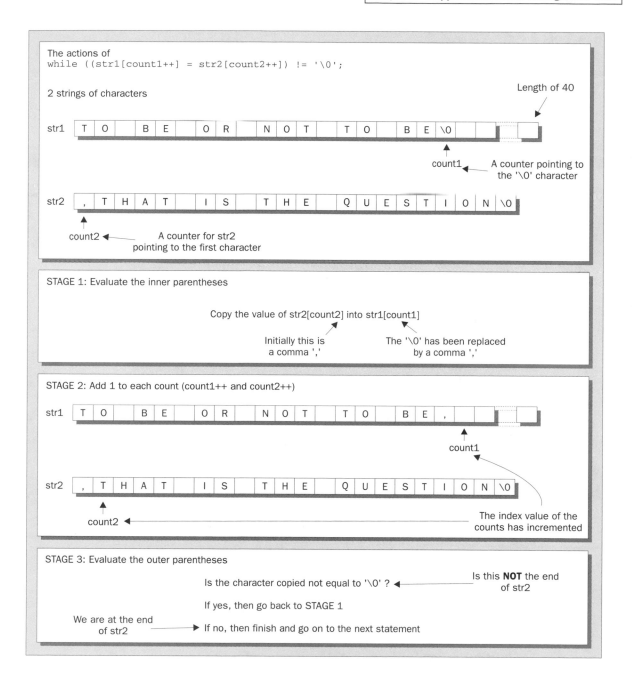

2 strings of characters

Length of 40

str1 | T | O | | B | E | | O | R | | N | O | T | | T | O | | B | E | \0 | | | | |

count1 — A counter pointing to the '\0' character

str2 | , | T | H | A | T | | I | S | | T | H | E | | Q | U | E | S | T | I | O | N | \0 |

count2 — A counter for str2 pointing to the first character

STAGE 1: Evaluate the inner parentheses

Copy the value of str2[count2] into str1[count1]

Initially this is a comma ','

The '\0' has been replaced by a comma ','

STAGE 2: Add 1 to each count (count1++ and count2++)

str1 | T | O | | B | E | | O | R | | N | O | T | | T | O | | B | E | , | | | | |

count1

str2 | , | T | H | A | T | | I | S | | T | H | E | | Q | U | E | S | T | I | O | N | \0 |

The index value of the counts has incremented

count2

STAGE 3: Evaluate the outer parentheses

Is the character copied not equal to '\0' ? ← Is this **NOT** the end of str2

If yes, then go back to STAGE 1

We are at the end of str2 → If no, then finish and go on to the next statement

205

Arrays of Strings

It may have occurred to you, by now, that we could use a two-dimensional array of type **char** to store strings, where each row is used to hold a separate string. In this way, we could arrange to store a whole bunch of strings - and refer to them through a single variable name. Let's change the last example to work in this way.

Try It Out - Arrays of Strings

```
/* Example 6.4 Arrays of strings */
#include <stdio.h>
void main()
{
   char str[2][40] = {
                        {"To be or not to be"   },
                        {",that is the question"}
                      };
   int count1 = 0;                  /* Length of first string  */
   int count2 = 0;                  /* Length of second string */

   /* find the length of the first string */
   /* Increment count till we reach the */
   while (str[0][count1] != '\0')
     count1++;          /* string terminating character */

   /* Find the length of the second string */
   /* Count characters in 2nd string     */
   while (str[1][count2] != '\0')
     count2++;

   /* Check that we have enough space for both strings  */
   if( sizeof str[0] < count1 + count2 + 1 )
     printf("\nYou can't put a quart into a pint pot.");
   else
   {
     /* Reset second counter */
     count2 = 0;

     /* copy 2nd to 1st */
     while ((str[0][count1++] = str[1][count2++]) != '\0');

     /* Output combined string */
     printf("\n%s", str[0]);
   }
}
```

Typical output from this program would be:

```
To be or not to be,that is the question
```

How it Works

Well, I have to admit, this isn't a great improvement on the previous version. We just declare a single two-dimensional **char** array, instead of the two one-dimensional arrays we had before:

```
char str[2][40] = {
                    {"To be or not to be"   },
                    {",that is the question"}
                  };
```

The first initializing string is stored with the index value of 0, and the second initializing string is stored with the index value of 1.

To access any particular string in the program, we just use an index to the appropriate array dimension: 0 for the first string, and 1 for the second. Otherwise, it's the same as the previous example.

We'd probably gain more from this method if we had twenty strings instead of two. On the downside, however, if we needed to cope with a variable number of strings, we would have no way of knowing how large to declare our string dimensions. Another disadvantage of this approach is that if our strings are significantly less than 40 characters long, we waste quite a bit of memory in the array.

String Library Functions

Now that we've struggled through the previous examples, laboriously copying strings from one variable to another, it's time to reveal that there's a standard library of string functions that can take care of all these little chores. Still, at least you'll know what's going on when you use the library functions!

The string functions are in the header file **string.h**, so you'll need to place this line into your code:

```
#include <string.h>
```

This instruction, like all pre-processor directives, comes at the beginning of your program whenever you want to use the relevant string library functions. The string library actually contains quite a lot of functions, and your compiler may provide an even more extensive range of string library capabilities. We'll discuss just a few of the essential functions, here, to demonstrate the basic idea. This leaves you with the rather interesting task of exploring all the other useful functions that are available with your C compiler.

Copying Strings Using a Library Function

First, let's return to copying strings. The **while** loop that we carefully created to do this must still be fresh in your mind. Well, we can do the same thing like this:

```
strcpy( string1, string2);
```

where the argument variables are **char** array names.

What the function actually does is to copy **string2** to **string1**, including the terminating **'\0'**. It's your responsibility to ensure that the array **string1** has sufficient space to accommodate **string2**. The function **strcpy()** has no way of checking the sizes of the arrays, so if it goes wrong it's your fault!

Determining String Length Using a Library Function

To find out the length of a string, we have the function **strlen()**, which returns the length of a string as an unsigned integer. In our example to do this we wrote:

```
/* Find the length of the second string */
/* Count characters in 2nd string      */
while (str[1][count2] != '\0')
   count2++;
```

Instead of this rigmarole we could simply write:

```
count2 = strlen(str2);
```

All the counting and searching that's necessary to find the end of the string is performed by the function, so you no longer have to worry about it. Note that it returns the length of the string *excluding* the **'\0'**. This is generally the most convenient result. It also returns the value as unsigned, so you may want to declare the variable to hold the result as unsigned as well.

Joining Strings Using a Library Function

In our Example 6.3, we also got into copying the second string to the end of the first, using this rather complex code:

```
/* Copy 2nd string to first  */
count2 = 0;                      /* Reset index for str2 to 0   */

while( str2[count2] != '\0' ) /* Copy up to null from str2   */
   str1[count1++] = str2[count2++];

str1[count1] = '\0';            /* Make sure we add terminator */
```

Well, the string library provides a slight simplification here, too. We can use a function that joins one string to the end of another, achieving the same result as above with this delightfully simple statement:

```
strcat(str1, str2);
```

This function finds the end of **str1**, and copies **str2** to the end of **str1**. The **strcat()** function is so called because it performs **string cat**enation. As well as appending **str2** to **str1**, the **strcat()** function also returns **str1**, which is the value we want.

Try It Out - Using the String Library

We now have enough tools to make a good job of rewriting Example 6.3:

```c
/* Example 6.5 Joining strings - revitalised */
#include <stdio.h>
#include <string.h>
#define STR_LENGTH 40

void main()
{
   char str1[STR_LENGTH] = "To be or not to be";
   char str2[STR_LENGTH] = ",that is the question";

   /* Enough space ? */
   if(STR_LENGTH > strlen(str1) + strlen(str2))
     /* yes, so display joined string */
     printf("\n%s", strcat(str1, str2));
   else
     printf("\nYou can't put a quart into a pint pot.");
}
```

This program will produce exactly the same output as before.

How it Works

Well, what a difference a library makes. It actually makes the problem trivial, doesn't it? We've defined a symbol for the size of the arrays, using a **#define** directive. If we want to change the array sizes in the program later, we can just modify the definition for **STR_LENGTH**. We check that we have enough space in our array by means of the **if** statement:

```c
   /* Enough space ? */
   if(STR_LENGTH > strlen(str1) + strlen(str2))
     /* yes, so display joined string */
     printf("\n%s", strcat(str1, str2));
   else
     printf("\nYou can't put a quart into a pint pot.");
```

If we do have enough space, we join the strings using the **strcat()** function within the argument to the **printf()**. Because the **strcat()** function returns **str1**, the **printf()** displays the result of joining the strings. If **str1** is too short, we just display a message.

Comparing Strings

The string library also provides us with a facility for comparing strings, and deciding whether one string is greater than or less than another. It may sound a bit odd to apply terms such as 'greater than' and 'less than' to strings, but the comparisons are quite straightforward and logical. Successive corresponding characters of the two strings are compared, based on the numerical value of their ASCII codes. This mechanism is illustrated graphically in the next figure, where the ASCII codes are shown as hexadecimal.

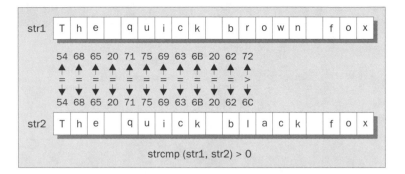

If the two strings are identical, then of course they are equal. The first pair of characters that are different determine whether the first string is less than or greater than the second. So if the ASCII code for the character in the first string is less than the ASCII code for the character in the second string, then the first string is said to be less than the first.

The function **strcmp(str1, str2)** compares two strings. It returns an **int** value that's less than, equal to, or greater than zero - corresponding to whether **str1** is less than, equal to, or greater than **str2**.

Try It Out - Comparing Strings

We can demonstrate the use of this in an example:

```c
/* Example 6.6 Comparing strings    */
#include <stdio.h>
#include <string.h>

void main()
{
   char word1[20];              /* Stores the first word  */
   char word2[20];              /* Stores the second word */

   printf("\nType in the first word:\n1: ");
   scanf("%s", word1);          /* Read the first word    */
   printf("Type in the second word:\n 2: ");
   scanf("%s", word2);          /* Read the second word   */

   /* Compare the two words */
   if(strcmp(word1,word2) == 0)
     printf("You have entered identical words");
   else
     printf("%s precedes %s",
                   (strcmp(word1, word2) < 0) ? word1 : word2,
                   (strcmp(word1, word2) < 0) ? word2 : word1);
}
```

This program will read in two words and then tell you which one is alphabetically before the other. The output looks something like this:

```
Type in two words:
1: apple
2: banana
apple precedes banana
```

How it Works

We've started the program with the **#include** statements for the header files for the standard input and output library, and the string handling library:

```
#include <stdio.h>
#include <string.h>
```

In the body of **main()**, we first we declare two character arrays to store the words we will read in from the keyboard:

```
char word1[20];          /* Stores the first word  */
char word2[20];          /* Stores the second word */
```

We set the size of the arrays to 20. This should be enough for our example, but I should give a word of warning: as with the **strcpy()** function, it's *your* responsibility to allocate enough space for what the user may key in. The function **scanf()** has no way to tell when it runs out of space, and it will happily overwrite things it shouldn't.

Our next task is to get two words from the user, so after a prompt, we use **scanf()** twice to get a couple of words.

```
printf("\nType in the first word:\n1: ");
scanf("%s", word1);          /* Read the first word    */
printf("Type in the second word:\n 2: ");
scanf("%s", word2);          /* Read the second word   */
```

Notice how, in this example, we haven't used an **&** before the variables. This is because the name of an array, by itself, is already an address: it corresponds to the address of the first element in the array. We could have written this explicitly, by writing:

```
scanf("%s", &word1[0]);
```

This means that **&word1[0] == word1**. Finally, we use the **strcmp()** function to compare the two words that were entered:

```
if(strcmp(word1,word2) == 0)
  printf("You have entered identical words");
else
  printf("%s precedes %s",
                  (strcmp(word1, word2) < 0) ? word1 : word2,
                  (strcmp(word1, word2) < 0) ? word2 : word1);
```

If the value returned by the **strcmp()** function is zero, then the two strings are equal, and we display a message to this effect. If not, then we print out a message specifying which word precedes the other. We do this using the conditional operator to specify which word we want to print first and which second.

Searching Text

There are several string-searching functions in the string library, and we'll take a good look at two of them here. Before we get into these, however, we need to take a peek at pointers, which are the subject of the next chapter.

The Idea of a Pointer

As we'll see in much greater detail in the next chapter, C provides us with a remarkably useful type of variable called a **pointer**. A pointer is a variable that contains an address; that is, it contains a reference to another location in memory that can contain a value. A pointer is described very simply in the next figure.

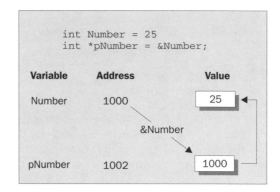

We declare a variable **Number** with the value 25, and a pointer, **pNumber**, which contains the address of **Number**. We can now use the variable **pNumber** in the expression ***pNumber** to obtain the value contained in **Number**.

The main reason I've introduced this idea now (rather than letting you read about it in the next chapter) is that the functions we're about to discuss return pointers. Pointers are a major topic in C programming, and in the next chapter we'll really get to grips with them. For now, though, I've told you enough about pointers for us to continue our discussion of strings and text.

String Search Functions

The first function we're going to look at is **strchr(str,c)**, which searches a given string for a specified character. Its first parameter is a **str**ing; the second parameter is an **int** variable used to store a character. **strchr()** will return a pointer to the first position in the string where the character is found.

strchr() is used as follows:

```
pGot_char = strchr(str, c);
```

The result of this is
illustrated in the figure here:

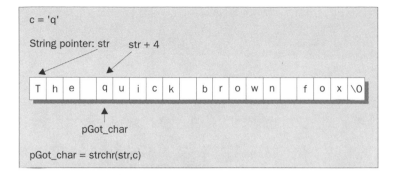

The second function, **strstr(str1, str2)**, is probably the most useful of all the searching functions in **string.h**. It searches one string for the first occurrence of another string, and it returns a pointer to the position in the first string where the second string is found.

If **strstr()** doesn't find a match, it returns **NULL**. **NULL** is a predefined constant that is the equivalent of zero for a pointer. If the value returned here isn't **NULL**, you can be sure that the searching function that you're using has found an occurrence of what it was searching for. The function **strstr()** is used as follows:

```
pFound = strstr(str1, str2);
```

The two arguments to the function are the string to be searched, and the string to be found, respectively.

Try It Out - Searching a String

We can see these string searching functions in action in the following example:

```
/* Example 6.7 A demonstration of seeking and finding  */
#include <stdio.h>
#include <string.h>
void main()
{
   char str1[] = "This string contains the holy grail.";
   char str2[] = "the holy grail";
   char str3[] = "the holy grill";

   /* Search str1 for the occurrence of str2 */
   if(strstr(str1, str2) == NULL)
     printf("\n\"%s\" was not found.", str2);
   else
     printf("\n\"%s\" was found in \"%s\"",str2, str1);

   /* Search str1 for the occurrence of str3 */
   if(strstr(str1, str3) == NULL)
     printf("\n\"%s\" was not found.", str3);
   else
     printf("\nWe shouldn't get to here!");
}
```

Typical output would be:

```
"the holy grail" was found in "This string contains the holy grail."
"the holy grill" was not found.
```

How it Works

We have three strings defined, **str1**, **str2**, and **str3**:

```
char str1[] = "This string contains the holy grail.";
char str2[] = "the holy grail";
char str3[] = "the holy grill";
```

In the first **if** statement we use the library function **strstr()** to search for the occurrence of the second string in the first:

```
if(strstr(str1, str2) == NULL)
  printf("\n\"%s\" was not found.", str2);
else
  printf("\n\"%s\" was found in \"%s\"",str2, str1);
```

We then display a message corresponding to the result by testing the returned value of **strstr()** against **NULL**. If the value returned is equal to **NULL**, this indicates the second string wasn't found in the first, so a message is displayed to that effect. If the second string *is* found then the **else** is executed. In this case, a message is displayed to indicate that the string was found.

We then repeat the process in the second **if** statement and check for the occurrence of the third string in the first:

```
if(strstr(str1, str3) == NULL)
  printf("\n\"%s\" was not found.", str3);
else
  printf("\nWe shouldn't get to here!");
```

If we get output from the first or the last **printf()** in the program, something is seriously wrong!

Analyzing Strings

If you need to examine the internal contents of a string, there's a set of standard library functions that are accessible if you include the header file, **ctype.h**, in your program. They provide you with a very flexible range of analytical functions that enable you to test what kind of character you have:

Function	Test	Function	Test
`isalpha()`	Alphabetic	`isupper()`	Upper-case
`isdigit()`	Numeric Digit	`islower()`	Lower-case
`isxdigit()`	Hexadecimal digit	`isspace()`	White space
`isalnum()`	Alphabetic or digit	`ispunct()`	Punctuation character
`isprint()`	Printable character	`isgraph()`	Printable but not space
`iscntrl()`	Control character		

The argument that you put between the parentheses when you use a function is the character to be tested. Functions return a non-zero value if the character is within the set that is being tested for, and zero otherwise. The return value is of type **int**.

Try It Out - Using the Character Classification Functions

We can demonstrate how they can be used with a simple example:

```
/* Example 6.8 Exercising ctype.h */
#include <stdio.h>
#include <ctype.h>
void main()
{
   char  Buffer[80];      /* Input buffer              */
   int i = 0;             /* Buffer index              */
   int num_letters = 0;   /* Number of letters in input */
   int num_digits = 0;    /* Number of digits in input  */

   printf("\nEnter an interesting string of less than 80"
                                       " characters:\n");
   gets(Buffer);          /* Read a string into Buffer */

   while(Buffer[i] != '\0')
   {
     if(isalpha(Buffer[i]) != 0)
       num_letters++;     /* Increment letter count    */
     if(isdigit(Buffer[i++]) != 0)
       num_digits++;      /* Increment digit count     */
   }
   printf("\nYour string contained %d letters and %d digits.\n",
                               num_letters, num_digits);
}
```

Typical output from this program is:

```
Enter an interesting string of less than 80 characters:
I was born on the 3rd of October 1965

Your string contained 24 letters and 5 digits.
```

How it Works

This example is quite straightforward. We read the string into the array, **Buffer**, with the statement:

```
gets(Buffer);
```

The string you enter is read into the array **Buffer** using the standard library function **gets()**. So far, we've used **scanf()** to accept input from the keyboard, but **scanf()** isn't very useful for reading strings - because it interprets a space as the end of an input value. The **gets()** function has the advantage that it will read all the characters entered from the keyboard, including blanks, up to when you press the *Enter* key. This is then stored as a string into the area specified by its argument, which in this case is the array **Buffer**. A **'\0'** will be appended to the string automatically.

The statements that analyze the string are:

```
    while(Buffer[i] != '\0')
    {
      if(isalpha(Buffer[i]) != 0)
        num_letters++;     /* Increment letter count     */
      if(isdigit(Buffer[i++]) != 0)
        num_digits++;      /* Increment digit count      */
    }
```

The input string is tested character by character in the **while** loop. Checks are made for alphabetic characters and digits, in turn, in the two **if** statements. When either is found, the appropriate counter is incremented. Note that we increment the index to the array **Buffer** in the second **if**. Remember, the check is made using the current value of **i**, and then **i** is incremented, afterwards, because we're using the postfix form of the increment operator.

You could implement this without using **if** statements:

```
    while(Buffer[i] != '\0')
    {
      num_letters += isalpha(Buffer[i]) != 0;
      num_digits += isdigit(Buffer[i++]) != 0;
    }
```

The test functions return a non-zero value if the argument belongs to the group of characters being tested for. The value of the logical expressions to the right of the assignment operators will be 1 if the character is what is sought, and 0 otherwise.

This isn't a particularly efficient way of doing things, since we test for a digit even if we've already discovered the current character is alphabetic. Do experiment here, and see if you can improve the code I've used.

Converting Characters

The standard library also includes two conversion functions that you access through **ctype.h**:

toupper()	Converts from lower-case to upper-case
tolower()	Converts from upper-case to lower-case

These functions will return the upper-case or lower-case equivalent, respectively, of the character that is sent to them. If the character you send is already in the correct case, then that character is simply returned. You can therefore convert a string to upper case using the statement,

```
for(i = 0 ; (Buffer[i] = toupper(Buffer[i])) != '\0' ; i++);
```

assuming, of course, that the index **i** has been declared appropriately. This loop will convert the entire string to upper-case by stepping through the string one character at a time, converting lower case to upper-case, and leaving upper-case characters unchanged. The loop stops when it reaches the string termination character **'\0'**.

Try It Out - Converting Characters

We could exercise the function **toupper()** together with the **strstr()** function, to find out how many times one string occurs in another, ignoring case. Look at the following example:

```
/* Example 6.9 Finding occurrences of one string in another  */
#include <stdio.h>
#include <string.h>
#include <ctype.h>

void main()
{
   char string1[100];      /* Input buffer for second string */
   char string2[40];       /* Input buffer for second string */
   int i = 0;              /* Index value & counter          */
   int str2_len = 0;       /* Length of string2              */
   char *pstr1 = string1;  /* Pointer to string1             */

   printf("\nEnter the string to be searched(less than 100"
                                         " characters):\n");
   gets ( string1 );
   printf("\nEnter the string sought (less than 40 characters ):\n");
   gets( string2 );

   /* Convert both strings to upper case. */
   for(i = 0 ; (string1[i] = toupper(string1[i])) != '\0' ; i++);
   for(i = 0 ; (string2[i] = toupper(string2[i])) != '\0' ; i++);

   str2_len = strlen(string2);   /* Get length of string2 */
   i=0;                          /* set counter to 0       */

   /* Loop until string2 not found */
   while ((pstr1 = strstr(pstr1, string2)) != NULL)
   {
     i++;                 /* Increment counter            */
     pstr1 += str2_len;   /* increment by string2 length  */
   }
   printf("\nThe second string was found %d times in the first.", i );
}
```

Typical operation of this example will produce:

```
Enter the string to be searched(less than 100 characters):
Smith, where Jones had had 'had had', had had 'had'. 'Had had' had had
the examiner's approval.

Enter the string sought (less than 40 characters):
had

The second string was found 11 times in the first.
```

How it Works

This program has three distinct phases: getting the input strings, converting both strings to upper-case, and searching the first string for occurrences of the second.

First of all, **printf()** displays messages to tell the user to enter two strings, and **gets()** is used to store the input in **string1** and **string2**:

```
    printf("\nEnter the string to be searched(less than 100"
                                        " characters):\n");
    gets ( string1 );
    printf("\nEnter the string sought (less than 40 characters ):\n");
    gets( string2 );
```

We use the function **gets()** because it will read in a string from the keyboard - including blanks. The conversion to upper-case is accomplished using the statements:

```
    for(i = 0 ; (string1[i] = toupper(string1[i])) != '\0' ; i++);
    for(i = 0 ; (string2[i] = toupper(string2[i])) != '\0' ; i++);
```

This uses **for** loops to do the conversion. The first **for** loop initializes **i** to 0 and then converts an element of **string1** to upper-case in the loop condition - and stores that result back in the same position in **string1**. The loop condition also checks to see whether the character stored is equal to **'\0'**. The index **i** is incremented in the third loop control expression. This ensures there is no confusion as to when the incrementing of **i** takes place. The second loop works in exactly the same way to convert **string2** to upper case

The function **strlen()** is used to find the length of **string2**, and the value is stored in the variable **str2_len**:

```
    str2_len = strlen(string2);    /* Get length of string2 */
```

Then the index **i** is reset to zero again for use in the final **while** loop.

```
    i=0;                                /* set counter to 0      */
```

The following statements count the occurrences of **string2** in **string1**:

```
    while ((pstr1 = strstr(pstr1, string2)) != NULL)
    {
      i++;                    /* Increment counter          */
```

```
      pstr1 += str2_len;  /* increment by string2 length  */
}
```

The search process may be a little confusing for you. If so, the mists will surely clear when you get to the next chapter. The function **strstr()** is used to search the first string for occurrences of the second. We've set the pointer variable **pstr1** to point to the beginning of **string1** at the start of the program. We then use this as a way to refer to the string to be searched (**string1**). The **while** loop will continue searching the first string for as long as **pstr1** is not equal to **NULL**; in other words, for as long as **string2** can be found in **pstr1**. Every time the second string is found in the first, the counter **i** is incremented. At the same time, **pstr1** is set to the position following the last occurrence of **string2** that was found, using the statement:

```
    pstr1 += str2_len;  /* increment by string2 length  */
```

After executing the loop condition first time through the loop, **pstr1** will point to the beginning of the first occurrence of **string2** in the array **string1**. Since **str2_len** contains the length of **string2**, this statement will move **pstr1** along **string1** by the length of **string2**. In other words it will move **pstr1** to point to the end of the first **"had"** in **string1** (assuming that **string2** holds the same data that was entered in the sample output above). So when the loop is re-entered, **strstr()** will re-start its search after the first **"had"** and start searching the remainder of the string for the next occurrence of **string2**. The loop continues until **string2** isn't found anywhere in the remainder of **string1**.

The program finally displays how many times the second string was found in the first:

```
    printf("\nThe second string was found %d times in the first.", i );
```

This whole process is illustrated in the figure below, where it is arbitrarily assumed that **string1** is stored starting at location 1000 in memory.

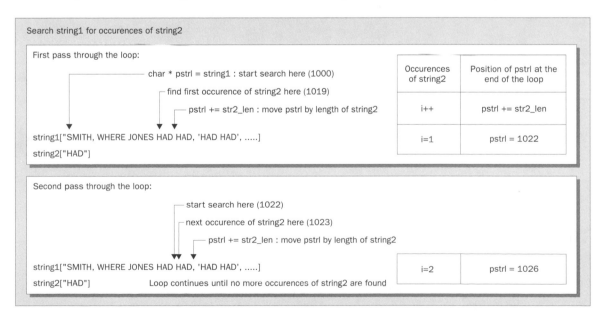

There is just one remaining statement that needs to be addressed, in this program, and it occurs near the top of the program:

```
char *pstr1 = string1;  /* Pointer to string1          */
```

This is the declaration for the pointer **pstr1**, which is a pointer to **char** type variables. The declaration ensures that **pstr1** is initialized with the *address* of the array **string1**. Don't worry about the details of this - we'll cover it all in the next chapter, which is all about pointers.

In the analysis above, you've seen how **pstr1** is used to move the point from where you start searching the string each time. If we didn't do this, then **strstr()** would always search from the start of the string, would always find the first, and only the first occurrence, and would repeat this process indefinitely. So, by increasing the value of **pstr1** each time we find an occurrence, we're able to search for all the instances of **string2** in **string1**.

Therefore, the first time through the loop, the string we are searching is:

```
"Smith, where Jones had had 'had had', had had 'had'. 'Had had' had had
the examiner's approval."
```

While the second time it is:

```
" had 'had had', had had 'had'. 'Had had' had had the examiner's
approval."
```

And so on, until we arrive at the string:

```
" the examiner's approval."
```

At this point, the contents of **string2** aren't found and the search process stops.

Designing a Program

We've almost come to the end of this chapter. It just remains for us to go through a larger program to use some of what we've learnt here.

The Problem

The problem we're going to solve is to write a program which will lock your computer until someone types in a password. You can use this code as a model when you want to prevent unauthorized access to other programs that you write.

The Analysis

We're not going to store the password as a normal string, as that would make it possible for someone to find out the password by looking at the program. We'll store the password internally in an encrypted form, so that even if you see the encrypted password, you won't be able to determine the original password entry too easily. Therefore, we'll write this program in two distinct parts. The first part will generate an encrypted password - this is the password entry process. The second part will prompt for a password entry to gain access to a program, and then encrypt the entry and compare it with the original encrypted version. If they are equal then access is granted.

Notice that we're actually writing two programs here. Although their code will be quite similar, the first program will run separately from the second. The steps are as follows:

1 Implement an encryption scheme, and use this to encrypt the password to be used in the program. This is our first program.

2 Use the above program as a base for our second program, which will offer the actual password protection facility.

This second program works by:

> Getting the password from the user

> Encrypting it

> Comparing it to the previously encrypted password, obtained from the first program

The Solution

1 The trickiest part of this program is implementing the encryption scheme. We'll provide for a password of up to twenty characters; but of course, a shorter password can be entered. We'll have a default string of 20 different characters, and the password entered will replace the default string, starting with the first default character. In this way, we ensure that we don't end up with a sequence of identical characters at the end - unless, of course, the user enters them. When we actually encrypt the password, we'll apply the encryption scheme to all twenty characters, regardless of how many characters were entered. This way, no one will know the true length of the original password.

Our encryption scheme will generate a final encrypted string containing only alphabetic characters. We'll encrypt the password by generating an encrypted character from each character in the original. The process will involve using one encrypted character in the process of encrypting the next. So we'll take each character in turn, encrypt it, and then use the result to encrypt the next character.

So how will we encrypt the first character? What we can do here is take the sum of the ASCII codes of all the characters, and calculate the remainder after dividing by 52. We'll use this value to generate a letter. For values between 0 and 25, we shall select the corresponding capital letter between 'A' and 'Z'. For values from 26 to 51, we'll select from 'a' to 'z'.

How will we encrypt the second and subsequent characters in the password? For that, we'll take the ASCII code for the previous encrypted character, multiply it by the ASCII code for the current character to be encrypted, and then take the remainder after dividing by 52. This produces a value from 0 to 51, which we'll use as we did for the first character in the password to select from 'A' to 'Z' and 'a' to 'z'. The following diagram should help to explain this more clearly.

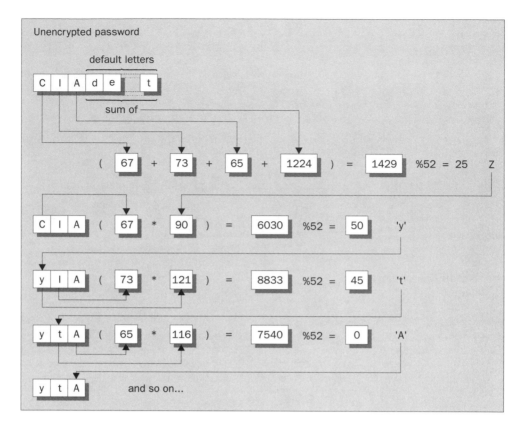

Let's put this into action. First, we need to set up the variables that our program is going to use, and get the password from the user:

```c
/* Example 6.10 Encrypting a password */
#include <stdio.h>

void main()
{
  /* Default password             */
  char unencrypted[] = "abcdefghijklmnopqrst";

  /* Stores encrypted password  */
  char encrypted[21];

  /* Input buffer               */
  char password[80];

  printf("\nEnter your password of up to 20"
                        " characters(no spaces):\n");

  /* Read the password          */
  scanf("%s", password);

  /* Plus the rest of the code  */
}
```

We've set the default, unencrypted password to **"abcdefghijklmnopqrst"** so that all the default characters that follow the entered password will be different. We'll store the encrypted password in the array named **encrypted**. We read the user's password into the array named **password**. This has a dimension of 80 to allow for overzealousness from the user. It's easy to enter 21 instead of 20 characters, but we shall only use the first 20 in any event.

Now, we need to copy **password** into **unencrypted**, missing off the terminating **'\0'** at the end of the string stored in **password**:

```
/* Example 6.10 Encrypting a password */
#include <stdio.h>

void main()
{
   /* Default password            */
   char unencrypted[] = "abcdefghijklmnopqrst";

   /* Stores encrypted password  */
   char encrypted[21];

   /* Input buffer               */
   char password[80];

   /* Loop counter               */
   int i = 0;

   printf("\nEnter your password of up to 20"
                        " characters(no spaces):\n");

   /* Read the password          */
   scanf("%s", password);

   /* Copy the input to the unencrypted array */
    for(i = 0; i < 20 && password[i] != '\0'; i++)
      unencrypted[i] = password[i];

   /* Plus the rest of the code  */
}
```

By putting the extra expression **i<20** in the loop condition expression, we ensure that we don't copy more than 20 characters from the input. Reaching **'\0'** or copying 20 characters will end the loop.

Now let's add the code to encrypt the password and display it:

```
/* Example 6.10 Encrypting a password */
#include <stdio.h>

void main()
{
   /* Default password             */
   char unencrypted[] = "abcdefghijklmnopqrst";
```

223

```
/* Stores encrypted password   */
char encrypted[21];

/* Input buffer              */
char password[80];

/* Loop counter              */
int i = 0;

/* Stores encrypted character */
long code = 0;

printf("\nEnter your password of up to 20"
                       " characters(no spaces):\n");

/* Read the password         */
scanf("%s", password);

/* Copy the input to the unencrypted array */
 for(i = 0; i < 20 && password[i] != '\0'; i++)
    unencrypted[i] = password[i];

/* Set up multiplier for first character encryption */
code = 0;
/* Sum all the characters     */
for (i = 0; i < 20; code += unencrypted[i++]);

/* Get the remainder */
code %=  52;

/* select a letter    */
code += code < 26 ? 'A' : ('a' - 26);

/* Encrypt the password string */
for (i = 0; i < 20; i++)
{
  /* multiply character to encrypt */
  code *= unencrypted[i];

  /* Get remainder */
  code %= 52;

  /* Select character */
  code += (code < 26) ? 'A' : ('a' - 26);

  /* Store character  */
  encrypted[i] = (char)code;
}

printf("\nEncrypted password is: %s", encrypted);
}
```

There are two steps in the encryption process. The first is to set up the multiplier that will encrypt the first character in the password. We get the sum of all the characters and store it in the variable **code**, and then get the remainder after dividing by 52. We use this value to select a letter. This uses a conditional operator. To see how this works, let's consider a couple of examples. Suppose the remainder in **code** is 3. The condition **code<26** will be true, so we'll add **'A'** to the current value of code, which will produce **'D'**. Values of code from 0 to 25 will produce **'A'** to **'Z'**; but suppose the remainder in code was 26. The condition **code<26** will be false, so we add **'a'-26** to **code**, which will result in **'a'**. Therefore, values 26 to 51 will produce **'a'** to **'z'**, which is what we want!

All 20 characters in the string are encrypted in the **for** loop. The initial value of **code** that we produced will be applied to the first character and, for subsequent characters, the encrypted version of the previous character (which is left in **code**) will be used. The process for selecting the encrypted letter, after multiplying **code** by the character to be encrypted, is the same as for the initial value of **code**.

Now that our first program is working, here's some sample output:

```
Enter your password of up to 20 characters(no spaces):
wroxpress

Encrypted password is: ZQvQYGvyfwtwXIrcHsRw
```

2 Now we have our encrypted version, we can change this code into the second program, which actually checks for a password. It will loop through, entering and checking the password until the encrypted password matches the saved version. For this example, we'll write in the encrypted password in the output sample given above (ZQvQYGvyfwtwXIrcHsRw) which is an encrypted password for wroxpress. It's important that when you type in your own encrypted word you get it right - otherwise, you'll never get control of your computer back!!

Actually, this isn't entirely true, since we have no way of disabling the *Break* key. This means that anyone can break your program using *Break* and gain access to the computer. Another flaw you need to be aware of is that the password attempt appears on the screen as you type, and remains there. There are ways around both of these problems, but they are a little beyond the scope of this book.

```
/* Example 6.11 Checking a password */
#include <stdio.h>
#include <string.h>

void main()
{
    /* Enter your own encrypted password here. */

    /* If you want to use this one the password is wroxpress */
    char encrypted[] = "ZQvQYGvyfwtwXIrcHsRw";  /* encoded password */

    char password[80];              /* Input buffer             */
    /* Default password          */
    char unencrypted[] = "abcdefghijklmnopqrst";
```

```c
    int i = 0;         /* Loop counter                    */
    long code = 0;     /* Stores encrypted character */

    for( ;; )
    {
      /* Initialize unencrypted       */
      strcpy(unencrypted, "abcdefghijklmnopqrst");

      printf("\nEnter your password of up to 20"
                                     " characters(no spaces):\n");
      scanf("%s", password);    /* Read the password */

      /* Copy the input to the unencrypted array */
      for(i = 0; i < 20 && password[i] != '\0'; i++)
        unencrypted[i] = password[i];

      /* Set up multiplier for first character encryption */
      code = 0;

      /* Sum all the characters */
      for (i = 0; i < 20; code += unencrypted[i++]);

      /* Get the remainder */
      code %=  52;

      /* select a letter */
      code += code < 26 ? 'A' : ('a' - 26);

      for (i = 0; i < 20; i++)
      {
        /* multiply character to encrypt */
        code *= unencrypted[i];

        /* Get remainder */
        code %= 52;
        code += (code < 26) ? 'A' : ('a' - 26);/* Select character */
        password[i] = (char)code;                    /* Store character  */
      }
      password[i] = '\0';
      if(strcmp(password, encrypted) != 0)
        printf("\nIncorrect password.\n");
      else
      {
        printf("\nPassword OK.\n");
        break;
      }
    }
}
```

The code here implements essentially the same mechanism as in the program to encrypt the password. The only difference is that the encryption of the password that's entered is done in an indefinite **for** loop. The loop repeats for as long as the password is entered incorrectly. When the correct password is entered, a message is displayed and the loop is exited using a **break** statement.

Sample output from this second program is:

```
Enter your password of up to 20 characters(no spaces):
wrexpross

Incorrect password.

Enter your password of up to 20 characters(no spaces):
wruxpriss

Incorrect password.

Enter your password of up to 20 characters(no spaces):
wroxpress

Password OK.
```

Summary

In this chapter, we've applied the techniques acquired in earlier chapters to the general problem of dealing with character strings. Strings present a different and perhaps more difficult set of problems than the numeric data types.

I've introduced you to two new libraries, **string.h** and **ctype.h**, which add considerable functionality when you're working with strings and individual characters, respectively. The functions in these libraries make programming string handling a lot easier by providing virtually all the basic functions that you're likely to need.

Most of this chapter has been about handling strings using arrays, but several times I've also mentioned pointers. These will provide you with even more flexibility in dealing with strings, and many other things besides - as you'll discover in the next chapter.

Pointers

In the last chapter, we had a glimpse of pointers, and just a small hint at what they can be used for. Here, we'll delve a lot deeper into the subject of pointers and see just what we can do with them.

We'll cover a lot of new concepts here, so you may need to repeat some things a few times. This is a long chapter, so spend some time on it; experiment with the examples. Remember that the basic ideas are very simple, but they can be applied to solving complicated problems. By the end of this chapter, you'll be equipped with an essential element for effective C programming.

In this chapter you'll learn:

- What a pointer is and how it is used
- What the relationship between pointers and arrays is
- How to use pointers with strings
- How you can declare and use arrays of pointers
- How to write an improved calculator program

A First Look at Pointers

We now come to one of the most extraordinarily powerful tools in the C language. It is also, potentially, the most confusing - so it's important you get the ideas straight in your mind at the outset, and maintain a clear idea of what's happening as we dig deeper.

Back in Chapters 2 and 5 we talked about memory. We talked about how your computer allocates an area of memory when you declare a variable. You refer to this area in memory using the variable name in your program, but once your program is compiled and running, your computer references it by the address of the memory location. This is the number that the computer uses to refer to the 'box' in which the value of the variable is stored.

Look at the following statement:

```
int number = 5L;
```

Here, we've allocated an area of memory for an integer and called it **number**. We've stored the value 5 in this area. The computer references the area using an address. The specific address where this data will be stored depends on your computer, and what operating system and compiler you're using. Even though the variable name is fixed in your source program, the address is likely to be different on different systems.

In C, there's a type of variable that's designed to hold an address. These variables are called **pointers**, and the address held in a pointer is usually that of another variable. This is illustrated in the following figure. We have a pointer **P** which contains the address of another variable, called **number**, which is an integer variable containing the value 5.

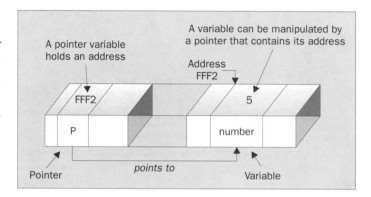

The first important thing to appreciate is that it's not enough to know that a particular variable, such as **P**, is a pointer. You, and more importantly, the compiler, must know the type of variable to which it points. Without this information it's virtually impossible to know how to handle the contents of the memory to which it points. A pointer to a value of type **char** is pointing to a value occupying one byte, whereas a pointer to a value of type **long** is usually pointing to a value occupying four bytes. This means that every pointer will be associated with a specific variable type, and can only be used to point to variables of that type. So pointers of type pointer to **int** can only point to **int** variables, **float** pointers to **float** variables, and so on.

Declaring Pointers

So much for the theory. Let's look at a small program to highlight the capabilities of this special kind of variable. When you've written a few programs like the one below, you should at least feel comfortable with what's actually going on when you use a pointer.

Try It Out - Declaring Pointers

In this example, we're simply going to declare a variable and a pointer. We'll then see how we can output their addresses and the values they contain:

```
/* Example 7.1 A simple program using pointers */

#include <stdio.h>

void main()
{
    int number = 0;        /* An variable of type int initialized to 0 */
    int *pointer = NULL;   /* A pointer that can point to type int     */
```

```
   number = 10;
   printf("\nnumber's address: %p", &number);   /* Output the address */
   printf("\nnumber's value: %d\n\n", number);   /* Output the value   */

   pointer = &number;      /* Store the address of number in pointer   */
   printf("pointer's address: %p", &pointer);   /* Output the address */

   /* Output the value (an address) */
   printf("\npointer's value: %p", pointer);

   printf("\nvalue pointed to: %d", *pointer); /* Value at the address */
}
```

The output from the program will look something like this. Remember, the actual address is likely to be different on your machine.

```
number's address: 0064FDF0
number's value: 10

pointer's address: 0064FDF4
pointer's value: 0064FDF0
value pointed to: 10
```

How It Works

Let's see what's happening here. We first declare a variable and a pointer:

```
   int number = 0;      /* An variable of type int initialized to 0 */
   int *pointer = NULL; /* A pointer that can point to type int      */
```

The variable called **number** is of type **int**, and the pointer called **pointer** is of type 'pointer to **int**'. Pointers need to be declared just like any other variable. To declare the pointer called **pointer** we put an asterisk (*****) in front of the variable name in the declaration. The asterisk defines **pointer** as a pointer, and the type, **int**, fixes it as a pointer to integer variables. The initial value, **NULL**, is the equivalent of zero for a pointer - it doesn't point to anything. There is nothing special about the declaration of a pointer. We can declare regular variables and pointers in the same statement. For example, the statement:

```
   double value, *pVal, fnum;
```

declares two double precision floating point variables, **value** and **fnum**, and a variable, **pVal**, of type 'pointer to **double**'.

After the declarations, we store the value 10 in the variable called **number**, and then output its address and its value with these statements:

```
   number = 10;
   printf("\nnumber's address: %p", &number);   /* Output the address */
   printf("\nnumber's value: %d\n\n", number);   /* Output the value   */
```

To output the address of the variable called **number**, we've used the output format specifier **%p**. This outputs the value, as a memory address, in hexadecimal form.

So how do we get a pointer to point to a variable? For that, we need the help of the **address of** operator, **&**. In this example, we wrote:

```
pointer = &number;      /* Store the address of number in pointer   */
```

This statement obtains the address of the variable **number** and stores that address in **pointer**. Remember, the only kind of value that you should store in **pointer** is an address.

Next, we have three **printf()** statements that output, respectively, the address of **pointer** (which is the memory location that **pointer** occupies), the value stored in **pointer** (which is the address of **number**), and the value stored at the address that **pointer** contains (which is the value stored in **number**):

```
    printf("pointer's address: %p", &pointer);    /* Output the address */

    /* Output the value (an address) */
    printf("\npointer's value: %p", pointer);

    printf("\nvalue pointed to: %d", *pointer);  /* Value at the address*/
```

Just to make sure we are clear about this, let's go through this line by line.

```
    printf("pointer's address: %p", &pointer);
```

Here, we are printing the address of the pointer. Remember, the pointer itself has an address, just like any other variable. We use **%p** as the conversion specifier to display an address, and we use the **&** (address of) operator to reference the address that the variable occupies.

```
    printf("\npointer's value: %p", pointer);
```

Now we get the actual value stored in **pointer**, which is the address of **number**. This is an address, so we use **%p** to display it; we use the variable name, **pointer**, to access the actual value.

```
    printf("\nvalue pointed to: %d", *pointer);
```

Here, we see something quite new to us. We're now using the pointer to access the actual value stored in **number**. The effect of the ***** operator is to access the data contained in the address stored at **pointer**. We use **%d** because we know it is an integer value. The variable **pointer** stores the address of **number**, so we can use that address to access the value stored in **number**. The ***** operator, here, is called the **indirection operator**, or sometimes the **dereferencing operator**.

The addresses shown will be different on different computers, and sometimes different at different times on the same computer. The addresses of **number** and **pointer** are where in the computer the variables are stored. Their values are what is actually stored at those addresses. For the variable called **number**, it is an actual integer value (**10**), but for the variable called **pointer**, it is the address of **number**. Using ***pointer** actually gives us access to the value of **number**. We are accessing the value of the variable, **number**, indirectly.

You may have noticed that our indirection operator, *****, is also the symbol, in C, for multiplication. Fortunately, there's no risk of confusion for the compiler. Depending on where the asterisk appears, the compiler will understand whether it should interpret it as an indirection operator or as a multiplication sign.

The figure illustrates using a pointer:

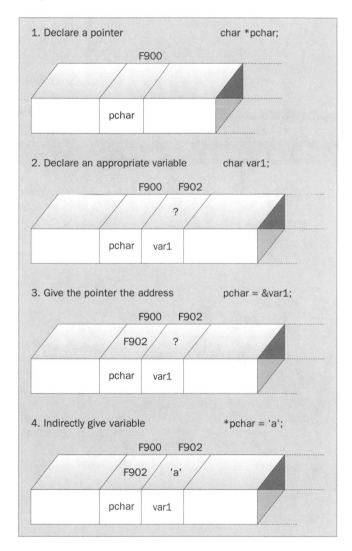

1. Declare a pointer   char *pchar;

2. Declare an appropriate variable   char var1;

3. Give the pointer the address   pchar = &var1;

4. Indirectly give variable   *pchar = 'a';

Using Pointers

Well, now we have **pointer** pointing at **number**, what can we do with it? You're probably wondering what use it is to be able to point to something. If we can access the contents of **number** through the pointer **pointer**; then the statement:

```
*pointer += 25;
```

increments the value of the variable called **number** by 25. The ***** indicates we're accessing the contents of whatever the variable called **pointer** is pointing to; in this case, the contents of the variable called **number**.

pointer can point to any variable of type **int**. This means we can change the variable that **pointer** points to by a statement such as this:

```
pointer = &AnotherNumber;
```

The same statement that we used previously:

```
*pointer += 25;
```

is now operating with the new variable, **AnotherNumber**. This means that a pointer can assume the guise of any variable of the same type; so we can use one pointer variable to change the values of many other variables, as long as they are of the same type as the pointer.

Try It Out - Using Pointers

Let's exercise this newfound facility in an example. We'll use pointers to increase values stored in variables.

```
/* Example 7.2   What's the pointer        */
#include <stdio.h>
void main()
{
   long num1 = 0;
   long num2 = 0;
   long *pnum = NULL;

   pnum = &num1;      /* Get address of num1        */
   *pnum = 2;         /* Set num1 to 2              */
   ++num2;            /* Increment num2             */
   num2 += *pnum;     /* Add num1 to num2           */

   pnum = &num2;      /* Get address of num2        */
   ++*pnum;           /* Increment num2 indirectly */

   printf ("\nnum1 = %ld   num2 = %ld   *pnum = %ld   *pnum + num2 = %ld",
                                  num1, num2, *pnum, *pnum + num2);
}
```

When you run this program, you should get the output:

```
num1 = 2   num2 = 4   *pnum = 4   *pnum + num2 = 8
```

How It Works

The comments should make the program easy to follow up to the **printf()**. First, in the body of **main()**, we have these declarations:

```
long num1 = 0;
long num2 = 0;
long *pnum = NULL;
```

This ensures that we set out with initial values for the two variables, **num1** and **num2,** at zero. It also declares an integer pointer, **pnum**, which is initialized with **NULL**.

> *It's important to initialize your pointers when you declare them. Using a pointer that isn't initialized to store an item of data is dangerous - who knows what you might overwrite?*

The next statement is an assignment:

```
    pnum = &num1;    /* Get address of num1        */
```

The pointer **pnum** is set to point to **num1** here, since we take the address of **num1** using the **address of** operator, and store it in **pnum**.

The next two statements are:

```
    *pnum = 2;       /* Set num1 to 2              */
    ++num2;          /* Increment num2             */
```

The first statement exploits our newfound power of the pointer, and we set **num1** to 2 indirectly. Then the variable **num2** gets incremented by 1 in the normal way, using the increment operator.

The statement:

```
    num2 += *pnum;   /* Add num1 to num2           */
```

adds the contents of the variable pointed to by **pnum**, to **num2**. Since **pnum** still points to **num1**, **num2** is being increased by the value of **num1**.

The next two statements are:

```
    pnum = &num2;    /* Get address of num2        */
    ++*pnum;         /* Increment num2 indirectly */
```

First, the pointer is reassigned to point to **num2**. The variable **num2** is then incremented indirectly through the pointer. You can see that the expression **++*pnum** increments the value pointed to by **pnum** without any problem. However, if we wanted to use the postfix form, we would have to write **(*pnum)++.** The parentheses are essential - assuming that we want to increment the value rather than the address. If we omit them, the increment would apply to the address contained in **pnum**. This is because the operators **++** and unary ***** (and also unary **&** for that matter) share the same precedence level and are evaluated right to left. The compiler would apply the **++** to **pnum** first, incrementing the address, and only then dereference it to get the value. This is a common source of error when incrementing values through pointers, so it's probably a good idea to use parentheses in any event.

Finally, we have a **printf()** statement:

```
    printf ("\nnum1 = %ld   num2 = %ld   *pnum = %ld   *pnum + num2 = %ld",
                                    num1, num2, *pnum, *pnum + num2);
```

This displays the values of **num1**, **num2**, **num2** through **pnum** and, lastly, **num2** in the guise of **pnum**, with the value of **num2** added.

Go through the program again slowly. Pointers can get confusing when you're just starting. You can work with addresses or values, pointers or variables - and sometimes it's hard to work out what exactly is going on. The best thing to do is keep writing short programs that use the things I've described, getting values using pointers, changing values, printing addresses, and so on. This is the only way to really get confident about using pointers.

I've mentioned the importance of operator precedence again in this discussion. We've accumulated a few more operators since the table back in Chapter 3, so let's put another table together with a more complete set of operators:

Operators	Associativity
( ) [] postfix **++** postfix **--** **->**	left to right
! **~** **sizeof** unary**+** unary**-** prefix **++** prefix **- -** unary***** (indirection operator) **&** (address of)	right to left
Type casts such as **(int)** and **(double)**	right to left
* **/** **%**	left to right
binary **+** binary **-**	left to right
<< >>	left to right
< **<=** **>** **>=**	left to right
== **!=**	left to right
&	left to right
^	left to right
|	left to right
&&	left to right
||	left to right
?: (conditional operator)	left to right
= **op=** (e.g. **+=** **-=** etc.)	right to left

This now includes all the operators we've seen. There's one operator that you haven't seen, **->**. You'll meet this operator in Chapter 11.

Let's come back to using pointers, and see how they work with input from the keyboard.

Try It Out - Using a Pointer with scanf()

Until now, when we've used **scanf()** to input values, we've used the **&** operator to obtain the address to be transferred to the function. When we have a pointer that already contains an address, we simply need to use the pointer name as a parameter. We can see this in the following example:

```
/* Example 7.3  Pointer argument to scanf */
#include <stdio.h>
void main()
{
   int value = 0;
   int *pvalue = NULL;

   pvalue = &value;                  /* Set pointer to refer to value   */

   printf ("Input an integer: ");
   scanf(" %d", pvalue);          /* Read into value via the pointer */

   printf("\nYou entered %d", value);   /* Output the value entered */
}
```

This program will just echo what you enter. How unimaginative can you get? Typical output could be something like this:

```
Input an integer: 10
You entered 10
```

How It Works

Everything should be pretty clear up to the **scanf()** statement:

```
   scanf(" %d", pvalue);
```

We normally store the value entered by the user at the address of the variable. Is this case, we could have used **&value**. But here, the pointer **pvalue** is used to hand over the address of **value** to **scanf()**. We've already stored the address of **value** in **pvalue** with this assignment:

```
   pvalue = &value;                  /* Set pointer to refer to value   */
```

pvalue and **&value** are the same, so we can use either!

We then just display **value**:

```
   printf("\nYou entered %d", value);
```

Although this is a rather trivial example, it illustrates how pointers and variables can work together. There's one thing I haven't explained fully, and that's the use of **NULL**; so let's look at this in a little more detail.

The Null Constant

The pointer declaration in the last example is:

```
   int *pvalue = NULL;
```

Here, we initialized **pvalue** with the value **NULL**. As I said earlier, **NULL** is a special constant in C, and it is the pointer equivalent to zero with ordinary numbers. The definition of **NULL** is contained in **stdio.h**, so if you use it, you must ensure that you include this header file.

We can use **NULL** as the value for a pointer that doesn't point to anything, since its value is guaranteed not to be the same as any real address value that might occur.

When you assign **NULL** to a pointer, it's the equivalent of setting it to 0. This provides some slight economy in the amount of keying, because if you want to test whether the pointer **pvalue** is **NULL** or not, you can write:

```
if(!pvalue)
{
    ...
}
```

rather than the statement:

```
if(pvalue == NULL)
{
    ...
}
```

To be on the safe side, I prefer to test pointer values against **NULL**, as this helps to make it clear that it's a pointer being checked - which makes the program much easier to follow.

> *It is possible to assign specific values to pointers, using numeric constants that are usually specified in hexadecimal notation. This means that you can access memory locations anywhere in the computer that may hold values of interest.*
>
> *This becomes very hazardous once you introduce the possibility of storing values in such specifically defined addresses. Unless you're absolutely sure what you're doing, the practice is best avoided.*

Naming Pointers

We've already started to write some quite large programs. As you can imagine, when your programs get even bigger, it's going to get even harder to remember which variables are normal variables and which are pointers. Therefore, it's quite a good idea to use names beginning with **p** for use as pointer names. If you follow this religiously, you'll never be in any doubt about which variables are pointers.

Arrays and Pointers

You'll need a clear head for this bit. Let's recap for a moment, and recall what an array is and what a pointer is:

▶ An array is a collection of objects of the same type that we can refer to using a single name. For example, an array called **scores[50]** could contain all our basketball scores for a 50-game season. We use a different index value to refer to each element in the array. **scores[0]** is our first score and **scores[49]** is our last. If we had 10 games each month, we could use a multi-dimensional array, **scores[12][10]**. If we start play in January, the third game in June would be referenced by **scores[5][2]**.

> A pointer is a variable that has as its value the address of another variable or constant of a given type. We can use a pointer to access different variables at different times, as long as they are all of the same type.

Actually, arrays and pointers are very closely tied together; and they can sometimes be used interchangeably. Let's consider strings. A string is just an array of type **char**. If we wanted to input a single character with **scanf()**, we could use:

```
char single;
scanf("%c", &single);
```

Here, we need the **address of** operator for **scanf()** to work. However, if we're reading in a string:

```
char multiple[10];
scanf("%s", multiple);
```

then we don't use the **&**. We're using the array name just like a pointer. If we use the array name in this way without an index value, then it refers to the address of the first element in the array.

However, there's an important difference: arrays are *not* pointers. You can change the address contained in a pointer, but you cannot change the address referenced by an array name.

Arrays and Pointers in Practice

Let's go through several examples to really see how arrays and pointers work together. The following examples all link together as a progression. With practical examples of how arrays and pointers can work together, you should find it fairly easy to get a grasp of the main ideas behind pointers and their relationship to arrays.

Try It Out - Arrays and Pointers

Just to further illustrate that an array name by itself refers to an address, try running the following program on your own computer:

```
/* Example 7.4  Arrays and pointers - A simple program*/
#include <stdio.h>

void main()
{
   char multiple[] = "I am a string";

   printf("\nUsing address of operator: %p", &multiple[0]);
   printf("\n     Without the operator: %p\n", multiple);
}
```

On my computer, the output is:

```
Using address of operator: 0064FDE8
    Without the operator: 0064FDE8
```

How It Works

We can conclude, from the output of this program, that **&multiple[0] = multiple**.

So let's take this a bit further. If **multiple** refers to the same thing as **&multiple[0]**, what does **multiple + 1** equal? Let's try the following example.

Try It Out - Arrays and Pointers Taken Further

```
/* Example 7.5a Arrays and pointers taken further */
#include <stdio.h>

void main()
{
   char multiple[] = "another string";

   printf("\n          value of second element: %c\n", multiple[1]);
   printf("value of multiple after adding 1: %c\n", *(multiple + 1));
}
```

The output is:

```
          value of second element: n
value of multiple after adding 1: n
```

How It Works

You can see that **multiple[1]** is the same as ***(multiple + 1)**. We can further confirm this if we display the addresses rather than the values:

```
/* Example 7.5b Arrays and pointers taken further */

#include <stdio.h>

void main()
{
   char multiple[] = "another string";

   printf("\n          address of second element: %p\n", &multiple[1]);
   printf("address of multiple after adding 1: %p\n", multiple + 1);
}
```

We would get:

```
          address of second element:    0064FDE9
address of multiple after adding 1:    0064FDE9
```

Nothing unusual there, nor is there anything unusual if we display the addresses of the first, second and third elements of the array:

```
/* Example 7.5c Arrays and pointers taken further */
#include <stdio.h>

void main()
{
    char multiple[] = "another string";

    printf(" first element: %p\n", multiple);
    printf("second element: %p\n", multiple + 1);
    printf(" third element: %p", multiple + 2);
}
```

```
  first element:  0064FDE8
 second element:  0064FDE9
  third element:  0064FDEA
```

Try It Out - Different Types of Arrays

Great, but we already knew that the computer could add numbers together without much problem. So let's change to a different type of array, and see what happens:

```
/* Example 7.6 Different types of arrays */

#include <stdio.h>

void main()
{
    long multiple[] = {1, 2, 3};

    printf(" first element address: %p value: %d\n",
                                        multiple, *multiple);
    printf("second element address: %p value: %d\n", multiple + 1,
                                        *(multiple + 1));
    printf(" third element address: %p value: %d", multiple + 2,
                                        *(multiple + 2));
}
```

If we compile and run this program, we get an entirely different story:

```
  first element address:  0064FDEC value: 1
 second element address:  0064FDF0 value: 2
  third element address:  0064FDF4 value: 3
```

How It Works

Look at the output: with this example, **multiple (64FDEC) + 1 = 64FDF0**! You can see that **64FDF0** is 4 greater than **64FDEC** although we only added **1**. This isn't a mistake. C realizes that when you add 1 to an address value, what you actually want to do is access the next variable of that type. This is why, when you declare a pointer, you have to specify the *type* of variable that's to be pointed to. Remember that **char** data is stored in one byte, and that variables declared as **long** typically occupy 4 bytes. As you can see, on my computer, variables declared as **long** are indeed 4 bytes.

> *Remember that although using an array name in this way means it behaves like a pointer, an array is not a pointer. An array has a fixed address.*

Multi-Dimensional Arrays

So far, we've looked at one-dimensional arrays; but is it the same story with multidimensional arrays? Well, to some extent it is. However, the difference between pointers and array names starts to become more apparent. Let's consider the array we used for the tic-tac-toe program at the end of Chapter 5. We declared the array as:

```
char board[3][3] = {
                        {'1','2','3'},
                        {'4','5','6'},
                        {'7','8','9'}
                    };
```

We'll use this array for the examples in this section - to explore multi-dimensional arrays in relation to pointers.

Try It Out - Using Two-Dimensional Arrays

We look first at some of the addresses related to our array, **board**, with this example:

```
/* Example 7.7 Two-Dimensional arrays */
#include <stdio.h>

void main()
{
   char board[3][3] = {
                           {'1','2','3'},
                           {'4','5','6'},
                           {'7','8','9'}
                       };

   printf("address of board        : %p\n", board);
   printf("address of board[0][0]  : %p\n", &board[0][0]);
   printf("but what is in board[0] : %p\n", board[0]);
}
```

The output might come as a bit of a surprise to you:

```
address of board        : 0064FDEC
address of board[0][0]  : 0064FDEC
but what is in board[0] : 0064FDEC
```

How It Works

As you can see, all three output values are the same; so what can we deduce from this? The answer is quite simple. When you declare a one-dimensional array, placing **[number1]** after the array name tells the compiler that it is an array of size **number1**. So placing another number, **[number2]**, after **[number1]**, actually tells the compiler to make an array of size **number1**, where each element is an array of size **number2**. When we declare a two-dimensional array, we are creating an array of sub-arrays. So, when accessing this two-dimensional array, if we use the array name with a single index value, **board[0]** for example, we're actually referencing the address of one of the sub-arrays. Using the two-dimensional array name by itself references the address of the beginning of the whole array of arrays, which is also the address of the beginning of the first sub-array!

> *To summarize this:*
>
> *board*
> *board[0]*
> *&board[0][0]*
>
> *all have the same value.*

This also means that **board[1]** actually contains the address of **board[1][0]**. This should be reasonably easy to understand. The problems start when we use pointer notation to get to the values within the array. We still have to use the indirection operator, but we must be careful. If we change the example above to display the value of the first element, you'll see why:

```
/* Example 7.7 Two-Dimensional arrays */

#include <stdio.h>

void main()
{
    char board[3][3] = {
                          {'1','2','3'},
                          {'4','5','6'},
                          {'7','8','9'}
                        };

    printf("value of board[0][0] : %c\n", board[0][0]);
    printf("value of board[0]    : %c\n", *board[0]);
    printf("value of board       : %c\n", **board);
}
```

The output for this program is as follows:

```
value of board[0][0] : 1
value of board[0]    : 1
value of board       : 1
```

As you can see, if we use **board** as a means of obtaining the value of the first element, then we need to use two indirection operators to get it: ****board.** We were able to use just one ***** in the previous program because we were dealing with a one-dimensional array. If we only used the one *****, we would get the address of the first element of the array of arrays, which is the address referenced by **board[0]**.

The relationship between our multi-dimensional array and its sub-arrays is shown in the following diagram:

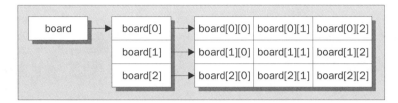

So, with this clearer picture of what's going on in our multi-dimensional array, let's see how we can use **board** to get to all the values in that array. We'll do this in the next example.

Try It Out - Getting All the Values in a Two-Dimensional Array

This example takes our previous example a bit further using a **for** loop:

```
/* Example 7.8  Getting the values in a two-dimensional array */
#include <stdio.h>

void main()
{
   int i = 0;          /* Loop counter */
   char board[3][3] = {
                        {'1','2','3'},
                        {'4','5','6'},
                        {'7','8','9'}
                      };

   /* List all elements of the array */
   for(i = 0; i < 9; i++)
     printf(" board: %c\n", *(*board + i));
}
```

The output from the program is:

```
board: 1
board: 2
board: 3
board: 4
board: 5
```

```
board: 6
board: 7
board: 8
board: 9
```

How It Works

The thing to notice about this program is the way we dereference **board** in the loop:

```
printf(" board: %c\n", *(*board + i));
```

As you can see, we used the expression ***(*board + counter)** to get the value of an array element. It's important that the brackets are included. Leaving them out would have given us the value pointed to by **board** (i.e. the value stored in the location referenced by the address stored in **board**) with the value of **i** added to this value. So if **i** had the value 2, we would simply output the value of the first element of the array plus 2. What we actually want to do, and what our expression does, is to add the value of **i** to the *address* contained in **board**, and then dereference this new address to obtain a value.

To make this clearer, let's see what happens if we omit the parentheses in the example. Try changing the initial values for the array so that the characters go from '9' to '1'. If you leave out the brackets in the expression in the **printf()** call, so that it reads like this:

```
printf(" board: %c\n", **board + i);
```

you should get output that looks something like this:

```
board: 9
board: :
board: ;
board: <
board: =
board: >
board: ?
board: @
board: A
```

This output results because we're adding the value of **i** to the contents of the first element of the array, **board**. The characters you get come from the ASCII table, starting at '9' and continuing to 'A'.

Also, if you used the expression ****(board + counter)**, this too would have given erroneous results. In this case, ****(board + 0)** points to **board[0][0]**, while ****(board + 1)** points to **board[1][0]**; and ****(board + 2)** points to **board[2][0]**. If we use higher increments, we would be accessing memory locations outside the array, because there isn't a fourth element in the array of arrays.

Multi-Dimensional Arrays and Pointers

So now we've used the array name using pointer notation for referencing a two-dimensional array, let's use a variable that we've declared as a pointer. As I've already stated, this is where there's a more noticeable difference. If we declare a pointer and assign the address of the array to it, then we can use that pointer to access the members of the array.

Try It Out - Multi-Dimensional Arrays and Pointers

We can see this in action in the next example:

```c
/* Example 7.9  Multi-dimensional arrays and pointers*/
#include <stdio.h>

void main()
{
   int i = 0;                    /* Loop counter      */
   char board[3][3] = {
                        {'1','2','3'},
                        {'4','5','6'},
                        {'7','8','9'}
                      };

   char *pointer = *board;    /* A pointer to char */

   for(i = 0; i < 9; i++)
     printf(" board: %c\n", *(pointer + i));
}
```

Here, we get the same output as before:

```
board: 1
board: 2
board: 3
board: 4
board: 5
board: 6
board: 7
board: 8
board: 9
```

How It Works

Here, we've initialized **pointer** to the address of first element of the array, and then just used normal pointer arithmetic to move through the array.

```c
   char *pointer = *board;    /* A pointer to char */

   for(i = 0; i < 9; i++)
     printf(" board: %c\n", *(pointer + i));
```

Note how we dereference **board** to obtain the address we want (with ***board**), because **board**, by itself, is the address of the array **board[0]**, not the address of an element. We could have initialized **pointer** by using:

```c
   char *pointer = &board[0][0];
```

This amounts to the same thing. You might think we could initialize **pointer** using the statement:

```
        pointer = board;
```

This is wrong. You should get a compiler warning if you do this. Strictly speaking, this isn't legal, because **pointer** and **board** have different levels of indirection. That's a great jargon phrase; what it means is that **pointer** refers to an address that contains a value of type **char**, whereas **board** refers to an address *that refers to an address* containing a value of type **char**. There's an extra level with **board** compared to **pointer**. Consequently, **pointer** needs one ***** to get to the value, and **board** needs two. Most compilers will allow you to get away with this, just giving a warning about what you've done. However, it's very bad practice, so you shouldn't do it!

Accessing Array Elements

Now we know that, for a two-dimensional array, we have several ways of accessing the elements in that array, let's list these ways of accessing our **board** array.

Board	0	1	2
0	board[0][0]	board[0][1]	board[0][2]
	*board[0]	*(board[0]+1)	*(board[0]+2)
	**board	*(*board+1)	*(*board+2)
1	board[1][0]	board[1][1]	board[1][2]
	*(board[0]+3)	*(board[0]+4)	*(board[0]+5)
	*board[1]	*(board[1]+1)	*(board[1]+2)
	*(*board+3)	*(*board+4)	*(*board+5)
2	board[2][0]	board[2][1]	board[2][2]
	*(board[0]+6)	*(board[0]+7)	*(board[0]+8)
	*(board[1]+3)	*(board[1]+4)	*(board[1]+5)
	*board[2]	*(board[2]+1)	*(board[2]+2)
	*(*board+6)	*(*board+7)	*(*board+8)

Let's see how we can apply what we've learnt so far about pointers in a program that we've already written without using pointers. Then we can see the differences. You'll recall that, in Chapter 5, we wrote an example that worked out your hat size. Let's see how we could have done things a little differently.

Try It Out - Know Your Hat Size Revisited

Here's a rewrite of the hat sizes example, using pointer notation:

```
/* Example 7.10  Understand pointers to your hat size - if you dare */
#include <stdio.h>
#define TRUE  1
#define FALSE 0
```

```
void main()
{
   char Size[3][12] = {      /* Hat sizes as characters */
       {'6', '6', '6', '6', '7', '7', '7', '7', '7', '7', '7', '7'},
       {'1', '5', '3', '7', ' ', '1', '1', '3', '1', '5', '3', '7'},
       {'2', '8', '4', '8', ' ', '8', '4', '8', '2', '8', '4', '8'}
                     };

   int Headsize[12] =        /* Values in 1/8 inches     */
       {164,166,169,172,175,178,181,184,188,191,194,197};

   float Cranium = 0.0;      /* Head circumference in decimal inches */
   int Your_Head = 0;        /* Headsize in whole eighths            */
   int i = 0;                /* Loop counter                         */
   int hat_found = FALSE;    /* Indicates when a hat is found to fit */
   int too_small = FALSE;    /* Indicates headsize is too small      */

   /* Get the circumference of the head */
   printf("\nEnter the circumference of your head above your eyebrows"
                                      " in inches as a decimal value: ");
   scanf(" %f", &Cranium);

   /* Convert to whole eighths of an inch */
   Your_Head = (int)(8.0* Cranium);

   /* Search for a hat size */
   for (i = 0 ; i < 12 ; i++)
   {
     /* Find head size in the Headsize array */
     if(Your_Head > *(Headsize+i))
       continue;

     /* If it is the first element and the head size is  */
     /* more than 1/8 smaller then the head is too small */
     /*  for a hat                                       */
     if((i == 0) && (Your_Head < (*Headsize)-1))
     {
       printf("\nYou are the proverbial pinhead. No hat for"
                                          " you I'm afraid.\n");
       too_small = TRUE;
       break;  /* Exit the loop */
     }

     /* If head size is more than 1/8 smaller than the current */
     /* element in Headsize array, take the next element down  */
     /* as the head size                                       */
     if( Your_Head < *(Headsize+i)-1 )
       i--;

     printf("\nYour hat size is %c %c%c%c",
                     *(*Size + i), *(Size[1] + i),
                     (i==4)?' ' : '/',  *(*Size+24+i));
```

```
         hat_found=TRUE;
         break;
      }
   if(!hat_found && !too_small)
      printf("\nYou, in technical parlance, are a fathead."
                            " No hat for you, I'm afraid.\n");

   }
```

The output from this program is the same as in Chapter 5 so I won't repeat it. It's the code that interests us, so let's look at the new elements in this program.

How It Works

This program works in essentially the same way as the example from Chapter 5. The first part, where we declare the arrays and the other variables that we need, is the same as in Example 5.6. The differences start in the **for** loop that searches the **Headsize** array. The value in **Your_Head** is compared with the values in the array in the statement:

```
      if(Your_Head > *(Headsize+i))
         continue;
```

The expression on the right hand size of the comparison, ***(Headsize+i)**, is equivalent to **Headsize[i]** in array notation. The bit between the parentheses adds **i** to the address of the beginning of the array. Remember that adding an integer **i** to an address will add **i** times the length of each element. Therefore, the sub-expression between parentheses produces the address of the element corresponding to the index value **i**. The de-reference operator, *****, then obtains the contents of this element for the comparison operation with the value in the variable **Your_Head**.

If you examine the **printf()** in the middle, you'll see that we mixed the notation a bit, just to show we can handle it:

```
      printf("\nYour hat size is %c %c%c%c",
                     *(*Size + i), *(Size[1] + i),
                     (i==4)?' ' : '/',  *(*Size+24+i));
```

Mixing array notation with pointers, as we've done here, is not recommended practice at all - it's just for illustration, here, to show you the various ways in which pointer arithmetic can be used. Let's look at how these expressions for the output values work.

The first is ***(*Size + i)**. Since **Size** is a two-dimensional array, **Size** by itself is a pointer to an array of pointers - each of which points to a row of the array. Therefore, ***Size+i** gives the address of the element in the first row of the array that has the index value **i**. De-referencing this in the expression ***(*Size + i)** produces the value stored in that element. This is equivalent to **Size[0][i]** in array notation.

The expression ***(Size[1] + i)** is equivalent to **Size[1][i]**. This is because **Size[1]** is a pointer to the second row of the array, and **Size[1]+i** is the address of the element in that row with index value **i**. The de-reference operator obtains the value stored.

The last expression in the **printf()** is ***(*Size+24+i)**. This is equivalent to **Size[2][i]**. Since ***Size** is a pointer to the first row, adding 24 produces the address of the first element in the third row. Adding **i** to that gives the address of the element in the third row with index value **i**. This is de-referenced using ***** to obtain the value.

Using Memory as you Go

Pointers are an extremely flexible and powerful tool for programming over a wide range of applications. The majority of programs in C use pointers to some extent. C also has a further facility that enhances the power of pointers, in that it permits memory to be allocated dynamically.

Think back to our program that averages students' scores (from Chapter 5). At the moment, it only works for 10 students. Suppose we wanted to write the program so that it would work without knowing the number of students in the class in advance, and wouldn't use any more memory than necessary for the number of student scores specified. **Dynamic memory allocation** allows us to do just that. We can produce arrays large enough to hold the right amount of data for the task we require.

Dynamic Memory Allocation - The malloc() Function

The standard library function to allocate memory as you go along is called **malloc()**, and you need to include the **stdlib.h** header file in your program when you use this function.

When you use the **malloc()** function, the number of bytes of memory that you want needs to be specified as an argument. The function returns the address of the first byte of memory allocated in response to your request. Since we get an address returned, a pointer is a useful place to put it.

A typical example of dynamic memory allocation might be:

```
int *pNumber = (int*)malloc(100);
```

Here, we've requested one hundred bytes of memory, and assigned the address of this memory block to **pNumber**. As long as we haven't modified it, any time we use the variable **pNumber** it will point to the first **int** location at the beginning of the one hundred bytes that were allocated. This whole block can hold 50 **int** values, assuming the typical **int** takes 2 bytes, or 25 **int** values on my computer - where they require 4 bytes each.

> Notice the cast, **(int*)**, that we've used to convert the address returned by the function to the type 'pointer to **int**'. We've done this because **malloc()** is a general purpose function that is used to allocate memory for any type of data. The function has no knowledge of what you want to use the memory for, so it actually returns a pointer of type 'pointer to **void**', which is written as **void***. The type **void** can best be described as an absence of type - so pointers of type **void*** can point to any kind of data. Many compilers will automatically cast the address returned by **malloc()** to the appropriate type, but it doesn't hurt to be specific.

We could request any number of bytes, subject only to the amount of free memory on the computer, and the limit on **malloc()** imposed by a particular implementation. If the memory that you request can't be allocated for any reason, **malloc()** returns a pointer with the value **NULL**. Remember that this is the equivalent of zero for pointers. It's always a good idea to check any dynamic memory request immediately, using an **if**, to make sure the memory is actually there before you try to use it. As with money, using memory you haven't got is generally catastrophic. For that reason, writing:

```
    if(pNumber == NULL)
      ...;
```

with a suitable action if the pointer is **NULL** is a good idea. For example, you could display a message **"not enough memory"** and terminate the program. In some instances, though, you may be able to free up a bit of memory that you've been using elsewhere, which might give you enough memory to continue.

Using the sizeof Operator

The previous example is all very well, but we don't usually deal in bytes: we deal in data of type **int** and type **double** and such like. It would be very useful to allocate memory for 75 items of type **int** for example. We can do this with the following statement:

```
    pNumber = (int*) malloc(75*sizeof(int));
```

As we've seen already, **sizeof** is actually an operator. It's part of the C language. It returns an unsigned integer that's the count of the number of bytes required to store its argument. It will accept a type keyword such as **int** or **float** as an argument between parentheses - in which case the value it returns will be the number of bytes required to store an item of that type. It will also accept a variable or array name as an argument. With an array name as an argument it returns the number of bytes required to store the whole array. In the example above we have asked for enough memory to store 75 data items of type **int**.

Try It Out - Dynamic Memory Allocation

We can put this into practice by using pointers to help calculate prime numbers. If you've forgotten, prime numbers are integers that are not divisible (without a remainder) by any lower integer, other than 1.

The process for finding a prime is quite simple. Firstly, we know by inspection that 2, 3, and 5 are the first three prime numbers, since they are not divisible by any lower number, other than 1. Since all the other prime numbers must be odd (otherwise they would be divisible by 2), we can work out the next number to check by starting at the last prime we have and adding 2. When we've checked out that number, we add another 2 to get the next to be checked, and so on.

To check whether a number is actually prime rather than just odd, we could divide by all the odd numbers less that the number that we're checking; but thankfully, we don't need to do as much work as that. If a number is *not* prime, it must be divisible by one of the primes lower than the number we're checking. Since we'll obtain the primes in sequence, it will be sufficient to check a candidate by testing whether any of the primes we've already found is an exact divisor.

We'll write this program using pointers and dynamic memory allocation:

```
/* Example 7.11  A dynamic prime example          */
#include <stdio.h>
#include <stdlib.h>
```

```c
void main()
{
   long *primes = NULL;    /* Pointer to primes storage area   */
   long trial = 0;         /* Integer to be tested             */

   int  i = 0;
   int found = 0;          /* Indicates when we find a prime   */
   int total = 0;          /* Number of primes required        */
   int count = 0;          /* Number of primes found           */

   printf("How many primes would you like?  ");
   scanf("%d", &total);    /* Total is how many we need to find */
   total = total<4 ? 4:total;   /* Make sure it is at least 4  */

   /* Allocate sufficient memory to store the number of
                                        primes required */
   primes = (long*)malloc(total*sizeof(long));
   if (primes == NULL)
   {
      printf("\nNot enough memory. Hasta la Vista, baby.\n");
      return;
   }


   /* We know the first three primes so let's give the
                                        program a start. */
   *primes = 2;            /* First prime   */
   *(primes+1) =3;         /* Second prime */
   *(primes+2) = 5;        /* Third prime   */
   count = 3;              /* Number of primes stored */
   trial = 5;              /* Set to the last prime we have */

   /* Find all the primes required */
   while(count<total)
   {
     trial += 2;          /* Next value for checking        */

     /* Try dividing by each of the primes we have      */
     /* If any divide exactly - the number is not prime */
     for(i = 0 ; i < count ; i++ )
       if(!(found = (trial % *(primes+i))))
         break;           /* Exit if no remainder           */

     if(found)            /* we got one - found is not 0    */
       *(primes+count++) = trial;  /* Store it and increment count  */
   }

   /* Display primes 5-up */
   for (i = 0 ; i < total ; i ++ )
   {
     if(!(i%5))
       printf("\n");      /* Newline after every 5          */
```

```
        printf ("%121d", *(primes+i));
    }
    printf("\n");          /* Newline for any stragglers    */
}
```

The output from this program looks something like this:

```
How many primes would you like?  25

        2            3            5            7           11
       13           17           19           23           29
       31           37           41           43           47
       53           59           61           67           71
       73           79           83           89           97
```

How It Works

With this example, you can enter how many prime numbers you want computed. The pointer variable, **primes**, will refer to a memory area that will be used to store the prime numbers as they are calculated. However, no memory is defined initially in the program. The space is allocated after you've entered the number of primes that you want:

```
    printf("How many primes would you like?  ");
    scanf("%d", &total);     /* Total is how many we need to find */
    total = total<4 ? 4:total;    /* Make sure it is at least 4   */
```

After the prompt, the number you enter is stored in **total**. The next statement then ensures that **total** is at least 4. This is because we'll define and store the three primes that we know (2, 3, and 5) by default.

We then use the value in **total** to allocate the appropriate amount of memory to store the primes:

```
    primes = (long*)malloc(total*sizeof(long));
    if (primes == NULL)
    {
        printf("\nNot enough memory. Hasta la Vista, baby.\n");
        return;
    }
```

Because we're going to store each prime as type **long**, the number of bytes we require is **total*sizeof(long)**. If the **malloc()** function returns **NULL**, no memory was allocated - so we display a message and end the program.

The maximum number of primes that you can specify depends on two things: the memory available on your computer, and the amount of memory that your compiler's implementation of **malloc()** can allocate at one time. The latter is probably the major constraint: you can generally rely on the **malloc()** function being able to allocate at least 32,767 bytes, but some C implementations will have a **malloc()** function supporting considerably more.

Once we have the memory allocated for the primes, we define the first three primes and store them in the first three positions in the memory area pointed to by **primes**:

```
    *primes = 2;         /* First prime  */
    *(primes+1) = 3;     /* Second prime */
    *(primes+2) = 5;     /* Third prime  */
```

As you can see, referencing successive memory locations is simple. Because **primes** is of type 'pointer to **long**', **primes+1** refers to the address of the second location - the address being **primes** plus the number of bytes required to store one data item of type **long**. To store each value, we use the indirection operator - otherwise we would be modifying the address itself.

Now we have three primes, we set the variable **count** to 3, and initialize the variable **trial** with the last prime we stored:

```
    count = 3;           /* Number of primes stored */
    trial = 5;           /* Set to the last prime we have */
```

The value in **trial** will be incremented by two to get the next value to be tested when we start searching for the next prime.

All the primes are found in the **while** loop:

```
    while(count<total)
    {
      ...
    }
```

The variable **count** is incremented within the loop as each prime is found, and when it reaches **total** the loop ends.

Within the **while** loop, we first increase the value in **trial** by 2, and then test whether the value is prime:

```
      trial += 2;          /* Next value for checking        */

    /* Try dividing by each of the primes we have        */
    /* If any divide exactly - the number is not prime   */
    for(i = 0 ; i < count ; i++ )
      if(!(found = (trial % *(primes+i))))
        break;             /* Exit if no remainder          */
```

The **for** loop does the testing. Within the loop, the remainder after dividing **trial** by each of the primes we have is stored in **found**. If the division is exact, the remainder - and therefore **found** - will be zero. This means that the value in **trial** is not a prime.

The value of an assignment is the value stored in the variable on the left of the assignment operator. Thus the value of the expression **(found = (trial % *(primes+i)))** will be the value stored in **found**. This will be 0 for an exact division, so the expression, **!(found = (trial % *(primes+i)))**, will be true in this case, and the **break** statement will be executed. Therefore, the **for** loop will end if any prime that we stored previously divides into **trial** exactly.

If none of the primes divides into **trial** exactly, the **for** loop will end when all the primes have been tried, and **found** will contain the last remainder value - which will be some positive integer. If **trial** had a factor, the loop will have ended via the **break** statement and **found** will contain 0. Therefore, we can use the value stored in **found** at the completion of the **for** loop to determine whether we have found a new prime or not:

```
if(found)              /* we got one - found is not 0   */
    *(primes+count++) = trial;  /* Store it and increment count   */
```

If **found** is positive - that is, true, we store the value of **trial** in the next available slot in the memory area. The address of the next available slot is **primes+count**. Remember that the first slot is **primes**, so when we have **count** number of primes, the last prime occupies the location **primes+count-1**. The statement storing the new prime also increments the value of **count** after the new prime has been stored.

The **while** loop just repeats the process until we have all the primes requested. We then output the primes five on a line:

```
for (i = 0 ; i < total ; i ++ )
{
  if(!(i%5))
    printf("\n");      /* Newline after every 5         */
  printf ("%12ld", *(primes+i));
}
printf("\n");           /* Newline for any stragglers    */
```

The **for** loop will output **total** number of primes. The **printf()** that displays each prime value just appends the output to the current line, but the **if** statement outputs a newline character after every fifth iteration, so there will be five primes displayed on each line. Since the number of primes may not be an exact multiple of five, we output a newline after the loop ends to ensure that there's always at least one newline character at the end of the output.

Handling Strings Using Pointers

We've used array variables of type **char** to store strings up to now, but we can also use a variable of type 'pointer to **char**' to reference a string. This approach will give us quite a lot of flexibility in handling strings, as we shall see. We can declare a variable of type 'pointer to **char**' with a statement such as:

```
char *pString = NULL;
```

At this point, it's worth remembering what a pointer is. A pointer is a variable containing the address of another memory location. So far, we've created a pointer, but not a place to store a string. To store a string, we need to allocate some memory. We can declare a block of memory that we intend to use to store string data, and then use pointers to keep track of where in this block we've stored the strings.

Try It Out - Pointers to Strings

We can try this in an example, and at the same time introduce another way of reading character data from the keyboard. Here's the code:

```
/* Example 7.12  Managing memory and storing strings */
#include <stdio.h>
#define BUFFER_LEN 500
void main()
{
   char Buffer[BUFFER_LEN];   /* Store for strings          */
   char *pS1 = NULL;          /* Pointer to first string   */
   char *pS2 = NULL;          /* Pointer to second string  */
   char *pS3 = NULL;          /* Pointer to third string   */
   char *pBuffer = Buffer;    /* Pointer to Buffer          */

   printf("\nEnter a message\n");

   /* Store address of first message */
   pS1 = pBuffer;

   /* Get input until Enter pressed    */
   while ((*pBuffer++ = getchar()) != '\n');

   /* Add string terminator            */
   *(pBuffer - 1) = '\0';

   printf("\nEnter another message\n");

   /* Store address of second message */
   pS2 = pBuffer;

   /* Get input till Enter pressed     */
   while ((*pBuffer++ = getchar()) != '\n');

   /* Add string terminator            */
   *(pBuffer - 1) = '\0';

   printf("\nEnter another message\n");

   /* Store address of third message   */
   pS3 = pBuffer;

   /* Get input till Enter pressed     */
   while((*pBuffer++ = getchar()) != '\n');

   /* Add string terminator            */
   *(pBuffer - 1) = '\0';

   printf("\nThe strings you entered are:\n\n%s\n%s\n%s",
                                        pS1, pS2, pS3);
```

```
     printf("\nThe buffer has %d characters unused.",
                          &Buffer[BUFFER_LEN - 1] - pBuffer + 1);
  }
```

Typical output from this would be:

```
Enter a message
Hello World!

Enter another message
Today is a great day for learning about pointers.

Enter another message
That's all.

The strings you entered are:
Hello World!
Today is a great day for learning about pointers.
That's all.
The buffer has 425 characters unused.
```

How It Works

The first thing of note in this example is that we use the symbol **BUFFER_LEN**, specified in the **#define** pre-processor directive, as the dimension for the array **Buffer**:

```
#define BUFFER_LEN 500
```

As we have seen before, the **#define** directive defines a value to be substituted for the symbol **BUFFER_LEN** wherever it's used in the code. This is a common technique when you want to be able to change values in a program easily.

The initial declarations for the program are:

```
     char Buffer[BUFFER_LEN];    /* Store for strings        */
     char *pS1 = NULL;           /* Pointer to first string  */
     char *pS2 = NULL;           /* Pointer to second string */
     char *pS3 = NULL;           /* Pointer to third string  */
     char *pBuffer = Buffer;     /* Pointer to Buffer        */
```

Here, we declare the string storage space as the array **Buffer** with the length determined by the **#define** directive for **BUFFER_LEN**. We declare three pointers to keep track of where we put the strings, and a pointer, **pBuffer**, to keep track of the current position in **Buffer** when working through it.

The basic operation of the program is to store messages in the array, **Buffer**, as they're entered. They are stored contiguously from the start of the array, and the end of each string is marked by the string terminator character, **'\0'**. The pointers, **pS1**, **pS2**, and **pS3,** keep track of the addresses of the beginning of each of the messages entered.

After outputting a prompt to the screen, we initialize **pS1** to the address of the first byte in **Buffer**:

```
printf("\nEnter a message\n");

/* Store address of first message */
pS1 = pBuffer;
```

We will use a new technique to read data into **pBuffer**, one character at a time. **pS1** is to point to the first string that we read. Since the first string that we read will start at the address currently in **pBuffer**, we store this in **pS1**.

We read in the first string one character at a time with the following statements:

```
/* Get input until Enter pressed    */
while ((*pBuffer++ = getchar()) != '\n');

/* Add string terminator             */
*(pBuffer - 1) = '\0';
```

The string is read in the **while** loop. The loop consists of just the condition - the loop statement itself being empty with just the semicolon at the end. The standard library function, **getchar()**, reads a single character from the keyboard and returns the character read. Thus each call of the function in the loop condition reads one character.

The loop condition stores the character returned by the function **getchar()** at the address pointed to by **pBuffer** and then increments the address in **pBuffer** to the next byte. This incrementing occurs after the whole of the loop condition has been evaluated. The loop condition also compares the character stored at **pBuffer** with **'\n'**, and when **'\n'** is read the loop ends. At the end of the loop, the **'\n'** character, which will have been the last character read, is stored at the address **pBuffer-1**, so we overwrite that character with the string terminator. Note how we increment **pBuffer** to point to the next free byte as we store each character. We couldn't use the name of the array here. Although we could use it as a pointer to access elements of the array, we couldn't change its value. Attempting to do so would cause an error.

Notice, also, how we can compute the address on the left-hand side of an assignment using the expression **(pBuffer -1)**. This expression computes the address in which we want to store the **'\0'** at the end of each string. We can only use an expression on the left-hand side of an assignment statement when it results in an address.

By reading the string using **getchar()** we have a great deal of control over the input process. This approach is not limited to just reading strings - you can use it for any input where you want to deal with it character by character. We could choose to remove spaces from the input, or look for special characters such as commas that you might use to separate one input value from the next.

The subsequent strings are processed in exactly the same way as the first string. Of course, the value of **pBuffer** will have changed each time, so that it points to the next free element in the array **Buffer**. The address of the first character of the second and the third strings are stored in the pointers, **pS2** and **pS3**. Managing the input in this way means that we are able to pack the strings tightly into the **Buffer** array, with no wasted characters between the end of one string and the beginning of the next.

258

In the last **printf()** we output the number of characters left in the string:

```
    printf("\nThe buffer has %d characters unused.",
                           &Buffer[BUFFER_LEN - 1] - pBuffer + 1);
```

This computation is illustrated graphically in the figure below.

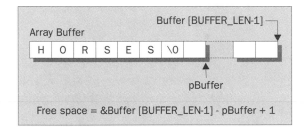

Remember that the last index value of the array is **BUFFER_LEN - 1**, since array indexing starts from zero. It's a very common error, particularly when using named constants, to put **BUFFER_LEN** as the last index value, rather than **BUFFER_LEN - 1**.

At the outset, we initialized our pointers to **NULL**. We can also initialize a pointer with the address of a constant string:

```
    char *pString = "To be or not to be";
```

This statement allocates sufficient memory for the string, places the constant string in the memory allocated, and after allocating space for it, sets the value of the pointer **pString** as the address of the first byte of the string. Contrast this with the declaration:

```
    char String[] = "To be or not to be";
```

These two statements are quite different in their effect, in spite of the apparent similarities. The first initializes the pointer, **pString**, to the address of a string constant. This string constant can't be changed, but the pointer can be set to point to something else. The second statement initializes the array with the character string as an initial value. This isn't a constant, and we can change the contents of the array whenever we wish. However, as we pointed out before, the address referenced by using the array name **String** can't be altered.

Arrays of Pointers

That last example was a bit repetitive. We used the same code for each string entered. If we could set up the pointers to the strings entered as an *array of pointers*, we could shorten the program quite a bit. Let's see how.

Try It Out - Arrays of Pointers

The following example is a rewrite of the previous program, and demonstrates how we could use an array of pointers:

```
/* Example 7.13 Arrays of Pointers to Strings */
#include <stdio.h>
#define BUFFER_LEN 500
void main()
{
   char Buffer[BUFFER_LEN];          /* Store for strings        */
   char *pS[3] = { NULL };           /* Array of string pointers */
   char *pBuffer = Buffer;           /* Pointer to Buffer        */
   int i = 0;                        /* loop counter             */


   /* Read the strings from the keyboard */
   for (i=0; i<3 ; i++)
   {
     printf("\nEnter %s message\n", i>0? "another" : "a" );
     *(pS + i) = pBuffer;     /* Save start of  string      */

     /* Get input till Enter pressed */
     while ((*pBuffer++ = getchar()) != '\n');

     /* Add terminator */
     *(pBuffer - 1) = '\0';
   }

   printf("\nThe strings you entered are:\n\n");
   for(i = 0 ; i<3 ;  i++)
     printf("%s\n", *(pS+i));

   printf("The buffer has %d characters unused.\n",
                   &Buffer[BUFFER_LEN - 1] - pBuffer + 1);
}
```

The output from this program is the same as the previous example.

How It Works

This is much neater isn't it? The declarations at the beginning are now:

```
   char Buffer[BUFFER_LEN];   /* Store for strings        */
   char *pS[3] = { NULL };    /* Array of string pointers */
   char *pBuffer = Buffer;    /* Pointer to Buffer        */
   int i = 0;                 /* loop counter             */
```

The difference, here, is that we now have an array of three pointers to **char**, called **pS**, each of which is initialized with **NULL**. We've also declared an extra integer variable, **i**, which we need as an index in the **for** loops to iterate through the array of pointers.

The first **for** loop reads in three strings. The first statement in the loop is:

```
     printf("\nEnter %s message\n", i>0? "another" : "a" );
```

Here, we use our snappy way to alter the prompt in the **printf()** after the first iteration of the **for** loop, using our old friend the conditional operator. This outputs **"a"** on the first iteration, and **"another"** on all subsequent iterations.

The next statement saves the address currently stored in **pBuffer**:

```
    *(pS + i) = pBuffer;    /* Save start of  string   */
```

The expression on the left hand side of the assignment, ***(pS + i)**, is equivalent to **pS[i]**, and is a pointer - since we have an array of pointers. This assignment statement is therefore storing, in an element of the **pS** pointer array, the address stored in the pointer **pBuffer**. If the left side of the expression didn't have the *****, it would be referring to the *address* of one of the elements of **pS**, which isn't the same thing at all!

> *In fact, if you try leaving out the indirection operator, the program won't compile. The most likely message from the compiler is that an lvalue is required. This sounds a bit obscure, but an lvalue is just somewhere you can store a result.*

The statements for reading the string and appending the string terminator are exactly as before:

```
    /* Get input till Enter pressed */
    while ((*pBuffer++ = getchar()) != '\n');

    /* Add terminator */
    *(pBuffer - 1) = '\0';
```

All the work is done in the **while** loop condition here. The statement to append **'\0'** is not in the loop: it follows it. When the loop ends, we output the strings in another **for** loop, after outputting an initial message:

```
    printf("\nThe strings you entered are:\n\n");
    for(i = 0 ; i<3 ; i++)
      printf("%s\n", *(pS+i));
```

In the loop, we first output ***pS**, then ***(pS+1)**, and finally ***(pS+2)**. These expressions reference each of the strings in turn, and the process of outputting the characters for each string is halted by the **'\0'** character that we appended to them.

If we developed this example just a little further, we would be able to allow input of an arbitrary number of messages, limited only by the number of string pointers provided for in the array.

Try It Out - Generalizing String Input

Let's try rewriting the example to generalize string input. We can extend the program to read an arbitrary number of strings up to a given limit, and ensure that we don't read strings that are longer than we've provided for. Here's the program:

```
/* Example 7.14 Generalizing string input */
#include <stdio.h>
#include <stdlib.h>
#define BUFFER_LEN 100    /* Length of input buffer        */
#define NUM_P 100         /* maximum number of strings     */
```

```
void main()
{
   char Buffer[BUFFER_LEN];         /* Input buffer                */
   char *pS[NUM_P] = { NULL };      /* Array of string pointers */
   char *pBuffer = Buffer;          /* Pointer to Buffer           */
   int i = 0;                       /* Loop counter                */
   int j = 0;                       /* Loop counter                */

   for (i = 0; i < NUM_P; i++)
   {
     pBuffer = Buffer ; /* Set pointer to beginning of buffer */
     printf("\nEnter %s message, or press Enter to end\n",
                                    i>0? "another" : "a");

     /* Read a string of up to BUFFER_LEN characters */
     while ((pBuffer-Buffer < BUFFER_LEN-1) &&
             ((*pBuffer++ = getchar()) != '\n'));

     /* check for empty line indicating end of input */
     if((pBuffer - Buffer) < 2)
       break;

     /* Check for string too long */
     if((pBuffer - Buffer) == BUFFER_LEN && *(pBuffer-1)!= '\n')
     {
       printf("String too long - maximum %d characters allowed.",
                                              BUFFER_LEN);

       i--;
       continue;
     }

     *(pBuffer - 1) = '\0'; /* Add terminator */

     /* Get memory for string       */
     pS[i] = (char*)malloc(pBuffer - Buffer);

     /* Check we actually got some... */
     if ( pS[i] == NULL )
     {
       printf("\nOut of memory - ending program.");
       return;            /* ...Exit if we didn't */
     }

     /* Copy string from Buffer to new memory */
     for(j = 0 ; (*(pS[i] + j) = Buffer[j]) != '\0' ; j++);
   }

   /* Output all the strings */
   printf("\nIn reverse order, the strings you entered are:\n");
   while (--i >= 0 )
   {
```

```
        printf("\n%s", *(pS + i) ); /* Display strings last to first */
        free(*(pS + i));        /* Release the memory we got          */
        *(pS + i) = NULL;       /* Set pointer back to NULL for safety */
    }
}
```

The output is very similar to the previous two examples:

```
Enter a message, or press Enter to end
Hello

Enter another message, or press Enter to end
World!

In reverse order, the strings you entered are:
World!
Hello
```

How It Works

This has expanded a little bit, but we've included quite a few extras compared to our original attempt at this. We now handle as many strings as you want, up to the number that we provide pointers for, in the array **pS**. The dimension of this array is defined at the beginning, to make it easy to change:

```
#define NUM_P 100           /* maximum number of strings         */
```

If you want to alter the maximum number of strings that the program will handle, you just need to change this directive.

At the beginning of **main()**, we have the declarations for the variables we need:

```
    char Buffer[BUFFER_LEN];        /* Input buffer              */
    char *pS[NUM_P] = { NULL };     /* Array of string pointers */
    char *pBuffer = Buffer;         /* Pointer to Buffer        */
    int i = 0;                      /* Loop counter             */
    int j = 0;                      /* Loop counter             */
```

The array **Buffer** is now just an input buffer, which will contain each string as we read it. Therefore, the **#define** directive for **BUFFER_LEN** now defines the maximum length of string we can accept. We then have the declaration for our pointer array of length **NUM_P**, and our pointer for working within **Buffer**, called ***pBuffer**. Finally, we have a couple of loop index variables.

The first **for** loop reads the strings and stores them. The loop control is:

```
    for (i = 0; i < NUM_P; i++)
```

This ensures that we can only input as many strings as there are pointers that we've declared. Once you've entered the maximum number of strings, the loop ends and you fall through to the output section of the program.

Within the loop, a string is entered using a similar mechanism with `getchar()` to those that we've seen before - but with an additional condition:

```
/* Read a string of up to BUFFER_LEN characters */
while ((pBuffer-Buffer < BUFFER_LEN-1) &&
        ((*pBuffer++ = getchar()) != '\n'));
```

The whole process takes place in the condition for the continuation of the **while** loop. A character obtained by `getchar()` is stored at the address pointed to by **pBuffer**, which starts out as the address of **Buffer**. **pBuffer** is then incremented to point to the next available space, and the character stored as a result of the assignment is compared with **'\n'**. If it is **'\n'** then the loop terminates. The loop will also end if the expression **pBuffer-Buffer < BUFFER_LEN-1** is false. This will occur if the next character to be stored will occupy the last position in the **Buffer** array.

The input process is followed by the check in the statement:

```
/* check for empty line indicating end of input */
if((pBuffer - Buffer) < 2)
  break;
```

This detects an empty line since, if you just press the *Enter* key, only one character will be entered - the **'\n'**. In this case, the break immediately exits the **for** loop, and begins the output process.

The next **if** checks whether you attempted to enter a string longer than the capacity of **Buffer**:

```
/* Check for string too long */
if((pBuffer - Buffer) == BUFFER_LEN && *(pBuffer-1)!= '\n')
{
  printf("String too long - maximum %d characters allowed.",
                                            BUFFER_LEN);
  i--;
  continue;
}
```

Because we end the **while** loop when the last position in the **Buffer** array has been used, if you attempt to enter more characters than the capacity of **Buffer** then the expression **pBuffer-Buffer** will be equal to **BUFFER_LEN**. Of course, this will also be the case if you enter a string that fits exactly, so we must also check the last character in **Buffer**, to see if it's **'\n'**. If it isn't, you tried to enter too many characters, so we decrement the loop counter after displaying a message, and go to the next iteration.

The next statement is:

```
*(pBuffer - 1) = '\0'; /* Add terminator */
```

This places the **'\0'** in the position occupied by the **'\n'** character, since **pBuffer** was left pointing to the first free element in the array **Buffer**.

Once a string has been entered, sufficient memory is requested, using **malloc()**, to hold the string exactly:

```
    /* Get memory for string      */
    pS[i] = (char*)malloc(pBuffer - Buffer);

    /* Check we actually got some… */
    if ( pS[i] == NULL )
    {
      printf("\nOut of memory - ending program.");
      return;              /* …Exit if we didn't */
    }
```

The number of bytes required is the difference between the address currently pointed to by **pBuffer**, which is the first vacant element in **Buffer**, and the address of the first element of **Buffer**. The pointer returned from **malloc()** is stored in the current element of the **pS** array, after casting it to type **char**. If we get a **NULL** pointer back from **malloc()**, we display a message and end the program.

We copy the string from the buffer to the new memory we have obtained using a **for** loop:

```
    /* Copy string from Buffer to new memory */
    for(j = 0 ; (*(pS[i] + j) = Buffer[j]) != '\0' ; j++);
```

The loop condition includes an assignment that stores the current element from **Buffer** in the new memory area. We get the address to store the character from **Buffer[j]** by adding **j** to the address in **pS[i].** The indirection operator indicates that we're modifying the contents of the location referenced by this address. The character stored is compared with **'\0'**, and when this character is stored the copying process ends.

Once we exit the loop, either because we entered an empty string or because we used all the pointers in the array **pS**, we generate the output:

```
    /* Output all the strings */
    printf("\nIn reverse order, the strings you entered are:\n");
    while (--i >= 0 )
    {
      printf("\n%s", *(pS + i) ); /* Display strings last to first */
      free(*(pS + i));       /* Release the memory we got         */
      *(pS + i) = NULL;     /* Set pointer back to NULL for safety */
    }
```

The index **i** will have a value one greater than the number of strings entered. So after the first loop condition check, we can use it to index the last string. The loop continues counting down from this value, and the last iteration will be with **i** at zero, which will index the first string.

The expression ***(pS + i)** *is equivalent to* **pS[i]** *in array notation. Using pointer notation on the array of pointers here is just for exercise.*

You can see we use a new function, **free()**, after the last **printf()**. This function is complementary to **malloc()**, and it releases memory previously allocated by **malloc()**. It only requires the pointer to the memory allocated as an argument. Although memory will be freed at the end of the program automatically, it's good practice to free memory as soon as you no longer need it. Of course, once you've freed memory in this way, you can't use it - so it's a good idea to set the pointer to **NULL** immediately, as we've done here.

> *Errors with pointers can produce catastrophic results. If an uninitialized pointer is used to store a value before it has been assigned an address value, the address used will be whatever happens to be stored in the pointer location. This could overwrite virtually anywhere in memory.*

Try It Out - Sorting Strings Using Pointers

Using the string library, we can demonstrate the effectiveness of using pointers by an example showing a simple method of sorting:

```c
/* Example 7.15 Sorting strings */
#include <stdio.h>
#include <stdlib.h>
#include <string.h>
#define BUFFER_LEN 100   /* Length of input buffer    */
#define NUM_P 100        /* maximum number of strings */
#define TRUE  1
#define FALSE 0

void main()
{
   char Buffer[BUFFER_LEN];    /* space to store an input string   */
   char *pS[NUM_P] = { NULL }; /* Array of string pointers         */
   char *pTemp = NULL;         /* Temporary pointer                */
   int i = 0;                  /* Loop counter                     */
   int sorted = FALSE;         /* Indicated when strings are sorted */
   int last_string = 0;        /* Index of last string entered     */

   printf("\nEnter successive lines, pressing Enter at the"
                  " end of each line. Just press Enter to end.\n\n");
   while((*gets(Buffer) != '\0') && (i < NUM_P))
   {
     pS[i] = (char*)malloc(strlen(Buffer) + 1);
     if(pS[i]==NULL)            /* Check for no memory allocated    */
     {
       printf(" Memory allocation failed. Program terminated.\n");
       return;
     }
     strcpy(pS[i++], Buffer);
   }
   last_string = i;            /* Save last string index           */

   /* Sort the strings in ascending order */
   while(!sorted)
   {
```

```
            sorted = TRUE;
            for (i = 0 ; i < last_string - 1 ; i++)
              if(strcmp(pS[i], pS[i + 1]) > 0)
              {
                sorted = FALSE;        /* We were out of order */
                pTemp= pS[i];          /* Swap pointers pS[i]  */
                pS[i] = pS[i + 1];    /*          and         */
                pS[i + 1]  = pTemp;  /*      pS[i + 1]        */
              }
          }

          /* Displayed the sorted strings */
          printf("\nYour input sorted in order is:\n\n");
          for (i = 0 ; i < last_string ; i++)
          {
            printf("%s\n", pS[i] );
            free( pS[i] );
            pS[i] = NULL;
          }
      }
```

Assuming you enter the same input data, the output from this program is:

```
Enter successive lines, pressing Enter at the end of each line.
Just press Enter to end.

Many a mickle makes a muckle.
A fool and your money are soon partners.
Every dog has his day.
Do unto others before they does it to you.
A nod is as good as a wink to a blind horse.


Your input sorted in order is:

A fool and your money are soon partners.
A nod is as good as a wink to a blind horse.
Do unto others before they does it to you.
Every dog has his day.
Many a mickle makes a muckle.
```

How It Works

This is quite an interesting example. It really will sort the wheat from the chaff. To simplify things a bit, we're using the input function **gets()**, which reads a complete string up to the point you press *Enter*, and then adds **'\0'** to the end. Its only argument is a pointer to the memory area where you want the string to be stored. Its return value is either the address where the input string is stored, or **NULL** if an error occurs. With the code as it is, though, we don't have any protection against exceeding the capacity of **Buffer**.

The overall operation of this program is quite simple, and involves three distinct activities:

- Read in all the input strings
- Sort them in order
- Display them in alphabetical order

After the initial prompt lines are displayed, the input process is handled by these statements:

```
while((*gets(Buffer) != '\0') && (i < NUM_P))
{
  pS[i] = (char*)malloc(strlen(Buffer) + 1);
  if(pS[i]==NULL)              /* Check for no memory allocated      */
  {
    printf(" Memory allocation failed. Program terminated.\n");
    return;
  }
  strcpy(pS[i++], Buffer);
}
```

The input process continues until an empty line is entered, or until you run out of space in the pointer array. Each line is read into **Buffer** using the **gets()** function. This is inside the **while** loop condition, which allows the loop to continue for as long as **gets()** does not read a string containing just **'\0'**, and the total number of lines entered does not exceed the pointer array dimension. The empty string with just **'\0'** will be a result of you pressing *Enter* without entering any text. We use the ***** to get at the contents of the pointer address return by **gets()**. This is the same as **Buffer**, of course.

As soon as we collect each input line in **Buffer**, we allocate the correct amount of memory using **malloc()**. We get the count of the number of bytes that we need by using the **strlen()** function to provide a count of the number of characters stored, and adding 1 for the **'\0'** at the end. After verifying that we did get the memory allocated, we copy the string from **Buffer** to the new memory, using the library function **strcpy()**.

We then save the index for the last string :

```
    last_string = i;              /* Save last string index          */
```

This is because we're going to reuse the loop counter, **i**, and we need to keep track of how many strings we have.

Once we have all our strings safely stowed away, we sort them using the simplest, and probably the most inefficient sort going - but it's easy to follow. This takes place within these statements:

```
    /* Sort the strings in ascending order */
    while(!sorted)
    {
      sorted = TRUE;
      for (i = 0 ; i < last_string - 1 ; i++)
        if(strcmp(pS[i], pS[i + 1]) > 0)
```

```
        {
          sorted = FALSE;      /* We were out of order */
          pTemp= pS[i];        /* Swap pointers pS[i]  */
          pS[i] = pS[i + 1];   /*         and          */
          pS[i + 1]  = pTemp; /*      pS[i + 1]        */
        }
      }
```

The sort takes place inside the **while** loop that continues as long as **sorted** is false. The sort proceeds by comparing successive pairs of strings using the **strcmp()** function inside the **for** loop. If the first string is greater than the second string, we swap pointer values. Using pointers, as we have here, is a very economical way of changing the order. The strings themselves remain undisturbed exactly where they were: it's just the sequence of their addresses that changes in the pointer array **pS**. This mechanism is illustrated in the following figure. The time needed to swap pointers is a fraction of that which would be required to move all the strings around.

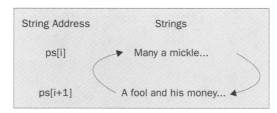

The swapping continues through all the string pointers. If we have to interchange any strings as we pass through them, we set **sorted** to **FALSE** to repeat the whole thing. It we repeat the whole thing without interchanging any, then they are in order - and we have finished the sort. We track the status of this with the integer variable **sorted**. This is set to **TRUE** at the beginning of each cycle, but if any interchange occurs then it gets set back to **FALSE**. If we exit a cycle with **sorted** still **TRUE**, it means that no interchanges occurred - so everything must be in order, and therefore we exit from the **while** loop.

The reason this sort isn't too good is that each pass through all the items only moves a value by one position in the list. In the worst case, when we have the first entry in the last position, the number of times we have to repeat the process is one less than the number of entries in the list. This inefficient, but nevertheless famous method of sorting is known as a **bubblesort**.

Handling strings and other kinds of data using pointers in this way is an extremely powerful mechanism in C. You can throw the basic data (the strings in this case) into a bucket of memory in any old order, and then you can process them in any sequence you like without moving the data at all. You just change the pointers! You could use ideas from this example as a base for programs for sorting any text. You'd do well to find a better sort of sort though!

Designing a Program

Congratulations! You have got through a really tough part of the C language, and now I can show you an application using some of what you have learnt. We'll follow the usual process, taking you through the analysis, design and writing step-by-step. Let's look at our final program for this chapter.

The Problem

The problem we'll address is to rewrite the calculator program that we wrote in Chapter 3 with some new features, but this time using pointers. The main improvements that we'll make are:

▶ Allow the use of signed decimal numbers including a decimal point with an optional leading sign, **–** or **+**, as well as signed integers

▶ Permit expressions to combine multiple operations such as **2.5+3.7-6/6**

▶ Add the **^** operator, which will be raise to a power. So **2^3** will produce **8**.

▶ Allow a line to operate on the previous result. If the previous result was 2.5, then writing **=*2 + 7** will produce the result 12. Any input line that starts with an assignment operator will automatically assume the left operand is the previous result.

We're also going to cheat a little by not taking into consideration the precedence of the operators. We'll simply evaluate the expression that's entered from left to right, applying each operator to the previous result and the right operand. This means that the expression:

```
1 + 2*3 - 4*-5
```

will be evaluated as:

```
((1 + 2)*3 - 4)*(-5)
```

The Analysis

We don't know in advance how long an expression is going to be, or how many numbers are going to be involved. We'll get a complete string from the user, and then analyze this to see what the numbers and operators are. We'll evaluate each intermediate result as soon as we have an operator with a left and a right operand.

The steps are:

1 Read an input string entered by the user and exit if it is **quit**

2 Search for operator followed by operand, executing each operator in turn until the end of the input string.

3 Display the result and go back to 1.

The Solution

1 As we saw earlier in this chapter, the **scanf()** function doesn't allow us to read a complete string that contains spaces, as it stops at the first whitespace character. We'll therefore read the input expression using the **gets()** function declared in the **stdio.h** library header file. This will read an entire line of input, including spaces. We can actually combine the input and the overall program loop together as follows:

```
/* Example 7.16 An improved calculator */
#include <stdio.h>            /* Standard input/output */
#include <string.h>           /* For string functions  */
void main()
{
   char input[256];           /* Input expression       */

   while(strcmp(gets(input), "quit") != 0)
   {
     /* Code to implement the calculator */
   }
}
```

We can do this because the function **strcmp()** expects to receive an argument that is a pointer to a string, and the function **gets()** actually returns a pointer to the string that the user has typed in, **&input[0]** in this case. The **strcmp()** function will compare the string that's entered with **"quit"**, and will return 0 if they are equal. This will end the loop.

We've set the input string to a length of 256. This should be enough as most computers' keyboard buffers are 255 characters. (This refers to the maximum number of characters that you can type in before having to press *Enter*.)

Once we have our string, we could start analyzing it straight away; but it would be better if we removed any spaces from the string. Since the input string is well defined, we don't need spaces to separate the operator from the operands. Let's add code inside the **while** loop to remove any spaces:

```
/* Example 7.16 An improved calculator */
#include <stdio.h>            /* Standard input/output */
#include <string.h>           /* For string functions  */
void main()
{
   char input[256];           /* Input expression       */
   /* Index of the current a character in input     */
   unsigned int index = 0;
   /* To index for copying input to itself          */
   unsigned int to = 0;
   /* Length of the string in input                 */
   unsigned int input_length = 0;

   while(strcmp(gets(input), "quit") != 0)
   {
     /* Get the input string length    */
     input_length = strlen(input);

     /* Remove all spaces from the input by copy the string to itself */
     /* including the string terminating character                    */
     for(to = 0, index = 0 ; index<=input_length ; index++)
     if(*(input+index) != ' ')                /* If it is not a space    */
       *(input+to++) = *(input+index);         /* Copy the character   */
```

```
      input_length = strlen(input);   /* Get the new string length   */
      index = 0;                       /* Start at the first character */

   /* Code to implement the calculator */
   }
}
```

We remove spaces by copying the string stored in **input** to itself. We need to keep track
of two indexes in the copy loop: one for the position in **input** where the next non-space
character is to be copied to, and one for the position of the next character to be copied. In
the loop we don't copy spaces. We just increment **index** to move to the next character.
The **to** index only gets incremented when a character is copied. After the loop is entered,
we store the new string length in **input_length**, and reset index to reference to the first
character in **input**.

We could equally well write the loop here using array notation:

```
   for(to = 0, index = 0 ; index<=input_length ; index++)
     if(input[index] != ' ')           /* If it is not a space */
       input[to++] = input[index];    /* Copy the character    */
```

For my taste, the code is clearer using array notation, but we'll continue using pointer
notation as we need the practice.

2 The input expression has two possible forms. It can start with an assignment operator,
indicating that the last result is to be taken as the left operand, or it can start with a
number with or without a sign. We can differentiate these two situations by looking for
the '=' character first. If we find one, the left operand is the previous result.

The code we need to add next in the **while** loop will look for an '=', and if one is not
found it will look for a substring that is numeric that will be the left operand:

```
/* Example 7.16 An improved calculator */
#include <stdio.h>        /* Standard input/output                */
#include <string.h>       /* For string functions                 */
#include <ctype.h>        /* For classifying characters           */
#include <stdlib.h>       /* For converting strings to numeric values */

void main()
{
  char input[256];        /* Input expression                     */
  char number_string[30]; /* Stores a number string from input */

  /* Index of the current a character in input    */
  unsigned int index = 0;
  /* To index for copying input to itself          */
  unsigned int to = 0;
  /* Length of the string in input                */
  unsigned int input_length = 0;
```

```
    /* Length of the string in number_string        */
    unsigned int number_length = 0;
    /* The result of an operation                    */
    double result = 0.0;
```

```
while(strcmp(gets(input), "quit") != 0)
{
   /* Get the input string length    */
   input_length = strlen(input);

   /* Remove all spaces from the input by copy the string to itself */
   /* including the string terminating character                    */
   for(to = 0, index = 0 ; index<=input_length ; index++)
     if(*(input+index) != ' ')                 /* If it is not a space   */
       *(input+to++) = *(input+index);           /* Copy the character  */

   input_length = strlen(input);     /* Get the new string length     */
   index = 0;                        /* Start at the first character */
```

```
    if(input[index]== '=')     /* Is there =? */
      index++;                 /* Yes so skip over it */
    else
    { /* No - look for the left operand */
      /* Look for a number that is the left operand for */
      /* the first operator                             */

      /* Check for sign and copy it */
      number_length = 0;        /* Initialize length       */

      /* Is it + or -?  */
      if(input[index]=='+' || input[index]=='-')
        /* Yes so copy it */
        *(number_string+number_length++) = *(input+index++);

      /* Copy all following digits */
      /* Is it a digit? */
      for( ; isdigit(*(input+index)) ; index++)
        /* Yes - Copy it  */
        *(number_string+number_length++) = *(input+index);

      /* copy any fractional part */
      /* Is it decimal point? */
      if(*(input+index)=='.')
      { /* Yes so copy the decimal point and the following digits */
        /* Copy point */
        *(number_string+number_length++) = *(input+index++);

        /* For each digit */
        for( ; isdigit(*(input+index)) ; index++)
          /* copy it        */
          *(number_string+number_length++) = *(input+index);
      }
```

```
      /* Append string terminator      */
      *(number_string+number_length) = '\0';

      /* If we have a left operand, the length of number_string */
      /* will be > 0. In this case convert to a double so we    */
      /* can use it in the calculation                          */
      if(number_length>0)
        /* Store first number as result */
        result = atof(number_string);
    }

    /* Code to analyze the operator and right operand */
    /* and produce the result                         */
  }
}
```

We include the **ctype.h** header for the character analysis functions, and the **stdlib.h** header because we use the function **atof()**, which converts a string passed as an argument to a floating-point value. We've added quite a chunk of code here, but it consists of a number of straightforward steps.

The **if** statement checks for '=' as the first character in the input:

```
  if(input[index]== '=')      /* Is there =? */
    index++;                  /* Yes so skip over it */
```

If we find one, we increment index to skip over it and go straight to looking for the operand. If '=' is not found, we execute the **else** which looks for a numeric left operand.

We'll copy all the characters that make up the number to the array **number_string**. The number may start with a unary sign, '-' or '+', so we first check for that in the **else** block - and if we find it then we copy it to **number_string**. This is done with the statement:

```
    /* Is it + or -?  */
    if(input[index]=='+' || input[index]=='-')
      /* Yes so copy it */
      *(number_string+number_length++) = *(input+index++);
```

If a sign is not found then **index** value, recording the current character to be analyzed in **input**, will be left exactly where it is. If a sign is found, it will be copied to **number_string** and the value of **index** will be incremented to point to the next character.

One or more digits should be next, so we have a **for** loop that copies however many digits there are to **number_string**:

```
    /* Is it a digit? */
    for( ; isdigit(*(input+index)) ; index++)
     /* Yes - Copy it  */
     *(number_string+number_length++) = *(input+index);
```

This will copy all the digits of an integer, and increment the value of index accordingly. Of course, if there are no digits, the value of index will be unchanged.

The number might not be an integer. In this case, there must be a decimal point next, which may be followed by more digits. The **if** statement checks for the decimal point; if there is one then the decimal point and any following digits will also be copied:

```
/* Is it decimal point? */
if(*(input+index)=='.')
{ /* Yes so copy the decimal point and the following digits */
  /* Copy point */
 *(number_string+number_length++) = *(input+index++);

  /* For each digit */
  for( ; isdigit(*(input+index)) ; index++)
    /* copy it          */
   *(number_string+number_length++) = *(input+index);
}
```

We must have finished copying the string for the first operand now, so we append a string terminating character to **number_string**.

```
/* Append string terminator    */
*(number_string+number_length) = '\0';
```

While there may not have been a value found, if we've copied a string representing a number to **number_string**, then the value of **number_length** must be positive - since there has to be at least one digit. Therefore, we use the value of **number_length** as an indicator that we have a number:

```
if(number_length>0)
   /* Store first number as result */
   result = atof(number_string);
```

The string is converted to a floating point value of type **double** by the **atof()** function. Note that we store the value of the string in **result**. We'll use the same variable later to store the result of an operation. This will ensure that **result** always contains the result of an operation, including that produced at the end of an entire string. If we haven't stored a value here, because there is no left operand, **result** will already contain the value from the previous input string.

At this point, what follows in the input string is very well defined. It must be an operator followed by a number. The operator will have the number we previously found as its left operand, or the previous result. This 'op-number' combination may also be followed by another, so we have a possible succession of 'op-number' combinations through to the end of the string. We can deal with this in a loop that will look for these combinations:

```
/* Example 7.16 An improved calculator */
#include <stdio.h>        /* Standard input/output              */
#include <string.h>       /* For string functions               */
#include <ctype.h>        /* For classifying characters          */
#include <stdlib.h>       /* For converting strings to numeric values */
```

```c
void main()
{
    char input[256];          /* Input expression                    */
    char number_string[30];   /* Stores a number string from input   */
    char op = 0;              /* Stores an operator                  */

    /* Index of the current a character in input    */
    unsigned int index = 0;
    /* To index for copying input to itself         */
    unsigned int to = 0;
    /* Length of the string in input                */
    unsigned int input_length = 0;

    /* Length of the string in number_string        */
    unsigned int number_length = 0;
    /* The result of an operation                   */
    double result = 0.0;

    /* Stores the value of number_string            */
    double number = 0.0;

    while(strcmp(gets(input), "quit") != 0)
    {
        /* Get the input string length   */
        input_length = strlen(input);

        /* Remove all spaces from the input by copy the string to itself */
        /* including the string terminating character                    */
        /* Code to remove spaces as before...                            */

        /* Code to check for '=' and analyze and store the */
        /* left operand as before.. */

        /* Now look for 'op number' combinations */
        for(;index < input_length;)
        {
            op = *(input+index++);      /* Get the operator */

            /* Copy the next operand and store it in number */
            number_length = 0;      /* Initialize the length  */

            /* Check for sign and copy it */
            /* Is it + or -?  */
            if(input[index]=='+' || input[index]=='-')
            /* Yes - copy it. */
            *(number_string+number_length++) = *(input+index++);

            /* Copy all following digits */
            /* For each digit */
            for( ; isdigit(*(input+index)) ; index++)
            /* copy it.       */
            *(number_string+number_length++) = *(input+index);
```

```
            /* copy any fractional part */
            /* Is is a decimal point? */
            if(*(input+index)=='.')
            { /* Copy the  decimal point and the following digits */
              /* Copy point       */
             *(number_string+number_length++) = *(input+index++);

              /* For each digit */
              for( ; isdigit(*(input+index)) ; index++)
                /* copy it.         */
               *(number_string+number_length++) = *(input+index);
            }

            /* terminate string */
            *(number_string+number_length) = '\0';

            /* Convert to a double so we can use it in the calculation */
            number = atof(number_string);
      }
    /* code to produce result */
      }
}
```

In the interests of not repeating the same code ad nauseam, there are some comments indicating where the previous bits of code that we added are located in the program. I'll list the complete source code with the next addition to the program.

The **for** loop continues until we reach the end of the input string, which will be when we have incremented **index** to be equal to **input_length**. On each iteration of the loop, we store the operator in the variable, **op**, of type **char**:

```
    op = *(input+index++);        /* Get the operator */
```

With the operator out of the way, we then extract the characters that form the next number. This will be the right operand for the operator. We haven't verified that the operator is valid here, so the code won't spot an invalid operator at this point.

The extraction of the string for the number that's the right operand is exactly the same as that for the left operand. The same code is repeated. This time though, the **double** value for the operand is stored in **number**:

```
    number = atof(number_string);
```

We now have the left operand stored in **result**, the operator stored in **op**, and the right operand stored in **number**. Consequently, we're now prepared to execute an operation of the form:

result=(result op number).

When we've added the code for this, the program will be complete.

3 We can use a **switch** statement to select the operation to be carried out based on the operand. This is essentially the same code that we used in the previous calculator. We'll also display the output and add a prompt at the beginning of the program on how the calculator is used. Here's the complete code for the program, with the last code we're adding shaded:

```
/* Example 7.16 An improved calculator */
#include <stdio.h>          /* Standard input/output                 */
#include <string.h>         /* For string functions                  */
#include <ctype.h>          /* For classifying characters            */
#include <stdlib.h>         /* For converting strings to numeric values */
#include <math.h>           /* For power() function                  */

void main()
{
   char input[256];         /* Input expression                      */
   char number_string[30];  /* Stores a number string from input */
   char op = 0;             /* Stores an operator                    */

   /* Index of the current a character in input     */
   unsigned int index = 0;
   /* To index for copying input to itself          */
   unsigned int to = 0;
   /* Length of the string in input                 */
   unsigned int input_length = 0;

   /* Length of the string in number_string         */
   unsigned int number_length = 0;
   /* The result of an operation                    */
   double result = 0.0;

   /* Stores the value of number_string             */
   double number = 0.0;

   printf("\nTo use this calculator, enter any expression with"
                                    " or without spaces");
   printf("\nAn expression may include the operators:");
   printf("\n          +, -, *, /, %%, or ^(raise to a power).");
   printf("\nUse = at the beginning of a line to operate on ");
   printf("the result of the previous calculation.");
   printf("\nUse quit by itself to stop the calculator.\n\n");

   /* The main calculator loop */
   while(strcmp(gets(input), "quit") != 0)
   {
      /* Get the input string length     */
      input_length = strlen(input);

      /* Remove all spaces from the input by copy the string to itself */
      /* including the string terminating character                     */
      for(to = 0, index = 0 ; index<=input_length ; index++)
```

```
      if(*(input+index) != ' ')              /* If it is not a space    */
         *(input+to++) = *(input+index);        /* Copy the character   */

   input_length = strlen(input);        /* Get the new string length  */
   index = 0;                           /* Start at the first character */

   if(input[index]== '=')               /* Is there =?                  */
     index++;                           /* Yes so skip over it          */
   else
   {                                    /* No - look for the left operand*/
      /* Look for a number that is the left operand for */
      /* the first operator                             */

      /* Check for sign and copy it */
      number_length = 0;        /* Initialize length        */

      /* Is it + or -?  */
      if(input[index]=='+' || input[index]=='-')
        /* Yes so copy it */
        *(number_string+number_length++) = *(input+index++);

      /* Copy all following digits */
      /* Is it a digit? */
      for( ; isdigit(*(input+index)) ; index++)
        /* Yes - Copy it  */
        *(number_string+number_length++) = *(input+index);

        /* copy any fractional part */
        /* Is it decimal point? */
      if(*(input+index)=='.')
      { /* Yes so copy the decimal point and the following digits */
        /* Copy point */
        *(number_string+number_length++) = *(input+index++);

        /* For each digit */
        for( ; isdigit(*(input+index)) ; index++)
          /* copy it        */
          *(number_string+number_length++) = *(input+index);
      }

     /* Append string terminator     */
     *(number_string+number_length) = '\0';
      /* If we have a left operand, the length of number_string */
      /* will be > 0. In this case convert to a double so we    */
      /* can use it in the calculation                          */
     if(number_length>0)
        /* Store first number as result */
        result = atof(number_string);
   }

   /* Now look for 'op number' combinations */
   for(;index < input_length;)
```

```
{
  op = *(input+index++);        /* Get the operator */

  /* Copy the next operand and store it in number */
  number_length = 0;      /* Initialize the length  */

  /* Check for sign and copy it */
  /* Is it + or -?  */
  if(input[index]=='+' || input[index]=='-')
    /* Yes - copy it. */
   *(number_string+number_length++) = *(input+index++);

  /* Copy all following digits */
  /* For each digit */
  for( ; isdigit(*(input+index)) ; index++)
    /* copy it.          */
     *(number_string+number_length++) = *(input+index);

  /* copy any fractional part */
  /* Is is a decimal point? */
  if(*(input+index)=='.')
  { /* Copy the  decimal point and the following digits */
    /* Copy point       */
   *(number_string+number_length++) = *(input+index++);
    /* For each digit */
    for( ; isdigit(*(input+index)) ; index++)
      /* copy it.          */
       *(number_string+number_length++) = *(input+index);
  }

  /* terminate string */
  *(number_string+number_length) = '\0';

  /* Convert to a double so we can use it in the calculation */
  number = atof(number_string);
```

```
  /* Execute operation, as 'result op= number' */
  switch(op)
  {
    case '+':        /* Addition            */
      result += number;
      break;
    case '-':         /* Subtraction        */
      result -= number;
      break;
    case '*':         /* Multiplication    */
      result *= number;
      break;
    case '/':         /* Division            */
      /* Check second operand for zero */
      if(number == 0)
        printf("\n\n\aDivision by zero error!\n");
```

```
          else
            result /= number;
          break;
        case '%':          /* Modulus operator - remainder   */
          /* Check second operand for zero */
          if((long)number == 0)
            printf("\n\n\aDivision by zero error!\n");
          else
            result = (double)((long)result % (long)number);
          break;
        case '^':          /* Raise to a power               */
          result = pow(result, number);
          break;
        default:           /* Invalid operation or bad input */
          printf("\n\n\aIllegal operation!\n");
      }
    }
    printf("= %f\n", result);  /* Output the result */
  }
}
```

The **switch** statement is essentially the same as the previous calculator program, but with some extra cases. Because we use the power function, **pow()**, to calculate **result**^{number}, we have to add a **#include** directive for the header file **math.h**.

Typical output from our calculator program is:

```
To use this calculator, enter any expression with or without spaces
An expression may include the operators:
                  +, -, *, /, %, or ^(raise to a power).
Use = at the beginning of a line to operate on the result of the
previous calculation.
Use quit by itself to stop the calculator.

2.5+3.3/2
= 2.900000
= *3
= 8.700000
= ^4
= 5728.976100
1.3+2.4-3.5+-7.8
= -7.600000
=*-2
= 15.200000
= *-2
= -30.400000
= +2
= -28.400000
quit
```

And there we have it!

Summary

In this chapter we've covered a lot of ground. We have explored pointers in detail. You should now understand the relationship between pointers and arrays (both one-dimensional and multi-dimensional arrays) and have a good grasp of their uses. We've introduced another function - the `malloc()` function for dynamically allocating memory, which provides the potential for your programs to use just enough memory for the data being processed in each run. You should have a clear idea of how you can use pointers with strings and, lastly, how you can use arrays of pointers.

The topics covered in this chapter are fundamental to a lot of what follows in the rest of the book, and of course to writing C programs effectively - so you should make sure that you're quite comfortable with what we've discussed. Once you feel comfortable with this material, we'll move on to the next chapter, which is all about structuring your programs.

Structuring Your Programs

I mentioned, in Chapter 1, that breaking a program up into reasonably self-contained units is basic to the development of any program of a practical nature. When confronted with a big task, the most sensible thing to do is break it up into manageable chunks. You can then deal with each small chunk fairly easily - and be sure that you've done it properly.

One of the key ideas in the C language is to segment a program into functions. Even with the relatively short examples that we've seen so far, which were written as a single function, **main()**, we've still used a variety of standard library functions for input and output, for mathematical operations, and for handling strings.

In this chapter, we'll be looking at how you can make your programs more effective, and easier to develop, by introducing more functions of your own.

In this chapter you will learn:

- More about functions
- How data is passed to a function
- How to return results from your functions
- How to define your own functions
- How pointers can be used with functions

Program Structure

As I said right at the outset, a C program consists of one or more functions, the most important of which is the function **main()**, where execution starts. We saw, when we used library functions such as **printf()** or **scanf()**, how one function was able to call up another function. Each function in a program is a self-contained unit. When a function is called, the code within the body of that function is executed; and when the function has finished, control returns to the point at which that function was called. This is illustrated in the next figure, where you can see an idealized representation of a C program structured as five functions. It doesn't show any details of the statements involved - just the sequence of execution.

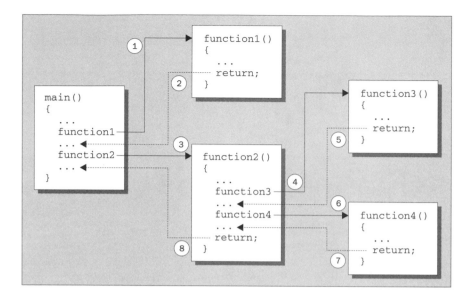

The program steps through the instructions in the normal way until it comes across a call to a particular function. At that point, execution moves to the start of that function – that is, the first statement in the body of the function. Execution of the program continues through the function statements until it hits a **return** statement. This signals that execution should go back to the point just after where the function was originally called.

The set of functions that make up a program link together, through the function calls and their **return** statements, to perform the various tasks necessary for the program to achieve its purpose.

Before we look in more detail at how we define our own functions, we need to look at a particular aspect of the way variables behave that we have glossed over so far.

Variable Scope

In all our examples up to now, we've declared the variables for the program at the beginning of the block that defines the body of the function **main()**. But we can actually define variables at the beginning of *any* block. Does this make a difference? "It most certainly does, Stanley", as Ollie would have said. Variables only exist within the block in which they are defined. They are created when they are declared, and they cease to exist at the next closing brace.

This also true of blocks that are inside other blocks. The variables declared at the beginning of an outer block also exist in the inner block. These variables are freely accessible, as long as there are no other variables with the same name in the inner block - as we'll see.

Variables that are created when they are declared and destroyed at the end of a block are called **automatic variables**, because they're automatically created and destroyed. The extent within a program where a given variable exists is called the variable's **scope**. When you use a variable within its scope, everything is OK. But if you try to reference a variable outside its scope, you'll get an error message when you compile the program - since the variable doesn't exist outside of its scope. The general idea is illustrated in the figure below.

```
{
  int a;

/* Reference to a is OK here */
/* Reference to b is an error here */

  {
    int b;

    /* Reference to a and b is OK here */

  }

/* Reference to b is an error here */
/* Reference to a is OK here */

}
```

Try It Out - Understanding Scope

Let's take a simple example that involves a nested block:

```
/* Example 8.1 A microscopic program about scope */
#include <stdio.h>
void main()
{
   int count1 = 1;     /* Declared in outer block */

   do
   {
     int count2 = 0; /* Declared in inner block */
     ++count2;
     printf("\ncount1 = %d     count2 = %d", count1,count2);
   }while( ++count1 <= 8 );

   /* count2 no longer exists */

   printf("\ncount1 = %d", count1);
}
```

Try running this program. You'll get this output:

```
count1 = 1     count2 = 1
count1 = 2     count2 = 1
count1 = 3     count2 = 1
count1 = 4     count2 = 1
count1 = 5     count2 = 1
count1 = 6     count2 = 1
count1 = 7     count2 = 1
count1 = 8     count2 = 1
count1 = 9
```

How It Works

The block that is the body of **main()** contains an inner block which is the **do-while** loop. We declare and define **count2** inside the loop block:

```
do
{
  int count2 = 0; /* Declared in inner block */
  ++count2;
  printf("\ncount1 = %d      count2 = %d", count1,count2);
}while( ++count1 <= 8 );
```

As a result, its value is never more than 1. During each iteration of the loop, the variable **count2** is created, initialized, incremented, and forgotten. It only exists from the statement that declares it down to the closing brace for the loop. The variable **count1**, on the other hand, exists at the **main()** block level. It continues to exist while it is incremented, so the last **printf()** produces the value 9.

Try modifying the program to make the last **printf()** output the value of **count2**. It won't compile. You'll get an error because, at the point where the last **printf()** is, **count2** no longer exists. From this you may guess, correctly, that failing to initialize automatic variables can cause untold chaos, because the memory they use may be reallocated to something else at the end of their existence. As a consequence, next time around, your uninitialized variables may contain anything but what you expect.

Try It Out - More About Scope

Let's try a slight modification of the last example:

```
/* Example 8.2 More scope in this one      */
#include <stdio.h>
void main()
{
   int count = 0;    /* Declared in outer block */
   do
   {
     int count = 0; /* This is another variable called count */
     ++count;         /* this applies to inner count          */
     printf("\ncount = %d ", count);
   }
   while( ++count <= 8 ); /* This works with outer count */

   /* Inner count is dead, this is outer */
   printf("\ncount = %d", count);
}
```

Now we've used the same variable name, **count**, at the **main()** block level and in the loop block. Observe what happens when you compile and run this.

```
count = 1
count = 1
```

```
count = 1
count = 1
count = 1
count = 1
count = 1
count = 1
count = 9
```

How It Works

The output is boring, but interesting at the same time. We actually have two variables called **count**, but inside the loop block the local variable will hide the version of **count** that exists at the **main()** block level. Inside the **while** loop, only the local version of **count** can be reached - so that is the variable that's being incremented. The **printf()** inside the loop block displays the local **count** value, which is always 1 - for the reasons given previously. As soon as we exit from the loop, the outer **count** variable becomes visible, and the last **printf()** displays its exit value from the loop as 9. Clearly, the variable controlling the loop is the one declared at the beginning of **main()**. This little example demonstrates why it isn't a good idea to use the same variable name for two different variables in a function, even though it is legal. At best, it is most confusing. At worst, you'll be thinking, "that's another fine mess I've got myself into".

Variable Scope and Functions

The last point to note, before we get into the detail of creating functions, is that the body of every function is a block (which may contain other blocks, of course). As a result, the automatic variables declared within a function are local to the function and do not exist elsewhere. Therefore, the variables declared within one function are quite independent of those declared in another function. There's nothing to prevent you from using the same name for variables in different functions: they will remain quite separate.

This becomes more significant when you are dealing with large programs where the problem of ensuring unique variables can become a little inconvenient. It's still a good idea to avoid any unnecessary or misleading overlapping of variable names in your various functions and, of course, you should try to use names that are meaningful to make your programs easy to follow. We'll see more about this as we explore functions in C more deeply.

Functions

In our programs so far, we've used built-in functions such as **printf()** and **strcpy()**. We've seen how these built-in functions were executed when we referenced them by name with suitable arguments. We transferred information to a function by using arguments in parentheses following the function name. With the **printf()** function, for instance, the first argument is usually a text string in quotes, and the succeeding arguments (of which there may be none) are a series of variables or expressions whose values are to be displayed.

We've also seen how we can receive information back from a function in two ways. The first way we saw we could do this was through one of the function arguments in parentheses. We provided an address of a variable through an argument to a function, and the function placed a value in that variable. When we use **scanf()** to read data from the keyboard, for instance, the input is stored in an address that we supply as an argument. The second way we saw that we could receive information back from a function was as a return value. With the **sqrt()** function, for instance, the square root of the argument that we supply appears in the program code in the position where the function call was made. Thus, in the expression **2.0*sqrt(25.0)**, the value **5.0** (which the function returns) replaces the function call in the expression. The expression will therefore amount to **2.0*5.0**. Where a function returns a value of a given type, the function call can appear as part of any expression where a variable of the same type could be used.

Since you've already written the function **main()** in all your programs already, you already have the basic knowledge of how a function is constructed. So let's move on and start defining some functions.

Defining a Function

To create a function, you need to specify a **function header** as the first line of the function definition, followed by the executable part that's called the **function body**, which is enclosed between braces.

> The function header defines the name of the function, the function parameters (in other words, what values are passed to the function when it's called) and the function's return value type.

> The function body determines what operations the function performs on the values passed to it.

The general form of a function is essentially the same as we've been using for **main()**, and looks like this:

```
Return_type  Function_name( Parameters - separated by commas )
{
    Statements;
}
```

The statements in the function body can be absent, but the braces must be present. If there are no statements in the body of a function, the return type must be **void**, and the function will have no effect. Although it may not be immediately apparent, presenting a function with a content-free body is often useful during the testing phase of a complicated program. This allows you to run the program with only selected functions actually doing something; you can then add the function bodies, step-by-step, until the whole thing works.

> *The statements in the body of a function can also contain nested blocks of statements. But you cannot define a function inside the body of another function.*

The general form for calling a function is this:

```
Function_name(  Parameters - separated by commas );
```

We simply use the function's name followed with a parameter list in parentheses - just as we've been calling functions such as **printf()** and **scanf()**. Notice that a call to a function must end with a semicolon.

Naming a Function

The function name, specified in the first line of our general representation of a function, can be any legal name in C that isn't a reserved word - such as **int**, **double** or **sizeof** - and which isn't the same as the name of another function. In particular, you should take care not to use the same names as the standard library functions, since this would prevent you from using the library function of the same name (as well as being very confusing).

One way of differentiating your function names is to start them with a capital letter - although some programmers find this rather too restricting. A legal name has the same form as that of a variable - a sequence of letters and digits, the first of which must be a letter. As with variable names, the underline character counts as a letter. Other than that, the name of a function can be anything you like but, ideally, you should give some clue as to what the function does. Examples of valid function names that you might create are:

    cube_root   FindLast   Explosion   Back2Front

You'll often want to define function names (and variable names, come to that) which consist of more than one word. There are two common approaches you can adopt (that happen to be illustrated in our first two examples above). These approaches are:

▶   Separate the words in a function name with an underline character

▶   Capitalize the first letter of each word

Both approaches work well. Which one you choose is up to you, but it's a good idea to pick an approach and stick to it. You can, of course, use one approach for functions and the other for variables. Within this book, both approaches have been sprinkled around to give you a feel for how they look. By the time you reach the end of the book, you'll probably have formed your own opinions.

Function Parameters

Function parameters are defined within the function header. The parameters are a list of variable names and their types, with successive parameters separated by commas. The entire list of parameters is enclosed between the parentheses that follow the function name.

Parameters provide the means to get information *from* the calling program *into* the function. These parameters are local to the function, and the values supplied to them when the function is called are referred to as **arguments**. The computation in the body of the function is then written using these parameters. Finally, when the computation has finished, the function will exit and return an appropriate value back to the original calling statement.

A typical function header is:

```
int SendMessage(char* text)
```

This function has one parameter, **text**, which is of type 'pointer to **char**', and it returns a value of type **int**.

A function is called by just using the function name followed by the arguments to the function in parentheses. When you actually call the function by referencing it in some part of your program, the arguments you specify in the call will be substituted for the parameters in the function.

As a result, when the function executes, the computation will proceed using the values supplied as arguments. The arguments that you specify when you call a function need to agree in type, number and sequence with the parameters specified in the function header. The relationship and information passing between the calling and called function is illustrated in the figure.

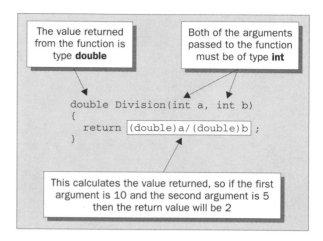

Return Value Type Specification

Let's take another look at the general form of a function:

```
Return_type  Function_name( Parameters - separated by commas )
{
    Statements;
}
```

Now the **Return_type** specifies the type of the value returned by the function. If the function is used in an expression, or as the right hand side of an assignment statement, the return value supplied by the function will effectively be substituted for the function in its position. The type of value to be returned by a function can be specified as any of the legal types in C, including pointers. The type can also be specified as **void**, meaning that no value is returned. Notice, then, that a function with a **void** return type can't be used in an expression, or anywhere in an assignment statement.

The return type can also be a pointer to **void**, which is a pointer value but with no specified type. This latter type is used when we want the flexibility to be able to return a pointer that may be used for a variety of purposes, as in the case of the **malloc()** function for allocating memory. The most common return types are shown in the following table:

Type	Meaning	Type	Meaning
int	integer, 2 or 4 bytes	**int***	pointer to **int**
short	integer, 2 bytes	**short***	pointer to **short**
long	integer, 4 bytes	**long***	pointer to **long**
char	character, 1 byte	**char***	pointer to **char**
float	floating point, 4 bytes	**float***	pointer to **float**
double	floating point, 8 bytes	**double***	pointer to **double**
void	no value	**void***	pointer to undefined type

The return Statement

The **return** statement provides the means of exiting from a function and resuming execution of the calling function at the point from which the call occurred. In its simplest form, the return statement is just this:

```
return;
```

In this form, the **return** statement is being used in a function where the return type has been declared as **void**. It doesn't return any value. However, the more general form of the **return** statement is:

```
return expression;
```

This form of **return** statement must be used when the return value type for the function has been declared as some type other than **void**.

> *You'll get an error if you compile a program that contains a function declared with a void return type that tries to return a value. Likewise, you'll get an error if you use a bare **return** in a function where the return type was declared to be something other than void.*

The **expression** can be any expression, but it should result in a value with the same type as that declared for the return value in the function header. If it isn't of the same type, the compiler will cast the type of the **expression** to the one required (where this is possible) along with a warning if the cast has the potential for losing information. The compiler will produce an error message if the cast is not possible.

There can be more than one **return** statement in a function, but each **return** statement must supply a value with the same type as that specified in the function header for the return value.

> *The calling function doesn't have to recognize or process the value returned from a called function. It's up to you how you use any values returned from function calls.*

Try It Out - Using Functions

It is always easier to understand with an example, so let's start with a trivial illustration of a program that consists of two functions. We'll write a function to compute the average of two floating-point variables, and we'll call that function from **main()**. This is more to illustrate the mechanism of writing and calling functions than to present a good example of their practical use.

```
/* Example 8.3 Average of two float values */
#include <stdio.h>

/* Definition of the function to calculate an average */
float average(float x, float y)
{
```

```
      return (x + y)/2.0f;
}

/* main program - execution always starts here */
void main()
{
   float average(float x, float y);   /* Function prototype */

   float value1 = 0.0F;
   float value2 = 0.0F;
   float value3 = 0.0F;

   printf("Enter two floating-point values separated by blanks: ");
   scanf("%f %f", &value1, &value2);
   value3 = average(value1, value2);
   printf("\nThe average is: %f",  value3);
}
```

Typical output of this program would be:

```
Enter two floating-point values separated by blanks: 2.34 4.567

The average is: 3.453500
```

How It Works

We'll go through this step by step. Look at the following figure. It describes the order of execution in our example.

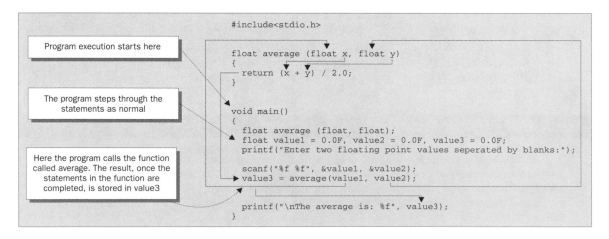

As we already know, execution begins at the first executable statement of our function **main()**. The first statement in the body of **main()** is:

```
      float average(float x, float y);   /* Function prototype */
```

This is not an executable statement. All we're doing is declaring the function. This is called a **function prototype**.

> *The purpose of a function prototype is to tell the compiler the essential specifications of a function. A function prototype includes specifications for the return type and any parameter types, in addition to the name of the function itself. Note that function prototypes require a semicolon at the end, just as variable declarations do.*

Our function prototype includes specifications for the return type (**float**) and the parameter types (**float** and **float**), as well as the name of the function, **average()**. Compare our prototype with the function header in the actual function definition, which *doesn't* have a semicolon:

```
float average(float x, float y)
```

The compiler is able to ensure that when we use the function, we provide arguments of the appropriate type, and that the return value is handled properly in any expression in which it's used.

The variables, **x** and **y** are local to the function **average()**, so we are free to use the same variable names in the calling function - or any other function for that matter. Note that the prototype doesn't need to use the same parameter names as in the function definition; in fact, you can even omit them altogether in the function prototype, like this:

```
float average(float, float); /* Function prototype */
```

This function declaration is not strictly necessary in our example. If you delete it, you'll see that the program will still compile and run. This is because the definition of the function **average()** *precedes* its use in **main()** - so the compiler already knows all about it. If the definition followed **main()**, however, then it would be essential to include the function declaration.

> *It's good practice to always include declarations for all of the functions in a program, regardless of where they are called. This approach will help your programs to be more consistent in design, and will prevent any errors occuring if, at any stage, you choose to call a function from another part of your program.*
>
> *Function declarations do not typically appear in the position shown in the example above. They usually appear at the beginning of a program file, preceding **main()** and the other functions in the program.*

Our first executable statement that actually does something is this:

```
printf("Enter two floating point values separated by blanks: ");
```

There's nothing new here; we simply make a call to the function **printf()** with one argument, which happens to be a string. The actual value transferred to **printf()** will be a pointer containing the address of the beginning of the string that we've specified as the argument. The **printf()** function will then display the string that we've supplied as that argument.

Our next statement is also a familiar one:

```
scanf("%f %f",&value1, &value2);
```

This is a call to the input function **scanf()**. This has three arguments: a string, which is therefore effectively a pointer (as in our previous statement); the addresses of the first variable - again, effectively a pointer; and the address of the second variable - again, effectively a pointer. As we've discussed, **scanf()** must have the addresses for those last two arguments, since we want the input data to be stored in them.

Once we've read in the two values, the assignment statement is executed:

```
value3 = average(value1, value2);
```

This calls our function **average()**, which expects two **float** type values as arguments - and we've correctly supplied **value1** and **value2**, which are both of type **float**.

There is a very important point to be made here, which is illustrated in the next figure.

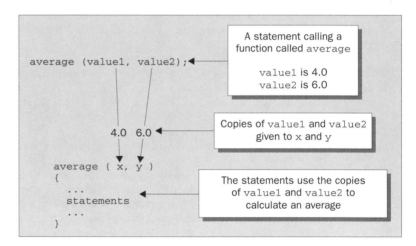

The important point is this: *copies* of the values of **value1** and **value2** are transferred to our function, *not the variables themselves*. This means that the function can't change **value1** or **value2**. For instance, if we input the values 4.0 and 6.0 for the two variables, the compiler will create separate copies of these two values to transfer to the function **average()** when it is called.

> *This mechanism is how all argument transfers to functions take place in C, and it is termed a call-by-value mechanism.*

The only way that a called function can change a variable belonging to the function that called it is by passing a parameter to the called function that's actually an address of the variable from the calling function. However, even when you pass an address like this, it is still only a copy of the address that's actually passed to the function, not the original. We'll come back to this point later in the chapter.

Our **average()** function is executed with the values from **value1** and **value2** substituted for the parameter names in the function - which are **x** and **y** respectively. Our function is defined by the statements:

```
float average(float x, float y)
{
  return (x + y)/2.0f;
}
```

The function body only has one statement, which is the **return** statement. But this **return** statement does all the work we need: it contains an expression for the value to be returned which works out the average of **x** and **y**. This value then appears in place of the function in the assignment statement back in **main()**. So, in effect, a function that returns a value acts like a variable of the same type as the return value.

Note that without the **f** on the constant **2.0**, this number would be **double** - and the whole expression would be evaluated as double. Since the compiler would then arrange to cast this to type **float** for the return value, we'd get a warning message - since data could be lost.

Instead of assigning the result of the function to **value3**, we could have written the last **printf()** statement as:

```
printf("\nThe average is: %f", average(value1, value2));
```

Here, the function **average()** would receive copies of the values of the argument. The return value from the function would be supplied to **printf()** directly, even though we hadn't explicitly specified a place to store it. The compiler would take care of assigning some memory to store the value returned from **average()**. It would also take the trouble to make a copy to hand over to the function **printf()** as an argument. Once the **printf()** had been executed, however, we would have had no means of accessing the value that was returned from the function **average()**.

Another possible option is to use explicit values in a function call. What happens then? Let's stretch our **printf()** out of context now and take, for example:

```
printf("\nThe average is: %f", average(4.0, 6.0));
```

In this case, the compiler would create a memory location to store each of the constant arguments to **average()**, and then supply copies of those values to the function - exactly as before. A copy of the result returned from the function **average()** would then be passed to **printf()**.

The next figure illustrates calling a function named **useful()** from **main()** and getting a value returned. The arrows in the figure show how the values correspond between **main()** and **useful()**. Notice that the value returned from **useful()** is finally stored in the variable **x** in **main()**.

```
void main()
{
   . . .
   x = useful ( y , z );
   . . .
}



long useful( int a , int b )
{
   long c; /* A local variable we are using to hold a result */
   . . .          /* In here would be useful statements */
   return c;
}
```

Function Declarations

As we saw in the previous example, the function declaration defines the essential characteristics of a function. It defines its name, its return value type, and the type of each of its parameters. You can actually write it exactly the same as the function header and just add a semicolon at the end if you want. A function declaration is also called a **function prototype**, because it models how you use the function. A function prototype enables the compiler to generate the appropriate instructions at each point where we use the function, and to check that we use it correctly in each case. When we include a header file in a program, the header file adds the function prototypes for library functions to the program. For example, the header file, **stdio.h** contains function prototypes for **printf()** and **scanf()** amongst others.

In a variation of our example, we could define the function **main()** first, and then the function **average()**:

```
#include <stdio.h>

void main()
{
  float average(float, float);
  ...
}

float average(float x, float y)
{
  return (x + y)/2.0;
}
```

In this case, we must put the declaration for the function **average()** at the beginning of the body of **main()**, since **main()** uses that function. Without it, the code would not compile.

> *The declaration for the function **average()**, here, is local to **main()**, because its scope is defined by the limits of the body of **main()**.*

If we wanted to use the function **average()** in several different functions in the same program, we could put the same declaration in the body of each.

However, there is another possibility - which also happens to be by far the most common method of handling function declarations in C. We could put the declaration of **average()** at the beginning of the file, along with our **#include** directives. The function declaration would then be external to all of our functions in that source file, and its scope would extend to the end of the source file - thereby allowing any of our function calls (to that particular function) to use that declaration, without further need of any declarations. This is the typical position for a function declaration, and I shall show this approach in the next example.

Pointers and Functions

We've already seen how it's possible to pass a pointer as an argument to a function. More than that, we've seen that this is actually quite necessary if a function is to modify the value of a variable defined in the calling function. In fact, this is the only way it can be done. So let's see how all this works out in practice.

Try It Out - Functions Using Ordinary Variables

Let's first take an elementary example that doesn't use a pointer argument. Here, we're going to try to change the contents of a variable by sending it as an argument to a function, changing it, and then returning it. We'll print its value both within the function and back in **main()** to see what the effect is:

```
/* Example 8.4 The change that doesn't  */
#include <stdio.h>

int change(int number);   /* Function prototype            */

void main()
{
   int number = 10;       /* Starting Value                */
   int result = 0;        /* Place to put the returned value */

   result = change(number);
   printf("\nIn main, result = %d\tnumber = %d", result, number);
}

/* Definition of the function change() */
int change(int number)
{
   number = 2 * number;
   printf("\nIn function change, number = %d", number);
   return number;
}
```

The output from this program is:

```
In function change, number = 20
In main, result = 20     number = 10
```

How It Works

This example demonstrates that we can't change the world without pointers. We can only change the values locally within the function.

The first thing of note about this example is that we've put the prototype for the function **change()** outside of **main()** along with our **#include** statement:

```
#include <stdio.h>

int change(int number);  /* Function prototype            */
```

This makes it *global*, and if we had other functions in the example, they would all be able to use this function.

In **main()** we set up an integer variable, **number,** with an initial value of 10. We also have a second variable, **result**, which we use to store the value we get back from the function **change()**:

```
int number = 10;        /* Starting Value             */
int result = 0;         /* Place to put the returned value */
```

We then call the function **change()** and send the value of the argument **number**:

```
result = change(number);
```

The function **change()** is defined as:

```
int change(int number)
{
    number = 2 * number;
    printf("\nIn function change, number = %d", number);
    return number;
}
```

Within the body of the function **change()**, the first statement doubles the value stored in the argument that's been passed to it from **main()**. We even use the same variable name in the function that we used in **main()**, to reinforce the idea that we want to change the original value. The function **change()** displays the new value of **number** before it sends it back to **main()** by means of the **return** statement.

In **main()** we also display what we got back from **change()**, and the value of **number**.

```
printf("\nIn main, result = %d\tnumber = %d", result, number);
```

Look at the output, though. It demonstrates how vain and pathetic our attempt to change a variable value by passing it to a function has been. Clearly, the variable **number** in **change()** has the value 20 on return from the function. It is displayed both in the function and as a returned value in **main()**. In spite of our transparent subterfuge of giving them the same name, the variables called **number** in **main()** and **change()** are evidently quite separate, so modifying one has no effect on the other.

Try It Out - Using Pointers in Functions

We can now modify the last example to use pointers, and with a following wind, we should succeed in modifying the value of a variable in **main()**.

```
/* Example 8.5 The change that does   */
#include <stdio.h>

int change(int* pnumber);    /* Function prototype                */

void main()
{
   int number = 10;          /* Starting Value                   */
   int* pnumber = &number;   /* Pointer to starting value        */
   int result = 0;           /* Place to put the returned value  */

   result = change(pnumber);
   printf("\nIn main, result = %d\tnumber = %d", result, number);
}

/* Definition of the function change() */
int change(int* pnumber)
{
   *pnumber *= 2;
   printf("\nIn function change, *pnumber = %d", *pnumber );
   return *pnumber;
}
```

The output from this program looks like this:

```
In function change, *pnumber = 20
In main, result = 20     number = 20
```

How It Works

There are relatively few changes to the last example. We've defined a pointer in **main()**, called
pnumber, which is initialized to the address of our variable **number**, which holds our starting
value:

```
   int* pnumber = &number;   /* Pointer to starting value        */
```

The prototype of the function **change()** has been modified to take account of the parameter
being a pointer:

```
int change(int* pnumber);    /* Function prototype                */
```

The definition of the function **change()** has been modified to use a pointer:

```
int change(int* pnumber)
{
   *pnumber *= 2;
   printf("\nIn function change, *pnumber = %d", *pnumber );
   return *pnumber;
}
```

This pointer, **pnumber**, has the same name as the pointer in **main()**, although this is of no consequence to the way the program works. We could call it anything we like, as long as it is a pointer of the correct type.

Within the function **change()**, the arithmetic statement has been changed to:

```
*pnumber *= 2;
```

Using the ***=** operator isn't strictly necessary, but it makes it a lot less confusing, provided you can remember what ***=** does at this point. It's exactly the same as:

```
*pnumber = 2*(*pnumber);
```

The output now demonstrates that the pointer mechanism is working correctly and that the function **change()** is indeed modifying the value of **number** in **main()**. Of course, when we submit a pointer as an argument, it's still passed by value. Therefore, the compiler does not pass the original pointer, but makes a copy of the pointer to hand over to the function. Since the copy will contain the same address as the original, it still refers to the variable **number**, so everything works OK.

If you're unconvinced of this, you can demonstrate it for yourself quite easily by adding a statement to the function **change()** that modifies the pointer **pnumber**. You could set it to **NULL** for instance. You can then check in **main()** that **pnumber** still points to **number**. Of course, you'll have to alter the **return** statement in **change()** to get the correct result.

Try It Out - Passing Data Using Pointers

We can exercise this method of passing data to a function using pointers in a slightly more practical way, with a revised version of our function for sorting strings from Chapter 7. You can see the complete code for the program here, and then we will discuss it in detail. The source code defines three functions in addition to **main()**:

```
/* Example 8.6 The functional approach to string sorting*/
#include <stdio.h>
#include <stdlib.h>
#include <string.h>
#define TRUE  1
#define FALSE 0

int str_in(char **);            /* Function prototype for str_in    */
void str_sort(char *[], int); /* Function prototype for str_sort  */
void str_out(char *[], int);  /* Function prototype for str_out   */

#define BUFFER_LEN 240
#define NUM_P 50

/* Function main - execution starts here */
void main()
{
   char *pS[NUM_P];               /* Array of string pointers      */
   int count = 0;                 /* Number of strings read        */
```

```
        printf("\nEnter successive lines, pressing Enter at the end of"
                        " each line. Just press Enter to end.\n");

   for(count = 0; count < NUM_P ; count++)   /* Max of NUM_P strings   */
     if(!str_in(&pS[count]) )                /* Read a string          */
       break;                                /* Stop input on 0 return */

   str_sort( pS, count );                    /* Sort strings           */
   str_out( pS, count );                     /* Output strings         */
}

/*****************************************************/
/*      String input routine                        */
/*  Argument is a pointer to a string pointer       */
/*   which is char**                                */
/*  Returns FALSE for empty string or if memory not */
/*  obtained, and returns TRUE otherwise.           */
/*****************************************************/
int str_in(char **pString)
{
   char Buffer[BUFFER_LEN];    /* Space to store input string  */

   if(gets(Buffer) == NULL )   /* NULL returned from gets()?   */
   {
     printf("\nError reading string.\n");
     return FALSE;             /* Read error                   */
   }

   if(Buffer[0] == '\0')       /* Empty string read?           */
     return FALSE;

   *pString = (char*)malloc(strlen(Buffer) + 1);

   if(*pString == NULL)        /* Check memory allocation      */
   {
     printf("\nOut of memory.");
     return FALSE;             /* No memory allocated          */
   }

   strcpy(*pString, Buffer);   /* Copy string read to argument */
   return TRUE;
}

/*****************************************************/
/*      String sort routine                         */
/* First argument is array of pointers to strings   */
/* which is type char**.                            */
/* Second argument is the number of elements in the */
/* pointer array - i.e. the number of strings       */
/*****************************************************/
void str_sort(char *P[], int N)
```

```
   {
      char *pTemp = NULL;        /* Temporary pointer              */
      int i = 0;                 /* Loop counter                   */
      int sorted = FALSE;        /* Strings sorted indicator       */
      while(!sorted)             /* Loop until there are no swaps   */
      {
        sorted = TRUE;           /* Initialize to indicate no swaps */
        for( i = 0 ; i < N - 1 ; i++ )
          if(strcmp(P[i], P[i + 1] ) > 0)
          {
            sorted = FALSE;      /* indicate we are out of order    */
            pTemp= P[i];         /* Swap pointers P[i]              */
            P[i] = P[i + 1];     /*                  and            */
            P[i + 1]  = pTemp;   /*                  P[i + 1]       */
          }
      }
   }


   /*****************************************************/
   /*         String output routine                     */
   /* First argument is an array of pointers to         */
   /* strings which is the same as char**               */
   /* The second argument is a count of the number of   */
   /* pointers in the array i.e. the number of strings  */
   /*****************************************************/
   void str_out(char *P[] , int N)
   {
      int i = 0;                 /* Loop counter                   */

      printf("\nYour input sorted in order is:\n\n");
      for (i = 0 ; i < N ; i++)
      {
        printf("%s\n", P[i]);    /* Display a string               */
        free(P[i]);              /* Free memory for the string     */
        P[i] = NULL;
      }
      return;
   }
```

Typical output would be:

```
Enter successive lines, pressing Enter at the end of each line. Just
press Enter to end.
Mike
Adam
Mary
Steve


Your input sorted in order is:
```

```
Adam
Mary
Mike
Steve
```

How It Works

This example works in a similar way to the sorting example in Chapter 7. It looks like a lot of code, but I've added quite a few comment lines in fancy boxes that occupy space. This is good practice for longer programs that use several functions, so that you can be sure you know what each section does.

The whole set of statements for all the functions makes up our source file. At the beginning of the program source file, before we define **main()**, we have our **#include** statements for the libraries we're using, our constant definitions, and our function prototypes. Each of these are effective from the point of their occurrence to the end of our file, since they're defined outside of all of the functions. They are therefore effective in all of our functions.

The program consists of three functions in addition to our function **main().** The prototypes of the functions we've defined are:

```
int str_in(char **);        /* Function prototype for str_in    */
void str_sort(char *[], int); /* Function prototype for str_sort  */
void str_out(char *[], int);  /* Function prototype for str_out   */
```

You can see that I haven't specified the parameter names here. You are not obliged to do so, but it is usually better if you do. I omitted them here to show that you can leave them out. You can also use different parameter names in the function prototype from those in the function definition.

> *It can be useful to use longer more explanatory names in the prototype, and shorter names in the function definition - to keep the code more concise.*

Our prototypes, in this example, declare a function to read in all the strings, called **str_in()**, a function to sort the strings, called **str_sort()**, and a function to output the sorted strings in their new sequence, called **str_out()**. Each of the function prototypes declares the types of the parameters and the return value type for that function.

Our first declaration is for **str_in()** and it declares the parameter as **char ****, which is a 'pointer to a pointer to **char**'. Sounds complicated? Well, let's have a closer look at exactly what's going on here, and you'll understand how simple this really is.

In **main()**, the argument to this function is **&pS[i]**. This is the address of **pS[i]**, or in other words, a pointer to **pS[i]**. And what is **pS[i]**? It's a pointer to **char**. Put these together and we have the type as declared: **char****. We have to declare it this way because we want to modify the contents of an element in the **pS** array from within the function **str_in**. This is the only way that the **str_in()** function can get access to the **pS** array. If we only used one ***** in the parameter type definition, and just used **pS[i]** as the argument, then the function would receive whatever was contained in **pS[i]**, which is not what we want at all! This mechanism is illustrated in the next figure.

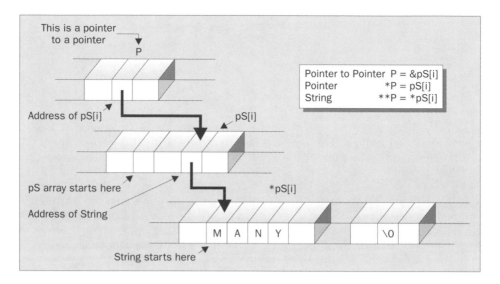

We can now take a look at the internal working of the function.

The str_in() Function

First, note our detailed comment at the beginning. This is a good way of starting out a function and highlighting its basic purpose. The function definition consists of:

```
/******************************************************/
/*       String input routine                         */
/*  Argument is a pointer to a string pointer          */
/*  which is char**                                    */
/*  Returns FALSE for empty string or if memory not    */
/*  obtained, and returns TRUE otherwise.              */
/******************************************************/
int str_in(char **pString)
{
   char Buffer[BUFFER_LEN];    /* Space to store input string */

   if(gets(Buffer) == NULL )   /* NULL returned from gets()?   */
   {
     printf("\nError reading string.\n");
      return FALSE;             /* Read error                   */
   }

   if(Buffer[0] == '\0')       /* Empty string read?           */
      return FALSE;

   *pString = (char*)malloc(strlen(Buffer) + 1);

   if(*pString == NULL)        /* Check memory allocation      */
   {
     printf("\nOut of memory.");
      return FALSE;             /* No memory allocated          */
   }
```

```
            strcpy(*pString, Buffer);     /* Copy string read to argument */
            return TRUE;
    }
```

The function **str_in()** receives from **main()** the address of **pS[i]**, which is the address of
the current free array element which is to receive the address of the next string entered. Within
the function, this is referred to as the parameter **pString**.

The input string is stored in **Buffer** by the function **gets()**. This function returns **NULL** if an
error occurred reading the input, so we first check for that. We then check the first character in
the string obtained by **gets()** against **'\0'**. The function replaces the newline character that
results from pressing the *Enter* key with **'\0'**, so if you just press the *Enter* key, the first
character of the string will be **'\0'**. If we get an empty string entered, we return the value
FALSE to **main()**. The symbols **TRUE** and **FALSE** are defined in pre-processor directives, after
the **#include** directives, so we can use these in any function within the source file.

Once we've read a string, we allocate space for it using the **malloc()** function and store its
address in ***pString**. After checking that we did actually get some memory, we copy the
contents of **Buffer** to the memory allocated. If **malloc()** fails to allocate memory, we simply
display a message and return **FALSE** to **main()**.

The function **str_in()** is called in **main()** within this loop:

```
        for(count = 0; count < NUM_P ; count++) /* Max of NUM_P strings   */
            if(!str_in(&pS[count]) )             /* Read a string           */
                break;                           /* Stop input on 0 return */
```

Since all the work is done in the function **str_in()**, all that's necessary here is to continue the
loop until we get **FALSE** returned from the function, whereupon the **break** is executed; or until
we fill up the pointer array **pS**, which is indicated by **count** reaching the value **NUM_P**, thus
ending the loop. The loop also counts how many strings are entered in **count**.

Having got all the strings safely stored, **main()** then calls the function **str_sort()** to sort the
strings with this statement:

```
        str_sort( pS, count );                          /* Sort strings          */
```

The first argument is the array name, **pS**, so the address of the first location of the array is
transferred to the function. The second argument is the index value of the last string entered, so
the function can know how many strings there are to work with. So let's now move on to the
str_sort() function.

The str_sort() Function

The function **str_sort()** is defined by these statements:

```
/****************************************************/
/*        String sort routine                       */
/* First argument is array of pointers to strings   */
/* which is type char**.                            */
/* Second argument is the number of elements in the */
/* pointer array - i.e. the number of strings       */
/****************************************************/
```

```
void str_sort(char *P[], int N)
{
   char *pTemp = NULL;            /* Temporary pointer            */
   int i = 0;                     /* Loop counter                 */
   int sorted = FALSE;            /* Strings sorted indicator     */
   while(!sorted)                 /* Loop until there are no swaps */
   {
     sorted = TRUE;               /* Initialize to indicate no swaps */
     for( i = 0 ; i < N - 1 ; i++ )
       if(strcmp(P[i], P[i + 1] ) > 0)
       {
         sorted = FALSE;          /* indicate we are out of order  */
         pTemp= P[i];             /* Swap pointers P[i]            */
         P[i] = P[i + 1];         /*                 and           */
         P[i + 1]  = pTemp;       /*                 P[i + 1]       */
       }
   }
}
```

Within the function, the parameter variable **P** has been defined as an array of pointers. This will be replaced, when the function is called, by the address for **pS** that's transferred as an argument. We haven't specified the dimension for **P**. This isn't necessary, since the array is one-dimensional - so only the address is passed to the function. The second argument defines the number of elements that we want to process. If the array had two or more dimensions, we would have had to specify all dimensions except the first. This would be necessary for the compiler to know the shape of the array. Of course, you can put the dimension in if you wish, but in general you're likely to want the function to handle arrays of various lengths anyway.

The second parameter, **N**, in the function **str_sort()**, is declared as **int**, and is replaced by the value of the argument **count** when the function is called. We declare a loop counter, **i**, and a variable named **sorted** that will have the value **TRUE** or **FALSE**. Remember that all the variables declared within the function body are local to that function. This means that the variable **i** in this function, for instance, isn't the same variable as the variable **i** in any other function.

The strings are sorted in the **for** loop. You can see how this works in the figure below. Notice that only the pointers are altered. In this illustration, I've used the input data we saw above, and the input is completely sorted in one pass - but if you try this process on paper with a more disordered sequence of the same input strings, you'll see that more than one pass is often required to reach the correct sequence.

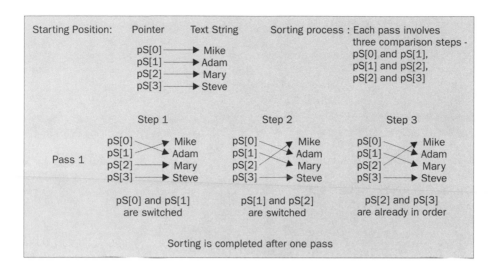

The str_out() Function

The last function called by **main()** is **str_out()**, which displays the sorted strings:

```
/****************************************************/
/*      String output routine                       */
/* First argument is an array of pointers to         */
/* strings which is the same as char**               */
/* The second argument is a count of the number of  */
/* pointers in the array i.e. the number of strings */
/****************************************************/
void str_out(char *P[] , int N)
{
  int i = 0;                  /* Loop counter                 */

  printf("\nYour input sorted in order is:\n\n");
  for (i = 0 ; i < N ; i++)
  {
    printf("%s\n", P[i]);   /* Display a string           */
    free(P[i]);             /* Free memory for the string */
    P[i] = NULL;
  }
  return;
}
```

In this function, the parameter **N** receives the value of **count**, and the strings are displayed using **N** as the count for the number of strings. The **for** loop outputs all the strings. Once a string has been displayed, we release the memory that it occupied by calling the library function **free()**, since the memory is no longer required. We also set the pointer to **NULL** to avoid any possibility of trying to refer to that memory again by mistake.

We've used a **return** statement, here, at the end of the function - but we could have left it out. Since the return type is **void**, reaching the end of the block enclosing the body of the function is the equivalent of **return**. (Remember, though, that this isn't the case for functions that return a value.)

309

Returning Pointer Values from a Function

We've seen how we can return numeric values from a function. We've just learnt how to use pointers as arguments, and how to store a pointer at an address passed as an argument. We can also return pointers from a function. Let's look first at a very simple example.

Try It Out - Returning Values from a Function

We can use increasing your salary as the basis for the example, as it's such a popular topic.

```
/* Example 8.7 A function to increase your salary */
#include <stdio.h>

long *IncomePlus(long* pPay);      /* Prototype for increase function */

void main()
{
   long Your_Pay = 30000L;          /* Starting salary             */
   long *pOld_Pay = &Your_Pay;      /* Pointer to pay value         */
   long *pNew_Pay = NULL;           /* Pointer to hold return value */

   pNew_Pay = IncomePlus( pOld_Pay );
   printf("\nOld pay = $%ld", *pOld_Pay);
   printf("\tNew pay = $%ld\n", *pNew_Pay);
}

/* Definition of function to increment pay */
long *IncomePlus(long *pPay)
{
   *pPay += 10000L;                 /* Increment the value for pay  */
   return pPay;                     /* Return the address           */
}
```

When you run the program, you'll get this output:

```
Old pay = $40000         New pay = $40000
```

How It Works

In **main()**, we set up an initial value in the variable **Your_Pay**, and define two pointers for use with the function **IncomePlus()**, which is going to increase **Your_Pay**. One pointer is initialized with the address of **Your_Pay**, while the other is initialized to **NULL,** since it's going to receive the address returned by the function **IncomePlus()**.

Look at the output. It seems a satisfactory result, except that there's something not quite right. If you overlook what you started with ($30000), it looks as though you didn't get any increase at all. Since the function **IncomePlus()** modifies the value of **Your_Pay** through the pointer **pOld_Pay**, the original value has been changed. Clearly, both our pointers, **pOld_Pay** and **pNew_Pay**, refer to the same location - **Your_Pay**. This is a result of the statement in the function **IncomePlus()**:

```
return pPay;
```

This returns the pointer value that the function received when it was called. This is the address contained in **pOld_Pay**. The result is that we inadvertently increase the original amount that we were payed - such is the power of pointers!

Try It Out - Using Local Storage

Let's look at what happens if we use local storage in the function **IncomePlus()**. After a small modification, our example becomes:

```
/* Example 8.8 A function to increase your salary that doesn't    */
#include <stdio.h>

long *IncomePlus(long* pPay);       /* Prototype for increase function */

void main()
{
    long Your_Pay = 30000L;         /* Starting salary               */
    long *pOld_Pay = &Your_Pay;     /* Pointer to pay value          */
    long *pNew_Pay = NULL;          /* Pointer to hold return value  */

    pNew_Pay = IncomePlus( pOld_Pay );
    printf("\nOld pay = $%ld", *pOld_Pay);
    printf("\tNew pay = $%ld\n", *pNew_Pay);
}

/* Definition of function to increment pay */
long *IncomePlus(long *pPay)
{
    long pay = 0;           /* Local variable for the result */

    pay = *pPay + 10000; /* Increment the value for pay    */
    return &pay;          /* Return the address             */
}
```

How It Works

We now get the following result (it may vary depending on your machine):

```
Old pay = $30000        New pay = $27467656
```

Numbers like **$27467656** with the word *pay* in the same sentence tend to be a bit startling. You would probably hesitate before complaining about this kind of error. However, you may get different results on your computer. You should get a warning from your compiler with this version of the program. With my compiler, I get the message, 'Suspicious pointer conversion'. This is because we're returning the address of the variable **pay**, which goes out of scope on exiting the function **IncomePlus()**. This is the cause of the remarkable value for the new value of pay - it's junk, just a spurious value left around by something. This is an easy mistake to make, but can be a hard one to find.

Try combining the two **printf()** statements in **main()** into one.

```
printf("\nOld pay = $%ld\tNew pay = $%ld\n", *pOld_Pay, *pNew_Pay);
```

On my computer it produces the output:

```
Old pay = $30000        New pay = $40000
```

This actually looks right, in spite of the fact that we know there's a serious error in the program. In this case, although the variable **pay** is out of scope and therefore no longer exists, the memory it occupied hasn't been re-used yet. In the earlier example, evidently something uses the memory previously used by the variable **pay**, and produces the enormous output value. Here is an absolutely 100% cast iron rule:

> *Never return the address of a local variable in a function.*

We'll turn to the more practical application of returning pointers by modifying Example 8.6. We could have written the routine **str_in()** in this example as:

```
char *str_in(void)
{
   char Buffer[BUFFER_LEN];     /* Space to store input string */
   char *pString = NULL;        /* Pointer to string           */

   if(gets(Buffer) == NULL)     /* NULL returned from gets()?   */
   {
     printf("\nError reading string.\n");
     return FALSE;              /* Read error                   */
   }

   if(Buffer[0] == '\0')        /* Empty string read?           */
     return NULL;

   pString = (char*)malloc( strlen(Buffer)  + 1);

   if(*pString == NULL)         /* Check memory allocation      */
   {
     printf("\nOut of memory.");
     abort();                               /* No memory allocated   */
   }
   return strcpy(pString, Buffer);  /* Return pString           */
}
```

Of course we would also have to modify the function prototype to:

```
char *str_in(void);
```

Now there are no parameters, since we've declared the parameter list as **void**, and the return value is now a pointer to a character string rather than an integer.

We would also need to modify the **for** loop in **main()** which invokes the function to:

```
for(count=0; count < NUM_P ; count++)   /* Max of NUM_P strings    */
{
  pS[count] = str_in();
  if(pS[count] == NULL)            /* Stop input on NULL return    */
    break;
}
```

We now compare the pointer returned from **str_in()** and stored in **pS[count]** with **NULL** - as this would indicate that an empty string had been entered, or that a string was not read because of a read error. The example would still work exactly as before, but the internal mechanism for input would be a little different. Now, the function returns the address of the allocated memory block into which the string has been copied. You might imagine that you could use the address of **Buffer**, instead, but remember that **Buffer** is local to the function - so it goes out of scope on return from the function. You could try it if you like, to see what happens.

If **malloc()** returns a **NULL** pointer, indicating that the memory for the string can't be allocated, we display a message as before, but this time we call the function **abort()** instead of returning from the function. This function, which is declared in **stdlib.h**, terminates the program immediately.

Choosing one version of the function **str_in()** or the other is, to some extent, a matter of taste; but on balance, this latter version is probably better, because it uses a simpler definition of the parameter, which makes it easier to understand.

Incrementing Pointers in a Function

When we use an array name as an argument to a function, a *copy* of the address of the beginning of the array is transferred to the function. As a result, we have the possibility of treating the value received as a pointer in the fullest sense, incrementing or decrementing the address as we wish. For example, we could rewrite the **str_out()** function in Example 8.6 as:

```
void str_out(char *P[] , int N)
{
   int i = 0;                  /* Loop counter                    */

   printf("\nYour input sorted in order is:\n\n");
   for (i = 0 ; i < N ; i++)
   {
     printf("%s\n", *P);       /* Display a string                */
     free(*P);                 /* Free memory for the string */
     *P++ = NULL; /* Set pointer to NULL and increment to next element */
   }
   return;
}
```

We've replaced the array notation with pointer notation in the **printf()** and **free()** function calls. We wouldn't be able to do this with an array declared within the function scope but, since we have a copy of the original array address, it's possible here. We can treat it just like a regular pointer. Because the address we have at this point is a copy of the original in **main()**, this doesn't interfere with the original array address **pS** in any way. There's little to choose between this version of the function and the original. The former version, using array notation, is probably just a little easier to follow.

Summary

This has been quite a long chapter, and it's a big topic. We haven't done with functions, yet, so we'll postpone diving into another chunky example until the end of the next chapter, which covers further aspects of using functions. So, let's pause for a moment, and summarize the key points that you need to keep in mind when creating and using functions:

▶ C programs consist of one or more functions, one of which is called **main()**. The function **main()** is where execution always starts and it's called by the operating system through a user command.

▶ A function is a self-contained, named block of code in a program. The name of a function is a unique sequence of letters and digits, the first of which must be a letter (an underline counts as a letter).

▶ A function definition consists of a header and a body. The header defines the name of the function, the type of the value returned from the function, and the types and names of all the parameters to the function. The body contains the executable statements for the function, which define what the function actually does.

▶ All the variables declared in a function are local to that function.

▶ Before you use a function in your source file, you should either define the function, or declare the function with a function prototype, which defines the return type, the parameter types for the function, and the function name. These must be the same as in the definition of the function. The function declaration must have a semicolon at the end. The function declaration must be placed before any function which calls the function itself.

▶ Arguments to a function must be of the same type as the corresponding parameters specified in its header. If you specify a parameter to be of type **int,** you can't then pass an argument of type **float**.

▶ A function that returns a value can be used in an expression just as if it were a value of the same type as the return value.

▶ Any function, other than **main()**, can be called as often as you need by using its name in a program.

▶ *Copies* of the argument values are transferred to a function, not the original values in the calling function. If you want a function to modify a variable in its calling function, the address of the variable needs to be transferred as an argument. This address can then be used in the called function as a pointer.

That covers the essentials of creating your own functions. In the next chapter, we'll add a few more techniques for using functions in addition to those that we have covered here. We'll also add a more substantial example of applying functions in a practical context.

More on Functions

Now that you've completed Chapter 8, you have a good grounding in the essentials of creating and using functions. In this chapter, we'll build on this by exploring how functions can be used and manipulated; in particular, we'll investigate how we can access a function through a pointer. We'll also get to grips with some more flexible methods of communicating between functions.

The topics we'll work with in this chapter include:

- Understanding what pointers to functions are, and how you use them
- Using static variables in functions
- Sharing variables between functions
- Understanding how functions can call themselves
- Writing an Othello-type game (also known as Reversi)

Pointers to Functions

Up to now, we've considered pointers as an exceptionally useful device for manipulating data and variables that contain data. It's a bit like handling things with a pair of tongs. We can manipulate a whole range of hot items with just one pair of tongs. However, we can also use pointers to handle *functions* at a distance. Since a function has an address in memory where it starts execution - its starting address - the basic information to be stored in a pointer to a function is going to be another address.

If you think about it, though, this isn't going to be enough. If a function is going to be called through a pointer, then information also has to be available about the number and type of the arguments to be supplied, and the type of return value that is to be expected. The compiler couldn't deduce these just from the address of the function. This means that declaring a pointer to a function is going to be a little more complicated than declaring a pointer to a data type.

Declaring a Pointer to a Function

The declaration for a pointer to a function looks a little strange, and can be confusing, so let's start with a simple example:

```
int (*pfunction) (int);
```

This declares a pointer to a function. The pointer's name is **pfunction**, and it's intended to point to functions with one argument, of type **int**, that return an **int** value to the calling program. Furthermore, we can *only* use this particular pointer to point to functions with these characteristics. If we wanted a pointer to functions that accept a **float** argument and return a **float** value then we would need to declare another pointer with the required characteristics. The components of our declaration are illustrated in the following diagram:

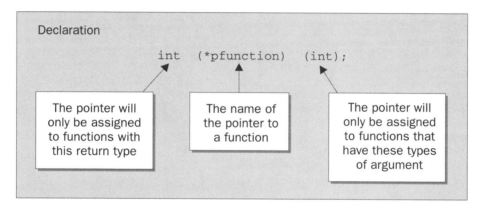

There are a lot of parentheses in a 'pointer to function' declaration. In our example here, the ***pfunction** part of the declaration must be between parentheses.

> *If you omit the parentheses, then you'll have a declaration for a function called* **pfunction()** *which returns a value that's a pointer to* **int***, which isn't what you want.*

With 'pointer to function' declarations, you must always put the ***** and the pointer name within parentheses. The second pair of parentheses just encloses the parameter list in the same way as they do with a standard function declaration.

Try It Out - Using Pointers to Functions

Let's try a simple example and see how it works. We'll define three functions that have the same parameter and return types, and use a pointer to a function to call each of them in turn:

```
/* Example 9.1 Pointing to functions */
#include <stdio.h>

/* Function prototypes */
int sum(int, int);
```

```
int product(int, int);
int difference(int, int);

void main()
{
   int a = 10;              /* Initial value for a            */
   int b = 5;               /* Initial value for b            */
   int result = 0;          /* Storage for results           */
   int (*pfun)(int, int);   /* Function pointer declaration   */

   pfun = sum;              /* Points to function sum()       */
   result = pfun(a, b);     /* Call sum() through pointer     */
   printf("\npfun = sum\t\tresult = %d", result );

   pfun = product;          /* Points to function product()   */
   result = pfun(a, b);     /* Call product() through pointer */
   printf("\npfun = product\t\tresult = %d", result );

   pfun = difference;       /* Points to function difference()   */
   result = pfun(a, b);     /* Call difference() through pointer */
   printf("\npfun = difference\tresult = %d", result );
}

/* Definition of the function sum   */
int sum(int x, int y)
{
   return x + y;
}

/* Definition of the function product   */
int product(int x, int y)
{
   return x * y;
}

/* Definition of the function difference   */
int difference(int x, int y)
{
   return x - y;
}
```

The output from this program looks like this:

```
pfun = sum              result = 15
pfun = product          result = 50
pfun = difference       result = 5
```

How It Works

We declare and define three different functions to return the sum, the product, and the difference between two integer arguments. Within **main()**, we declare a pointer to a function with this statement:

```
int (*pfun)(int, int); /* Function pointer declaration    */
```

This pointer can be assigned to point to any function which accepts two **int** arguments and also returns a value of type **int**. Notice the way we assign a value to the pointer:

```
pfun = sum;                     /* Points to function sum()        */
```

We just use a regular assignment statement that has the name of the function, completely unadorned, on the right hand side! We don't need to put the parameter list or anything. If we did, it would be wrong, since it would then be a function call, not an address, and the compiler will complain. A function is very much like an array in its usage here. If you want the address, you just use the name by itself.

In **main()**, we assign the address of each function, in turn, to the function pointer **pfun**. We then call each function using the pointer **pfun**, and display the result. You can see how to call a function using the pointer in this statement:

```
result = pfun(a, b);    /* Call sum() through pointer       */
```

You just use the name of the pointer as though it were a function name, followed by the argument list between parentheses. Here, we're using the 'pointer to function' variable name as though it were the original function name, so the argument list must correspond with the parameters in the function header for the function you are calling. This is illustrated graphically in the following figure:

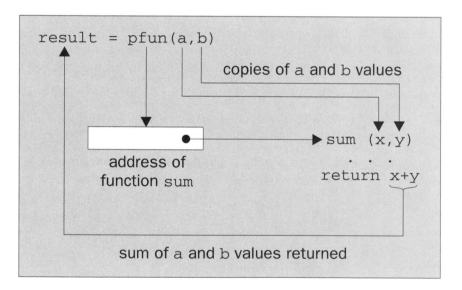

Arrays of Pointers to Functions

Of course, a function pointer is a variable like any other. We can therefore create an array of pointers to functions. Let's see how this would work in practice.

Try It Out - Arrays of Pointers to Functions

We can demonstrate this with a variation on the last example:

```c
/* Example 9.2 Arrays of Pointers to functions   */
#include <stdio.h>

/* Function prototypes    */
int sum(int, int);
int product(int, int);
int difference(int, int);

void main()
{
   int i = 0;                    /* Loop counter                      */
   int a = 10;                   /* Initial value for a               */
   int b = 5;                    /* Initial value for b               */
   int result = 0;               /* Storage for results               */
   int (*pfun[3])(int, int);  /* Function pointer array declaration */

   /* Initialize pointers */
   pfun[0] = sum;
   pfun[1] = product;
   pfun[2] = difference;

   /* Execute each function pointed to */
   for( i = 0 ; i < 3 ; i++)
   {
     result = pfun[i](a, b);  /* Call the function through a pointer */
     printf("\nresult = %d", result);       /* Display the result    */
   }

   /* Call all three functions through pointers in an expression */
   result = pfun[1](pfun[0](a, b), pfun[2](a, b));
   printf("\n\nThe product of the sum and the difference = %d", result );
}

/* Definition of the function sum         */
int sum(int x, int y)
{
   return x + y;
}

/* Definition of the function product     */
int product(int x, int y)
{
   return x * y;
}
```

```
/* Definition of the function difference */
int difference(int x, int y)
{
    return x - y;
}
```

The output from this program is:

```
result = 15
result = 50
result = 5

The product of the sum and the difference = 75
```

How It Works

The major difference to the last example is our pointer array, declared as:

```
int (*pfun[3])(int, int);   /* Function pointer array declaration */
```

This is similar to the previous declaration for a single pointer variable, but with the addition of the array dimension in square brackets following the pointer name. If we wanted a two-dimensional array, two sets of square brackets would have to appear here, just like declarations for ordinary array types. We still enclose the parameter list between parentheses, as we did in the declaration of a single pointer. Again, in parallel with what happens for ordinary arrays, all the elements of our array of 'pointers to functions' are of the same type and will only accept the argument list specified. So, in our example, they can all only point to functions that take two arguments of type **int**, and return an **int** value.

When we want to assign a value to a pointer within the array, we write it in the same way as an element of any other array:

```
pfun[0] = sum;
```

Apart from the function name on the right of the equals sign, this could be a normal data array. It's used in exactly the same way. We could have chosen to initialize all the elements of the array of pointers within the declaration itself:

```
int (*pfun[3])(int, int) = { sum, product, difference };
```

This would have initialized all three elements and would have eliminated the need for the assignment statements that perform the initialization. In fact, we could have left out the array dimension, too, and got it by default:

```
int (*pfun[])(int, int) = { sum, product, difference };
```

The number of initializing values between the braces would determine the number of elements.

When it comes to calling a function that an array element points to, we write it as:

```
result = pfun[i](a, b);   /* Call the function through a pointer */
```

This, again, is very like our previous example, with just the addition of the index value in square brackets that follows the pointer name. We index this array with the loop variable, **i**, as we have done many times before with ordinary data arrays.

Look at the output. The first three lines are generated in the **for** loop, where the functions **sum()**, **product()**, and **difference()** are each called, in turn, through the corresponding element of the pointer array. The last line of output is produced using the value **result** from the statement:

```
result = pfun[1](pfun[0](a, b), pfun[2](a, b));
```

This statement shows that we can incorporate function calls through pointers into expressions, in the same way that we might use a normal function call. Here, we've called two of the functions through pointers, and their results are used as arguments to a third function that's called through a pointer. Because the elements of the array correspond to the functions **sum()**, **product()**, and **difference()** in sequence, this statement is equivalent to:

```
result = product(sum(a, b), difference(a, b));
```

The sequence of events in this statement is:

1 Execute **sum(a, b)** and **difference(a, b)** and save the return values

2 Execute the function **product()** with the returned values from step 1 as arguments, and save the value returned

3 Store the value obtained from step 2 in the variable **result**.

Pointers to Functions as Arguments

We can also pass a pointer to a function as an argument. This allows a different function to be called - depending on which function is addressed by the pointer that's passed.

Try It Out - Pointers to Functions as Arguments

We could produce a variant of the last example, using this technique, as follows (some of the code is the same as in the previous example - only the new sections are highlighted):

```
/* Example 9.3 Passing a Pointer to a function    */
#include <stdio.h>

/* Function prototypes */
int sum(int,int);
int product(int,int);
int difference(int,int);
int any_function(int(*pfun)(int, int), int x, int y);

void main()
{
```

```
    int a = 10;                      /* Initial value for a */
    int b = 5;                       /* Initial value for b */
    int result = 0;                  /* Storage for results */
    int (*pf)(int, int) = sum;    /* Pointer to function */

    /* Passing a pointer to a function */
    result = any_function(pf, a, b);

    printf("\nresult = %d", result );

    /* Passing the address of a function        */
    result = any_function(product,a, b);

    printf("\nresult = %d", result );

    printf("\nresult = %d", any_function(difference, a, b));
}

/* Definition of a function to call a function */
int any_function(int(*pfun)(int, int), int x, int y)
{
    return pfun(x, y);
}

/* Definition of the function sum        */
int sum(int x, int y)
{
    return x + y;
}

/* Definition of the function product     */
int product(int x, int y)
{
    return x * y;
}

/* Definition of the function difference */
int difference(int x, int y)
{
    return x - y;
}
```

The output looks like this:

```
result = 15
result = 50
result = 5
```

How It Works

The function which will accept a 'pointer to a function' as an argument is **any_function()**. It is declared in this statement:

```
int any_function(int(*pfun)(int, int), int x, int y);
```

Our function named **any_function()** has three parameters. The first parameter type is a pointer to a function that accepts two integer arguments and returns an integer. The last two parameters are integers that will be used in the call of the function specified by the first parameter. **any_function()** itself returns an integer value that will be the value obtained by calling the function indicated by the first argument.

Within the definition of **any_function()**, the function specified by the pointer argument is called in the **return** statement:

```
/* Definition of a function to call a function */
int any_function(int(*pfun)(int, int), int x, int y)
{
    return pfun(x, y);
}
```

The name of the pointer **pfun** is used, followed by the other two parameters as arguments to the function to be called. The value of **pfun**, and the values of the other two parameters **x** and **y**, all originate in **main()**.

Notice how we initialize the function pointer **pf** that we've declared in **main()**:

```
    int (*pf)(int, int) = sum;    /* Pointer to function */
```

We've placed the name of the function **sum()** as the initializer after the equals sign. As we saw earlier, we can initialize function pointers to the addresses of specific functions just by putting the function name as an initializing value.

The first call to **any_function()** involves passing the value of the pointer **pf** and the values of the variables **a** and **b** to **any_function()**:

```
    result = any_function(pf, a, b);
```

The pointer is used as an argument in the usual way, and the value returned by **any_function()** is stored in the variable **result**. Because of the initial value of **pf**, the function **sum()** will be called in **any_function()**, so the returned value will be the sum of the values of **a** and **b**.

The next call to **any_function()** is in this statement:

```
    result = any_function(product, a, b);
```

Here, we've explicitly entered the name of a function, **product()**, as the first argument, so within **any_function()** the function **product()** will be called with the values of **a** and **b** as arguments. In this case, we're effectively persuading the compiler to create an internal pointer to the function **product()**, and passing it to **any_function()**.

The final call of **any_function()** takes place in the argument to the **printf()** call:

```
    printf("\nresult = %d", any_function(difference, a, b));
```

325

In this case, we're also explicitly specifying the name of a function, **difference()**, as an argument to **any_function()**. The compiler knows from the prototype of **any_function()** that the first argument should be a pointer to a function. Since we've specified the function name, **difference()**, explicitly as an argument, the compiler will generate a pointer to this function for us, and pass that pointer to the **any_function()**. Lastly, the value returned by **any_function()** is passed as an argument to the function **printf()**. When all this unwinds, we eventually get the difference between the values of **a** and **b** displayed.

Take care not to confuse the idea of passing an address of a function to a function, as in this expression:

```
any_function(product, a, b)
```

with the idea of passing a value returned from a function, as in the statement:

```
printf("\n%d", product(a, b));
```

In the former case, we're passing the address of the function **product()** as an argument, and if and when it gets called depends on what goes on inside the body of the function **any_function()**. In the latter case, however, we're calling the function **product()** before we call **printf()**, and passing the result obtained to **printf()**.

Variables in Functions

Structuring a program into functions not only simplifies the process of developing the program, but it also extends the power of the language to solve problems. The power of the language is further enhanced by the properties of variables within a function - and some extra capabilities that C provides in declaring variables. We'll take a look at some of these now.

Static Variables - Keeping Track within a Function

So far, all the variables we've used have gone out of scope at the end of the block in which they were defined, and their memory has then become free for reallocation. These are called **automatic variables**, because they are automatically created at the point where they are declared, and automatically destroyed when program execution leaves the block in which they were declared. This is a very efficient, since the memory containing data in a function is only retained for as long as we're executing statements within the function in which the variable was declared.

However, there are some circumstances in which you might want to retain information from one function call to the next within a program. You may wish to maintain a count of something within a function, such as the number of times the function has been called, or the number of lines of output that have been written. With automatic variables, we have no way of doing this using functions.

However, C does provide us with a way to do this with **static variables**. We could declare a **static** counter, for example, with this declaration:

```
static int count = 0;
```

The word **static** in this statement is a keyword in C. The variable declared in this statement differs from an automatic variable in two ways. First of all, despite the fact that it may be defined within the scope of a function, this **static** variable does not get destroyed when execution leaves the function. Secondly, whereas an automatic variable is initialized each time its scope is entered, the initialization of a variable declared as **static** occurs only once, right at the beginning of the program.

> *You can make any type of variable within a function a **static** variable.*

Try It Out - Using Static Variables

We can see static variables in action with a very simple example, as follows:

```
/* Example 9.4 Static versus automatic variables */
#include <stdio.h>

/* Function prototypes */
void test1(void);
void test2(void);

void main()
{
   int i = 0;

   for( i = 0; i < 5; i++ )
   {
     test1();
     test2();
   }
}

/* Function test1 with an automatic variable */
void test1(void)
{
   int count = 0;
   printf("\ntest1   count = %d ", ++count );
}

/* Function test2 with a static variable */
void test2(void)
{
   static int count = 0;
   printf("\ntest2   count = %d ", ++count );
}
```

This produces the output:

```
test1   count = 1
test2   count = 1
test1   count = 1
```

```
test2   count = 2
test1   count = 1
test2   count = 3
test1   count = 1
test2   count = 4
test1   count = 1
test2   count = 5
```

How It Works

As you can see, the two variables called **count** are quite separate. The changes in the values of each show clearly that they are independent of one another. The **static** variable, **count**, is declared in the function **test2()**:

```
static int count = 0;
```

Although we specify an initial value here, the variable would have been initialized to zero anyway, because we have declared it as static.

> *All static variables are initialized to zero unless you initialize them with some other value.*

The **static** variable **count** is used to count the number of times the function is called. This is initialized when program execution starts, and its current value when the function is exited is maintained. It is not re-initialized on subsequent calls to the function. Because it has been declared as **static**, the compiler arranges things so that it will only be initialized once, when program execution starts.

The automatic variable **count** in the function **test1()** is declared as:

```
int count = 0;
```

Since this is an automatic variable, it isn't initialized by default - and if we don't specify an initial value, it will contain a junk value. This variable gets re-initialized to zero at each entry to the function, and it is discarded on exit from **test1()**; therefore, it never reaches a value higher than 1.

> *Although a **static** variable will persist for as long as the program is running, it will only be visible within the scope in which it was declared, and it cannot be referenced outside of that original scope.*

Sharing Variables Between Functions

We also have a way of sharing variables between all our functions. In the same way that we can declare constants at the beginning of a program file, so that they are outside the scope of the functions making up the program, we can also declare variables like this. These are called **global variables** as they are accessible anywhere. Global variables are declared in the normal way; it is the position of the declaration that is significant.

Try It Out - Using Global Variables

By way of a demonstration, we can modify our previous example to share **count** between functions:

```
/* Example 9.5 Global variables */
#include <stdio.h>

int count = 0;                    /* Declare a global variable    */

/* Function prototypes */
void test1(void);
void test2(void);

void main()
{
   int count = 0;                 /* This hides the global count */

   for( ; count < 5; count++)
   {
     test1();
     test2();
   }
}

/* Function test1 using the global variable    */
void test1(void)
{
   printf("\ntest1   count = %d ", ++count);
}

/* Function test2 using a static variable */
void test2(void)
{
   static int count;              /* This hides the global count */
   printf("\ntest2   count = %d ", ++count);
}
```

The output will be:

```
test1   count = 1
test2   count = 1
test1   count = 2
test2   count = 2
test1   count = 3
test2   count = 3
test1   count = 4
test2   count = 4
test1   count = 5
test2   count = 5
```

How It Works

In this example, we now have three separate variables called **count**! The first of these is the global variable **count** declared at the beginning of the file:

```
#include <stdio.h>

int count = 0;
```

This is not a **static** variable (although we could make it **static** if we wanted to) so we must initialize it. It is potentially accessible in any function from the point where it's declared to the end of the file - so it's accessible in any of our functions here.

The second is an automatic variable **count** declared in **main()**:

```
    int count = 0;                  /* This hides the global count */
```

Because this is the same name as the global variable, the global variable **count** cannot be accessed from **main()**. The local variable **count** *hides* the global variable.

The third is a static variable **count** that's declared in the function **test2()**:

```
      static int count;             /* This hides the global count */
```

Because this is a **static** variable, it will be initialized to zero by default. This variable also hides the global variable of the same name, so only the static variable **count** is accessible in **test2()**.

The function **test1()** works using the global **count**. The functions **main()** and **test2()** use their local versions of **count**, since the local declaration hides the global variable of the same name.

Clearly, the **count** variable in **main()** is incremented from 0 to 4, since we have 5 calls to each of the functions **test1()** and **test2()**. This has to be different from the **count** variables in either of the called functions; otherwise, they could not have the values 1 to 5 that are displayed in the output.

We can further demonstrate that this is indeed the case by simply removing the declaration for **count** in **test2()** as a **static** variable. We'll then have made **test1()** and **test2()** share the global **count**, and the values displayed will run from 1 to 10. If you then put a declaration back in **test2()** for **count** as an initialized automatic variable with the statement:

```
    int count = 0;
```

the output from **test1()** will run from 1 to 5, and the output from **test2()** will remain at 1, since the variable is now automatic and will be re-initialized on each entry to the function.

Global variables can replace the need for function arguments and return values. They look very tempting as the complete alternative to automatic variables. However, you should use global variables sparingly. They can be a major asset in simplifying and shortening some programs, but if you use them excessively it will make your programs prone to errors. It's very easy to modify a global variable and forget what consequences it might have throughout your program. The bigger the program, the more difficult it becomes to avoid erroneous references to global variables. The use of local variables provides very effective insulation, for each function, against the possibility of interference from the activities of other functions. You could try removing the declaration of the local variable, **count** from **main()** in Example 9.5, to see the effect on the output of such an oversight.

> *As a rule, it is unwise to use the same names in C for local and global variables. There is no particular advantage to be gained, other than to demonstrate the effect, as we have done with our example. Using local and global variables with the same name also makes programs more error-prone, and certainly makes them harder to follow.*

Functions That Call Themselves - Recursion

It's possible for a function to call itself. This is termed **recursion**. You're unlikely to come across a need for this very often, so we won't dwell on it, but it can be a very effective technique in some contexts. There are also a few bad jokes based on the notion of recursion, but we won't dwell on those either.

Try It Out - Recursion

The primary uses of recursion tend to arise in complicated problems, so it is hard to come up with original but simple examples to show how it works. Therefore, we'll follow the crowd and use the standard illustration: the calculation of the factorial of an integer. A factorial of any integer is the product of all the integers from 1 up to the integer itself. So here we go:

```
/* Example 9.6 Calculating factorials using recursion */
#include <stdio.h>

long factorial(long);

void main()
{
   long number = 0;
   printf("\nEnter an integer value: ");
   scanf(" %ld", &number);
   printf("\nThe factorial of %ld is %ld\n", number, factorial(number));
}

/* Our recursive factorial function */
long factorial(long N)
{
   if(N < 2)
     return N;
   else
     return N*factorial(N - 1);
}
```

Typical output from the program would look like this:

```
Enter an integer value: 4

The factorial of 4 is 24
```

How It Works

This is very simple once you get your mind round what's happening. Let's go through a simple example of how it works. Assume you enter the value 4. The sequence of events is shown in the following figure.

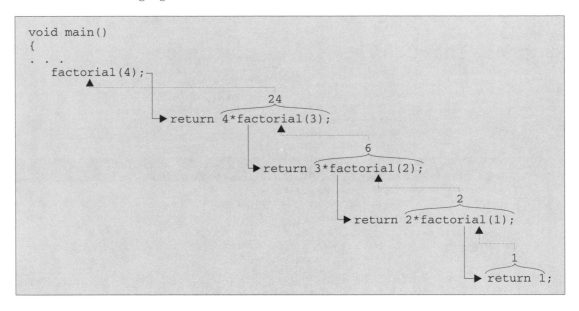

Within the statement:

```
printf("\nThe factorial of %ld is %ld", number, factorial(number));
```

the function **factorial()** gets called from **main()** with **number** having the value 4 as the argument.

Within the **factorial()** function itself, since the argument is greater than 1, the statement executed is:

```
return N*factorial(N - 1);
```

This is the second **return** statement in the function, and it calls **factorial()** again with the argument value 3 from within the arithmetic expression. This expression cannot be evaluated and the return can't occur until the value is returned from this call to the function **factorial()** with the argument 3.

This continues, as shown in the above figure, until the argument in the last call is 1. In this case, the first return statement:

```
    return N;
```

is executed and the value 1 is returned to the previous call point. This call point is, in fact, inside the second return in the **factorial()** function, which can now calculate 2*1 and return to the previous call.

In this way, the whole process unwinds, ending up with the value required being returned to **main()** where it is displayed. So for any given number **n**, we will have **n** calls to the function **factorial()**. For each call, a copy of the argument is created, and the location to be returned to is stored. This can get expensive on memory if there are a lot of levels of recursion. A loop to do the same thing would be cheaper and faster. If you do need or want to use recursion, the most important thing to remember is that there has to be a way to get back. In other words, there must be a mechanism for *not* repeating the recursive call. In our example, we use a check for the argument supplied being 1.

Notice how factorial values grow very quickly. With quite modest input values, you will exceed the capacity of a **long** integer and start getting the wrong results.

Libraries of Functions - Header Files

I've already mentioned that your compiler comes with a wide range of standard functions declared in **header files**, sometimes called **include files**. These represent a rich source of help for you when you're developing your own applications. We've already met some of these - since header files are such a fundamental component of programming in C. So far, we've used functions from the following header files:

stdio.h	Input/Output Functions
math.h	Mathematical Floating-Point Functions
stdlib.h	Memory Allocation Functions
string.h	String Handling Functions
ctype.h	Character Conversion Functions

All the header files above contain declarations for a range of functions, as well as definitions for various constants. They are all ANSI standard libraries (and ISO for that matter), so all ANSI-conforming compilers will support them and provide at least the basic set of functions; but typically, they will supply much more. To comprehensively discuss the contents of even the ANSI standard library header files and functions could double the size of this book, so I'll just mention the most important aspects of the ANSI header files, and leave you to browse the documentation that came with your compiler.

The header file **stdio.h** contains declarations for quite a large range of high-level input/output functions, so we'll devote the whole of Chapter 10 to explore some of these.

As well as memory allocation functions, **stdlib.h** provides facilities for converting character strings to their numerical equivalents from the ASCII table. There are also functions for sorting and searching. Functions that generate random numbers are also available through **stdlib.h**.

We described and used the **string.h** file in Chapter 6. With some compilers, this header file also declares functions for managing buffers, as there's a strong affinity between these functions and the general process of handling strings. They generally compare, copy, and move fixed length blocks of memory, whereas the functions we discussed in Chapter 6 were oriented towards variable length strings.

A header file providing a very useful range of functions also related to string processing is **ctype.h**, which we saw in Chapter 6. **ctype.h** includes functions to convert characters from upper to lower-case, and vice versa, and a number of functions checking for alphabetic characters, numeric digits, and so on. These provide an extensive toolkit for you to do your own detailed analysis of the contents of a string, which is particularly useful for dealing with user input.

I strongly recommend that you invest some time becoming familiar with the contents of these header files and the libraries that are supplied with your compiler. This familiarity will greatly increase the ease with which you can develop applications in C.

> *Conveniently, each header file provides the necessary declarations for all the functions that it includes, so you don't have to write declarations yourself for the functions that you use from a library. What could be easier?*

Designing a Program

At this point, we've finished with functions - and you're quite a way through the capabilities of C. So a practical example of reasonable complexity would not come amiss. In this program, we're going to put to use the various elements of C that we've covered so far in the book.

The Problem

The problem we're going to solve is to write another game. There are several reasons for choosing to write a game. First, games tend to be just as complex, if not more so, than other types of programs, even when the game is simple. And, secondly, games are more fun!

The game is in the same vein as Othello, or, if you remember Microsoft Windows 3.0, Reversi. The game is played by two players who take turns to place a colored counter on a square board. One player has black counters and the other has white counters. The board has an even number of squares along a side. The starting position, followed by five successive moves, is shown next.

You can only place a counter adjacent to an opponent's counter, such that one or more of your opponent's counters - in a line diagonally, horizontally, or vertically - are enclosed between two of your own counters. The opponent's counters are then changed to counters of your own color.

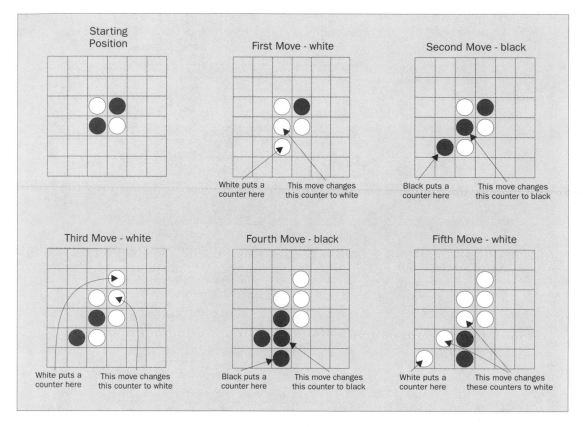

The person with the most counters on the board at the end of the game wins. The game ends when all the squares are occupied by counters. The game can also end if neither side can place a counter legally - which can occur if you or your opponent manage to convert all the counters to the same color.

The game can be played with any size of board, but we'll implement it here on a 6x6 board. We'll also implement it as a game that you play against the computer.

The Analysis

The analysis of this problem is a little different from that which we've used up to now. The whole point of this chapter is to introduce the concept of structured programming: in other words, breaking a problem into small pieces - which is why we've spent so long looking at functions.

A good way to start is with a diagram. We'll start with a single box, which represents the whole program - or the **main()** function, if you like. Developing from this, on the next level down we'll show the functions that will need to be directly called by the **main()** function, and we'll indicate what these functions have to do. Below that, we'll show the functions that those functions, in turn, have to use. We don't have to show the actual functions: we can just show the tasks that need to be accomplished. However, these tasks *do* tend to be functions, so this is a great way to design our program. Let's see what our diagram looks like:

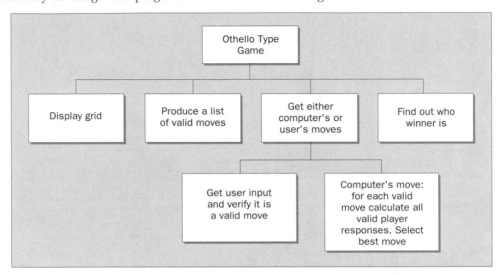

We can now go a stage further than this, and begin to think about the actual sequence of actions, or functions, that the program is going to perform. The next figure, which is a flowchart, describes the same set of functions - but in a more sequential, logical manner. We're moving closer, now, to a general description of the actual program.

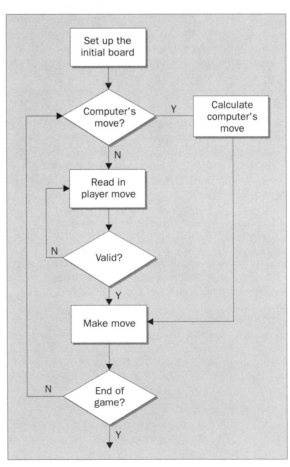

This is not absolutely fixed, of course. There's a lot of detail that we'll need to fill in. This sort of diagram can help us get the logic of the program clear in our minds - and from there, we can progress to a more detailed definition of how the program will work.

The Solution

1   The first thing to do is to set up and display the initial board. We'll use a smaller than normal board (6 by 6) as this makes the games shorter, but we'll implement the program with the board size as a symbol defined by a pre-processor directive. We'll then be able to change the size later if we want. We'll display the board using a separate function, as this is a self-contained activity.

So: let's declare, initialize and display the grid. The computer will use `'@'` as a counter, and the player will have `'O'` for their counter:

```
/* Example 9.7 REVERSAL An Othello type game */
#include <stdio.h>

#define SIZE 6   /* Board size - must be even */

/* Function prototypes */
void display(char board[][SIZE]);

void main()
{
   char board [SIZE][SIZE] = { 0 };   /* The board         */
   int row = 0;                       /* Board row index    */
   int col = 0;                       /* Board column index */

   /* Blank all the board squares */
   for(row = 0; row < SIZE; row++)
     for(col = 0; col < SIZE; col++)
       board[row][col] = ' ';

   /* Place the initial four counters in the center */
   board[SIZE/2 - 1][SIZE/2 - 1] = board[SIZE/2][SIZE/2] = 'O';
   board[SIZE/2 - 1][SIZE/2] = board[SIZE/2][SIZE/2 - 1] = '@';

   display(board);                    /* Display the board  */
}

/***********************************************/
/* Function to display the board in it's       */
/* current state with row numbers and column   */
/* letters to identify squares.                */
/* Parameter is the board array.               */
/***********************************************/
void display(char board[][SIZE])
{
   int row  = 0;              /* Row index       */
```

```
    int col = 0;              /* Column index   */
    char col_label = 'a';  /* Column label   */

    printf("\n ");            /* Start top line */
    for(col = 0 ; col<SIZE ;col++)
      printf("   %c", col_label+col); /* Display the top line */
    printf("\n");                      /* End the top line      */

    /* Display the intermediate rows */
    for(row = 0; row < SIZE; row++)
    {
      printf("   +");
      for(col = 0; col<SIZE; col++)
        printf("---+");
      printf("\n%2d|",row + 1);

      for(col = 0; col<SIZE; col++)
        printf(" %c |", board[row][col]);  /* Display counters in row */
      printf("\n");
    }

    printf("   +");                     /* Start the bottom line   */
    for(col = 0 ; col<SIZE ;col++)
      printf("---+");                   /* Display the bottom line */
    printf("\n");                       /* End the bottom  line    */
}
```

The function **display()** outputs the board with row numbers to identify the rows, and the letters from **'a'** onwards to identify each column. This will be the reference system by which the user will select a square to place their counter.

The code looks complicated, but it's quite straightforward. The first loop outputs the top line with the column label, from **'a'** to **'f'** with our board size. The next loop outputs the squares that can contain counters, a row at a time, with a row number at the start of each row. The last loop outputs the bottom of the last row. Notice how we've passed the array **board** as a parameter to the function **display()**, rather than making **board** a global variable. This is to prevent other functions from modifying the contents of **board** accidentally. Our function will display a board of any size.

2 We need a function to generate all the possible moves that can be made for the current player. This function has two uses: first, it allows us to check that the move the user enters is valid; second, it will help us to determine what moves the computer can make. But first, we must decide how we're going to represent and store this list of moves.

So what information do we need to store, and what options do we have? Well, we've defined the grid in such a way that any cell can be referenced by a row number and a column letter. We could therefore store moves as a string consisting of a number and a letter. We would then need to deal with a list of varying length, though, just in case the user chooses to change the dimensions of the board to 10 by 10 or greater.

There is an easier option. We can create a second array with the same dimensions as the board, and store a 1 for positions where there is a valid move, and 0 otherwise. We can store values of type **int** in this array. Our function will need three parameters: the **board** array, so that it can check for vacant squares; the **moves** array in which the valid moves are to be recorded; and the identity of the current player, which will be the character used as a counter for the player.

The strategy will be this: for each blank square, search the squares around that square for an opponent counter. If we find an opponent counter, then follow a line of opponent counters (horizontal, vertical, and diagonal) until we find a player counter. If we do in fact find a player counter along that line, then we know that the original blank square is a valid move for the current player.

We can add our function definition to the file following the definition of the **display()** function:

```
/* Example 9.7 REVERSAL An Othello type game */
#include <stdio.h>

#define SIZE 6   /* Board size - must be even */

/* Function prototypes */
void display(char board[][SIZE]);
int valid_moves(char board[][SIZE], int moves[][SIZE], char player);

void main()
{
    char board [SIZE][SIZE] = { 0 };   /* The board          */
    int moves[SIZE][SIZE] = { 0 };     /* Valid moves        */
    int row = 0;                       /* Board row index    */
    int col = 0;                       /* Board column index */

    /* Other code for main as before... */
}

/* Code for definition of display() as before... */

/************************************************/
/* Calculates which squares are valid moves     */
/* for player. Valid moves are recorded in the  */
/* moves array - 1 indicates a valid move,       */
/* 0 indicates an invalid move.                 */
/* First parameter is the board array           */
/* Second parameter is the moves array          */
/* Third parameter identifies the player        */
/* to make the move.                            */
/* Returns valid move count.                    */
/************************************************/
int valid_moves(char board[][SIZE], int moves[][SIZE], char player)
{
    int rowdelta = 0;    /* Row increment around a square    */
```

Beginning C

```
      int coldelta = 0;       /* Column increment around a square */
      int row = 0;            /* Row index                        */
      int col = 0;            /* Column index                     */
      int x = 0;              /* Row index when searching         */
      int y = 0;              /* Column index when searching      */
      int no_of_moves = 0;    /* Number of valid moves            */


      /* Set the opponent            */
      char opponent = (player == 'O')? '@' : 'O';


      /* Initialize moves array to zero */
      for(row = 0; row < SIZE; row++)
        for(col = 0; col < SIZE; col++)
          moves[row][col] = 0;


      /* Find squares for valid moves.                            */
      /* A valid move must be on a blank square and must enclose */
      /* at least one opponent square between two player squares */
      for(row = 0; row < SIZE; row++)
        for(col = 0; col < SIZE; col++)
        {
          if(board[row][col] != ' ')   /* Is it a blank square?  */
            continue;                   /* No - so on to the next */

          /* Check all the squares around the blank square  */
          /* for the opponents counter                      */
          for(rowdelta = -1; rowdelta <= 1; rowdelta++)
            for(coldelta = -1; coldelta <= 1; coldelta++)
            {
              /* Don't check outside the array, or the current square */
              if(row + rowdelta < 0 || row + rowdelta >= SIZE ||
                 col + coldelta < 0 || col + coldelta >= SIZE ||
                                       (rowdelta==0 && coldelta==0))
                continue;

              /* Now check the square */
              if(board[row + rowdelta][col + coldelta] == opponent)
              {
                /* If we find the opponent, move in the delta direction  */
                /* over opponent counters searching for a player counter */
                x = row + rowdelta;                    /* Move to        */
                y = col + coldelta;                    /* opponent square */

                /* Look for a player square in the delta direction */
                for(;;)
                {
                  x += rowdelta;                       /* Go to next square */
                  y += coldelta;                       /* in delta direction*/

                  /* If we move outside the array, give up */
                  if(x < 0 || x >= SIZE || y < 0 || y >= SIZE)
                    break;
```

```
            /* If we find a blank square, give up */
        if(board[x][y] == ' ')
          break;
        /*  If the square has a player counter */
        /*  then we have a valid move          */
        if(board[x][y] == player)
        {
          moves[row][col] = 1;    /* Mark as valid */
          no_of_moves++;          /* Increase valid moves count */
          break;                  /* Go check another square    */
        }
      }
    }
   }
  }
  return no_of_moves;
}
```

We've added a prototype for the **valid_moves()** function, and added a declaration for the array **moves** in **main()**.

Since the counters are either **'O'** or **'@'** we can set the opponent counter in the **valid_moves()** function as the one that is *not* the player counter that's passed as an argument. We do this with the conditional operator. We then zero the **moves** array in the first nested loop - so we only have to set valid positions to 1. The second nested loop iterates through all the squares on the board, looking for those that are blank. When we find a blank square, we search for an opponent counter in the inner loop:

```
/* Check all the squares around the blank square  */
/* for the opponents counter                      */
for(rowdelta = -1; rowdelta <= 1; rowdelta++)
  for(coldelta = -1; coldelta <= 1; coldelta++)
    ...
```

This will iterate through all the squares that surround the blank square, and will include the blank square itself - so we skip the blank square or any squares that are off the board with this **if** statement:

```
/* Don't check outside the array, or the current square */
if(row + rowdelta < 0 || row + rowdelta >= SIZE ||
   col + coldelta < 0 || col + coldelta >= SIZE ||
                      (rowdelta==0 && coldelta==0))
  continue;
```

If we get past this point, we've found a non-blank square that's on the board. If it contains the opponent's counter, then we move in the same direction - looking for either more opponent counters or a player counter. If we find a player counter, the original blank square was a valid move so we record it. If we find a blank or run off the board, then it is not a valid move so we look for another blank square.

The function returns a count of the number of valid moves, so we can use this value to indicate whether the function returns any valid moves or not. Remember - any positive integer is true and zero is false.

3 Now that we can produce an array that contains all the valid moves, we can fill in the game loop in **main()**. We'll base this on the flowchart that we saw earlier. We can start by adding two nested **do-while** loops: the outer one will initialize each game, and the inner one will iterate through player and computer turns:

```
/* Example 9.7 REVERSAL An Othello type game */
#include <stdio.h>

#define SIZE 6   /* Board size - must be even */

/* Function prototypes */
void display(char board[][SIZE]);
int valid_moves(char board[][SIZE], int moves[][SIZE], char player);

void main()
{
    char board [SIZE][SIZE] = { 0 };   /* The board           */
    int moves[SIZE][SIZE] = { 0 };     /* Valid moves         */
    int row = 0;                       /* Board row index     */
    int col = 0;                       /* Board column index  */
    int no_of_games = 0;               /* Number of games     */
    int no_of_moves = 0;               /* Count of moves      */
    int invalid_moves = 0;             /* Invalid move count  */
    int comp_score = 0;                /* Computer score      */
    int user_score = 0;                /* Player score        */
    char again = 0;                    /* Replay choice input */
    int player = 0;                    /* Player indicator    */
    int i=0;                           /* loop counter        */
    int j=0;                           /* loop counter        */

    /* The main game loop */
    do
    {
      /* On even games the player starts; */
      /* on odd games the computer starts */
      player = ++no_of_games % 2;
      no_of_moves = 4;                 /* Starts with four counters */

        /* Blank all the board squares */
        for(row = 0; row < SIZE; row++)
          for(col = 0; col < SIZE; col++)
            board[row][col] = ' ';

        /* Place the initial four counters in the center */
        board[SIZE/2 - 1][SIZE/2 - 1] = board[SIZE/2][SIZE/2] = 'O';
        board[SIZE/2 - 1][SIZE/2] = board[SIZE/2][SIZE/2 - 1] = '@';
```

```
   /* The game play loop */
   do
   {
     display(board);                 /* Display the board   */
     if(player++ % 2)
     { /*   It is the player's turn                          */
       /* Code to get the player's move and execute it */
     }
     else
     { /* It is the computer's turn                          */
       /* Code to make the computer's move                   */
     }
   }while(no_of_moves < SIZE*SIZE && invalid_moves<2);

   /* Game is over */
   display(board); /* Show final board   */

   /* Get final scores and display them */
   comp_score = user_score = 0;
   for(i = 0; i < SIZE; i++)
     for(j = 0; j < SIZE; j++)
     {
       comp_score += board[i][j] == '@';
       user_score += board[i][j] == 'O';
     }
   printf("The final score is:\n");
   printf("Computer %d\n    User %d\n\n", comp_score, user_score);

   fflush(stdin);               /* Flush the input buffer */
   printf("Do you want to play again (y/n): ");
   scanf("%c", &again);         /* Get y or n              */
 }while(again == 'y');          /* Go again on y           */

 printf("\nGoodbye\n");
}

/* Code for definition of display() */

/* Code for definition of valid_moves() */
```

I don't recommend that you run this program yet: since we haven't written the code to handle input from the user, or moves from the computer, it will just loop infinitely, printing a board with no new moves being made. We'll sort those parts of the program out next.

The variable **player** determines whose turn it is. When player is 0, it's the computer's turn, and when it's 1, it's the player's turn. This is set, initially, to the remainder when the game count is divided by 2, so that the computer and the player will take the first turn on alternate games. To determine who takes the next turn, we increment the variable **player** and take the remainder modulo 2, and then test it in the **if** statement, which will allow us to alternate between the computer and the player automatically.

The game ends when the count of the number of counters in **no_of_moves** reaches **SIZE*SIZE**, the number of squares on the board. It will also end if **invalid_moves** reaches 2. We set **invalid_moves** to zero when a valid move is made and increment it each time no valid move is possible. Thus it will reach 2 if, for two successive moves, there's no valid option, which means that neither player can go. At the end of a game, we output the final board and the results, and offer the option of another game.

We can now add the code to **main()** that will make the player and computer moves:

```
/* Example 9.7 REVERSAL An Othello type game */
#include <stdio.h>
#include <ctype.h>

#define SIZE 6  /* Board size - must be even */

/* Function prototypes */
void display(char board[][SIZE]);
int valid_moves(char board[][SIZE], int moves[][SIZE], char player);
void make_move(char board[][SIZE], int row, int col, char player);
void computer_move(char board[][SIZE], int moves[][SIZE], char player);

void main()
{
   char board [SIZE][SIZE] = { 0 };   /* The board            */
   int moves[SIZE][SIZE] = { 0 };     /* Valid moves          */
   int row = 0;                       /* Board row index      */
   int col = 0;                       /* Board column index   */
   int no_of_games = 0;               /* Number of games      */
   int no_of_moves = 0;               /* Count of moves       */
   int invalid_moves = 0;             /* Invalid move count   */
   int comp_score = 0;                /* Computer score       */
   int user_score = 0;                /* Player score         */
   char y = 0;                        /* Column letter        */
   int x = 0;                         /* Row number           */
   char again = 0;                    /* Replay choice input  */
   int player = 0;                    /* Player indicator     */
   int i=0;                           /* loop counter         */
   int j=0;                           /* loop counter         */

   /* The main game loop */
   do
   {
     /* On even games the player starts; */
     /* on odd games the computer starts */
     player = ++no_of_games % 2;
     no_of_moves = 4;                 /* Starts with four counters */

     /* Blank all the board squares */
     for(row = 0; row < SIZE; row++)
       for(col = 0; col < SIZE; col++)
         board[row][col] = ' ';
```

```
  /* Place the initial four counters in the center */
board[SIZE/2 - 1][SIZE/2 - 1] = board[SIZE/2][SIZE/2] = 'O';
board[SIZE/2 - 1][SIZE/2] = board[SIZE/2][SIZE/2 - 1] = '@';

/* The game play loop */
do
{
  display(board);                    /* Display the board  */
  if(player++ % 2)
  { /*    It is the player's turn                        */
    if(valid_moves(board, moves, 'O'))
    {
      /* Read player moves until a valid move is entered */
      for(;;)
      {
        fflush(stdin);                /* Flush the keyboard buffer */
        printf("Please enter your move: "); /* Prompt for entry   */
        scanf("%d%c", &x, &y);               /* Read input        */
        y = tolower(y) - 'a';         /* Convert to column index */
        x--;                          /* Convert to row index    */
        if( x>=0 && y>=0 && x<SIZE && y<SIZE && moves[x][y])
        {
          make_move(board, x, y, 'O');
          no_of_moves++;              /* Increment move count */
          break;
        }
        else
          printf("Not a valid move, try again.\n");
      }
    }
    else                              /* No valid moves */
      if(++invalid_moves<2)
      {
        fflush(stdin);
        printf("\nYou have to pass, press return");
        scanf("%c", &again);
      }
      else
        printf("\nNeither of us can go, so the game is over.\n");
  }
  else
  { /* It is the computer's turn                         */
    if(valid_moves(board, moves, '@')) /* Check for valid moves */
    {
      invalid_moves = 0;              /* Reset invalid count    */
      computer_move(board, moves, '@');
      no_of_moves++;                  /* Increment move count   */
    }
    else
    {
      if(++invalid_moves<2)
        printf("\nI have to pass, your go\n"); /* No valid move */
```

```
            else
              printf("\nNeither of us can go, so the game is over.\n");
          }
        }
    }while(no_of_moves < SIZE*SIZE && invalid_moves<2);

    /* Game is over */
    display(board);  /* Show final board */

    /* Get final scores and display them */
    comp_score = user_score = 0;
    for(i = 0; i < SIZE; i++)
      for(j = 0; j < SIZE; j++)
      {
        comp_score += board[i][j] == '@';
        user_score += board[i][j] == 'O';
      }
    printf("The final score is:\n");
    printf("Computer %d\n    User %d\n\n", comp_score, user_score);

    fflush(stdin);              /* Flush the input buffer */
    printf("Do you want to play again (y/n): ");
    scanf("%c", &again);        /* Get y or n              */
  }while(again == 'y');         /* Go again on y           */

  printf("\nGoodbye\n");
}

/* Code for definition of display() */

/* Code for definition of valid_moves() */
```

The code to deal with game moves uses two new functions, for which we have added prototypes. The function **make_move()** will execute a move, and the **computer_move()** function will calculate the computer's move. For the player, we calculate the **moves** array for the valid moves in the **if** statement:

```
      if(valid_moves(board, moves, 'O'))
      ...
```

If the return value is positive then there are valid moves - so we read the row number and column letter for the square selected:

```
        printf("Please enter your move: "); /* Prompt for entry  */
        scanf("%d%c", &x, &y);               /* Read input        */
```

We convert the row number to an index by subtracting 1, and the letter to an index by subtracting **'a'**. We call **tolower()** just to be sure the value in **y** is lower case. Of course, we must include the **ctype.h** header for this function. For a valid move, the index values must be within the bounds of the array, and **moves[x][y]** must be 1:

```
         if( x>=0 && y>=0 && x<SIZE && y<SIZE && moves[x][y])
         ...
```

If we have a valid move then we execute it by calling the function **make_move()**, which we will write in a moment (notice that the code won't compile, yet, because we make a call to this function without having defined it in the program).

If there are no valid moves for the player, we increment **invalid_moves**. If this is still less than 2 then we output a message that the player cannot go, and go to the next iteration for the computer's move. If **invalid_moves** is not less than 2, however, then we output a message that the game is over, and the **do-while** loop condition controlling game moves will be false.

For the computer move, if there are valid moves, we call the **computer_move()** function to make the move, and increment the move count. The circumstances where there are no valid moves are handled in the same way as for the player.

Let's add the definition of the **make_move()** function next. To make a move, we must place the appropriate counter on the selected square, and flip any adjacent rows of opponent counters that are bounded at the opposite end by a player counter. You can add the code for this function at the end of the source file – I won't repeat all the other code:

```
/*********************************************************************/
/* Makes a move. This places the counter on a square,and reverses    */
/* all the opponent's counters affected by the move.                 */
/* First parameter is the board array.                               */
/* Second and third parameters are the row and column indices.       */
/* Fourth parameter identifies the player.                           */
/*********************************************************************/
void make_move(char board[][SIZE], int row, int col, char player)
{
   int rowdelta = 0;                    /* Row increment            */
   int coldelta = 0;                    /* Column increment         */
   int x = 0;                           /* Row index for searching  */
   int y = 0;                           /* Column index for searching */
   char opponent = (player == 'O')? '@' : 'O';  /* Identify opponent */

   board[row][col] = player;            /* Place the player counter  */

   /* Check all the squares around this square */
   /* for the opponents counter               */
   for(rowdelta = -1; rowdelta <= 1; rowdelta++)
     for(coldelta = -1; coldelta <= 1; coldelta++)
     {
       /* Don't check off the board, or the current square */
       if(row + rowdelta < 0 || row + rowdelta >= SIZE ||
          col + coldelta < 0 || col + coldelta >= SIZE ||
                           (rowdelta==0 && coldelta== 0))
         continue;
```

```
              /* Now check the square */
          if(board[row + rowdelta][col + coldelta] == opponent)
          {
            /* If we find the opponent, search in the same direction */
            /* for a player counter                                  */
            x = row + rowdelta;          /* Move to opponent */
            y = col + coldelta;          /* square           */

            for(;;)
            {
              x += rowdelta;             /* Move to the    */
              y += coldelta;             /* next square    */

              /* If we are off the board give up */
              if(x < 0 || x >= SIZE || y < 0 || y >= SIZE)
                break;

              /* If the square is blank give up */
              if(board[x][y] == ' ')
                break;

              /* If we find the player counter, go backwards from here */
              /* changing all the opponents counters to player         */
              if(board[x][y] == player)
              {
                while(board[x-=rowdelta][y-=coldelta]==opponent)
                  board[x][y] = player;     /* Opponent? Yes, change it */
                break;                       /* We are done    */
              }
            }
          }
        }
      }
    }
}
```

The logic here is similar to that in the **valid_moves()** function for checking that a square is a valid move. The first step is to search the squares around the square indexed by the parameters **row** and **col** for an opponent counter. This is done in the nested loops:

```
for(rowdelta = -1; rowdelta <= 1; rowdelta++)
  for(coldelta = -1; coldelta <= 1; coldelta++)
  {
    ...
  }
```

When we find an opponent counter, we head off in the same direction looking for a player counter in the indefinite **for** loop. If we fall off the edge of the board, or find a blank square, we break out of the **for** loop, and continue the outer loop to move to the next square around the selected square. If we do find a player counter, however, then we back up, changing all the opponent counters to player counters.

```
                   /* If we find the player counter, go backwards from here */
                   /* changing all the opponents counters to player          */
                   if(board[x][y] == player)
                   {
                     while(board[x-=rowdelta][y-=coldelta]==opponent)
                       board[x][y] = player;      /* Opponent? Yes, change it */
                     break;                        /* We are done      */
                   }
```

The break here breaks out of the indefinite **for** loop.

Now that we have this function, we can move on to the trickiest part of the program, which is implementing the function to make the computer's move. We'll adopt a relatively simple strategy for determining the computer's move. We'll evaluate each of the possible valid moves for the computer. For each valid computer move, we'll determine what is the best move that the player could make, and determine a score for that. We'll then choose the computer move for which the player's best move produces the lowest score.

Before we get to write **computer_move()**, we'll implement a couple of helper functions. The first will be the function **get_score()** that will calculate the score for a given board position. You can add the following code to the end of the source file:

```
/****************************************************************/
/* Calculates the score for the current board position for the  */
/* player. player counters score +1, opponent counters score -1 */
/* First parameter is the board array                           */
/* Second parameter identifies the player                       */
/* Return value is the score.                                   */
/****************************************************************/
int get_score(char board[][SIZE], char player)
{
   int score = 0;      /* Score for current position */
   int row = 0;        /* Row index               */
   int col = 0;        /* Column index            */
   char opponent = player == 'O' ? '@' : 'O';  /* Identify opponent */

   /* Check all board squares */
   for(row = 0; row < SIZE; row++)
     for(col = 0; col < SIZE; col++)
     {
       score -= board[row][col] == opponent; /* Decrement for opponent */
       score += board[row][col] == player;   /* Increment for player   */
     }
   return score;
}
```

This is quite simple. The score is calculated by adding 1 for every player counter on the board, and subtracting one for each opponent counter on the board.

The next helper function is **best_move()**, which will calculate and return the score for the best move of the current set of valid moves for a player. The code for this is as follows:

```c
/*******************************************************************/
/* Calculates the score for the best move out of the valid moves  */
/* for player in the current position.                            */
/* First parameter is the board array                            */
/* Second paramter is the moves array defining valid moves.       */
/* Third parameter identifies the player                         */
/* The score for the best move is returned                       */
/*******************************************************************/
int best_move(char board[][SIZE], int moves[][SIZE], char player)
{
   int row = 0;      /* Row index    */
   int col = 0;      /* Column index */
   int i = 0;        /* Loop index   */
   int j = 0;        /* Loop index   */

   char opponent = player=='O'?'@':'O'; /* Identify opponent */

   char new_board[SIZE][SIZE] = { 0 };  /* Local copy of board  */
   int score = 0;                        /* Best score          */
   int new_score = 0;                    /* Score for current move */

   /* Check all valid moves to find the best */
   for(row = 0 ; row<SIZE ; row++)
     for(col = 0 ; col<SIZE ; col++)
     {
       if(!moves[row][col])            /* Not a valid move?    */
         continue;                      /* Go to the next       */

       /* Copy the board */
       for(i = 0 ; i<SIZE ; i++)
         for(j = 0 ; j<SIZE ; j++)
           new_board[i][j] = board[i][j];

       /* Make move on the board copy */
       make_move(new_board, row, col, player);

       /* Get score for move          */
       new_score = get_score(new_board, player);

       if(score<new_score)            /* Is it better?         */
             score = new_score;  /* Yes, save it as best score */
     }
   return score;                       /* Return best score     */
}
```

Remember that we must add function prototypes for both of these helper functions to the other function prototypes in **main()**:

```
/* Function prototypes */
void display(char board[][SIZE]);
int valid_moves(char board[][SIZE], int moves[][SIZE], char player);
void make_move(char board[][SIZE], int row, int col, char player);
void computer_move(char board[][SIZE], int moves[][SIZE], char player);
int best_move(char board[][SIZE], int moves[][SIZE], char player);
int get_score(char board[][SIZE], char player);
```

4 The last piece to complete the program is the implementation of the **computer_move()** function. The code for this is as follows:

```
/***************************************************************/
/* Finds the best move for the computer. This is the move for  */
/* which the opponent's best possible move score is a minimum.  */
/* First parameter is the board array.                          */
/* Second parameter is the moves array containing valid moves.  */
/* Third parameter identifies the computer.                     */
/***************************************************************/
void computer_move(char board[][SIZE], int moves[][SIZE], char player)
{
    int row = 0;                        /* Row index              */
    int col = 0;                        /* Column index           */
    int best_row = 0;                   /* Best row index         */
    int best_col = 0;                   /* Best column index      */
    int i = 0;                          /* Loop index             */
    int j = 0;                          /* Loop index             */
    int new_score = 0;                  /* Score for current move */
    int score = 100;                    /* Minimum opponent score */
    char temp_board[SIZE][SIZE];        /* Local copy of board    */
    int temp_moves[SIZE][SIZE];         /* Local valid moves array */
    char opponent = (player == 'O')? '@' : 'O'; /* Identify opponent */

    /* Go through all valid moves */
    for(row = 0; row < SIZE; row++)
      for(col = 0; col < SIZE; col++)
      {
        if(moves[row][col] == 0)
          continue;

        /* First make copies of the board and moves arrays */
        for(i = 0; i < SIZE; i++)
          for(j = 0; j < SIZE; j++)
            temp_board[i][j] = board[i][j];

        /* Now make this move on the temporary board */
        make_move(temp_board, row, col, player);
```

```
        /* find valid moves for the opponent after this move */
        valid_moves(temp_board, temp_moves, opponent);

        /* Now find the score for the opponents best move */
        new_score = best_move(temp_board, temp_moves, opponent);

        if(new_score<score)      /* Is it worse?                */
        {                        /* Yes, so save this move */
          score = new_score;     /* Record new lowest opponent score */
          best_row = row;  /* Record best move row              */
          best_col = col;  /* and column                        */
        }
      }

    /* Make the best move */
    make_move(board, best_row, best_col, player);
}
```

This is not difficult with the two helper functions. Remember that we're going to choose the move for which the opponent's subsequent best move is a minimum.

In the main loop, controlled by the counters **row** and **col**, we make each valid move, in turn, on the copy of the current board that's stored in the local array **temp_board**. After each move, we call the **valid_moves()** function to calculate the valid moves for the opponent in that position, and store the results in the **temp_moves** array. We then call the **best_move()** function to get the score for the best opponent move from the valid set stored in the array **temp_moves**. If that score is less than any previous score, we save the score, the row, and the column index for that computer move as a possible best move.

The variable **score** is initialized with a value that's higher than any possible score, and we go about trying to minimize this (since it's the strength of the opponent's next move) to find the best possible move for the computer. After all of the valid computer moves have been tried, **best_row** and **best_col** contain the row and column index for the move that minimizes the opponent's next move. We then call **make_move()** to make the best move for the computer.

You can now compile and execute the game. The games starts something like this:

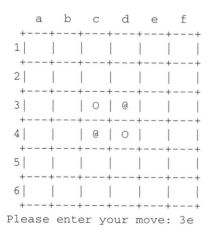

```
     a   b   c   d   e   f
   +---+---+---+---+---+---+
 1 |   |   |   |   |   |   |
   +---+---+---+---+---+---+
 2 |   |   |   |   |   |   |
   +---+---+---+---+---+---+
 3 |   |   | O | @ |   |   |
   +---+---+---+---+---+---+
 4 |   |   | @ | O |   |   |
   +---+---+---+---+---+---+
 5 |   |   |   |   |   |   |
   +---+---+---+---+---+---+
 6 |   |   |   |   |   |   |
   +---+---+---+---+---+---+
Please enter your move: 3e
```

352

```
     a   b   c   d   e   f
   +---+---+---+---+---+---+
 1 |   |   |   |   |   |   |
   +---+---+---+---+---+---+
 2 |   |   |   |   |   |   |
   +---+---+---+---+---+---+
 3 |   |   | O | O | O |   |
   +---+---+---+---+---+---+
 4 |   |   | @ | O |   |   |
   +---+---+---+---+---+---+
 5 |   |   |   |   |   |   |
   +---+---+---+---+---+---+
 6 |   |   |   |   |   |   |
   +---+---+---+---+---+---+
```

The computer doesn't play too well, since it only looks one move ahead, and it doesn't have any favoritism for edge and corner cells.

Also, the board is only 6 by 6. If you want to change the board size, then just change the value of **SIZE** to another even number. The program will work just as well.

Summary

If you've arrived at this point without too much trouble, you're well on your way to being a competent C programmer. This chapter, and the previous one, have included all you really need to write well structured C programs. A functional structure is inherent to the C language, and you should keep your functions short with a well-defined purpose. This is the essence of good C code. You should now be able to approach your own programming problems with a functional structure in mind, right from the outset.

Don't forget the flexible power that pointers give you as a C programmer. They can greatly simplify many programming problems, and you should frequently find yourself using them as function arguments and return values. After a while, it will be a natural inclination. The real teacher is experience, so going over the programs in this chapter again will be extremely useful if you don't feel completely confident. And once you feel confident with what's in this book, you should be raring to have a go at some problems of your own.

There's still one major new piece of language territory in C that we've yet to deal with so far, and that's all about data and how to structure it. We'll look at data in Chapter 11. But before we do that, we need to cover input/output in rather more detail than we have done so far. Handling input and output is an important and fascinating aspect of programming, and so that's where we're headed next.

Essential Input and Output Operations

In this chapter, we're going to look in more detail at input from the keyboard, output to the screen, and output to a printer. The good news is that everything in this chapter is fairly easy, although there may be moments when you feel it's all becoming a bit of a memory test. Treat this as a breather from the last two chapters; after all, you don't have to memorize everything you see here: you can always come back to it when you need it!

The C language has no inherent input or output capability. All operations of this kind are provided by functions from standard libraries. We've been using many of these functions to provide input from the keyboard, and output to the screen, in all the preceding chapters.

This chapter will miraculously put all the pieces together into some semblance of order, and round it out with the aspects I haven't explained so far. I'll also add a bit about printing, since it's usually a fairly essential facility for a program. There's no program in this chapter, for the simple reason that we don't really cover anything that requires any practice (it's that easy).

In this chapter you will learn:

- How to read data from the keyboard
- How to format data for output on the screen
- How to deal with character output
- How to output data to a printer

Input and Output Streams

Up to now, we've used **scanf()** for keyboard input and **printf()** for output to the screen. Actually, there's been nothing in particular about the way we've used these functions to specify where the input came from, or where the output went. The information that **scanf()** received could have come from anywhere, as long as it was a suitable stream of characters. Similarly, the output from **printf()** could have been going anywhere that could accept a stream of characters. This is no accident: the standard input/output functions in C have been designed to be device independent, so that the transfer of data to or from a specific device isn't the concern of the programmer. The C library functions and the operating system make sure that operations with a specific device are executed correctly, which is good news for us.

Each input source and output destination in C is called a **stream**. A stream is independent of the physical piece of equipment involved, such as the monitor or the keyboard. Each device that a program uses will usually have one or more streams associated with it, depending on whether it's simply an input or an output device, such as a printer or a keyboard, or a device that can have both input and output operations, such as a disk drive. This is illustrated in the next figure.

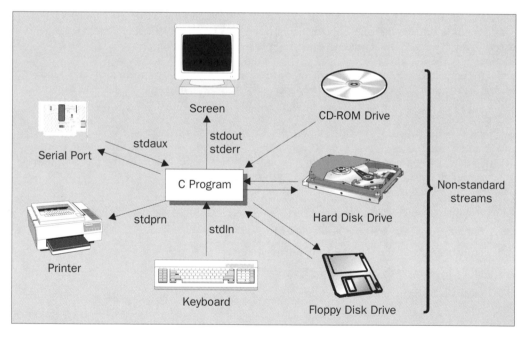

A disk drive can have multiple input and output streams, since it can contain multiple files. The correspondence is between a stream and a file, not between a stream and the device. A stream can be associated with a specific file on the disk, in which case that stream could be an **input stream** (that could only read from the file), an **output stream** (where you could write to the file), or both an **input and output stream** (where reading and writing to the file are both possible). You could also associate a stream with a file on a CD-ROM drive. Since this device is typically read only, the stream would, of necessity, be an input stream.

There are two further kinds of streams: **character streams** and **binary streams**. The main difference between these is that data transferred to or from character streams is modified by the library routine concerned, according to a format specification, whereas data transferred to or from binary streams is not modified. We'll discuss binary streams in Chapter 12 when we discuss disk file input/output.

Standard Streams

C has three predefined **standard streams** that are automatically available in any program - provided, of course, that you've included the header file necessary for their definition, which is the **stdio.h** header. These standard streams are **stdin**, **stdout**, and **stderr**. There are two other streams that are supported by many systems, which are **stdprn** and **stdaux**.

No initialization or preparation is necessary to use these streams. You just have to apply the appropriate library function that sends data to them. They are each pre-assigned to a specific physical device, as follows:

stdin	Keyboard
stdout	Display Screen
stderr	Display Screen
stdprn	Printer
stdaux	Serial Port

We shall concentrate on the standard input stream, **stdin**, the standard output stream, **stdout**, and the printer stream, **stdprn**.

The stream **stderr** is simply the one to which error messages from the C library are sent, and you can direct your own error messages to **stderr** if you wish. We shan't discuss this, other than to say it points to the display screen and can't be redirected to another device. Output to the stream **stdaux** is directed to the serial port and is outside the scope of this book - for reasons of space rather than complexity.

Both **stdin** and **stdout** can be re-assigned to files, instead of the default of keyboard and screen, by using operating system commands. When you do this, however, error conditions can arise which wouldn't normally arise with the default devices - and that's a pretty good reason not to do it for the moment.

Input from the Keyboard

There are two forms of input from the keyboard on **stdin** that we've already seen in previous chapters. There is **formatted input**, which is provided principally by **scanf()**, and there is **unformatted input**, where we receive the raw character data from a function like **getchar()**. There's rather more to both of these possibilities, so let's look at them in detail.

Formatted Keyboard Input

As we know, the function **scanf()** reads characters from the stream **stdin** and converts them to one or more internal variable values according to the format specifiers in a format control string. The general form of the function **scanf()** is:

```
int scanf(char *format, pointer_1, pointer_2,..., pointer_n )
```

The format control string parameter is actually of type **char *** - a pointer to a character string, as shown here. However, this usually appears as an explicit argument in the function call, such as in:

```
scanf("%lf", &variable);
```

But there's nothing to prevent you writing:

```
char str[] = "%lf";
scanf(str, &variable);
```

The format control string is basically a coded description of how **scanf()** should convert the incoming character stream to the values required. Following the format control string, we can have one or more arguments - each of which is an address where a corresponding converted input value is to be stored. As we've seen, this implies that the arguments must be the variable name preceded by **&** to define the address of the variable rather than its value. Of course, pointer variables and array names usually appear as arguments without the **&**.

The function **scanf()** reads from **stdin** until it comes to the end of the format control string, or until an error condition stops the input process. This sort of error would occur as the result of input that didn't correspond to what was expected with the current format specifier, as we shall see. Something that we have not previously noted is that **scanf()** returns a value: the count of the number of input values read.

Input Format Control Strings

The format control string used with **scanf()** is not precisely the same as that used with **printf()**. For one thing, blanks and tab characters are ignored. These are also called **whitespace characters**. You can use spaces and tabs to separate the format specifiers and thereby make the control string more readable. There are other differences too, as we shall see when we get to discuss formatted output a bit later in this chapter.

The most general form of a format specifier is shown in the next figure:

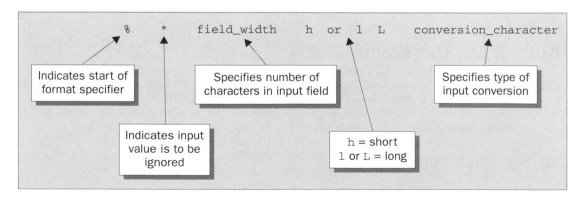

Let's take a look at the various parts of this general form.

▶ The **%** sign simply indicates the start of the format specifier.

▶ The next ***** is optional. If it's included, it indicates the next input value is to be ignored. This isn't normally used with input from the keyboard. It does become useful, however, when the keyboard input has been re-assigned to a file and you don't want to process all the values that appear within the file in your program.

▶ The field width is optional. It is an integer specifying the number of characters that **scanf()** should assume makes up the current value being input. This allows you to input a sequence of values without spaces between them. It's also often quite useful when reading files.

▶ The next character is also optional, and can be **h**, **L** or **l** (the letter). If it's **h**, it can only be included with an integer conversion specifier (**d**, **i**, **o**, **u** or **x**) and indicates that the input is to be converted as **short**. If it's **l** or **L** then it indicates **long** when preceding an **int** conversion specifier, and **double** when preceding a **float** conversion specifier.

▶ The conversion character specifies the type of conversion to be carried out on the input stream. The possible characters and their meaning are shown in the following table:

Conversion Character	Meaning
d	Convert input to **int**.
i	Convert input to **int**. If preceded by **0** then assume octal digits input, if preceded by **0x** or **0X**, then assume hexadecimal digits input.
o	Convert input to **int** and assume all digits are octal.
u	Convert input to **unsigned int**.
x	Convert to **int** and assume all digits are hexadecimal.
c	Input the next character as **char** (including blank).
s	Input the string of non-whitespace characters, starting with the next non-whitespace character.
e, f, or g	Convert input to **float**. A decimal point and an exponent in the input are optional.

Try It Out - Exercising Formatted Input

We can now exercise some of these format control strings with practical examples:

```
/* Example 10.1     Exercising formatted input */
#include <stdio.h>

void main()
{
    int i = 0;
    int j = 0;
    int k = 0;
    float fp1 = 0.0;
```

```
    k = scanf("%f %d %d", &fp1, &i , &j);
    printf("\nReturn value = %d\n", k);
    printf("\nfp1 = %f\ti = %d\tj = %d\n", fp1, i, j);
  }
```

How It Works

Execute this program and key the input as:

```
3.14159  7  8
```

You should get the output:

```
Return value = 3

fp1 = 3.141590   i = 7   j = 8
```

The value of **k** is the count of the number of values processed. The remaining variables are what you might expect. The **\t** in the **printf()** statement is the tab character.

It isn't essential that you enter all the data on a single line. If you key the first two values and press *Enter*, the **scanf()** function will wait for you to enter the next value on the next line.

Now let's change the program a little bit by altering one statement. Replace the input statement by:

```
    k = scanf("%3f %2d %2d", &fp1, &i, &j);
```

Now run the program with exactly the same input line as before. You should get the output:

```
Return value = 3

fp1 = 3.10000   i = 41   j = 59
```

Because we specified a field width of 3 for the floating-point value, the first three characters are taken as defining the value of our first input variable. The following two integer values to be input have a field width definition of 2, so they have values defined by the successive pairs of characters from what was our first input value in the previous example. The consequence of this is that **i** has the value 41, and **j** has the value 59.

Let's try another simple variation. Change the input statement to:

```
    k = scanf("%6f %2d %2d", &fp1, &i, &j);
```

With exactly the same input line as before, you should now get the output:

```
Return value = 3

fp1 = 3.141500   i = 9   j = 7
```

So what can we conclude from this case? The first floating-point value has clearly been defined by the first six characters of input. The next two values result in integers 9 and 7. This shows that in spite of the fact that we specified a field width of 2 in each case, it appears to have been overridden. This is a consequence of the blank following each of the two digits involved, terminating the input scanning for the value being read. So whatever value we put as a field width, the scanning of the input line for a given value stops as soon as we meet the first blank. We could change the specifiers for the integer values to **%12d** and the result would still be the same for the given input.

We could demonstrate one further aspect of numerical input processing by running the last version of the previous example with the input line:

```
3.1415A7        8
```

You should now get the output:

```
Return value = 1

fp1 = 3.141500  i = 0  j = 0
```

The count of the number of input values is 1, corresponding to a value for the variable **fp1** being input. The **A** in the input stream is invalid in numerical input, and so the whole process stops dead. No values for variables **i** and **j** are processed. This demonstrates how unforgiving **scanf()** really is. A single invalid character in the input stream will stop your program in its tracks. If you want to be able to recover the situation when invalid input is entered, you can use the return value from **scanf()** as a measure of whether all the necessary input has been processed correctly, and include some code to retrieve the situation when necessary.

The simplest approach would perhaps be to print an irritable message and then demand the whole input be repeated. But beware of errors in your code getting you into a permanent loop in this circumstance. You'll need to think through all of the possible ways that things might go wrong if you're going to produce a robust program.

Characters in the Input Format String

We can include a character string that isn't a format conversion specifier within the input format string. If you do this, you're indicating that you expect the same characters to appear in the input. These have to be matched exactly, character for character, by the data in the input stream. Any variation will terminate the input scanning process in **scanf()**.

Try It Out - Characters in the Input Format String

We can illustrate this by modifying the previous example to the following:

```
/* Example 10.2 Characters in the format control string */
#include <stdio.h>

void main()
{
   int i = 0;
   int j = 0;
   int k = 0;
   float fp1 = 0.0;
```

```
    k = scanf("fp1 = %f i = %d %d", &fp1, &i , &j);
    printf("\nReturn value = %d\n", k);
    printf("\nfp1 = %f\ti = %d\tj = %d\n", fp1, i, j);
}
```

How It Works

If you enter the input string:

```
fp1=3.14159   i = 7  8
```

then you'll get this output:

```
Return value = 3

fp1 = 3.141590  i = 7  j = 8
```

It doesn't matter whether the blanks before and after the **=** are included in the input or not: they're whitespace characters and are therefore ignored. The important thing is to include the same characters that appear in the format control string, in the correct sequence and at the correct place in the input. Try the input line:

```
fp1 = 3.14159  i = 7  j = 8
```

and you'll get this output:

```
Return value = 2

fp1 = 3.141590  i = 7  j = 0
```

This is because the character **j** in the input stops processing immediately, and no value is received by the variable **j**. The input processing of characters by **scanf()** is also case-sensitive. If you input **Fp1=** instead of **fp1=**, no values will be processed at all, since the mismatch with the capital **F** will stop scanning before any values are entered.

Floating-Point Input

The next aspect of formatted input using **scanf()** that we'll look at is the variety of possible input forms for floating-point values.

Try It Out - Floating-Point Input

We'll go straight to a simple example:

```
/* Example 10.3 Floating Point Input */
#include <stdio.h>

void main()
{
    float fp1 = 0.0f;
```

```
        float fp2 = 0.0f;
        float fp3 = 0.0f;

        printf("\nReturn value = %d\n", scanf("%f %f %f", &fp1, &fp2, &fp3));
        printf("\nfp1 = %f\tfp2 = %f\tfp3 = %f", fp1, fp2, fp3);
    }
```

How It Works

In this example, we've put the **scanf()** call as the argument to the first **printf()**, just to show that it can be done - although I actually think that it makes the code rather inelegant and harder to follow, so I don't recommend it as a rule!

You might run this program with the input:

```
    3.14    .314E1 .0314e+02
```

And you'll get this output:

```
    Return value = 3

    fp1 = 3.140000        fp2 = 3.140000        fp3 = 3.140000
```

I've demonstrated, here, three different ways of entering the same value. The first is a straightforward decimal value; the second has an exponent value defined by the **E1**, which indicates that the value is to be multiplied by 10; and the third has an exponent value of **e+02** and is to be multiplied by 10^2. We have the option of whether or not to include an exponent. If we do include an exponent, we can define it beginning with either an **e** or an **E**. We can also include a sign for the exponent value if we want. There are countless variations possible here.

I recommend that you experiment with the various possibilities, here; in particular, try experimenting with floating-point numbers and the field width specifiers that we used for reading integers.

Reading Hexadecimal and Octal Values

We can read hexadecimal values from the input stream using the format specifier **%x**. For octal values we use **%o**.

Try It Out - Reading Hexadecimal and Octal Values

Try the following example:

```
/* Example 10.4 Reading hexadecimal and octal values */
#include <stdio.h>

void main()
{
    int i = 0;
    int j = 0;
```

```
        int k = 0;
        int m = 0;

        m = scanf(" %d %x %o", &i , &j, &k );
        printf("\n%d values read.\n", m);
        printf("\ni = %d\tj = %d\tk = %d\n", i, j, k );
    }
```

How It Works

If you enter the values:

```
    12      12      12
```

then you'll get this output:

```
    3 values read.

    12      18      10
```

We read the three values 12, first with a decimal format specifier **%d**, second using a hexadecimal format specifier **%x**, and last using an octal format specifier **%o**. The output shows that 12 in hexadecimal is 18 in decimal notation, while 12 in octal is 10 in decimal notation.

Hexadecimal data entry can be useful when you want to enter bit patterns (sequences of 1's and 0's) as they're easier to specify in hexadecimal than in decimal. Each hexadecimal digit corresponds to four bits, so you can specify a 16-bit word as four hexadecimal digits. Octal is hardly ever used these days, and it appears here mainly for historical reasons.

Reading Characters Using scanf()

There are two format specifiers for reading characters. You can read a single character using the format specifier **%c**. For a string of characters you use the specifier **%s**.

Try It Out - Reading Characters Using scanf()

We can show these character reading functions in operation with the following example:

```
/* Example 10.5 Reading characters with scanf() */
#include <stdio.h>

void main()
{
    char initial = ' ';
    char name[80] = { 0 };

    printf("\nEnter your first initial: ");
    scanf("%c", &initial );
    printf("\nEnter your first name:" );
    scanf("%s", name );
```

```
      if(initial != name[0])
        printf("\n%s,you got your initial wrong.", name);
      else
        printf("\nHi, %s. Your initial is correct. Well done!", name );
    }
```

How It Works

This program expects you to enter your first initial and then your first name. It checks that the first letter of your name is the same as the initial you entered. Here's the output I get from telling the program about my name:

```
Enter your first initial: I

Enter your first name:Ivor

Hi, Ivor. Your initial is correct. Well done!
```

If you try a couple of variations on the input, however, you'll see some of the limitations of **scanf()**. Try entering a space, then your initial. The program will treat the blank as the value for **initial**, and the single character you entered as your **name**. The first character you enter when using the **%c** specifier is taken to be the character, whatever you've typed.

You could also try entering a valid initial, and then your full name, including surname. You'll find that only your first name is recognized. The blank between your first and second name will signal the end of the input with the **%s** specifier.

> *You can't read strings containing blanks with* ***scanf()***.
>
> *If you want to read a complete line, including blanks, in one go then you have to use the* ***gets()*** *function, which we'll discuss in the next section.*

Pitfalls with scanf()

There are two very common mistakes that are made when using **scanf()** that you should keep in mind:

➤ Don't forget that the arguments must be pointers. Perhaps the most common error is to forget the ampersand when specifying single variables as arguments to **scanf()**, particularly since you don't need them with **printf()**. Of course, the **&** isn't necessary if the argument is an array name or a pointer variable.

➤ When inputting a string using **%s**, remember to ensure that there's enough space for the string to be read in, *plus* the terminating **'\0'**. If you don't remember to do this, you'll overwrite some data, possibly even some of your program code.

String Input From the Keyboard

There's a function in **stdio.h** that will read a complete line of text as a string. The general syntax of the function is:

```
char *gets(char *str);
```

This function reads characters into the memory pointed to by **str** until you press the *Enter* key. It appends the terminating null, **'\0'**, in place of the newline character generated when you press *Enter*. The return value is identical to the argument, which is the address where the string has been stored.

Try It Out - Reading a String with gets()

We could modify the previous example to use **gets()** instead of **scanf()**:

```
/* Example 10.6 Reading a string with gets() */
#include <stdio.h>

void main()
{
   char initial[2] = {0};
   char name[80] = {0};

   printf("\nEnter your first initial: ");
   gets( initial );
   printf("\nEnter your name: " );
   gets(name);
   if(initial[0] != name[0])
     printf("\n%s,you got your initial wrong,", name);
   else
     printf("\nHi, %s. Your initial is correct. Well done!", name);
}
```

How It Works

As you can see, all we needed to do to produce this example was to replace the two calls to **scanf()** in the last example with two calls to **gets()**, after changing the variable **initial** to an array with two elements. This last change is necessary because the function **gets()** will append **'\0'** even if only one character is read. Typical output from the program is:

```
Enter your first initial: M

Enter your name: Mephistopheles

Hi, Mephistopheles. Your initial is correct. Well done!
```

It works extremely simply, since there is no format specification involved. Because **gets()** will read characters until you press *Enter*, you can now enter your full name if you wish.

For string input, using **gets()** is usually the preferred approach. However, **gets()** isn't quite so useful when you only want one character, as we do for reading an initial. Also, if you enter a space before you enter your initial, then you'll overwrite some memory, because more space will be required than we've allocated in the array **initial**.

Unformatted Input from the Keyboard

The function **getchar()** allows us to read from **stdin** character by character. **getchar()** is also defined in **stdio.h**, and its general syntax is:

```
int getchar(void)
```

getchar() requires no arguments, and it returns the character read from the input stream. Note that this character is returned as **int**, and that it's displayed on the screen.

With many systems, the header file **conio.h** is often provided. This provides additional functions for character input and output. One of the most useful of these is **getch()**, which reads a character from the keyboard without displaying it on the screen. This is particularly useful when you need to prevent others being able to see what's being keyed in, such as when a password is being entered.

Output To The Screen

Output to the screen is much easier than input from the keyboard. You know what data you are outputting, whereas with input you have all the vagaries of possible miskeying. The primary function to realize formatted output to the **stdout** stream is **printf()**.

Fortunately, or unfortunately, depending how you view the chore of getting familiar with this stuff, **printf()** provides a myriad of possible variations for the output you can obtain - much more than the scope of the format specifiers associated with **scanf()**.

Formatted Output To The Screen - Using printf()

The **printf()** function is defined in the header file **stdio.h**, and its general form is as follows:

```
int printf(char *format, argument_1, argument_2,...,argument_n)
```

The first parameter, here, is the format control string, which can be a pointer to a string specified elsewhere. This is apparent from the representation on the previous page, although usually it's entered as an explicit string constant argument - as we have seen in previous examples. The succeeding parameters are the values to be output in sequence, and they must correspond with the format conversion specifiers appearing in the first argument.

Of course, as we have also seen in earlier examples, if the output is simply the text that appears in the control string, then there are no additional arguments after the first. But where there are argument values to be output, there must be *at least* as many arguments as there are format specifiers. If not, the results are unpredictable. If there are *more* arguments than specifiers, then the excess is ignored. This is because the function uses the format string as the determinant of how many arguments follow, and what type they have.

This is also the reason why you get the wrong result with a %d specifier combined with a **long** *argument on systems where* **int** *is two bytes rather than four.*

The format conversion specifiers for **printf()** are a little more complicated than those used for input with **scanf()**. The general form of the format specifier is shown in the following figure:

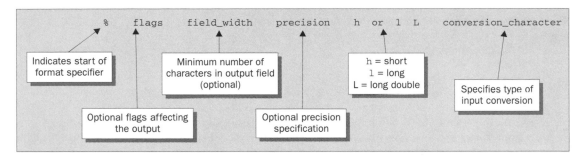

Let's take a quick pass through the elements of this general format specifier:

▶ The **%** sign indicates the start of the specifier, as it does for output.

▶ The optional flag characters are **+**, **-**, **#**, and blank. These affect the output as follows:

Character	Use
+	Ensures that, for signed output values, there's always a sign preceding the output value - either a plus or a minus sign.
-	Specifies that the output value is to be left justified in the output field, and padded with blanks on the right. The default positioning of the output is right-justified.
#	Specifies that **0** is to precede an octal output value, **0x**, or **0X** is to precede a hexadecimal output value, or that a floating-point output value will contain a decimal point. For **g** or **G** floating-point conversion characters, trailing zeros will also be omitted.
blank	Specifies that positive or zero output values will be preceded by a blank rather than a plus sign.

▶ The optional **field_width** specifies the minimum number of characters for the output value. If the value requires more characters, the field is simply expanded. If it requires less than the minimum specified, then it is padded with blanks - unless the field width is specified with a leading zero, as in 09, for example, where it would be filled on the left with zeros.

▶ The precision specifier is also optional and is generally used with floating-point output values. A specifier of **.n** indicates that **n** decimal places are to be output. If the value to be output has more than **n** significant digits, it is rounded or truncated.

▶ We use the **h**, **l** (the letter), or **L** specification to specify that the output conversion is being applied to **short**, **long** or **long double** values, respectively.

▶ The conversion character that you use defines how the output is to be converted for a particular type of value to be output. Conversion characters are defined in the next table.

Conversion Character	Output Produced
Applicable to integers:	
d	Signed decimal integer value
o	Unsigned octal integer value
u	Unsigned decimal integer value
x	Unsigned hexadecimal integer value with lower case digits, **a, b, c, d, e, f**
X	As **x** but with upper case digits **A, B, C, D, E, F**
Applicable to floating point:	
f	Signed decimal value
e	Signed decimal value with exponent
E	As **e** but with **E** for exponent instead of **e**
g	As **e** or **f** depending on size of value and precision
G	As **g** but with **E** for exponent values
Applicable to characters:	
c	Single character
s	All characters until **'\0'** is reached or **precision** characters have been output

Believe it or not, this set of output options includes only the really important ones. If you consult the documentation accompanying your compiler, you'll find a few more!

Let's take a look at some of the variations we haven't identified so far. Those with field width and precision specifiers are probably the most interesting.

Escape Sequences

We can include whitespace characters in the format control string for **printf()**. The characters that are referred to as whitespace are: newline, carriage return, formfeed characters, blank (a space), and tab. Some of these are represented by escape sequences that begin with \. Here are the most common escape sequences:

\a	Bell - sound a beep on your computer
\b	Backspace
\f	Formfeed or page eject
\n	Newline
\r	Carriage return (for printers) or move to the beginning of the current line for output to the screen
\t	Horizontal tab

You use the escape sequence \\ in format control strings when you want to output the backslash character, \. If this were not the case then it would be impossible to output a backslash, since it would always be assumed that a backslash was the start of an escape sequence.

> *Escape sequences can be used within any string, not just in the context of the format string for the* ***printf ()*** *function.*

Different Output

Let's look at some examples of the different ways of outputting information.

Try It Out - Outputting Integers

We can try a sample of integer output formats first:

```
/* Example 10.7 Integer output variations */
#include <stdio.h>

void main()
{
   int i = 15;
   int j = 345;
   int k = 4567;
   long li = 56789L;
   long lj = 678912L;
   long lk = 23456789L;

   printf("\ni = %d\tj = %d\tk = %d\ti = %6.3d\tj = %6.3d\tk = %6.3d\n",
          i ,j, k, i, j, k);
   printf("\ni = %-d\tj = %+d\tk = %-d\ti = %-6.3d\tj = %-6.3d\tk ="
          " %-6.3d\n",i ,j, k, i, j, k);
   printf("\nli = %d\tlj = %d\tlk = %d\n", li, lj, lk);
   printf("\nli = %ld\tlj = %ld\tlk = %ld\n", li, lj, lk);
}
```

How It Works

When you execute the example above, you should see something like this:

```
i = 15   j = 345 k = 4567      i =     015    j =     345    k =     4567

i = 15   j = +345       k = 4567      i = 015       j = 345       k = 4567

li = -8747    lj = 0       lk = 23552

li = 56789    lj = 678912  lk = 23456789
```

This example illustrates a miscellany of options for integer output. You can see the effects of the **minus** flag by comparing the first two lines produced by these statements:

```
   printf("\ni = %d\tj = %d\tk = %d\ti = %6.3d\tj = %6.3d\tk = %6.3d\n",
          i ,j, k, i, j, k);
   printf("\ni = %-d\tj = %+d\tk = %-d\ti = %-6.3d\tj = %-6.3d\tk ="
          " %-6.3d\n",i ,j, k, i, j, k);
```

The minus flag, **-**, causes the output to be left justified. The effect of the field width specifier is also apparent from the spacing of the last three outputs in each group of six.

We get a leading plus in the output of **j** on the second line because of the flag modifier. You can use more than one flag modifier if you want. With the second output of the value of **i,** we have a leading zero inserted due to the minimum precision being specified as 3. We could also have obtained leading zeros by preceding the minimum width value with a zero in the format specification.

The third output line is produced by the statement:

```
printf("\nli = %d\tlj - %d\tlk = %d\n", li, lj, lk);
```

Here, you can see that failure to insert the **l** (the small letter L) modifier when outputting long integers results in apparent garbage, because the output value is assumed to be a two byte integer. Of course, if your system implements type **int** as a four byte integer, the values will be correct here: the problem only arises if **long** and **int** are differentiated.

We get the correct values from the statement:

```
printf("\nli = %ld\tlj = %ld\tlk = %ld\n", li, lj, lk);
```

It's unwise to specify inadequate values for the width and the precision of the values to be displayed. Weird and wonderful results may be produced if you do. Try experimenting with this example to see just how much variation you can get.

Try It Out - Variations on a Single Integer

We'll try one more integer example to run the gamut of possibilities with a single integer value:

```
/*       Example 10.8 Variations on a single integer */
#include <stdio.h>
void main()
{
   int k = 678;

   printf("\n%%d\t%%o\t%%x\t%%X");        /* Display format as heading */
   printf("\n%d\t%o\t%x\t%X", k, k, k, k );         /* Display values */

   /* Display format as heading then display the values */
   printf("\n\n%%8d      %%-8d      %%+8d      %%08d      %%-+8d");
   printf("\n%8d  %-8d  %-+8d  %08d  %-+8d", k, k, k, k, k );
}
```

How It Works

This program may look a little confusing at first, since the first of each pair of **printf()** statements displays the format used to output the number appearing immediately below. The **%%** specifier simply outputs the **%** character. When you execute this example you should get something like this:

```
%d        %o        %x        %X
678       1246      2a6       2A6

%8d          %-8d       %+8d        %08d        %-+8d
     678     678        +678        00000678    +678
```

The first row of output values are produced by this statement:

```
printf("\n%d\t%o\t%x\t%X", k, k, k, k );          /* Display values */
```

The outputs are decimal, octal, and two varieties of hexadecimal, for the value 678, with default width specification. The corresponding format appears above each value in the output.

The next row of output values is produced by:

```
printf("\n%8d  %-8d  %-+8d  %08d  %-+8d", k, k, k, k, k );
```

This statement includes a variety of flag settings with a width specification of **8**. The first is normal right justification in the field. The second is left justified, because of the **–** flag. The third has a sign, because of the **+** flag. The fourth has leading zeros, because the width is specified as **08** instead of **8**, and also has a sign because of the **+** flag. The last output value uses a specifier with all the trimmings, **%-+8d**, so the output is left justified in the field, and also has a leading sign.

> *When you're outputting multiple rows of values on the screen, using a width specification - possibly with tabs - will enable you to line them up in columns.*

Outputting Floating-Point Values

If plowing through the integer options hasn't got you nodding off, then we can take a quick look at the floating-point output options.

Try It Out - Outputting Floating-Point Values

Look at the following example:

```
/* Example 10.9 Outputting floating-point values */
 #include <stdio.h>

void main()
{
   float fp1 = 345.678f;
   float fp2 = 1.234E6f;
   double fp3 = 234567898.0;
   double fp4 = 11.22334455e-6;

   printf("\n%f\t%+f\t%-10.4f\t%6.4f\n", fp1, fp2, fp1, fp2);
   printf("\n%e\t%+E\n", fp1, fp2);
   printf("\n%f\t%g\t%#+f\t%8.4f\t%10.4g\n", fp3,fp3, fp3, fp3, fp4);
}
```

How It Works

With my compiler, I get this output:

```
345.678009        +1234000.000000 345.6780          1234000.0000

3.456780e+002    +1.234000E+006

234567898.000000          2.34568e+008    +234567898.000000
234567898.0000 1.122e-005
```

It's possible that you may not get exactly the same output, but it should be close. You may have only two-digit exponent values, for example. Most of the output is a straightforward demonstration of the effects of the format conversion specifiers that we've discussed; but a few points are worthy of note.

The value of the first output for **fp1** differs slightly from the value that we assigned to the variable. This is typical of the kind of small difference that can creep in when floating-point numbers are converted from decimal to binary. With fractional decimal values there isn't always an exact equivalent in binary floating-point.

In the output from the statement:

```
printf("\n%f\t%+f\t%-10.4f\t%6.4f\n", fp1, fp2, fp1, fp2);
```

the second output value for **fp1** shows how the number of decimal places after the point can be constrained. The output in this case is left justified in the field. The second output of **fp2** has a field width specified that is too small for the number of decimal places required, and is therefore overridden.

The second **printf()** statement is:

```
printf("\n%e\t%+E\n", fp1, fp2);
```

This outputs the same values in floating-point format with an exponent. Whether you get a capital **E** or a small **e** for the exponent indicator depends on how you write the format specifier.

In the last line, you can see how the **g**-specified output of **fp3** has been rounded-up compared to the **f**-specified output.

> *There are a huge number of possible variations for the output obtainable with **printf()**. It would be very educational for you to play around with the options, trying various ways of outputting the same information.*

Character Output

Now that we've looked at the various possibilities of outputting numbers, let's have a look at outputting characters.

Outputting Strings

In addition to the string output capabilities of **printf()**, we have the function **puts()** in **stdio.h**, which complements the **gets()** function. The general form of **puts()** is as follows:

```
int puts(char *string)
```

The **puts()** function accepts a pointer to a string as an argument and displays **string** on **stdout**. The string must be terminated by **'\0'**. It returns a non-negative value if no errors occur on output. **puts()** is very useful for outputting single line messages, as in:

```
puts("Is there no end to input and output?");
```

This will output the line appearing as an argument, and then move the cursor to the next line. The function **printf()** requires an explicit **'\n'** to be included at the end of the string.

> *The function **puts()** will, of course, also process embedded **'\n'** characters to generate new lines.*

Unformatted Output to the Screen

Also included in **stdio.h**, and complementing the function **getchar()**, is the function **putchar()**. This has the general form:

```
int putchar(int c)
```

putchar() outputs a single character, **c**, to **stdout**, and returns the character displayed. This allows you to output a message one character at a time, which can make your programs a bit bigger. For example, you could write:

```
char string[] = "Jabberwocky!\n";
puts(string);
```

or you could write:

```
char string[] = "Jabberwocky!\n";
int i = 0;
while( string[i] != '\0')
  putchar(string[i++]);
```

Both of these will output the same thought-provoking message. Of course, the real purpose of these functions is to give you complete control of input and output operations - if and when you need it. With **putchar()**, for instance, you could choose to output a selected sequence of characters from the middle of a string. You wouldn't be able to do this very easily with just **puts()**.

Sending Output to the Printer

To print, we just need to use a more generalized form of the **printf()** function, called **fprintf()**. This is actually designed to send formatted output to *any* stream, but we'll stick to printing for now. For the purpose of printing, the general form of **fprintf()** is:

```
int fprintf(stdprn, format_string, argument_1, argument_2,..,argument_n)
```

With the exception of the first parameter, and the extra **f** in the function name, **fprintf()** looks exactly like **printf()**. And so it is. If you don't have **stdprn** defined with your compiler and library, you'll need to consult your documentation to see how to handle printing, but most systems do support **stdprn**. You can use the same format string with the same set of specifiers to output data to your printer, in exactly the same way that you display results with **printf()**. However, there are a couple of minor variations you need to be aware of, and I'll illustrate these in the next example.

Try It Out - Printing On a Printer

This program shows how we can get programs to output to a printer.

```
/* Example 10.10 Printing on a printer - where else? */
#include <stdio.h>
void main()
{
   fprintf( stdprn, "The barber shaves all those who do not"
                                      " shave themselves.");
   fprintf(stdprn, "\n\rQuestion: Who shaves the barber?\n\r");
   fprintf(stdprn, "\n\rAnswer: She doesn't need to shave.\f");
}
```

How It Works

The only oddities here are the new escape sequences **\r** and **\f**. The sequence **\n\r** is equivalent to new line/carriage return on a printer, and the **\f** is form feed - which produces a page-eject on printers where this is necessary.

Summary

Although the various formatting codes that we've seen in this chapter have been chosen with the idea of being as meaningful as possible, there are a lot of them. The only way you're going to become comfortable with them is with practice. This generally needs to be in a practical context. Understanding the various codes is one thing, but they'll probably only become really familiar to you once you've used them a few times in real programs. Naturally, then, I recommend that you go and find practical uses for these formatting codes. In the meantime, you can always look them up here!

Structuring Data

So far, we've learned how to declare and define variables that can hold various types of data, including integers, floating-point values and characters. We also have the means to create arrays of any of these types, and arrays of pointers to memory locations containing data of the types available to us. While these have proved very useful, there are many applications where we need even more flexibility.

For instance, suppose we wanted to write a program that processed data about breeding horses. We'd need information about each horse - such as its name, its date of birth, its coloring, its height, its parentage, and so on. Some items are strings and some are numeric. Clearly, we could set up arrays for each data type, and store them quite easily. However, this has its limitations. It doesn't allow us to refer to Dobbin's date of birth or Trigger's height particularly easily. We'd need to synchronize our arrays by relating data items through a common index. Amazingly, C provides us with a better way of doing this, and that's what we're going to discuss here.

In this chapter you will learn:

> What structures are
> How to declare and define data structures
> How to use structures and pointers to structures
> How you can use pointers as structure members
> How to share memory between variables
> How to define your own data types
> How to write a program that produces bar charts from your data

Data Structures - Using struct

The keyword **struct** enables us to define a collection of variables, of various types, that we can treat as a unit. This will be clearer if we go straight into a simple example of a structure declaration:

```
struct horse
{
    int age;
    int height;
} Silver;
```

We've declared a **structure** type called **horse**. This is not a variable name: it's a new type. This type name is usually referred to as a **structure tag**, or a **tag name**. The naming of the structure tag follows the same rules as for a variable name, which you should be familiar with by now.

> *It's actually legal to use the same name for a structure tag name and another variable. However, I don't recommended that you do this, because it significantly increases the chances of confusion in your program.*

The variable names within the structure, **age** and **height**, are called **structure members**. In this case, they're both of type **int**. The members of the structure appear between the braces that follow the **struct** tag name **horse**.

In our example, an instance of the structure, called **Silver**, is declared at the same time that the structure is defined. **Silver** is a variable of type **horse**. Now, whenever we use the variable name **Silver**, it includes both members of the structure: the member **age**, and the member **height**.

Let's look at the declaration of a slightly more complicated version of the structure type **horse**:

```
struct horse
{
    int age;
    int height;
    char name[20];
    char father[20];
    char mother[20];
} Dobbin = {
            24, 17, "Dobbin", "Trigger", "Flossie"
           };
```

Any kind of variable can appear as a member of a structure, including arrays. As you can see, there are five members to this version of the structure we've called **horse**: the integer members **age** and **height**, and the arrays **name[]**, **father[]**, and **mother[]**. Each member declaration is essentially the same as a normal variable declaration, with the type followed by the name and terminated by a semicolon. Note that initialization values can't be placed here, because we aren't declaring variables - we're defining members of a type called **horse**. This is a kind of specification, or blueprint, that can then be used to define variables. So initial values *can* be assigned when we define instances of the type **horse**.

We define an instance of the structure **horse** after the closing brace of the structure definition. This is the variable **Dobbin**. Initial values are also assigned to the member variables of **Dobbin**, in a manner similar to that used to initialize arrays.

In our declaration of **Dobbin**, the values appearing between the final pair of braces apply, in sequence, to the member variable **age** (24), **height** (17), **name[]** ("Dobbin"), **father[]**

(**"Trigger"**), and **mother** (**"Flossie"**). The statement is finally terminated with a semicolon. The variable **Dobbin** now refers to the complete collection of members included in the structure. The memory occupied by the structure **Dobbin** is shown in the following figure. You can always find out the amount of memory occupied by a structure using the operator **sizeof**.

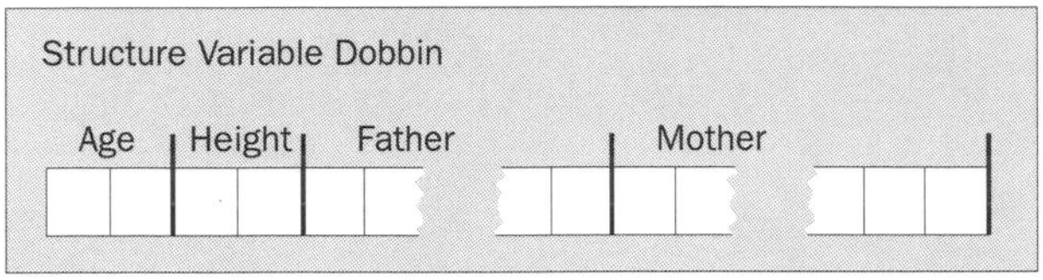

Structure Definition and Structure Variable Declaration

We could have separated the declaration of the structure from the declaration of the structure variable. Instead of the statements we saw above, we could have written:

```
struct horse
{
    int age;
    int height;
    char name[20];
    char father[20];
    char mother[20];
};

struct horse Dobbin = {
                       24, 17,"Dobbin", "Trigger", "Flossie"
                      };
```

We now have two separate statements, the definition of the structure tag **horse**, and the declaration of one variable of that type, **Dobbin**. Both the structure declaration and the structure variable definition statements end with a semicolon.

> *Notice that we've spread the definition of the variable* **Dobbin** *across several lines for readability.*

We could also add a third statement to our previous two examples that would define another variable of type **horse**:

```
struct horse Trigger = {
                        30, 15, "Trigger", "Smith", "Wesson"
                       };
```

Now we have a variable **Trigger** that holds the details of the father of **Dobbin**, where it's clear that the ancestors of **Trigger** are **"Smith"** and **"Wesson"**.

Of course, we can also declare multiple structure variables in a single statement. This is almost as easy as declaring variables of one of the standard C types. For example:

```
struct horse Piebald, Bandy;
```

379

This declares two variables of type **horse**. The only additional item in the declaration, compared with standard types, is the keyword **struct**. We haven't initialized the values - to keep the statement simple - but in general it's wise to do so.

Accessing Structure Members

Now we know how to define a structure and declare structure variables, we need to be able to refer to the members of a structure. A structure variable name is *not* a pointer. We need a special syntax to access the members.

We refer to a member of a structure by writing the structure variable name followed by a period, followed by the member variable name. For example, if we found that **Dobbin** had lied about his age, and was actually much younger than the initializing value would suggest, we could amend the value by writing:

```
Dobbin.age = 12;
```

This sets the age member of the structure **Dobbin** to 12. Structure members are just the same as variables of the same type. You can set their values and use them in expressions just the same as ordinary variables.

Try It Out - Using Structures

We can try out what we've covered so far about structures in a simple example that's designed to appeal to the horse enthusiast:

```
/* Example 11.1 Exercising the horse */
#include <stdio.h>

void main()
{
   /* Structure declaration */
   struct horse
   {
     int age;
     int height;
     char name[20];
     char father[20];
     char mother[20];
   };

   struct horse My_first_horse;  /* Structure variable declaration   */

   /* Initialize  the structure variable from input data */
   printf("\nEnter the name of the horse: " );
   scanf("%s", My_first_horse.name );     /* Read the horse's name   */

   printf("\nHow old is %s? ", My_first_horse.name );
   scanf("%d", &My_first_horse.age );     /* Read the horse's age    */
```

```
      printf("\nHow high is %s ( in hands )? ", My_first_horse.name );
      scanf("%d", &My_first_horse.height );   /* Read the horse's height */

      printf("\nWho is %s's father? ", My_first_horse.name );
      scanf("%s", My_first_horse.father );    /* Get the father's name   */

      printf("\nWho is %s's mother? ", My_first_horse.name );
      scanf("%s", My_first_horse.mother );    /* Get the mother's name    */

      /* Now tell them what we know */
      printf("\n\n%s is %d years old, %d hands high,",
         My_first_horse.name, My_first_horse.age, My_first_horse.height);
      printf(" and has %s and %s as parents.", My_first_horse.father,
                                           My_first_horse.mother );
}
```

Depending on what data you key in, you should get output approximating to:

```
Enter the name of the horse: Neddy

How old is Neddy? 12

How high is Neddy ( in hands )? 14

Who is Neddy's father? Bertie

Who is Neddy's mother? Nellie


Neddy is 12 years old, 14 hands high, and has Bertie and Nellie as
parents.
```

How It Works

The way we reference members of a structure makes it very easy to follow what's going on in this example. We've declared structure **horse** with the statement:

```
struct horse
{
   int age;
   int height;
   char name[20];
   char father[20];
   char mother[20];
};
```

Our structure has two integer members, **age** and **height**, and three **char** array members, **name[]**, **father[]**, and **mother[]**. Since there's just a semicolon following the closing brace, no variables of type **horse** are declared here.

After declaring the structure **horse**, we have the statement:

```
    struct horse My_first_horse;   /* Structure variable declaration    */
```

This declares one variable of type **horse**, which is **My_first_horse**. This variable has no initial values assigned in the declaration.

We then read in the data for the **name** member of the structure **My_first_horse**, with this statement:

```
    scanf("%s", My_first_horse.name );        /* Read the horse's name    */
```

No **address of** operator (**&**) is necessary here, because the member name is an array - so we implicitly transfer the address of the first array element to the function **scanf()**. We reference the member by writing the structure name, **My_first_horse**, followed by a period, followed by the member name, **name**. Other than the notation used to access it, using a structure member is the same as using any other variable.

The next value we read in is for the age of the horse:

```
    scanf("%d", &My_first_horse.age );        /* Read the horse's age     */
```

This member is a variable of type **int**, so here we must put the **&** to pass the address of the structure member.

> *Note that, when using the address of operator (&) for a member name, we place the &
> in front of the whole reference to the member, not in front of the member name.*

The following statements read the data for each of the other members of the structure in exactly the same manner, prompting for the input in each case. Once input is complete, the values read are output to the display as a single line using the statements:

```
    printf("\n\n%s is %d years old, %d hands high,",
        My_first_horse.name, My_first_horse.age, My_first_horse.height);
    printf(" and has %s and %s as parents.", My_first_horse.father,
                                               My_first_horse.mother );
```

The long names necessary to refer to the members of the structure tend to make this statement appear complicated, but it's really very straightforward. We have the names of the member variables as the arguments to the function following the first argument - which is the standard sort of format control string that you've seen many times before.

Unnamed Structures

We don't have to give a structure a tag name. When we declare a structure (and any instances of that structure) in a single statement, we can omit the tag name. In the last example, instead of the structure declaration for type **horse**, followed by the instance declaration for **My_first_horse**, we could have written this statement:

```
    struct
    {                       /* Structure declaration and... */
       int age;
       int height;
       char name[20];
```

```
      char father[20];
      char mother[20];
   } My_first_horse;  /* ...structure variable declaration combined */
```

A serious disadvantage with this approach is that we can no longer define further instances of the structure in another statement. All the variables of this structure type that you want in your program must be defined in the one statement.

Arrays of Structures

Our basic approach to keeping horse data is fine as far as it goes. But it'll probably begin to be a bit cumbersome by the time we've accumulated 50 or 100 horses. We need a more stable method for handling a lot of horses. It's exactly the same problem that we had with variables, which we solved using an array. And we can do the same here: we can declare a **horse** array.

Try It Out - Using Arrays of Structures

Let's saddle up and extend the previous example to handle several horses:

```
/* Example 11.2    Exercising the horse */
#include <stdio.h>
void main()
{
   struct horse      /* Structure declaration */
   {
     int age;
     int height;
     char name[20];
     char father[20];
     char mother[20];
   };

   struct horse My_horses[50]; /* Structure array declaration   */
   int hcount = 0;             /* Count of the number of horses */
   int i = 0;                  /* Loop counter                  */
   char test = '\0';           /* Test value for ending         */

   for(hcount = 0; hcount < 50 ; hcount++ )
   {
     printf("\nDo you want to enter details of a%s horse (Y or N)? ",
                                          hcount?"nother " : "" );
     scanf(" %c", &test );
     if(test == 'N' || test == 'n')
        break;

     printf("\nEnter the name of the horse: " );
     scanf("%s", My_horses[hcount].name );  /* Read the horse's name */

     printf("\nHow old is %s? ", My_horses[hcount].name );
```

```
        scanf("%d", &My_horses[hcount].age );   /* Read the horse's age  */

    printf("\nHow high is %s ( in hands )? ", My_horses[hcount].name );

    /* Read the horse's height*/
    scanf("%d", &My_horses[hcount].height );

    printf("\nWho is %s's father? ", My_horses[hcount].name );

    /* Get the father's name */
    scanf("%s", My_horses[hcount].father );

    printf("\nWho is %s's mother? ", My_horses[hcount].name );

    /* Get the mother's name  */
    scanf("%s", My_horses[hcount].mother );
  }

  /* Now tell them what we know. */
  for (i = 0 ; i < hcount ; i++ )
  {
    printf("\n\n%s is %d years old, %d hands high,",
             My_horses[i].name, My_horses[i].age, My_horses[i].height);
    printf(" and has %s and %s as parents.", My_horses[i].father,
                                              My_horses[i].mother );

  }
}
```

The output from this program is little different to the previous example we saw that dealt with a single horse. The main addition is the prompt for input data for each horse. Once all the data has been entered (or if you have the stamina, data on 50 horses has been entered) the program outputs a summary of all the data entered, one line per horse. The whole mechanism works very well in the mane (almost an unbridled success, you might say).

How It Works

In this version of equine data processing, we first declare the **horse** structure, and this is followed by the declaration:

```
struct horse My_horses[50]; /* Structure array declaration    */
```

This declares the variable **My_horses**, which is an array of fifty **horse** structures. Apart from the keyword **struct**, it's just like any other array declaration.

We then have a **for** loop controlled by:

```
for(hcount = 0; hcount < 50 ; hcount++ )
```

This creates the potential for the program to read in data for up to 50 horses. The loop control variable **hcount** is used to accumulate the total number of **horse** structures entered. The first action in the loop is in these statements:

```
        printf("\nDo you want to enter details of a%s horse (Y or N)? ",
                                            hcount?"nother " : "" );
    scanf(" %c", &test );
    if(test == 'N' || test == 'n')
        break;
```

On each iteration, the user is prompted to indicate whether or not they want to enter data for another horse - by entering **'Y'** or **'N'**. The **printf()** statement for this uses the conditional operator to insert **"nother"** into the output on every iteration after the first. After reading the character that the user enters, using **scanf()**, the **if** statement executes a **break**, which immediately exits from the loop if the response is negative.

The succeeding sequence of **printf()** and **scanf()** statements is much the same as before, but there are two points of note in these. Look at this statement:

```
    scanf("%s", My_horses[hcount].name );  /* Read the horse's name */
```

You can see the method for referencing the member of one element of an array of structures is easier to write than to say! The structure array name has an index in square brackets, to which a period and the member name are appended. If we wanted to reference the third element of the **name** array for the fourth structure element, then we would write **My_horses[3].name[2]**.

> *Of course, the index values start from zero, as with arrays of other types, so the fourth element of the structure array has the index value 3, and the third element of the member array is accessed by the index value 2.*

Now look at this statement from our example:

```
    scanf("%d", &My_horses[hcount].age );  /* Read the horse's age  */
```

Notice that the arguments to **scanf()** don't need the **&** for the string array variables, such as **My_horses[hcount].name**, but they *do* require them for the integer arguments **My_horses[hcount].age** and **My_horses[hcount].height**. It's very easy to forget the **address of** operator when reading values for variables like these.

Don't be misled, at this point, and think that these techniques are limited to equine applications. They can perfectly well be applied to porcine problems.

Structures in Expressions

A member of a structure that is one of the built-in types can be used as any other variable in an expression. Using the structure from Example 11.2, we could write this rather meaningless computation:

```
    My_horses[1].height = (My_horses[2].height + My_horses[3].height)/2;
```

I can think of no good reason why the height of one horse should be the average of two other horses' heights (unless there's some Frankenstein-like assembly going on) but it is a legal statement.

385

We can also use a complete structure element in an assignment statement:

```
My_horses[1] = My_horses[2];
```

This statement causes *all* the members of the structure **My_horses[2]** to be copied to the structure **My_horses[1]**, which means that the two structures become identical. The only other operation that's possible with a whole structure is to take its address - using the **&** operator. You can't add, compare, or perform any other operations with a complete structure.

Pointers to Structures

The ability to obtain the address of a structure raises the question of whether we can have pointers to a structure. Since we can take the address of a structure, the possibility of declaring a pointer to a structure does, indeed, naturally follow. We use the notation that we've already seen with other types of variables:

```
struct horse *phorse;
```

This declares a pointer, **phorse**, to a structure of type **horse**. We can now set **phorse** to have the value of the address of a particular structure, using exactly the same kind of statement that we've been using for other types of pointer. For example:

```
phorse = &My_horses[1];
```

Now **phorse** points to the structure **My_horses[1]**. We can immediately reference elements of this structure through our pointer. So if we wanted to display the name member of this structure, we could write:

```
printf("\nThe name is %s.", (*phorse).name);
```

The parentheses around the dereferenced pointer are essential, because the precedence of the member selection operator (the period) is higher than that of the pointer dereferencing operator, *****.

However, there's another way of doing this, and it's much more readable and intuitive. We could write the previous statement as:

```
printf("\nThe name is %s.", phorse->name );
```

So we don't need parentheses or an asterisk. You construct the operator **->** from a minus sign immediately followed by the symbol for greater than. This notation is almost invariably used in preference to the usual pointer-dereferencing notation we used at first, because it makes your programs so much easier to read.

Dynamic Memory Allocation for Structures

We have virtually all the tools we need to rewrite Example 11.2 with much a more economical use of memory. In the original version we allocated the memory for an array of 50 **horse** structures, even when, in practice, we probably didn't need anything like that amount.

To create dynamically allocated memory for structures, the only tool that's missing is an array of pointers to structures - which is declared very easily, as you can see in this statement:

```
struct horse *phorse[50];
```

This declares an array of 50 pointers to structures of type **horse**. Only memory for the pointers has been allocated by this statement. We must still allocate the memory necessary to store the actual members of each structure that we need.

Try It Out - Using Pointers with Structures

We can see the dynamic memory allocation of structures at work in the following example:

```c
/* Example 11.3 Pointing out the horses */
#include <stdio.h>
#include <stdlib.h>

void main()
{
   struct horse         /* Structure declaration */
   {
     int age;
     int height;
     char name[20];
     char father[20];
     char mother[20];
   };

   struct horse *phorse[50]; /* pointer to structure array declaration */
   int hcount = 0;            /* Count of the number of horses         */
   int i = 0;                 /* Loop counter                          */
   char test = '\0';          /* Test value for ending input           */

   for(hcount = 0; hcount < 50 ; hcount++ )
   {
     printf("\nDo you want to enter details of a%s horse (Y or N)? ",
                                        hcount?"nother " : "" );
     scanf(" %c", &test );
     if(test == 'N' || test == 'n')
       break;

     /* allocate memory to hold a structure     */
     phorse[hcount] = (struct horse*) malloc(sizeof(struct horse));

     printf("\nEnter the name of the horse: " );
     scanf("%s", phorse[hcount]->name );  /* Read the horse's name */

     printf("\nHow old is %s? ", phorse[hcount]->name );
     scanf("%d", &phorse[hcount]->age );  /* Read the horse's age  */
```

```
      printf("\nHow high is %s ( in hands )? ", phorse[hcount]->name );

      /* Read the horse's height    */
      scanf("%d", &phorse[hcount]->height );

      printf("\nWho is %s's father? ", phorse[hcount]->name );
      /* Get the father's name      */
      scanf("%s", phorse[hcount]->father );

      printf("\nWho is %s's mother? ", phorse[hcount]->name );
      scanf("%s", phorse[hcount]->mother ); /* Get the mother's name   */
    }

    /* Now tell them what we know. */
    for (i = 0 ; i < hcount ; i++ )
    {
      printf("\n\n%s is %d years old, %d hands high,",
                  phorse[i]->name, phorse[i]->age, phorse[i]->height);
      printf(" and has %s and %s as parents.",
                               phorse[i]->father, phorse[i]->mother);
    }
  }
```

The output should be exactly the same as that from Example 11.2, given the same input.

How It Works

This looks very similar to the previous version, but it operates rather differently. Initially, we don't have any memory allocated to any structures. The declaration:

```
    struct horse *phorse[50]; /* pointer to structure array declaration */
```

only defines 50 pointers to structures of type **horse**. We still have to find somewhere to put the structures to which we are going to point:

```
    phorse[hcount] = (struct horse*) malloc(sizeof(struct horse));
```

In this statement, we allocate the space for each structure as it is required. Let's have a quick review of how the **malloc()** function works. The **malloc()** function allocates the number of bytes specified by its argument, and returns the address of the block of memory allocated as a pointer to type **void**. In our case, we use the **sizeof** operator to provide the value required.

It's very important to use **sizeof** when we need the number of bytes occupied by a structure. It doesn't necessarily correspond to the sum of the bytes occupied by each of its individual members, so you're likely to get it wrong if you try to work it out yourself.

Variables other than type **char** are often stored beginning at an address which is a multiple of 2 for two byte variables, a multiple of 4 for four-byte variables, and so on. This can result in unused bytes occurring between member variables of different types, depending on their sequence. These have to be accounted for in the number of bytes allocated for a structure. An illustration of how this can occur is in the following figure.

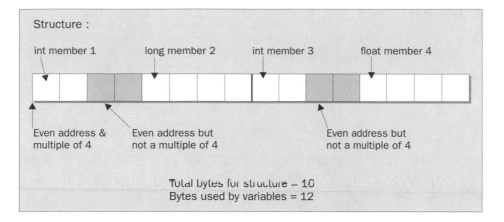

As the value returned by **malloc()** is a pointer to **void**, we then cast this to the type we require with the expression **(struct horse*)**. This enables the pointer to be incremented or decremented correctly, if required.

```
scanf("%s", phorse[hcount]->name );   /* Read the horse's name    */
```

In this statement, we use the new notation for selecting members of a structure through a pointer. It's much clearer than **(*phorse[hcount]).name.** All subsequent references to members of a specific **horse** structure use this new notation.

Lastly, in this program, we display a summary of all the data entered for each horse.

More on Structure Members

So far, we've seen that any of the basic data types, including arrays, can be members of a structure. But there's more. You can also make a structure a member of a structure. Furthermore, not only can pointers be members of a structure, but a pointer to a structure can also be a member.

This opens up a whole new range of possibilities in programming with structures and, at the same time, increases the potential for confusion. Let's look at each of these possibilities in sequence, and see what they have to offer. Maybe it won't be a can of worms after all.

Structures as Members of a Structure

When we started this chapter, we discussed the needs of horse breeders and, in particular, the necessity to manage a variety of details about each horse - including name, height, date of birth, and so on. We then went on to look at Example 11.1, which carefully avoided date of birth and substituted age instead. This was partly because dates are messy things to deal with, since they're represented by three numbers and hold all the complications of leap years. However, we're now ready to tackle dates, using a structure that's a member of another structure.

We can define a structure type designed to hold dates. We can specify a suitable structure with the tag name **Date** with this statement:

```
struct Date
{
   int day;
   int month;
   int year;
};
```

Now we can define our structure, **horse**, including a date of birth variable, like this:

```
struct horse
{
   struct Date dob;
   int height;
   char name[20];
   char father[20];
   char mother[20];
};
```

Now we have a single variable member within the structure that represents the date of birth of a horse, and this member is itself a structure. Now we can define an instance of the structure **horse** with the usual statement:

```
struct horse Dobbin;
```

We can define the value of the member **height** with the same sort of statement that we've already seen:

```
Dobbin.height = 14;
```

If we want to set the date of birth in a series of assignment statements then we can use the logical extension of this notation:

```
Dobbin.dob.day = 5;
Dobbin.dob.month = 12;
Dobbin.dob.year = 1962;
```

We have a very old horse. The expression **Dobbin.dob.day** is referencing an **int** variable, so we can happily use it in arithmetic or comparative expressions. But if we're going to use the expression **Dobbin.dob** then we'd be referring to a **struct** variable of type **Date**. Since this is clearly not a basic type, but a structure, we can only use it in an assignment such as:

```
Trigger.dob = Dobbin.dob;
```

This *could* mean they're twins, but it doesn't guarantee it!

If you can find a good reason to do it, you can extend the notion of structures that are members of a structure, to a structure that is a member of a structure that is a member of a structure. In fact, if you can make sense of it, you can continue with further levels of structure.

Your C system is likely to provide for at least 15 levels of such convolution. But beware: if you reach this depth of structure nesting, you're likely to be in for a bout of repetitive strain injury just typing the references to members.

Declaring a Structure within a Structure

We could have declared the **Date** structure within the horse structure definition, as in the following code:

```
struct horse
{
   struct Date
   {
     int day;
     int month;
     int year;
   } dob;

   int height;
   char name[20];
   char father[20];
   char mother[20];
};
```

This has an interesting effect. Because the declaration is enclosed within the scope of the **horse** structure definition, it doesn't exist outside it, and so it becomes impossible to declare a **Date** variable external to the **horse** structure. Of course, each instance of a **horse** type variable would contain the **Date** type member, **dob**. But a statement such as this:

```
struct Date my_date;
```

would cause a compiler error. The message generated will say that the structure type **Date** is undefined. If you need to use **Date** outside the structure **horse** then its definition must be placed outside of the **horse** structure.

Pointers to Structures as Structure Members

Any pointer can be a member of a structure. This includes pointers that point to structures. A pointer structure member that points to the same type of structure is also permitted. For example, our **horse** type structure could contain a pointer to a **horse** type structure. Interesting, but is it of any use? Well, as it happens: yes.

Try It Out - Pointers to Structures as Structure Members

We can demonstrate this with a modification of the last example:

```
/* Example 11.4   Daisy chaining the horses */
#include <stdio.h>
#include <stdlib.h>
```

```c
void main()
{
  struct horse                /* Structure declaration      */
  {
    int age;
    int height;
    char name[20];
    char father[20];
    char mother[20];
    struct horse *next;  /* Pointer to next structure    */
  };

  struct horse *first = NULL;    /* Pointer to first horse      */
  struct horse *current = NULL;  /* Pointer to current horse    */
  struct horse *previous = NULL; /* Pointer to previous horse   */

  char test = '\0';                     /* Test value for ending input */

  for( ; ; )
  {
    printf("\nDo you want to enter details of a%s horse (Y or N)? ",
                                     first != NULL?"nother " : "" );
    scanf(" %c", &test );
    if(test == 'N' || test == 'n')
      break;

    /* Allocate memory for a structure */
    current = (struct horse*) malloc(sizeof(struct horse));

    if(first == NULL)
      first = current;              /* Set pointer to first horse  */

    if(previous != NULL)
      /* Set next pointer for previous horse */
      previous -> next = current;

    printf("\nEnter the name of the horse: ");
    scanf("%s", current -> name); /* Read the horse's name       */

    printf("\nHow old is %s? ", current -> name);
    scanf("%d", &current -> age); /* Read the horse's age        */

    printf("\nHow high is %s ( in hands )? ", current -> name );
    scanf("%d", &current -> height);  /* Read the horse's height */

    printf("\nWho is %s's father? ", current -> name);
    scanf("%s", current -> father);   /* Get the father's name   */

    printf("\nWho is %s's mother? ", current -> name);
    scanf("%s", current -> mother);   /* Get the mother's name   */
```

```
        current->next = NULL;              /* In case its the last...   */
        previous = current;               /* Save address of last horse */
    }


    /* Now tell them what we know. */
    current = first;                      /* Start at the beginning      */

    while (current != NULL)       /* As long as we have a valid pointer */
    { /* Output the data*/
      printf("\n\n%s is %d years old, %d hands high,",
                        current->name, current->age, current->height);
      printf(" and has %s and %s as parents.", current->father,
                                               current->mother);
        previous = current;     /* Save the pointer so we can free memory */
        current = current->next;          /* Get the pointer to the next */
        free(previous);                   /* Free memory for the old one */
    }
  }
```

This example should produce the same output as Example 11.3 (given the same input) but here we have yet another mode of operation.

How It Works

This time, not only do we have no space for structures allocated, but we have only three pointers defined initially. These are declared and defined in the statements:

```
    struct horse *first = NULL;    /* Pointer to first horse      */
    struct horse *current = NULL;  /* Pointer to current horse    */
    struct horse *previous = NULL; /* Pointer to previous horse   */
```

Each of these pointers has been defined as a pointer to a **horse** structure. The pointer **first** is used solely to store the address of the first structure. The second and third pointers are working storage; **current** holds the address of the current **horse** structure we're dealing with, and **previous** keep track of the address of the previous structure that was processed.

We've added a member to our structure **horse**, with the name **next**, which is a pointer to a **horse** type structure. This will be used to link all the horses we have together, where each **horse** structure will have a pointer containing the address of the next. The last structure will be an exception of, course: its **next** pointer will be **NULL**. The structure is otherwise exactly as we had previously. It's shown in the following figure:

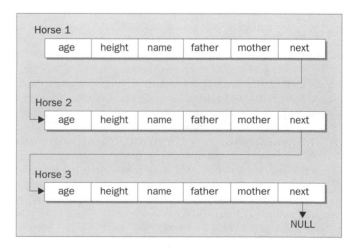

Our input loop is controlled by:

```
for( ; ; )
```

Our input loop is now an indefinite loop, since we don't have an array to worry about. We don't need to mess about with indexes. It's also unnecessary to keep count of how many sets of data are read in, so we don't need the variable **hcount** or the loop variable **i**. Since we allocate memory for each horse, we can just take them as they come.

The initial statements in the loop are:

```
printf("\nDo you want to enter details of a%s horse (Y or N)? ",
                              first != NULL?"nother " : "" );
scanf(" %c", &test );
if(test == 'N' || test == 'n')
  break;
```

After the prompt, we exit from the loop if the response **'N'** or **'n'** is detected. Otherwise, we expect another set of structure members to be entered. We use the pointer **first** to get a slightly different prompt on the second and subsequent iterations, since the only time it will be **NULL** is on the first loop iteration.

Assuming we get past the initial question in the loop, we execute these statements:

```
current = (struct horse*) malloc(sizeof(struct horse));

if(first == NULL)
  first = current;               /* Set pointer to first horse  */

if(previous != NULL)
  /* Set next pointer for previous horse */
  previous -> next = current;
```

On each iteration, we allocate the memory necessary for the current structure. To keep things short, we don't check for a **NULL** return from **malloc()**, although really we ought to do this in practice.

If the pointer **first** is **NULL**, we must be on the first loop iteration, and this must be the first structure about to be entered. Consequently, we set the pointer **first** to the pointer value that we've just obtained from **malloc()**, which was stored in the variable **current**. The address in **first** is our key to accessing the first horse in the chain. We can get to any of the others by starting with the address in **first** and then looking in the member pointer **next** to obtain the address of the next structure, and so on.

The **next** pointer needs to point to the next structure, but the address of the next structure can only be determined once we actually have the next structure. Therefore, on the second and subsequent iterations, we store the address of the current structure in the member **next** of the previous structure, whose address we will have saved in **previous**. On the first iteration, the pointer **previous** will be **NULL** at this point, so of course we do nothing.

At the end of the loop, following all the input statements, we have these statements:

```
        current->next = NULL;            /* In case its the last...    */
        previous = current;             /* Save address of last horse */
```

The pointer **next** in the structure pointed to by **current**, that we are presently working with, is set to **NULL** - in case this is the last structure and there's no next structure. If there is a next structure, this pointer **next** will be filled in on the next iteration. The pointer **previous** is set to **current**, ready for the next iteration, when the **current** structure will indeed be the **previous** structure.

The strategy of the program is to generate a daisy chain of **horse** structures, where the **next** member of each structure points to the next structure in the chain. The last is an exception since there is no next **horse**, so the **next** pointer contains **NULL**. The jargon name for this arrangement is a **linked list**.

Once we have our **horse** data in a linked list, we process it by starting with the first structure, then getting the next structure through the pointer member **next**. When the pointer **next** is **NULL**, we know that we've reached the end of the list. This is how we generate the output list of all the input.

Linked lists are invaluable in applications where we need to process an unknown number of structures, such as we have here. The main advantages of a linked list are with memory usage and ease of handling. We only occupy the minimum memory necessary to store and process the list. Even though the memory used may be fragmented, we have no problem progressing from one structure to the next. As a consequence, in a practical situation where you may need to deal with several different types of objects simultaneously, each can be handled using its own linked list, with the result that memory use is optimized. There is one small cloud associated with this - as there is with any silver lining - and it's that you pay a penalty in slower access to the data.

The output process shows how a linked list is accessed, as it steps through the linked list we have created, with these statements:

```
    current = first;                        /* Start at the beginning      */

    while (current != NULL)       /* As long as we have a valid pointer */
    { /* Output the data*/
      printf("\n\n%s is %d years old, %d hands high,",
                       current->name, current->age, current->height);
      printf(" and has %s and %s as parents.", current->father,
                                                current->mother);
      previous = current;     /* Save the pointer so we can free memory */
      current = current->next;           /* Get the pointer to the next */
      free(previous);                    /* Free memory for the old one */
    }
```

The pointer **current** controls the output loop, and it is set to **first** at the outset. Remember that the pointer **first** contains the first structure in the list. The loop steps through the list, and as the members of each structure are displayed, the address stored in the member **next**, which points to the next structure, is assigned to **current**.

The memory for the structure just displayed is then freed. It's obviously fairly essential that we only free the memory for a structure once we have no further need to reference it. It's easy to fall into the trap of putting the call of the function **free()** straight after we've output all of the member values for the current structure; this would create some problems, since then we couldn't legally reference the current structure's **next** member to get the pointer to the next horse structure.

For the last structure in the linked list, the pointer **next** will contain **NULL** and the loop will terminate.

Doubly Linked Lists

A disadvantage of the linked list is that you can only go forwards. However, a small modification of the idea gives us the **doubly linked list**, which will allow us to go through a list in either direction. The trick is to include an extra pointer in each structure to store the address of the previous structure.

Try It Out - Doubly Linked Lists

You can see a double linked list in action in a modified version of Example 11.4:

```
/*   Example 11.5 Daisy chaining the horses both ways */
#include <stdio.h>
#include <stdlib.h>

void main()
{
   struct horse  /* Structure declaration */
   {
     int age;
     int height;
     char name[20];
     char father[20];
     char mother[20];
     struct horse *next;     /* Pointer to next structure      */
     struct horse *previous; /* Pointer to previous structure  */
   };

   struct horse *first = NULL;     /* Pointer to first horse    */
   struct horse *current = NULL;   /* Pointer to current horse  */
   struct horse *last = NULL;      /* Pointer to previous horse */

   char test = '\0';               /* Test value for ending input */

   for( ; ; )
   {
     printf("\nDo you want to enter details of a%s horse (Y or N)? ",
                               first == NULL?"nother " : "");
     scanf(" %c", &test );
```

```
    if(test == 'N' || test == 'n')
      break;

    /* Allocate memory for each new horse structure */
    current = (struct horse*)malloc(sizeof(struct horse));

    if( first == NULL )
    {
      first = current;              /* Set pointer to first horse   */
      current->previous = NULL;
    }
    else
    {
      /* Set next address for previous horse */
      last->next = current;                 .

      /* Previous address for current horse  */
      current->previous = last;
    }

    printf("\nEnter the name of the horse: ");
    scanf("%s", current -> name );        /* Read the horse's name    */

    printf("\nHow old is %s? ", current -> name);
    scanf("%d", &current -> age);         /* Read the horse's age     */

    printf("\nHow high is %s ( in hands )? ", current -> name);
    scanf("%d", &current -> height);     /* Read the horse's height */

    printf("\nWho is %s's father? ", current -> name);
    scanf("%s", current -> father);       /* Get the father's name    */

    printf("\nWho is %s's mother? ", current -> name);
    scanf("%s", current -> mother);        /* Get the mother's name    */

    current -> next = NULL;   /* In case its the last horse...*/
    last = current;           /* Save address of last horse   */
  }

  /* Now tell them what we know. */
  while(current != NULL)      /* Output horse data in reverse order */
  {
    printf("\n\n%s is %d years old, %d hands high,",
             current->name, current->age, current->height);
    printf(" and has %s and %s as parents.", current->father,
                                        current->mother);

    /* Save pointer to enable memory to be freed */
    last = current;

    /* current points to previous in list        */
    current = current->previous;
```

```
            /* Free memory for the horse we output       */
      free(last);
    }
  }
```

For the same input, this program should produce the same output as before, except that the data on horses entered is displayed in reverse order to that of entry - just to show that we can do it.

How It Works

Our initial pointer declarations are now:

```
    struct horse *first = NULL;     /* Pointer to first horse     */
    struct horse *current = NULL;   /* Pointer to current horse   */
    struct horse *last = NULL;      /* Pointer to previous horse  */
```

We've changed the name of the pointer recording the **horse** structure entered on the previous iteration of the loop to **last**. This name change is not strictly necessary, but it does help to avoid confusion with the structure member **previous**.

The structure **horse** is declared as:

```
    struct horse  /* Structure declaration */
    {
      int age;
      int height;
      char name[20];
      char father[20];
      char mother[20];
      struct horse *next;     /* Pointer to next structure       */
      struct horse *previous; /* Pointer to previous structure   */
    };
```

The structure **horse** now contains two pointers: one to point forwards in the list, called **next**, the other to point backwards to the preceding structure, called **previous**. This allows the list to be traversed in either direction, as we demonstrate by the fact that we output the data at the end of the program in reverse order.

Aside from the output, the only changes to the program are to add the statements that take care of the entries for the pointer structure member **previous**. At the beginning of the input loop we have:

```
    if( first == NULL )
    {
      first = current;                /* Set pointer to first horse   */
      current->previous = NULL;
    }
    else
    {
      /* Set next address for previous horse */
      last->next = current;
```

```
            /* Previous address for current horse   */
        current->previous = last;
    }
```

Here, we've taken the option of writing an **if** with an **else**, rather than the two **if**s we had in the previous version. The only material difference is setting the value of the structure member **previous**. For the first structure, **previous** is set to **NULL**, and for all subsequent structures it is set to the pointer **last**, whose value was saved on the preceding iteration.

The other change is at the end of the input loop:

```
    last = current;                 /* Save address of last horse   */
```

This statement is added to allow the pointer **previous** in the next structure to be set to the appropriate value, which is the **current** structure that we're recording in the variable **last**.

The output process is virtually the same as in the previous example, except that we start from the last structure in the list, and work back to the first.

Bit-Fields in a Structure

Bit-fields provide a mechanism that allows us to define variables that are each one or more binary bits within a single integer word, which you can nevertheless refer to explicitly with an individual member name for each one.

> *Bit-fields are used when memory is at a premium and you're in a situation where you must use it as sparingly as possible.*
>
> *Bit-fields will slow your program down appreciably compared to using standard variable types. You must therefore assess each situation upon its merits to decide whether the saving in memory offered by bit-fields is worth this price in execution speed for your programs.*

An example of declaring a bit-field is shown here:

```
    struct
    {
        unsigned int flag1 : 1;
        unsigned int flag2 : 1;
        unsigned int flag3 : 2;
        unsigned int flag4 : 3;
    } indicators;
```

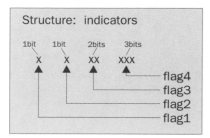

This defines an instance of a structure with the name **indicators** which contains four bit-fields with the names **flag1** through **flag4**. These will all be stored in a single word, as illustrated in the following figure.

The first two bit-fields, being a single bit specified by the 1 in their definition, can only assume the values 0 or 1. The third bit-field, **flag3**, has 2 bits and so it can have a value from 0 to 3. The last bit-field, **flag4**, can have values from 0 to 7, since it has 3 bits. These bit-fields are referenced in the same manner as other structure members. For example:

```
indicators.flag4 = 5;
indicators.flag3 = indicators.flag1 = 1;
```

You'll rarely, if ever, have any need for this facility. I've have included bit-fields here for the sake of completeness and for that strange off-chance that, one day, bit-fields will be just what you need in a particularly tight memory situation.

Structures and Functions

Since structures represent such a powerful feature of the C language, their use with functions is very important. We'll now look at how we can pass structures as arguments to a function, and how we can return a structure from a function.

Structures as Arguments to Functions

There's nothing unusual in the method for passing a structure as an argument to a function. It's exactly the same as passing any other variable. Analogous to our **horse** structure, we could create this structure:

```
struct family
{
   char name[20];
   int age;
   char father[20];
   char mother[20];
};
```

We could then construct a function to test whether two members of the type **family** were siblings:

```
int siblings(struct family member1, struct family member2)
{
   if(strcmp(member1.mother, member2.mother) == 0)
     return 1;
   else
     return 0;
}
```

This function has two arguments, each of which is a structure. It simply compares the strings corresponding to the member **mother** for each structure. If they are the same, they are siblings and 1 is returned. Otherwise, they can't be siblings so 0 is returned. We're ignoring the effects of divorce, in vitro fertilization, cloning, and any other possibilities that may make this test inadequate.

Pointers to Structures as Function Arguments

Remember that a copy of the value of an argument is transferred to a function when it's called. If the argument is a large structure, this can take quite a time, as well as occupying whatever memory that a copy of the structure takes. Under these circumstances, you should use a pointer to a structure as an argument. This avoids the memory consumption and the copying time, since now only a copy of the pointer is made. The function will access the original structure directly through the pointer. More often than not, structures are passed to a function using a pointer, just for these reasons of efficiency. We could rewrite the **siblings()** function like this:

```
int siblings(struct family *member1, struct family *member2)
{
   if(strcmp(member1->mother, member2->mother) == 0)
     return 1;
   else
     return 0;
}
```

Now there is a downside to this. The pass-by-value mechanism provides good protection against accidental modification of values from within a called function. You lose this if you pass a pointer to a function. On the upside, if you don't need to modify the values pointed to by a pointer argument (you just want to access and use them, for instance) then there is a technique for getting a degree of protection, even though you're passing pointers to a function.

Have another look at the last function **siblings()**. It doesn't need to modify the structures passed to it; in fact, it only needs to compare members. We could therefore rewrite it as this:

```
int siblings(struct family const *pmember1, struct family const
                                                        *pmember2)
{
   if(strcmp(pmember1->mother, pmember2->mother) == 0)
     return 1;
   else
     return 0;
}
```

You'll recall the **const** modifier from earlier in the book, where we used it to make a variable effectively a constant. This function declaration specifies the parameters as type 'pointers to constant **family** structures'. This implies that the structures pointed to by the pointers transferred to the function will be treated as constants within the function. Any attempt to change those structures will cause an error message during compilation. Of course, this doesn't affect their status as variables in the calling program, since the **const** keyword only applies to the values while the function is executing.

Note the difference between the previous definition of the function and this one:

```
int siblings(struct family *const pmember1, struct family *const
                                                        pmember2)
{
   if(strcmp(pmember1->mother, pmember2->mother) == 0)
     return 1;
```

```
      else
        return 0;
  }
```

The indirection operator in each parameter definition is now in front of the keyword **const**, rather than in front of the pointer name as it was before. Does this make a difference? You bet it does. The parameters here are 'constant pointers to structures of type **family**', not 'pointers to constant structures'. Now we are free to alter the structures themselves in the function, but we must not modify the addresses stored in the pointers. It is the pointers that are protected here, not the structures to which they point.

A Structure as a Function Return Value

There's nothing unusual about returning a structure from a function, either; the function prototype merely has to indicate this return value in the normal way. For example:

```
struct horse my_fun(void);
```

This is a prototype for a function taking no arguments that returns a structure of type **horse**. While we can return a structure from a function, like this, it's often more convenient to return a pointer to a structure.

Try It Out - Returning a Pointer to a Structure

To demonstrate how this works, let's rewrite our previous **horse** example in terms of humans, and perform the input in a separate function:

```
/* Example 11.6 Basics of a family tree */
#include <stdio.h>
#include <stdlib.h>

struct Family *get_person(void);  /* Prototype for input function    */

struct Date
{
   int day;
   int month;
   int year;
};

struct Family                           /* Family structure declaration   */
{
   struct Date dob;
   char name[20];
   char father[20];
   char mother[20];
   struct Family *next;                 /* Pointer to next structure      */
   struct Family *previous;             /* Pointer to previous structure  */
};
```

```
void main()
{
   struct Family *first = NULL;     /* Pointer to first person        */
   struct Family *current = NULL;   /* Pointer to current person      */
   struct Family *last = NULL;      /* Pointer to previous person     */

   char more = '\0';                /* Test value for ending input    */

   for( ; ; )
   {
     printf("\nDo you want to enter details of a%s person (Y or N)? ",
                                     first != NULL?"nother " : "" );
     scanf(" %c", &more);
     if(more == 'N' || more == 'n')
       break;

     current = get_person();

     if(first == NULL)
     {
       first = current;              /* Set pointer to first Family    */
       last = current;               /* Remember for next iteration     */
     }
     else
     {
       /* Set next address for previous Family */
       last->next = current;
       /* Set previous address for current      */
       current->previous = last;
       /* Remember for next iteration           */
       last = current;
     }
   }

   /* Now tell them what we know */

   /* Output Family data in reverse order */
   while (current  != NULL)
   {
     printf("\n%s was born %d/%d/%d, and has %s and %s as parents.",
             current->name, current->dob.day, current->dob.month,
             current->dob. year, current->father,  current->mother );

     last = current;      /* Save pointer to enable memory to be freed */
     current = current->previous;  /* current points to previous list */
     free(last);          /* Free memory for the Family we output      */
   }
}

/*   Function to input data on Family members    */
struct Family *get_person(void)
```

```
{
    struct Family *temp;            /* Define temporary structure pointer */

    /* Allocate memory for a structure */
    temp = (struct Family*) malloc(sizeof(struct Family));

    printf("\nEnter the name of the person: ");
    scanf("%s", temp -> name );   /* Read the Family's name          */

    printf("\nEnter %s's date of birth (day month year); ", temp->name);
    scanf("%d %d %d", &temp->dob.day, &temp->dob.month, &temp->dob.year);

    printf("\nWho is %s's father? ", temp->name );
    scanf("%s", temp->father );       /* Get the father's name       */

    printf("\nWho is %s's mother? ", temp -> name );
    scanf("%s", temp -> mother );   /* Get the mother's name         */

    temp->next = temp->previous = NULL;   /* Set pointers to NULL     */

    return temp;                    /* Return address of Family structure */
}
```

How It Works

Although this looks like a lot of code, you should find this example quite straightforward. It operates very similarly to the previous example, but is organized as two functions instead of one.

The structure declaration:

```
struct Date
{
    int day;
    int month;
    int year;
};
```

defines a structure type **Date** with three members: **day**, **month**, and **year**, which are all declared as integers. No instances of the structure are declared at this point.

The next structure declaration:

```
struct Family                       /* Family structure declaration  */
{
    struct Date dob;
    char name[20];
    char father[20];
    char mother[20];
    struct Family *next;            /* Pointer to next structure      */
    struct Family *previous;        /* Pointer to previous structure  */
};
```

404

defines a structure type **Family**, which has a **Date** type structure as its first member. It then has three conventional **char** arrays as members. The last two members are pointers to structures. They are intended to allow a doubly linked list to be constructed, being pointers to the next and previous structures in the list, respectively.

An important difference between this and the previous examples is that both structure declarations are external to all the functions, and are therefore available globally. This is necessary because we want to define **Family** structure variables in both the functions **main()** and **get_person()**.

> *Only the specification of the structure type is accessible globally. All the variables of type **Family** declared within each function are local in scope to the function in which they are declared.*

The function **get_person()** has this prototype:

```
struct Family *get_person(void);  /* Prototype for input function  */
```

which indicates that it accepts no arguments, but returns a pointer to a **Family** structure.

The process parallels the operation of Example 11.5, with the difference that we have global structure type declarations, and we input a structure within a separate function.

After verifying that the user wants to enter data, by checking their response in **more**, our function **main()** calls the function **get_person()**. Within the function **get_person()**, we declare this pointer:

```
struct Family *temp;          /* Define temporary structure pointer */
```

This is a 'pointer to a **Family** type structure', and has local scope. The fact that the declaration of the structure type is global has no bearing on the scope of actual instances of the structure. The scope of each instance that we declare will depend on where the declaration is placed in the program.

The first action within the function **get_person()** is:

```
temp = (struct Family*) malloc(sizeof(struct Family));
```

This obtains sufficient memory, through **malloc()**, to store a **Family** type structure, and stores the address returned in the pointer variable, **temp**. Although **temp** is local, and will go out of scope at the end of the function **get_person()**, the memory allocated by **malloc()** is more permanent. It remains until you free it yourself within the program somewhere, or until you exit from the program completely.

The function **get_person()** reads in all the basic data for a person, and stores that data in the structure pointed to by **temp**.

The last statement in the function **get_person()** is:

```
return temp;                    /* Return address of Family structure */
```

405

This returns a copy of the pointer to the structure that it has created. Even though **temp** will no longer exist after the return, the address that it contained, pointing to the memory block obtained from **malloc()**, is still valid.

Back in **main()**, this returned pointer is stored in the variable **current**, and is also saved in the variable **first** if this is the first iteration. We do this because we don't want to lose track of the first structure in the list. We also save the pointer **current** in the variable **last**, so that on the next iteration we can fill in the backward pointer member, **previous**, for the current person whose data we've just obtained.

After all the input data has been read, the program outputs a summary to the screen in reverse order, in a similar fashion to the previous examples.

An Exercise in Program Modification

Perhaps we ought to produce an example combining both the use of pointers to structures as arguments, and the use of pointers to structures as return values. We can declare some additional pointers, **p_to_pa** and **p_to_ma** in the structure type **Family** in the previous example, by changing that structure declaration to:

```
struct Family                        /* Family structure declaration  */
{
   struct Date dob;
   char name[20];
   char father[20];
   char mother[20];
   struct Family *next;              /* Pointer to next structure     */
   struct Family *previous;          /* Pointer to previous structure */
   struct Family *p_to_pa;           /* Pointer to father structure    */
   struct Family *p_to_ma;           /* Pointer to mother structure    */
};
```

This allows us to note the addresses of related structures in the pointer members **p_to_pa** and **p_to_ma**. We'll need to set them to **NULL** in the **get_person()** function by adding the statement:

```
        temp->p_to_pa = temp->p_to_ma = NULL;    /* Set pointers to NULL  */
```

just before the **return** statement.

We can now augment our program with some additional functions that will fill in our new pointers **p_to_pa** and and **p_to_ma**, once data for everybody has been entered. We could code this by adding the following two functions:

```
char set_ancestry(struct Family *pmember1, struct Family *pmember2)
{
   if(strcmp(pmember1->father, pmember2->name) == 0)
   {
     pmember1->p_to_pa = pmember2;
     return 1;
   }
```

```
      if( strcmp(pmember1->mother, pmember2->name) == 0)
      {
        pmember1->p_to_ma = pmember2;
        return 1;
      }
      else
        return 0;
  }
```

```
  /* Fill in pointers for mother or father relationships */
  char related (struct Family *pmember1, struct Family *pmember2)
  {
      return set_ancestry(pmember1, pmember2) ||
                          set_ancestry(pmember2, pmember1);
  }
```

The first of these functions, **set_ancestry()**, accepts pointers to **Family** structures as arguments, and checks whether the structure pointed to by **pmember2** is the father or mother of the structure pointed to by **pmember1**. If it is, the appropriate pointer is updated to reflect this, and 1 is returned; otherwise, 0 is returned.

Since we use the **strcmp()** function, we need to add a **#include** statement at the beginning of our program for **string.h**:

```
  #include <string.h>
```

The second function, **related()**, calls **set_ancestry()** twice in the **return** statement - to test all possibilities of relationship. The return value will be 1 if either of the calls to **set_ancestry()** return the value 1. The calling program can use the return value from **related()** to determine whether a pointer has been filled in or not.

We now need to add some code to the **main()** we created in Example 11.6 to use the function **related()** to fill in all the pointers in all the structures where valid addresses can be found. The following code should be inserted into **main()** directly after the loop that inputs all the initial data:

```
  current = first;

  while(current->next != NULL)  /* Check for relation for each person */
  {                            /* in the list up to second to last       */
    int parents = 0;           /* Declare parent count local to this block */
    last = current;            /* Get the pointer to the current          */

    while(last->next != NULL)   /* This loop tests current person         */
    {                          /* against all the remainder in the list  */
      if(related(current, last->next))   /* Found a parent ?              */
        if(++parents == 2)     /* Yes, update count and check it          */
          break;               /* Exit inner loop if both parents found  */
```

```
        last = last->next;      /* Get the address of the next      */
    }
    current = current->next;  /* Next in the list to check         */
}
```

```
/* Now tell them what we know etc. */
/* rest of output code etc.  ...   */
```

This is a relatively self-contained block of code to fill in the parent pointers where possible. Starting with the first structure, a check is made with each of the succeeding structures to see if a parent relationship exists. The checking stops for a given structure if two parents have been found (which would have filled in both pointers) or the end of the list is reached.

Of necessity, some structures will have pointers where the values can't be updated. Since we don't have an infinite list, and barring some very strange family history, there will always be someone whose parent records are not included. The process will take each of the structures in the list and check it against all the following structures to see if they are related - at least, up to the point where the two parents have been discovered.

Of course, we also need to insert prototypes for our functions **related()** and **test()** at the beginning of the program, immediately after the prototype for the function **get_person()**. These would look like this:

```
char related(struct Family *pmember1, struct Family *pmember2);
char set_ancestry(struct Family *pmember1, struct Family *pmember2);
```

To show that the pointers have been successfully inserted, we can extend the final output to display information about the parents of each person by adding some additional statements immediately after the last **printf()**. We can also amend the output loop to start from **first** in a similar manner to that employed in Example 11.4; the output loop will thus be:

```
/* Output Family data in correct order */

current = first;

while (current != NULL)  /* Output Family data in correct order  */
{
  printf("\n%s was born %d/%d/%d, and has %s and %s as parents.",
            current->name, current->dob.day, current->dob.month,
          current->dob. year, current->father,  current->mother);
  if(current->p_to_pa != NULL )
    printf("\n\t%s's birth date is %d/%d/%d  ",
            current->father, current->p_to_pa->dob.day,
                             current->p_to_pa->dob.month,
                             current->p_to_pa->dob.year);
  if(current->p_to_ma != NULL)
    printf("and %s's birth date is %d/%d/%d.\n  ",
            current->mother, current->p_to_ma->dob.day,
                             current->p_to_ma->dob.month,
                             current->p_to_ma->dob.year);

  current = current->next;  /* current points to next in list      */
}
```

This should then produce the dates of birth of both parents for each person using the pointers to the parents' structures - but only if the pointers have been set to valid addresses. Note that we don't free the memory in the loop. If we did this, the additional statements to output the parents' dates of birth would produce junk output when the parent structure appeared earlier in the list. So finally, we must add a separate loop at the end of **main()** to delete the memory when the output is complete:

```
/* Now free the memory */
current = first;
while(current != NULL)
{
  last = current;      /* Save pointer to enable memory to be freed */
  current = current->next; /* current points to next in list        */
  free(last);          /* Free memory for last                      */
}
```

If you've assembled all the pieces into a new example, you should have a sizeable new program to play with. The sort of output that you should get is as follows:

```
Do you want to enter details of an  person (Y or N)? y

Enter the name of the person: Jack

Enter Jack's date of birth (day month year); 1 1 65

Who is Jack's father? Bill

Who is Jack's mother? Nell

Do you want to enter details of another  person (Y or N)? y

Enter the name of the person: Mary

Enter Mary's date of birth (day month year); 3 3 67

Who is Mary's father? Bert

Who is Mary's mother? Moll

Do you want to enter details of another  person (Y or N)? y

Enter the name of the person: Ben

Enter Ben's date of birth (day month year); 2 2 89

Who is Ben's father? Jack

Who is Ben's mother? Mary

Do you want to enter details of another  person (Y or N)? n
```

```
Jack was born 1/1/65, and has Bill and Nell as parents.
Mary was born 3/3/67, and has Bert and Moll as parents.
Ben was born 2/2/89, and has Jack and Mary as parents.
        Jack's birth date is 1/1/65  and Mary's birth date is 3/3/67.
```

You could try to modify the program to output everybody in chronological order, or possibly work out how many offspring each person has.

Sharing Memory

We've already seen how economies in the use of memory can be made with the use of bit-fields, which are typically applied to logical variables. C has a further capability that allows us to place several variables in the same memory area. This can be applied much more widely than bit-fields when memory is short, since circumstances frequently arise in practice where you're working with several variables, but only one of them holds a valid value at any given moment.

Another instance where you can share memory between a number of variables to some advantage is when your program processes a number of different kinds of data record, but only one kind at a time - and the kind to be processed is determined at execution time. A third possibility is that you want to access the same data at different times, and assume it's of a different type on different occasions. You might have a group of variables of numeric data types, for instance, that you want to treat as simply an array of type **char** so that you can move them about as a single chunk of data.

Unions

The facility in C that allows the same memory area to be shared by a number of different variables is called a **union**. The syntax for declaring a **union** is similar to that used for structures, and a union is usually given a tag name in the same way. For example, the following statement declares a union to be shared by three variables:

```
union u_example
{
   float decval;
   int *pnum;
   double my_value;
} U1;
```

This statement declares a union with the tag name **u_example**, which shares memory between a floating point value **decval**, a pointer to an integer **pnum**, and a double precision floating-point variable **my_value**. The statement also defines one instance of the union with a variable name of **U1**. We can declare further instances of this union with a statement such as this:

```
union u_example U2, U3;
```

Members of a union are accessed in exactly the same way as members of a structure. For example, to assign values to members of **U1** and **U2**, we can write:

```
U1.decval = 2.5;
U2.decval = 3.5 * U1.decval;
```

Try It Out - Using Unions

Look at the following example:

```
/* Example 11.7 The operation of a union */
#include <stdio.h>

void main()
{
   union u_example
   {
     float decval;
     int pnum;
     double my_value;
   } U1;

   U1.my_value = 125.5;
   U1.pnum = 10;
   U1.decval = 1000.5f;
   printf("\ndecval = %f\tpnum = %d\tmy_value = %lf",
                      U1.decval, U1.pnum, U1.my_value);

   printf("\nU1 size = %d\ndecval size = %d\tpnum size = %d\tmy_value"
                    " size = %d",sizeof U1, sizeof U1.decval,
                           sizeof U1.pnum, sizeof U1.my_value);
}
```

How It Works

This example is intended to demonstrate the structure and operation of a union. We declare our union **U1** as:

```
union u_example
{
   float decval;
   int pnum;
   double my_value;
} U1;
```

The three members are each of different types, and they each require a different amount of storage (assuming our compiler assigns two bytes to variables of type **int**).

With the assignment statements we assign a value to each of the members of the union instance **U1** in turn:

```
   U1.my_value = 125.5;
   U1.pnum = 10;
   U1.decval = 1000.5f;
```

Notice that we reference each member of the union in the same way as for members of a structure.

The next two statements output each of the three member values, the size of the union **U1**, and the size of each of its members. We get this output (or something close if your machine assigns four bytes to variables of type **int**):

```
decval = 1000.500000      pnum = 8192        my_value = 125.50016
U1 size = 8
decval size = 4           pnum size = 2      my_value size = 8
```

The first thing to note is that the last variable that was assigned a value is correct, and the other two have been corrupted. This is to be expected, since they all share the same memory space. The second thing to notice is how little the member **my_value** has been corrupted. This is because only the least significant part of **my_value** is being modified. In a practical situation, such a small error could easily be overlooked, but the ultimate consequences could be dire. You need to take great care, when using unions, that you are not using invalid data.

> You can see from the output of the sizes of the union and its members that the size of the union is the same as the size of the largest member.

Pointers to Unions

You can also define a pointer to a union with a statement such as this:

```
union u_example *pU;
```

Once the pointer has been defined, you can modify members of the union, via the pointer, with these statements:

```
pU = &U2;
U1.decval = pU->decval;
```

The expression on the right of the second assignment is equivalent to **U2.decval**.

Initializing Unions

If you wish to initialize an instance of a union when you declare it, you can only initialize it with a constant of the same type as the first variable in the union. The union that we've just declared, **u_example**, can only be initialized with a **float** constant, as in:

```
union u_example U4 = 3.14f;
```

> You can always rearrange the sequence of members in a definition of a union so that the member that you want to initialize occurs first. The sequence of members has no other significance, since all members overlap in the same memory area.

Structures as Union Members

Structures and arrays can be members of a union. It's also possible for a union to be a member of a structure. To illustrate this, we could write:

```
struct my_structure
{
   int num1;
   float num2;
   union
   {
     int *pnum;
     float *pfnum;
   } my_U;
} samples[5];
```

Here, we've declared a structure type, **my_structure**, which contains a union without a tag name - so instances of the union can only exist within instances of the structure. We've also defined an array of 5 instances of the structure, referenced by the variable name **samples**. The union within the structure shares memory between two pointers. To reference members of the union, you use the same notation that we used for nested structures. For example, to access the pointer to **int** in the third element of the structure array, we would use the expression appearing on the left in the following statement:

```
samples[2].my_U.pnum = &my_num;
```

We're assuming, here, that the variable **my_num** has been declared as type **int**.

It's important to realize that when using a value stored in a union, we always retrieve the last value assigned. This may seem obvious, but in practice it's all too easy to use a value as **float** which has most recently been stored as an integer - and sometimes the error can be quite subtle, as shown by the curious output of **my_value** in Example 11.7. Naturally, we'll often end up with garbage if we do this.

Defining Your Own Data Types

With structures we have come pretty close to defining our own data types. However, it doesn't look quite right because we must use the keyword **struct** in our declarations of structure variables. Declaration of a variable for a built-in type is simpler. However, there is a feature of the C language which permits you to get over this and make the declaration of variables of types you have defined follow exactly the same syntax as for the built-in types. We have already seen this in Chapter 4, but here, with structures, it really comes into its own.

Structures and the typedef Facility

Suppose we have a structure for geometric points with three coordinates, x, y, and z, that we declare with the statement:

```
struct pts
{
   int x;
   int y;
   int z;
};
```

We can now define an alternative name for declaring such structures using **typedef**, as in the following statement:

```
typedef struct pts Point;
```

When we want to declare some instances of the structure **pts**, we can now use a statement such as this:

```
Point start_pt;
Point end_pt;
```

Here, we declare the two structure variables **start_pt** and **end_pt**. The **struct** keyword isn't necessary, and we have a very natural way of declaring structure variables. The appearance of the statement is exactly the same form as a declaration for a **float** or an **int**.

We could actually have combined the **typedef** and the structure declaration as:

```
typedef struct pts
{
   int x;
   int y;
   int z;
} Point;
```

Don't confuse this with a basic **struct** declaration. Here, **Point** is not a structure variable name: this is a type name we're defining. When we need to declare structure variables, as we have just seen, we can use a statement such as this:

```
Point my_pt;
```

There's nothing to prevent us from having several types defined that pertain to a single structure type, although this is likely to be confusing in most situations.

There are other useful applications of **typedef** relating to a given structure type. Suppose we had occasion to frequently define pointers to the structure **pts**. We could define a type to do this for us with this statement:

```
typedef struct pts *pPoint;
```

Now, when we wanted to declare some pointers we would just write:

```
pPoint pfirst;
pPoint plast;
```

The two variables declared are both pointers to structures of type **pts**.

Simplifying Code using typedef

In Chapter 9 we discussed pointers to functions, which are declared with a somewhat complicated notation. In one of our examples we had the pointer declaration:

```
    int(*pfun)(int, int);              /* Function pointer declaration      */
```

If we were expecting to use several pointers to functions of this kind in a program, we could use **typedef** to declare a generic type for such declarations with the statement:

```
    typedef int (*pFN)(int, int);  /* Function pointer type declaration */
```

This doesn't declare a variable of type 'pointer to a function'. This declares **pFN** as a type that you can use to declare a 'pointer to function', so we could replace our original declaration of **pfun** with this statement:

```
    pFN pfun;
```

This is evidently much simpler than what we started with. The benefit in simplicity is even more marked if we have several such pointers to declare, since we can declare three pointers to functions with the statements:

```
    pFN pfun1;
    pFN pfun2;
    pFN pfun3;
```

Of course, we can also initialize them - so if we assume we have the functions **sum()**, **product()**, and **difference()**, we can declare and initialize our pointers with:

```
    pFN pfun1 = sum;
    pFN pfun2 = difference;
    pFN pfun3 = product;
```

The type we have defined naturally only applies to 'pointers to functions' with the arguments and return type that we specified in the **typedef** statement. If we want something different then we can simply define another type.

Designing a Program

We've reached the end of another long chapter and it's time to see how we can put what we've learnt into practice in the context of a more substantial example.

The Problem

The problem we're going tackle is to write a program that produces a vertical bar chart from a set of data values.

The Analysis

We won't be making any assumptions about the size of the 'page' that we're going to output to, or the number of columns, or even the scale of the chart. Instead, we'll just write a function that accepts a dimension for the output page, and then makes the set of bars fit the page if possible. This will make the function useful in virtually any situation. We'll store the values in a sequence of structures in a linked list. In this way, we'll just need to pass the first structure to the function, and the function will be able to get at them all. We'll keep the structure very simple, but you can embellish it later with other information of your own design.

We will assume that the order in which the bars are to appear in the chart is going to be the same as the order in which the data values were entered, so we won't need to sort them. There will be two functions in our program: a function that generates the bar chart, and a function **main()** that will exercise the bar chart generation process.

These are the steps that are required:

1 Write the bar-chart function

2 Write a **main()** function to test the bar-chart function once it's been written

The Solution

1 The first stage is to design the structure that we'll use throughout the program. We'll use a **typedef** so that we don't have to keep re-using **struct**:

```
/* Example 11.8 Generating a bar chart */
#include <stdio.h>

typedef struct barTAG
{
   double value;
   struct barTAG *pnextbar;
}bar;

void main()
{
   /* Code for main */
}

/* Definition of the bar-chart function */
```

Notice how we've defined the pointer in the structure to the next structure. You may have thought that the **typedef** statement would mean that we could use the type name, **bar**, which we're defining here. However, we have to use **struct barTAG** here because, at this point, the compiler hasn't finished processing the **typedef** yet - so **bar** is not defined. In other words, the structure **barTAG** is declared first, and then the **typedef** is performed.

Now we can specify the function prototype for the bar chart function and put the skeleton of the definition for the function. It will need to have parameters for a pointer to the first bar in the linked list, the page height and width, and the title for the chart to be produced:

```
/* Example 11.8 Generating a bar chart */
#include <stdio.h>
```

```
#define PAGE_HEIGHT   20
#define PAGE_WIDTH    40

typedef struct barTAG
{
   double value;
   struct barTAG *pnextbar;
}bar;

typedef unsigned int uint;        /* Type definition */

/* Function prototype */
int bar_chart(bar *pfirstbar, uint page_width, uint page_height,
                                             char *title);

void main()
{
   /* Code for main */
}

int bar_chart(bar *pfirstbar, uint page_width, uint page_height,
                                             char *title)
{
   /* Code for function... */
   return 0;
}
```

We've added a **typedef** to define **uint** as an alternative to **unsigned int**. This will shorten statements that declare **unsigned int** variables.

Next, we can add some declarations and code for the basic data we need for the bar chart. We'll need the maximum and minimum values for the bars, and the vertical height of the chart, which will be determined by the difference between the maximum and minimum values. We also need to calculate the width of a bar, given the page width and the number of bars, and we must adjust the height to accommodate a horizontal axis and the title:

```
/* Example 11.8 Generating a bar chart */
#include <stdio.h>

#define PAGE_HEIGHT   20
#define PAGE_WIDTH    40

typedef struct barTAG
{
   double value;
   struct barTAG *pnextbar;
}bar;

typedef unsigned int uint;        /* Type definition */

/* Function prototype */
int bar_chart(bar *pfirstbar, uint page_width, uint page_height,
                                             char *title);
```

417

```
void main()
{
   /* Code for main */
}

int bar_chart(bar *pfirstbar, uint page_width, uint page_height,
                                                char *title)
{
   bar *plastbar = pfirstbar;    /* Pointer to previous bar         */
   double max = 0.0;             /* Maximum bar value               */
   double min = 0.0;             /* Minimum bar value               */
   double vert_scale = 0.0;      /* Unit step in vertical direction */
   uint bar_count = 1;           /* Number of bars - at least 1     */
   uint barwidth = 0;            /* Width of a bar                  */
   uint space = 2;               /* spaces between bars             */

   /* Find maximum and minimum of all bar values */

   /* Set max and min to first bar value */
   max = min = plastbar->value;

   while((plastbar = plastbar->pnextbar) != NULL)
   {
     bar_count++;                /* Increment bar count */
     max = (max < plastbar->value)? plastbar->value : max;
     min = (min > plastbar->value)? plastbar->value : min;
   }
   vert_scale = (max - min)/page_height; /* Calculate step length */

   /* Check bar width */
   if((barwidth = page_width/bar_count - space) < 1)
   {
     printf("\nPage width too narrow.\n");
     return -1;
   }

   /* Code for rest of the function...  */
   return 0;
}
```

The variable **space** stores the number of spaces separating one bar from the next, and we have arbitrarily assigned the value 2 for this.

We will, of necessity, be outputting the chart a row at a time. Therefore, we'll need a string that corresponds to a section across a bar that we can use to draw that bar row by row - and a string of the same length, containing spaces to use when there is no bar at a particular position across the page. Let's add the code to create these:

```
/* Example 11.8 Generating a bar chart */
#include <stdio.h>
#include <stdlib.h>
```

```
#define PAGE_HEIGHT   20
#define PAGE_WIDTH    40

typedef struct barTAG
{
   double value;
   struct barTAG *pnextbar;
}bar;

typedef unsigned int uint;      /* Type definition */

/* Function prototype */
int bar_chart(bar *pfirstbar, uint page_width, uint page_height,
                                                   char *title);

void main()
{
   /* Code for main */
}

int bar_chart(bar *pfirstbar, uint page_width, uint page_height,
                                                   char *title)
{
   bar *plastbar = pfirstbar;   /* Pointer to previous bar        */
   double max = 0.0;            /* Maximum bar value              */
   double min = 0.0;            /* Minimum bar value              */
   double vert_scale = 0.0;     /* Unit step in vertical direction */
   uint bar_count = 1;          /* Number of bars - at least 1    */
   uint barwidth = 0;           /* Width of a bar                 */
   uint space = 2;              /* spaces between bars            */
   uint i = 0;                  /* Loop counter                   */
   char *column = NULL;         /* Pointer to bar column section  */
   char *blank = NULL;          /* Blank string for bar+space     */

   /* Find maximum and minimum of all bar values */

   /* Set max and min to first bar value */
   max = min = plastbar->value;

   while((plastbar = plastbar->pnextbar) != NULL)
   {
     bar_count++;                    /* Increment bar count */
     max = (max < plastbar->value)? plastbar->value : max;
     min = (min > plastbar->value)? plastbar->value : min;
   }
   vert_scale = (max - min)/page_height; /* Calculate step length */

   /* Check bar width */
   if((barwidth = page_width/bar_count - space) < 1)
   {
     printf("\nPage width too narrow.\n");
     return -1;
   }
```

419

```
      /* Set up a string which will be used to build the columns */

      /* Get the memory */
      if((column = malloc(barwidth + space + 1)) == NULL)
      {
        printf("\nFailed to allocate memory in barchart()"
                         " - terminating program.\n");
        abort();
      }
      for(i = 0 ; i < space ; i++)
        *(column+i)=' ';           /* Blank the space between bars */
      for( ; i < space+barwidth ; i++)
        *(column+i)='#';           /* Enter the bar characters     */
      *(column+i) = '\0';          /* Add string terminator        */

      /* Set up a string which will be used as a blank column */

      /* Get the memory */
      if((blank = malloc(barwidth + space + 1)) == NULL)
      {
        printf("\nFailed to allocate memory in barchart()"
                         " - terminating program.\n");
        abort();
      }

      for(i = 0 ; i < space+barwidth ; i++)
        *(blank+i) = ' ';          /* Blank total width of bar+space */

      *(blank+i) = '\0';           /* Add string terminator          */

    /* Code for rest of the function...  */
    free(blank);                   /* Free memory for blank string   */
    free(column);                  /* Free memory for column string  */
    return 0;
}
```

We'll draw a bar using **'#'** characters. When we draw a bar we will write a string containing **space** spaces and **barwidth** **'#'** characters. We allocate the memory for this dynamically using the library function **malloc()**, so we must add a **#include** directive for the header file **stdlib.h**. The string that we'll use to draw a bar is **column**, and the same length string containing spaces is **blank**. After the bar chart has been drawn, and just before we exit, we free the memory occupied by **column** and **blank**.

Next we can add the final piece of code that draws the chart.

```
/* Example 11.8 Generating a bar chart */
#include <stdio.h>
#include <stdlib.h>

#define PAGE_HEIGHT  20
#define PAGE_WIDTH   40
#define TRUE  1
#define FALSE 0
```

```
typedef struct barTAG
{
   double value;
   struct barTAG *pnextbar;
}bar;

typedef unsigned int uint;       /* Type definition */

/* Function prototype */
int bar_chart(bar *pfirstbar, uint page_width, uint page_height,
                                               char *title);
void main()
{
   /* Code for main */
}


int bar_chart(bar *pfirstbar, uint page_width, uint page_height,
                                               char *title)
{
   bar *plastbar = pfirstbar;   /* Pointer to previous bar          */
   double max = 0.0;            /* Maximum bar value                */
   double min = 0.0;            /* Minimum bar value                */
   double vert_scale = 0.0;     /* Unit step in vertical direction  */
   double position = 0.0;       /* Current vertical position on chart */
   uint bar_count = 1;          /* Number of bars - at least 1      */
   uint barwidth = 0;           /* Width of a bar                   */
   uint space = 2;              /* spaces between bars              */
   uint i = 0;                  /* Loop counter                     */
   uint bars = 0;               /* Loop counter through bars        */
   char *column = NULL;         /* Pointer to bar column section    */
   char *blank = NULL;          /* Blank string for bar+space       */
   int axis = FALSE;            /* Indicates axis drawn             */

   /* Find maximum and minimum of all bar values */

   /* Set max and min to first bar value */
   max = min = plastbar->value;

   while((plastbar = plastbar->pnextbar) != NULL)
   {
     bar_count++;               /* Increment bar count */
     max = (max < plastbar->value)? plastbar->value : max;
     min = (min > plastbar->value)? plastbar->value : min;
   }
   vert_scale = (max - min)/page_height; /* Calculate step length */

   /* Check bar width */
   if((barwidth = page_width/bar_count - space) < 1)
   {
     printf("\nPage width too narrow.\n");
     return -1;
   }
```

```
/* Set up a string which will be used to build the columns */

/* Get the memory */
if((column = malloc(barwidth + space + 1)) == NULL)
{
  printf("\nFailed to allocate memory in barchart()"
                      " - terminating program.\n");
  abort();
}
for(i = 0 ; i < space ; i++)
  *(column+i)=' ';            /* Blank the space between bars */
for( ; i < space+barwidth ; i++)
  *(column+i)='#';            /* Enter the bar characters      */
*(column+i) = '\0';           /* Add string terminator         */

/* Set up a string which will be used as a blank column */

/* Get the memory */
if((blank = malloc(barwidth + space + 1)) == NULL)
{
  printf("\nFailed to allocate memory in barchart()"
                      " - terminating program.\n");
  abort();
}

for(i = 0 ; i < space+barwidth ; i++)
  *(blank+i) = ' ';           /* Blank total width of bar+space */
*(blank+i) = '\0';            /* Add string terminator          */
```

```
  printf("^ %s\n", title);   /* Output the chart title      */

/* Draw the bar chart */
position = max;
for(i = 0 ; i <= page_height ; i++)
{
  /* Check if we need to output the horizontal axis */
  if(position <= 0.0 && !axis)
  {
    printf("+");              /* Start of horizontal axis     */
    for(bars = 0; bars < bar_count*(barwidth+space); bars++)
      printf("-");            /* Output horizontal axis       */
    printf(">\n");
    axis = TRUE;              /* Axis was drawn               */
    position -= vert_scale;/* Decrement position           */
    continue;
  }
  printf("|");                /* Output vertical axis         */
  plastbar = pfirstbar;       /* start with the first bar     */

  /* For each bar... */
  for(bars = 1; bars <= bar_count; bars++)
  {
```

```
        /* If position is between axis and value, output column */
        /* otherwise output blank                               */
        printf("%s", position <= plastbar->value &&
                   plastbar->value >= 0.0 && position > 0.0 ||
                   position >= plastbar->value &&
                   plastbar->value <= 0.0 &&
                   position <= 0.0 ? column: blank);
      plastbar = plastbar->pnextbar;
    }
    printf("\n");                /* End the line of output      */
    position -= vert_scale;  /* Decrement position          */
  }
  if(!axis)                 /* Have we output the horizontal axis? */
  {                         /* No, so do it now                    */
    printf("+");
    for(bars = 0; bars < bar_count*(barwidth+space); bars++)
      printf("-");
    printf(">\n");
  }

  free(blank);             /* Free memory for blank string   */
  free(column);            /* Free memory for column string  */
  return 0;
}
```

The **for** loop outputs **page_height** lines of characters. Each line will represent a distance of **vert_scale** on the vertical axis - we get this value by dividing **page_height** by the difference between the maximum and minimum values. Therefore, the first line of output corresponds to **position** having the value **max**, and it is decremented by **vert_scale** on each iteration until it reaches **min**.

On each line, we must decide first whether we need to output the horizontal axis. This will be necessary when **position** is less than or equal to zero, and we have not already displayed the axis.

On lines other than the horizontal axis, we must decide what to display for each bar position. This is done in the inner **for** loop that repeats for each bar. The conditional operator in the **printf()** call outputs either **column** or **blank**. We output **column** if **position** is between the value of the bar and zero, and we output **blank** otherwise. Having output a complete row of bar segments, we output **'\n'** to end the line, and decrement **position**.

It's possible that all the bars could be positive, in which case we need to make sure that the horizontal axis is output after the loop is complete, since it will not be output from within the loop.

2 Now we just need to implement **main()** to exercise the **bar_chart()** function:

```
/* Example 11.8 Generating a bar chart */
#include <stdio.h>
#include <string.h>
#include <stdlib.h>
```

```
#define PAGE_HEIGHT   20
#define PAGE_WIDTH    40
#define TRUE   1
#define FALSE  0

typedef struct barTAG           /* Bar structure        */
{
   double value;                /* Value of bar         */
   struct barTAG *pnextbar;     /* Pointer to next bar */
}bar;                           /* Type for a bar       */

typedef unsigned int uint;      /* Type definition      */

/* Function prototype */
int bar_chart(bar *pfirstbar, uint page_width, uint page_height, char
*title);
```

```
int main()
{
   bar firstbar;              /* First bar structure */
   bar *plastbar = NULL;      /* Pointer to last bar */
   char value[80];            /* Input buffer        */
   char title[80];            /* Chart title         */

   printf("\nEnter the chart title: ");
   gets(title);               /* Read chart title    */

   for( ;; )                  /* Loop for bar input  */
   {
     printf("Enter the value of the bar, or use quit to end: ");
     gets(value);

     if(strcmp(value, "quit") == 0)   /* quit entered?        */
      break;                          /* then input finished */

     /* Store in next bar */
     if(plastbar == NULL)             /* First time?          */
     {
       firstbar.pnextbar = NULL;  /* Initialize next pointer */
       plastbar = &firstbar;      /* Use the first           */
     }
     else
     {
       /* Get memory */
       if((plastbar->pnextbar = malloc(sizeof(bar))) == NULL)
       {
         printf("Oops! Couldn't allocate memory\n");
         return -1;
       }
       plastbar = plastbar->pnextbar;    /* Old next is new bar  */
       plastbar->pnextbar = NULL;        /* New bar next is NULL */
     }
```

```
      plastbar->value = atof(value);        /* Store the value      */
    }

    /* Create bar-chart */
    bar_chart(&firstbar, PAGE_WIDTH, PAGE_HEIGHT, title);

    /* We are done, so release all the memory we allocated */
    while(firstbar.pnextbar != NULL)
    {
      plastbar = firstbar.pnextbar;             /* Save pointer to next */
      firstbar.pnextbar = plastbar->pnextbar; /* Get one after next    */
      free(plastbar);                           /* Free next memory      */
    }
    return 0;
}

int bar_chart(bar *pfirstbar, uint page_width, uint page_height, char
*title)
{
  /* Implementation of function as before... */
}
```

After reading the chart title using **gets()**, we read successive values in the **for** loop. For each value, other than the first, we allocate the memory for a new bar structure before storing the value. Of course, we keep track of the first structure, **firstbar**, because this is the link to all the others, and we track the pointer to the last structure that we added, so we can update its **pnextbar** pointer when we add another. Once we have all the values, we call **bar_chart()** to produce the chart. Finally, we delete the memory for the bars. Note that we need to take care not to try to delete **firstbar**, as we did not allocate the memory for this dynamically. We need a **#include** directive for **string.h**, as we use the function **gets()**.

All we do then is add a line to **main()** that actually prints the chart from the values typed in.

Typical output from the example is shown below:

```
Enter the chart title: Trial Bar Chart
Enter the value of the bar, or use quit to end: 6
Enter the value of the bar, or use quit to end: 3
Enter the value of the bar, or use quit to end: -5
Enter the value of the bar, or use quit to end: -7
Enter the value of the bar, or use quit to end: 9
Enter the value of the bar, or use quit to end: 4
Enter the value of the bar, or use quit to end: quit
```

```
^  Trial Bar Chart
|                                        ####
|                                        ####
|                                        ####
|                                        ####
|    ####                                ####
|    ####                                ####
|    ####                                ####
|    ####                                ####   ####
|    ####   ####                         ####   ####
|    ####   ####                         ####   ####
|    ####   ####                         ####   ####
|    ####   ####                         ####   ####
+----------------------------------------------->
|                   ####   ####
|                   ####   ####
|                   ####   ####
|                   ####   ####
|                   ####   ####
|                          ####
|                          ####
|                          ####
```

Summary

This has been something of a marathon chapter, but the topic is extremely important. Having a good grasp of structures rates alongside pointers and functions in importance if you want to use C effectively.

Most real world applications deal with things such as people, cars, or materials, which require several different values to represent them. Structures in C provide a ready tool for dealing with these sorts of complex objects. Although some of the operations may seem a little complicated, remember that you're dealing with complicated entities - so the complexity is built in to some extent.

In the next chapter, we'll be looking at how we can store data in external files. This will, of course, include the ability to store structures.

Managing Large Amounts of Data

If your computer could only ever process data stored within the main memory of the machine, the scope and variety of applications that you could deal with would be severely limited. Virtually all serious business applications require more data than would fit into main memory, and depend on the ability to process data that's stored on an external device, such as a fixed disk drive. In this chapter, we're going to explore how we can process data stored on an external device.

C provides a range of functions in the header file **stdio.h** for writing to and reading from an external device. The external device is typically a fixed disk drive or a floppy disk - but not exclusively. Since, consistent with the philosophy of the C language, the facilities that we shall use are device-independent, they apply to virtually any external storage device. However, we shall assume in our examples that we're dealing with disk files throughout.

In this chapter you will learn:

- What a file is in C
- How files are processed
- How to write and read formatted files and binary files
- How to retrieve data from a file by direct random access to the information
- How to use temporary work files in a program
- How to write a file viewer program

The Concept of a File

With all the examples we've seen up to now, any data that the user entered when the program was executed was lost once the program had finished running. At the moment, if the user wants to run the program with the same data, they must enter it again each time. There are lots of occasions when this is not just inconvenient, but it actually makes the programming task impossible.

If we want to maintain a directory of names, addresses and telephone numbers, for instance, a program where you have to enter all the names, addresses and telephone numbers each time is worse than useless! The answer is to store data on permanent storage that continues to be maintained after your computer is switched off. As I'm sure you know, this storage technique is called a **file**, and is usually stored on a hard disk.

You're probably familiar with the basic mechanics of how a disk works. If so, this can be helpful in recognizing when a particular approach to file usage is efficient, and when it isn't. On the other hand, if you know nothing about disk file mechanics, don't worry at this point. There's nothing in the concept of file processing in C that depends on any knowledge of physical storage devices.

A file in C is essentially a serial sequence of bytes, as illustrated in the following figure.

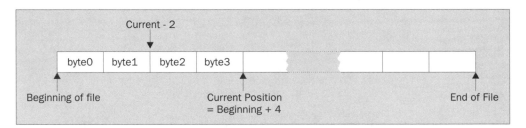

A file has a beginning and an end, and it has a **current position**, typically defined as so many bytes from the beginning. The current position is where any file action (a read from the file or a write to the file) will take place. We can move the current position to any other point in the file. A new current position can be specified as an offset from the beginning of the file, or, in some circumstances, as a positive or negative offset from the previous current position.

Of course, we can write any data we like to a file. As we shall see, there are various ways that data can be written to a file, but it ends up as just a series of bytes in the end. This means that when the file is read, the program must know what sort of data the file represents. We've seen, many times now, that exactly what a series of bytes represents is dependent upon how you interpret it. A sequence of twelve bytes could be twelve ASCII characters, twelve 8-bit signed integers, twelve 8-bit unsigned integers, six 16-bit signed integers, and so on. All of these will be perfectly valid interpretations of the data, so it's important that a program reading a file has the correct assumptions about how it was written.

Processing Files

The files resident on your disk drive each have a name. On a PC running DOS, for example, the name is up to eight characters, which can be followed by a period and an extension of up to three characters.

When we write a program to process a file, it wouldn't be particularly convenient if the program would only work with a specific file with a particular name. If it did, we would need to produce a different program for each file we might want to process. For this reason, when we process a file in C, our program references a file through a **file pointer**. A file pointer is associated with a particular file when the program is run so that, on different occasions, the program can work with different files. In the examples in this chapter, we'll use DOS file names. If you're using some other operating system environment, such as UNIX, you'll need to adjust the names of the files appropriately.

If we want to use several files simultaneously, we need a separate file pointer for each file, although as soon as we've finished using a file, we can associate the file pointer with another file. So if we need to process several files, but we'll be working with them one at a time, then really we only need the one file pointer.

Opening a File

We associate a specific external file name with an internal file pointer variable through a process referred to as **opening** a file. This is achieved through the standard library function **fopen()**, which returns the file pointer for a specific external file. The function **fopen()** is defined in **stdio.h**, and it has this prototype:

```
FILE *fopen(char *name, char* mode);
```

The first argument to the function is a pointer to the name of the external file that we want to process, stored as a text string. We can specify the name explicitly as an argument, or we can use an array, or a pointer to a **char** variable in which we've stored the character string that defines the file name. We typically obtain the file name through some external means, or perhaps defined as a constant at the beginning of the program, or maybe we arrange to read it in from the keyboard.

The second argument to the function **fopen()** is a character string which specifies what we want to do with the file. This is called the **file mode**. As we shall see, this spans a whole range of possibilities, but for the moment we'll look at just three file modes (which nonetheless comprise the basic set of operations on a file). These three file modes are:

"w"	Open a file for **w**rite operations
"a"	Open a file for **a**ppend operations (adding to the end of the file, for example)
"r"	Open a file for **r**ead operations

Notice that these mode specifiers are character strings defined between double quotes, not single characters defined between single quotes.

Assuming the call to **fopen()** is successful, it returns a pointer that we can now use to reference the file in further input/output operations, using other functions in the library.

> *The pointer returned by **fopen()** is referred to as a file pointer, or a stream pointer.*

So, a call to **fopen()** does two things for us: it creates a file pointer indicating the specific file that our program is going to operate on, and it determines what we can do with that file within our program.

The pointer returned by **fopen()** is of type 'pointer to **FILE**', where **FILE** specifies a structure that has been predefined in the header file **stdio.h** through a **typedef**. Because it has been defined using a **typedef**, a declaration of a file pointer only requires the use of the keyword **FILE**. The structure associated with a file pointer will contain information about the file. This could be the mode specified, the address of the buffer in memory to be used, and a pointer to the current position in the file for the next operation. We don't need to worry about the contents of this structure in practice. It's all taken care of by the input/output functions.

However, if you really want to know about the FILE structure, you can browse through the library header file.

As we've seen, when we want to have several files open at once, they must each have their own file pointer variable declared, and they are each opened with a separate call to `fopen()` with the value returned stored in a separate file pointer.

If we wanted to write to an existing file with the name `myfile.txt`, we would use these statements:

```
FILE *pfile = NULL;                  /* Declaration of file pointer     */
pfile = fopen("myfile.txt", "w");  /* Open file myfile.txt to write it */
```

The first statement is a declaration for our file pointer of type **FILE**. We've initialized the pointer to **NULL** to be on the safe side. The second statement opens the file and associates the physical file specified by the file name `myfile.txt` with our internal pointer `pfile`. Because we've specified the mode as `"w"`, we can only write to the file, we cannot read from it.

If the file name `myfile.txt` doesn't already exist, the function `fopen()` will create it.

So here we have the facility to create a new file. Simply call fopen() with mode "w" and the first argument specifying the name you want to assign to the new file.

On opening a file for writing, the file is positioned at the beginning of any existing data for the first operation. This means that any data previous written to the file will be overwritten when you initiate any write operations.

If we want to add to an existing file rather than overwrite it, we specify mode `"a"`, which is the append mode of operation. This positions the file at the end of any previously written data. If the file specified doesn't exist, as in the case of mode `"w"`, a new file will be created. Using the file pointer we declared above, to open the file to add data to the end, we would use the statement:

```
pfile = fopen("myfile.txt", "a"); /* Open file myfile.txt to add to it */
```

If we want to read a file, once we have declared our file pointer, we would open it using this statement:

```
pfile = fopen("myfile.txt", "r");
```

Since we've specified the mode argument as `"r"`, indicating that we want to read the file, we cannot write to this file. The file position will be set to the beginning of the data in the file.

Clearly, if we're going to read the file, it must already exist. If we inadvertently try to open a file for reading that doesn't exist, `fopen()` will return **NULL**. It's therefore a good idea to check the value returned from `fopen()` in an `if` statement, to make sure that we really are accessing the file we want.

Writing to a File

Once we've opened a file for writing, we can write to it any time from anywhere in our program, provided we have access to the pointer for the file which has been set by **fopen()**. So, if we want to be able to access a file from anywhere in a program that contains multiple functions, we need to ensure the file pointer has global scope.

> *As you'll recall, this is achieved by placing the declaration outside of all of the functions, usually at the beginning of the program code.*

The simplest write operation is provided by the function **fputc()**, which writes a single character to a file. It has the following prototype:

```
int fputc(int c, FILE *pfile);
```

fputc() writes the character specified by the first argument to the file defined by the file pointer, which is entered as the second argument. If the write is successful, it returns the character written. Otherwise it returns **EOF**.

> *EOF is a special character called the 'end of file' character. In fact, the symbol **EOF** is defined in **stdio.h** and usually has the value -1. However, this is not necessarily always the case, so you should use **EOF** in your programs rather than an explicit value.*

In practice, characters aren't written to the physical file one by one. This would be extremely inefficient. Hidden from your program and managed by the output routine, output characters are written to an area of memory called a **buffer** until a reasonable number have been accumulated, when they are written to the file in one go. This mechanism is illustrated in the next figure.

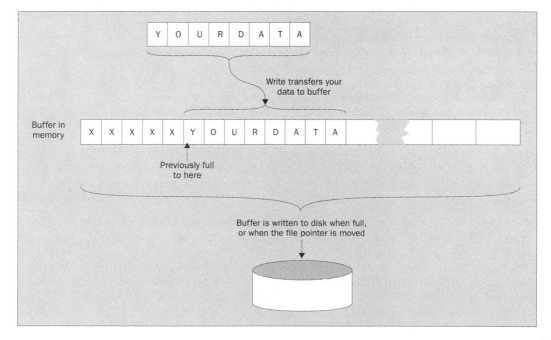

Note that the function **putc()** is equivalent to **fputc()**. It requires the same arguments and the return type is the same. The difference between them is that **putc()** may be implemented as a macro whereas **fputc()** is a function.

Reading from a File

The complementary function to **fputc()** is **fgetc()**, which reads a character from a file that has been opened for reading. It takes the file pointer as its only argument, and returns the character read as an **int** type if the read is successful; otherwise it returns **EOF**. The typical use of **fgetc()** is illustrated by the statement:

```
mchar = fgetc(pfile);          /* Reads a character into mchar */
```

We're assuming, here, that the variable **mchar** has been declared to be of type **int**.

Behind the scenes, the actual mechanism for reading a file is the inverse of writing to a file. A whole block of characters is read into a buffer. The characters are then handed over to your program one at a time as you request them, until the buffer is empty - whereupon another block is read. This makes the process very fast, since most **fgetc()** operations won't involve reading the disk, but simply moving a character from the buffer in main memory to the place where you want to store it.

Note that the function **getc()** that is equivalent to **fgetc()** is also available. It requires an argument of type **FILE*** and returns the character read as type **int**, so it is virtually identical to **fgetc()**. The only difference between them is that **getc()** may be implemented as a macro whereas **fgetc()** is a function.

> *Don't confuse the function **getc()** with the function **gets()**. They are quite different in operation - **getc()** reads a single character from the stream specified by its argument whereas **gets()** reads a whole line of input from the standard input stream, which is the keyboard. We have already used the **gets()** function in previous chapters for reading a string from the keyboard.*

Closing a File

When we've finished with a file, we need to tell the operating system that this is the case and free up our file pointer. This is referred to as **closing** a file. We do this through the function, **fclose()**, which accepts a file pointer as an argument and returns an **int** value which is set to **EOF** if an error occurs and 0 otherwise. Typical usage would be:

```
fclose(pfile);          /* Close the file associated with pfile */
```

The result of executing this statement is that the connection between the pointer, **pfile**, and the physical file name is broken, so **pfile** can no longer be used to access the physical file it represented. If the file was being written, then the contents of the output buffer are written to the file to ensure that data is not lost.

It's good programming practice to close a file as soon as you've finished with it. This protects against losing output data, which could occur if an error in another part of our program caused the execution to be stopped in an abnormal fashion. This could result in the contents of the output buffer being lost, as the file wouldn't be closed properly.

Another reason for closing files as soon as you have finished with them is that the operating system will usually limit the number of files you may have open at one time. Closing files as soon as you have finished with them will minimize the chances of you falling foul of the operating system in this respect.

There is a function in **stdio.h** that will force any unwritten data left in a buffer to be written to a file. This is the function **fflush()**, which we've already used in previous chapters to flush the input buffer. With our file pointer **pfile**, we could force any data left in the output buffer to be written to the file by using this statement:

```
fflush(pfile);
```

The **fflush()** function returns a value of type **int** that is normally zero, but will be set to **EOF** if an error occurs.

Try It Out - Using a Simple File

We now have enough knowledge of the file input/output capabilities in C to write a simple program that writes and then uses a simple file. So let's do just that:

```
/* Example 12.1 Writing a file a character at a time  */
#include <stdio.h>
#include <string.h>

void main()
{
   char mystr[80];         /* Input string          */
   int i = 0;              /* Loop counter          */
   int lstr = 0;           /* Length of input string */
   int mychar = 0;         /* Character for output  */
   FILE *pfile = NULL;     /* File pointer          */

   printf("\nEnter an interesting string.\n");
   gets(mystr);            /* Read in a string      */

   /* Create a new file we can write */
   pfile = fopen("C:\\myfile.txt", "w");
   lstr = strlen( mystr );

   for(i = lstr-1 ; i >= 0 ; i--)
     fputc(mystr[i], pfile);  /* Write string to file backwards */

   fclose(pfile);             /* Close the file              */
```

```
        /* Open the file for reading */
    pfile = fopen("c:\\myfile.txt", "r");

        /* Read a character from the file */
    while((mychar = fgetc(pfile)) != EOF)
      putchar(mychar);               /* Output character from the file */

    fclose(pfile);                   /* Close the file              */
    remove("c:\\myfile.txt");        /* Delete the physical file    */
  }
```

How It Works

Before running this program, or indeed any of the examples working with files, make sure you don't have an existing file of the same name. If you have, you should change the file name in the example otherwise your existing file will be overwritten. This program provides a very simple illustration of writing a file character by character.

After displaying a prompt, the program reads a string from the keyboard. It then executes the statement:

```
    /* Create a new file we can write */
    pfile = fopen("C:\\myfile.txt", "w");
```

This calls **fopen()** to create the new file **myfile.txt** on drive C, and opens it for writing. Note that we must use the escape sequence, ****, to get a backslash character. If we forget to do this, the compiler will think that we're writing an escape sequence, **'\m'**, which it won't recognize as valid. The second argument to **fopen()** determines the mode as writing the file.

After determining the length of the string, using **strlen()**, and storing the result in **lstr**, we have a loop defined by these statements:

```
    for(i = lstr-1 ; i >= 0 ; i--)
      fputc(mystr[i], pfile);   /* Write string to file backwards */
```

The loop index is varied from a value corresponding to the last character in the string, **lstr-1**, back to zero. Therefore, the **fputc()** function call within the loop writes to the new file character-by-character, in reverse order. The particular file we're writing is specified by the pointer **pfile** as the second argument to the function call.

After closing the file with a call to **fclose()**, it's re-opened in reading mode by the statement:

```
    /* Open the file for reading */
    pfile = fopen("c:\\myfile.txt", "r");
```

Here, the mode specification **"r"** indicates that we intend to read the file; so the file position is set to the beginning of the file.

Next, we use the **fgetc()** function to read characters from the file within the **while** loop condition:

```
        /* Read a character from the file */
   while((mychar = fgetc(pfile)) != EOF)
     putchar(mychar);               /* Output character from the file */
```

The file is read character-by-character. The read operation actually takes place within the loop continuation condition. As each character is read, it's displayed on the screen using the function **putchar()** within the loop. The process stops when **EOF** is returned by **getc()** at the end of the file.

The last two statements in the program are:

```
   fclose(pfile);                   /* Close the file          */
   remove("c:\\myfile.txt");        /* Delete the physical file */
```

These provide the necessary final tidying up, now we have finished with the file. After closing the file the program calls a library function, **remove()**, that is new to us. This function will delete the file identified by the argument. Here, this function deletes the file that we've created in order to avoid cluttering up the disk with stray files.

Writing a String to a File

Analogous to the function **puts()** for writing a string to **stdout**, we have the function **fputs()** for writing a string to a file. Its prototype is:

```
   int fputs(char *pstr, FILE *pfile);
```

This accepts as its arguments a pointer to the character string to be output, and a file pointer. The operation of the function is slightly odd, in that it continues to copy a string until it reaches a **'\0'** character, which it doesn't copy to the file. This can complicate the reading of variable length strings. It returns **EOF** if an error occurs, and 0 under normal circumstances. It is used in the same way as **puts()**. For example:

```
   fputs("The higher the fewer", pfile);
```

This will output the string appearing as the first argument to the file pointed to by **pfile**.

Reading a String from a File

Complementing **fputs()** is the function **fgets()** for reading a string from a file. It has the prototype:

```
   char *fgets(char *pstr, int nchars, FILE *pfile);
```

fgets() differs from **fputs()** in that it has three parameters. The function will read a string into the area pointed to by **pstr**, from the file specified by **pfile**. Characters are read from the file until a **'\n'** is read, or **nchars-1** characters have been read from the file.

If a newline character is read, it is retained in the string. The **'\0'** is appended to the end of the string in memory. If there is no error, **fgets()** will return the pointer **pstr**, otherwise **NULL** is returned. This function enables us to ensure that we don't overrun the memory area we've assigned for input in your program. To prevent the capacity of our data input area being exceeded, we just specify the length of the area or the array that will receive the input data as the second argument to the function.

Try It Out - Transferring Strings To and From a File

We can exercise the functions to transfer strings to and from a file in an example which also uses the append mode:

```c
/* Example 12.2      As the saying goes...it comes back! */
#include <stdio.h>

void main()
{
   char *proverbs[] =
              {  "Many a mickle makes a muckle.\n",
                 "Too many cooks spoil the broth.\n",
                 "He who laughs last didn't get the joke in"
                                          " the first place.\n"
              };

   char more[60] = "A nod is a good as a wink to a blind horse.\n";
   FILE *pfile = NULL;             /* File pointer */
   int i = 0;                      /* Loop counter */

   /* Create a new file( if myfile.txt does not exist */
   pfile = fopen("c:\\myfile.txt", "w" );

   /* Write our first three sayings. */
   for(i = 0 ; i < sizeof proverbs/sizeof proverbs[0] ; i++)
     fputs(proverbs[i], pfile);

   fclose(pfile);                  /* Close the file */

   /* Open it again to append data */
   pfile = fopen("C:\\myfile.txt", "a");

   /* Write another proverb        */
   fputs(more, pfile);

   /* Close the file               */
   fclose(pfile);

   /* Open the file to read it      */
   pfile = fopen("C:\\myfile.txt", "r");

   /* Read a proverb                */
   while(fgets(more, 60, pfile) != NULL)
   /* and display it                */
   printf("\n%s", more);
```

```
    fclose(pfile);              /* Close the file */
    remove("c:\\myfile.txt");   /* and remove it  */
}
```

How It Works

In this example, we've used a novel way of initializing the array of pointers **proverbs[]** in the statement:

```
char *proverbs[] =
        {  "Many a mickle makes a muckle.\n",
           "Too many cooks spoil the broth.\n",
           "He who laughs last didn't get the joke in"
                                " the first place.\n"
        };
```

We specify the three sayings as initial values, which causes the compiler to allocate the space necessary to store each string, and then we put the address of the space allocated for each in the appropriate element of the pointer array. The compiler will automatically fill in the dimension for the array to provide sufficient pointers for the number of strings specified as initializing values. Each string has **'\n'** as the last character, so that **fgets()** will be able to recognize the end of each string.

We have a further declaration:

```
char more[60] = "A nod is a good as a wink to a blind horse.\n";
```

This initializes a conventional **char** array with another proverb. We also include **'\n'** at the end - for the same reason as before.

After creating and opening a file on drive **C:** for writing, the program executes the loop:

```
/* Write our first three sayings. */
for(i = 0 ; i < sizeof proverbs/sizeof proverbs[0] ; i++)
  fputs(proverbs[i], pfile);
```

The contents of each of the memory areas pointed to by elements of the **proverbs[]** array are written to the file in the **for** loop using the function **fputs()**. This function is extremely easy to use: it just requires a pointer to the string as the first argument, and a pointer to the file as the second.

The number of iterations is set with the expression:

```
sizeof proverbs/sizeof proverbs[0]
```

sizeof proverbs will evaluate to the total number of bytes occupied by the complete array, and **sizeof proverbs[0]** will result in the number of bytes required for a single pointer in one element of the array. Therefore, the whole expression will evaluate to the number of elements in the pointer array. We could have manually counted how many initializing strings we supplied, of course, but doing it this way means that the correct number of iterations is determined automatically, and this expression will still be correct even if the array dimension is changed by adding more initializing strings.

Once the first set of proverbs has been written the file is closed, and then re-opened with the statement:

```
    /* Open it again to append data */
    pfile = fopen("C:\\myfile.txt", "a");
```

Because we have the mode specified as **"a"**, the file is opened in append mode. Note that the current position for the file is automatically set at the end of the file in this mode.

We then write to the file with the statement:

```
    /* Write another proverb       */
    fputs(more, pfile);
```

The additional proverb stored in the character array **more[]** is then written to the file using **fputs()**. As you can see, the function **fputs()** is just as easy to use with an array as it is with a pointer. Since we're in append mode, the new proverb will be added at the end of the existing data in the file.

Having written the file, it's closed and then re-opened for reading using the mode specifier **"r"**. We then have the loop:

```
    /* Read a proverb              */
    while(fgets(more, 60, pfile) != NULL)
    /* and display it              */
    printf("\n%s", more);
```

We read strings successively from the file into the array **more[]** within the loop continuation condition. After each string is read, we display it on the screen by the call to **printf()** within the loop. The reading of each proverb by **fgets()** is terminated by detecting the **'\n'** character at the end of each string. The loop terminates when the function **fgets()** returns **NULL**.

Finally, the file is closed and then deleted from drive **C:** using the function **remove()** in the same fashion as the previous example.

Formatted File Input and Output

Writing files one character at a time isn't really adequate for most purposes; neither is the ability to output a string, as in **fputs()**. What we need is a way to store away big chunks of data at a time, which will usually run the whole gamut of data types. We may also want to ensure the output is structured in a very specific manner. One mechanism for doing just this is provided by the functions for formatted file input and output.

Formatted Output to a File

We've already met the function for formatted output to a file when we discussed standard streams back in Chapter 10. It's virtually the same as the **printf()** statement, with one extra parameter and a slight name change. Its typical usage is:

```
   fprintf(pfile, "%12d%12d%14f", num1, num2, fnum1);
```

As you can see, the function name has an additional **f** (for file), compared with **printf()**, and the first argument is a file pointer specifying the destination of the output. The file pointer obviously needs to be set through a call to **fopen()** first. The remaining arguments are identical to that of **printf()**. This example writes the values of the three variables **num1**, **num2**, and **num3**, to the file specified by the file pointer **pfile**, under control of the format string specified as the second argument. Therefore, the first two variables are of type **int**, and are to be written with a field width of 12, and the third variable is of type **float**, and is to be written to the file with a field width of 14.

Formatted Input from a File

We get formatted input from a file by using the function **fscanf()**. To read three variable values from a file **pfile** we would write:

```
   fscanf(pfile, "%12d%12d%14f", &num1, &num2, &fnum1);
```

This function works in exactly the same way as **scanf()** does with **stdin**, except that here we are obtaining input from a file specified by the first argument. The same rules govern the specification of the format string and the operation of the function as apply to **scanf()**. The function returns **EOF** if an error occurs such that no input is read; otherwise, it returns the number of values read as an **int** value.

Try It Out - Using Formatted Input and Output Functions

We can exercise the formatted input and output functions with an example that will also demonstrate what's happening to the data in these operations:

```
/* Example 12.3 Messing about with formatted file I/O */
#include <stdio.h>

void main()
{
   long num1 = 234567L;    /* Input values...              */
   long num2 = 345123L;
   long num3 = 789234L;

   long num4 = 0L;         /* Values read from the file... */
   long num5 = 0L;
   long num6 = 0L;

   float fnum = 0.0f;      /* Value read from the file     */
   int   ival[6] = { 0 };  /* Values read from the file    */
   int i = 0;              /* Loop counter                 */
   FILE *pfile = NULL;     /* File pointer                 */

   /* Create file to be written */
   pfile = fopen("C:\\myfile.txt", "w");
```

441

```
   /* Write file         */
   fprintf(pfile, "%61d%61d%61d", num1, num2, num3);

   /* Close file         */
   fclose(pfile);

   /* Display values written   */
   printf("\n %61d %61d %61d", num1, num2, num3);

   /* Open file to read        */
   pfile = fopen("C:\\myfile.txt", "r");

   /* Read back          */
   fscanf(pfile, "%61d%61d%61d", &num4, &num5 ,&num6);

   /* Display what we got     */
   printf("\n %61d %61d %61d", num4, num5, num6);

   /* Go to the beginning of the file */
   rewind(pfile);

   /* Read it again          */
   fscanf(pfile, "%2d%3d%3d%3d%2d%2d%3f", &ival[0], &ival[1],
          &ival[2], &ival[3], &ival[4] , &ival[5], &fnum);

   fclose(pfile);                /* Close the file and      */
   remove("C:\\myfile.txt");     /* delete physical file.   */
   printf("\n\n");

   /* Output the results */
   for( i = 0 ; i < 6 ; i++ )
     printf("%sival[%d] = %d", i == 4 ? "\n\t" : "\t", i, ival[i]);
   printf("\nfnum = %f", fnum);
}
```

Output from this example would be:

```
234567 345123 789234
234567 345123 789234

        ival[0] = 23    ival[1] = 456    ival[2] = 734    ival[3] = 512
        ival[4] = 37    ival[5] = 89
fnum = 234.000000
```

How It Works

This example writes the values of **num1**, **num2**, and **num3**, which are defined and assigned values in their declaration, to the file **myfile.txt** on drive **C:**. This is referenced through the pointer **pfile**. The file is closed and re-opened for reading, and the values are read from the file in the same format as they were written. We then have the statement:

```
                /* Go to the beginning of the file */
        rewind(pfile);
```

This calls the function **rewind()**, which simply moves the current position back to the beginning of the file so that we can read it again. We could have achieved the same thing by closing the file then re-opening it again, but with **rewind()** we do it with one function call.

Having repositioned the file, we read the file again with the statement:

```
        /* Read it again           */
        fscanf(pfile, "%2d%3d%3d%3d%2d%2d%3f", &ival[0], &ival[1],
                &ival[2], &ival[3], &ival[4] , &ival[5], &fnum);
```

This reads the same data into the array **ival[]** and the variable **fnum**, but with different formats from those that we used for writing the file. You can see, from the effects of this, that the file consists of just a string of characters once it has been written, exactly the same as the output to the screen from **printf()**.

> *You can lose information if you choose a format specifier which outputs fewer digits precision than the stored value holds.*

You can see that the values you get back from the file when you read it will depend on both the format string that we use and upon the variable list that we specify in the **fscanf()** function.

None of the intrinsic source information that existed when you wrote the file is necessarily maintained. Once the data is in the file, it is just a sequence of bytes where the meaning is determined by how you interpret them. This is demonstrated quite clearly by our example, where we have converted our original three values into eight new values.

Lastly, in this program, we leave everything neat and tidy by closing the file and using the function **remove()** to delete it from drive **C:**.

Dealing with Errors

Our examples haven't included much in the way of error checking and reporting, since it tends to take up a lot of space in the book and make the programs look rather complicated. In real world programs, however, it's essential that we do check for error returns from library functions.

Generally, we should write our error messages to **stderr**, which is automatically available to your program and always points to your display screen. Even though **stdout** may be redirected to a file by an operating system command, **stderr** continues to be assigned to the screen. It's particularly important to check that a file we want to read does in fact exist.

> *It's a good idea to define your file names as string constants: then you can refer to them in your error output.*

For example, to check that the file **myfile.txt** on drive **C:** has been successfully opened, we could use the code:

```
char * myfile = "C:\MYFILE.TXT";            /* File name    */
FILE *pfile = NULL;                         /* File pointer */
....
if(pfile = fopen(myfile, "r") == NULL)
  fprintf(stderr, "\nCannot open %s.", myfile );
```

It's wise to include some basic error checking and reporting code in all of your programs. Once you've written a few programs, you'll find that including some standard bits of code for each type of operation warranting error checks is no hardship. With a standard approach, you can copy most of what you need from one program to another.

Further File Operation Modes

We've only processed files as text files so far, where information is written as strings of characters. Text mode is generally the default mode of operation, but you can specify explicitly that file operations are in text mode if you want to be sure about it. You do this by adding a **t** at the end of the existing specifiers. This gives us mode specifiers **"wt"**, **"rt"**, and **"at"** instead of our original three.

We can also open a file for update; that is, for both reading and writing, using the specifier **"r+"**. If we wanted the mode to be specified explicitly as a text operation, it would become **"r+t"** or **"rt+"**. Either specification for the file mode is perfectly acceptable. We can also specify the mode **"w+"** if we want to both read and write a new file, or when you want to discard the original contents of an existing file before you start. To specify text mode explicitly this would become **"wt+"** or **"w+t"**.

As I've said, in update mode we can both read and write the file. However, we can't write to the file immediately after reading it, or read from the file immediately after writing it, unless **EOF** has been reached, or the position in the file has been changed by some means. (This involves calling a function such as **rewind()**, or some other functions that we'll see later in this chapter.)

The reason for this is that writing to a file doesn't necessarily write the data to the external device. It simply transfers it to a buffer in memory that's written to the file once it's full, or when some other event causes it to be written. Similarly, the first read from a file will fill a buffer area in memory, and subsequent reads will transfer data from the buffer until it's empty, whereupon another file read to fill the buffer will be initiated. This is illustrated in the following figure.

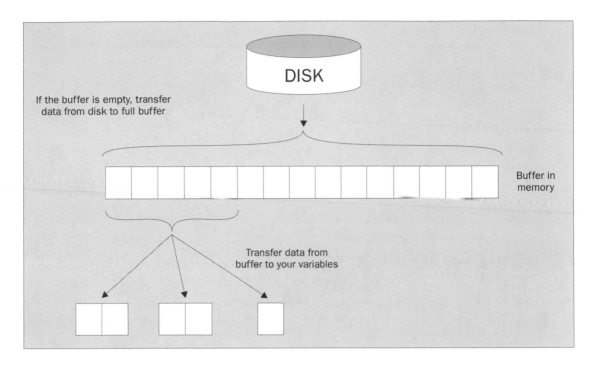

This means that if we switch immediately from write mode to read mode, data will be lost, since it will be left in the buffer. In the case of switching from read mode to write mode, the current position in the file may be different from what we imagine it to be, and we may inadvertently overwrite data on the file. A switch from read to write or vice versa, therefore, requires an intervening event that implicitly flushes the buffers. The function **fflush()**, that I mentioned earlier in this chapter, will cause bytes remaining in an output buffer to be written to an output file.

Unformatted File Input/Output

The alternative to text mode operations on a file is binary mode. In this mode, no transformation of the data takes place, and there's no need for a format string to control input or output - so it's much simpler than text mode. The binary data as it appears in memory is transferred directly to the file. Characters such as **'\n'** and **'\0'** that have specific significance in text mode are of no consequence in binary mode.

Binary mode has the advantage that no data is transformed, or precision lost, as can happen with text mode due to the formatting process. It's also somewhat faster than text mode, because no transformation operations are performed. The two modes are contrasted in the next figure.

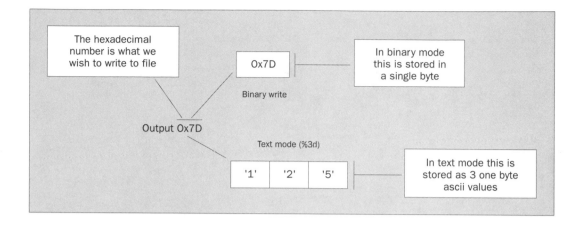

Specifying Binary Mode

We specify binary mode by appending a **"b"** to the basic mode specifiers. Therefore, we have the additional specifiers **"wb"** for writing a binary file, **"rb"** to read a binary file, **"ab"** to append data to the end of a binary file, and **"rb+"** to enable reading and writing of a binary file.

Since binary mode involves handling the data to be transferred to and from the file in a different way from text mode, we have a new set of functions to perform input and output.

Writing a Binary File

To write a binary file, you use the function **fwrite()**. This is best explained with an example of its use. Assuming we open the file to be written with the statement:

```
pfile = fopen("C:\\myfile.txt", "wb");
```

where **pfile** has been declared as a pointer to an object of type **FILE** as before, then we could write to the file with this statement:

```
wcount = fwrite(pdata, size, num_items, pfile);
```

The function operates on the principle of writing a specified number of data items to a file, where each item is a given number of bytes long. The first argument, **pdata**, is a pointer containing the starting address in memory of the data objects to be written. The second argument, **size**, specifies the size of each object to be written. The third argument, **num_items**, defines a count of the number of items to be written to the file specified by the last argument, **pfile**. The function **fwrite()** returns the count of the number of items actually written. If the operation was unsuccessful, this value will be less than **num_items**.

The return value, and the arguments **size** and **num_items**, are all of the same type as that returned by the **sizeof** operator. This is defined as type **size_t**, which is essentially an unsigned integer type.

Let's assume that we want to write objects stored at an address specified by **pdata**, where **pdata** has been declared as a pointer of some kind with a declaration such as:

```
long *pdata = NULL;
```

Once **pdata** has been assigned a suitable valid address, we can specify the write operation from the area pointed to by **pdata** as:

```
wcount = fwrite(pdata, sizeof(*pdata), num_items, pfile);
```

Therefore, we can use the **sizeof** operator to specify the size in bytes of the objects to be transferred. This is a good way of specifying this value, particularly for structures where it isn't always obvious how many bytes are involved. Of course, in a real context, we should also check the return value in **wcount**, to be sure the write was successful.

This means that our function for binary writes to a file is geared to writing a number of objects of any length. You can write in units of your own structures as easily as you can write **int** values, values of type **double**, or sequences of individual bytes.

Reading a Binary File

To read a binary file once it has been opened in read mode, we use the function **fread()**. Using the same variables as in our example of writing a binary file, to read the file we would use a statement such as:

```
wcount = fread( pdata, size, num_items, pfile);
```

This operates exactly as the inverse of the write operation. Starting at the address specified by **pdata**, the function reads **num_items** objects, each of size **size** bytes, and returns the count of the number of objects read. If the read isn't completely successful, the count will be less than the number of objects requested. Of course, you'd probably write the **size** argument as **sizeof(*pdata)**.

Try It Out - Reading a Binary File

We could apply the binary file operations to a version of the program we first saw in Chapter 7 for calculating primes. This time, we'll use a disk file as a buffer to calculate a larger number of primes. We can make the program automatically spill primes on to a disk file if the array assigned to store the primes is insufficient for the number required. In this version of the program to find primes, we'll use array notation throughout and improve the checking process a little.

In addition to the function **main()**, which will contain the prime finding loop, we'll write a function to test whether a value is prime called **test_prime()**, a helper function that will check a given value against a block of primes called **check()**, and a function called **put_primes()** which will retrieve the primes from the file and display them.

As this program consists of several functions, let's take a look at **main()** first:

```
/* Example 12.4  A prime example using binary files */
#include <stdio.h>
#include <stdlib.h>
#include <math.h >        /* For square root function sqrt()      */
```

```
#define MEM_PRIMES 100   /* Count of number of primes in memory */

/* Function prototypes */
int test_prime(unsigned long N);
void put_primes(void);
int check(unsigned long buffer[], int count, unsigned long N);

/* Global variables */
char myfile[] = "C:\\myfile.bin";    /* Physical file name      */
FILE *pfile = NULL;                  /* File pointer            */

/* Array to store primes   */
unsigned long primes[MEM_PRIMES] = { 2UL,3UL,5UL };

int index = 3;  /* Index of free location in array primes */
int nrec = 0;   /* Number of file records   */

void main()
{
   unsigned long trial = 5UL; /* Prime candidate */
   long num_primes = 3L;      /* Prime count     */
   long total = 0L;           /* Total required  */
   int i = 0;                 /* Loop counter    */

   printf("How many primes would you like?  ");
   scanf("%d", &total);    /* Total is how many we need to find */
   total = total<4 ? 4:total;    /* Make sure it is at least 4 */

   /* Prime finding and storing loop */
   while(num_primes < total) /* Loop until we get total required  */
   {
     trial += 2;                    /* Next value for checking         */

     if(test_prime(trial))    /* Check if trial is prime         */
     {                        /* Positive value means prime      */
       primes[index++] = trial;  /* so store it                  */
       num_primes++;             /* Increment total number of primes */

       if(index == MEM_PRIMES) /* Check if array is full          */
       {
         /* File opened OK?   */
         if((pfile = fopen(myfile, "ab")) == NULL)
         { /* No, so explain and end the program */
           printf("\nUnable to open %s to append\n", myfile);
           abort();
         }
         /* Write the array     */
         fwrite(primes, sizeof(long), MEM_PRIMES, pfile);

         /* Close the file      */
         fclose(pfile);
```

```
           /* Reset count of primes in memory  */
           index = 0;

           /* Increment file record count       */
           nrec++;
      }
    }
  }

  if(total>MEM_PRIMES)    /* If we wrote some to file          */
    put_primes();         /* Display the contents of the file */
  if(index)               /* Display any left in memory        */
    for(i = 0; i<index ; i++)
    {
      if(i%5 == 0)
        printf("\n");                 /* Newline after five     */
      printf("%12lu", primes[i]);  /* Output a prime          */
    }

  if(total>MEM_PRIMES)                  /* Did we need a file? */
    if(remove(myfile))                  /* then delete it.      */
      printf("\nFailed to delete %s\n", myfile); /* Delete failed */
    else
      printf("\nFile %s deleted.\n",myfile);    /* Delete OK      */
}
```

How It Works

After the usual **#include** statements, we have the definition for **MEM_PRIMES**, which is the maximum number of primes to be held in memory. Once more than this number of primes have been computed, the primes in memory will be written to a disk file automatically by the program. If you request less than this number, none will be written to disk.

The prototypes for three functions used in the program are:

```
int test_prime(unsigned long N);
void put_primes(void);
int check(unsigned long buffer[], int count, unsigned long N);
```

Within the prototypes, we could have written just the parameter types, without using a parameter name. Function prototypes can be written either with or without parameter names, but the parameter types must be specified. Generally, it's better to include names, because they give a clue to the purpose of the parameter. The names in the prototype can be different from the names used in the definition of the function, but you should only do this if it helps to make the code more readable.

The following statements are the declarations for the global variables:

```
/* Global variables */
char myfile[] = "C:\\myfile.bin";    /* Physical file name    */
FILE *pfile = NULL;                   /* File pointer          */
```

```
/* Array to store primes   */
unsigned long primes[MEM_PRIMES] = { 2UL,3UL,5UL };

int index = 3;   /* Index of free location in array primes */
int nrec = 0;    /* Number of file records  */
```

These can all be accessed by any function in the program. The first declaration defines a **char** array containing the name of the external file to be used. You need the double backslash to get a backslash character in the string. You should change this file name to suit your environment.

We've included the file pointer **pfile** and the character array **myfile**, which holds the external file name, as global variables so that we can use input and output operations on the file from anywhere in the program. This allows the function **put_primes()** to be defined without parameters. We also define the array to hold primes in memory as global, and insert the first three primes as initial values.

The function **main()** starts following the global declarations. When the program executes, you enter the number of primes you want to find, and this value controls the main iteration for testing prime candidates. Checking for a prime is performed by the function **test_prime()**, which is called in the **if** statement condition within the loop. The function returns 1 if the value tested is prime, and 0 otherwise. If a prime is found then we execute the statements:

```
primes[index++] = trial;   /* so store it                        */
num_primes++;              /* Increment total number of primes  */
```

The first statement, here, stores the prime that we have found in the **primes[]** array. We keep track of how many primes we have in total with the variable **num_primes**, and the variable **index** counts how many we have in memory at any given time.

Every time we find a prime and add it to the **primes[]** array, we perform the following check:

```
if(index == MEM_PRIMES) /* Check if array is full              */
{
  /* File opened OK?   */
  if((pfile = fopen(myfile, "ab")) == NULL)
  { /* No, so explain and end the program */
    printf("\nUnable to open %s to append\n", myfile);
    abort();
  }
  /* Write the array   */
  fwrite(primes, sizeof(long), MEM_PRIMES, pfile);

  /* Close the file    */
  fclose(pfile);

  /* Reset count of primes in memory  */
  index = 0;

  /* Increment file record count       */
  nrec++;
}
```

If we have filled the array **primes[]**, the **if** condition will be true and we'll execute the associated statement block. In this case, the file is opened in binary mode to append data. The first time this occurs, a new file will be created. On subsequent file opens to append data, the file will be positioned at the end of any existing data in the file, ready for the next block to be written. After writing a block, the file is closed - as it will be necessary to open it for reading in the function that performs the checking of prime candidates.

Finally, in this group of statements, the count of the number of primes in memory is reset to zero, since they have all been safely stowed away, and the count of the number of blocks of primes written to the file is incremented.

When sufficient primes have been found to fulfill the number requested, we display the primes with the statements:

```
    if(total>MEM_PRIMES)      /* If we wrote some to file     */
      put_primes();           /* Display the contents of the file */
    if(index)                 /* Display any left in memory   */
      for(i = 0; i<index ; i++)
      {
        if(i%5 == 0)
          printf("\n");                  /* Newline after five   */
        printf("%12lu", primes[i]);  /* Output a prime       */
      }
```

It's quite possible that the number of primes requested could be accommodated in memory, in which case we won't write to a file at all. We must therefore check whether **total** exceeded **MEM_PRIMES** before calling the function **put_primes()** that outputs the primes in the file. If the value of **index** is positive, then there are primes in the array **primes[]** that have not been written to the file. In this case, we display these in the **for** loop, five to a line.

Finally in **main()** we remove the file from the disk with the statements:

```
    if(total>MEM_PRIMES)                /* Did we need a file? */
      if(remove(myfile))                /* then delete it.     */
        printf("\nFailed to delete %s\n", myfile); /* Delete failed */
      else
        printf("\nFile %s deleted.\n",myfile);      /* Delete OK      */
```

The first **if** ensures that we don't attempt to delete the file if we did not create one.

The function to check whether a value is prime or not is as follows:

```
/***************************************************************/
/* Function to test if a number, N, is prime using primes in   */
/* memory and on file                                          */
/* First parameter N - value to be tested                      */
/* Return value - a positive value for a prime, zero otherwise */
/***************************************************************/
int test_prime(unsigned long N)
{
   /* local buffer for primes from the file */
   unsigned long buffer[MEM_PRIMES];
```

```
      /* Loop counter */
      int i = 0;
      int k = 0;

      if(nrec > 0)            /* Have we written records? */
      {
        if((pfile = fopen(myfile, "rb")) == NULL)  /* Then open the file */
        {
          printf("\nUnable to open %s to read\n", myfile);
          abort();
        }

        for(i = 0; i < nrec ; i++)
        { /* Check against primes on file first */

          /* Read primes */
          fread(buffer, sizeof(long), MEM_PRIMES, pfile);

          if((k = check(buffer, MEM_PRIMES, N)) >= 0)    /* Prime or not? */
          {
            fclose(pfile);                         /* Yes, so close the file */
            return k;                              /* 1 for prime, 0 for not */
          }
        }
        fclose(pfile);                             /* Close the file         */
      }

      return check(primes, index, N);  /* Check against primes in memory */
    }
```

The function **test_prime()** accepts a candidate value as an argument, and returns 1 if it is prime, and 0 if it isn't.

If we've written anything to the file, this will be indicated by a positive value of **nrec**. In this case, the primes in the file need to be used as divisors first, since they are lower than those in memory as we compute them in sequence.

> *As you may remember, a prime is a number with no factors other than 1 and itself. It's sufficient to check whether a number is divisible by any of the primes less than the square root of the number, to verify that it is prime. This follows from the simple logic that any exact divisor greater than the square root must have an associated factor (the result of the division) that is less than the square root.*

To read the file, the function executes this statement:

```
      fread(buffer, sizeof(long), MEM_PRIMES, pfile);
```

This reads one block of primes from the file into the array **buffer**. The second argument defines the size of each object to be read, and **MEM_PRIMES** defines the number of objects of the specified size to be read.

Having read a block, the following check is executed:

```
if((k = check(buffer, MEM_PRIMES, N)) >= 0)    /* Prime or not? */
{
  fclose(pfile);                               /* Yes, so close the file */
  return k;                                    /* 1 for prime, 0 for not */
}
```

Within the **if** condition, the function **check()** is called to determine whether any of the array elements divide into the prime candidate with no remainder. This function returns 0 if an exact division is found, indicating the candidate is not prime. If no exact division is found with primes up to the square root of the candidate value, 1 is returned indicating that the candidate must be prime. If the value returned from **check()** is 0 or 1, in both cases we have finished checking so the file is closed and the same value is returned to **main()**.

The value -1 is returned from **check()** if no exact division has been found, but the square root of the test value has not been exceeded. We don't need to check for the -1 return explicitly, since it is the only possibility left if it isn't 0 or 1. In this case, the next block, if there is one, is read from the file in the next iteration of the **for** loop.

If the contents of the file have been exhausted without determining whether **N** is prime or not, the **for** loop will end, we will close the file, and execute the statement:

```
return check(primes, index, N);  /* Check against primes in memory */
```

Here, the test value is tried against any primes in the array **primes[]** in memory by the function **check()**. If a prime is found, the **check()** function will return 1 and this value will be returned. Otherwise the function will return 0.

The code for the function **check()** is as follows:

```
/***************************************************************/
/* Function to check whether an integer, N, is divisble by any */
/* of the elements in the array pbuffer up to the square root of N.*/
/* First parameter buffer - an array of primes                 */
/* second parameter count - number of elements in pbuffer      */
/* Third parameter N - the value to be checked                 */
/* Return value - 1 if N is prime, zero if N is not a prime,   */
/*                -1 for more checks                           */
/***************************************************************/
int check(unsigned long buffer[], int count, unsigned long N)
{
   int i = 0;           /* Loop counter */
   /* Upper limit */
   unsigned long root_N = (unsigned long)(1.0 + sqrt((double)N));

   for(i = 0 ; i<count ; i++)
   {
     if(N % buffer[i] == 0UL ) /* Exact division?            */
       return 0;               /* Then not a prime           */
```

```
      if(buffer[i] > root_N)     /* Divisor exceeds square root? */
        return 1;                /* Then must be a prime         */
    }
  return -1;                     /* More checks necessary...     */
}
```

The role of this function is to check whether any of the primes contained in the array, **buffer[]**, divide exactly into the test value supplied as the second argument. The local variables in the function are declared in the statements:

```
    int i = 0;            /* Loop counter */
    /* Upper limit */
    unsigned long root_N = (unsigned long)(1.0 + sqrt((double)N));
```

The integer variable, **root_N**, will hold the upper limit for divisors to be checked against the trial value. Only divisors less than the square root of the test value **N** are tried.

The checking is done in the **for** loop:

```
    for(i = 0 ; i<count ; i++)
    {
      if(N % buffer[i] == 0UL ) /* Exact division?              */
        return 0;               /* Then not a prime             */

      if(buffer[i] > root_N)    /* Divisor exceeds square root? */
        return 1;               /* Then must be a prime         */
    }
```

This steps through each of the divisors in the **buffer[]** array. If a divisor is found, the function will end and return 0 to indicate that the value is not prime. If we arrive at a divisor that is greater than **root_N**, we've tried all those lower than this value so **N** must be prime and we return 1. If the loop ends, we have not found an exact divisor, but we haven't tried all values up to **root_N**, so the function returns -1 to indicate there is more checking to be done.

The last function we need to define is designed to output all the primes written to the file:

```
/* Function to output primes from the file */
void put_primes(void)
{
   unsigned long buffer[MEM_PRIMES]; /* Buffer for a block of primes */
   int i = 0;                        /* Loop counter                 */
   int j = 0;                        /* Loop counter                 */

   if((pfile = fopen( myfile, "rb"))==NULL) /* Open the file         */
   {
     printf("\nUnable to open %s to read primes for output\n", myfile);
     abort();
   }

   for (i = 0 ; i< nrec ; i++)
   {
```

```
        /* Read a block of primes    */
        fread(buffer, sizeof(long), MEM_PRIMES, pfile);

        for(j = 0 ; j<MEM_PRIMES ; j++)   /* Display the primes */
        {
          if(j%5 == 0)                     /* Five to a line      */
            printf("\n");
          printf("%12lu", buffer[j]);      /* Output a prime      */
        }
      }
      fclose(pfile);                       /* Close the file      */
    }
```

The operation of the function **put_primes()** is very simple. Once the file is opened, blocks of primes are read into the array **buffer[]**, and as each is read, the **for** loop outputs the values to the screen, five to a line with a field width of 12. After all records have been read, the file is closed.

To run the program, you need to assemble all the functions that we've described into a single file, and compile it. You'll be able to get as many primes as your computer and your patience will permit.

A disadvantage with this program, when you have a large number of primes, is that the output whizzes by on the screen before you can inspect it. Several things could be done to fix this. You could write the output to the printer for a permanent record, instead of writing it to the screen. Or perhaps you could arrange for the program to display a prompt and wait for the user to press a key, between the output of one block and the next.

Moving around in a File

For many applications, we need to be able to access data in a file, other than in the sequential order we have used up to now. We can always find some information stored in the middle of a file by reading from the beginning, and continuing in sequence until you find what you want. But if we've written a few million items to the file, this may take some time.

Of course, to access data in random sequence requires that we have some means of knowing where the data we'd like to retrieve is stored in the file. Arranging for this is a complicated topic, in general. There are many different ways of constructing pointers or indexes to make direct access to the data in a file faster and easier. The basic idea is similar to that of an index to a book. You have a table of keys that identify the contents of each record in the file you might want, and each key has an associated position in the file defined where the data is stored.

Let's look at the basic tools in the library that we need to enable you to deal with this kind of file input/output.

File Positioning Operations

There are two aspects to file positioning: finding out where we are at a given point in a file; and moving to a given point in a file. The former is basic to the latter: if we never know where we are, we can never decide where we want to go.

455

A random point in a file can be accessed regardless of whether the file concerned was written in binary or text mode. However, working with text mode files can get rather complicated if you're using DOS on a PC. This results from the fact that the number of characters recorded in the file can be greater than the number you actually wrote. This is due to a `'\n'` character in memory translating into two characters when written to a file in text mode (carriage return - CR, and line feed - LF). Of course, your C library sorts everything out when you read the data back. The problem arises when you think a point in the file is 100 bytes from the beginning. If you subsequently write some different data that is the same length in memory, it will only be the same length on the file if it contains the same number of `'\n'` characters. For this reason, we shall side-step the complications of moving about in text files and concentrate our examples on the much more useful - and easier - context of binary files.

Finding Out Where You Are

We have two functions to tell us where we are, which are both very similar - but not identical. They each complement a different positioning function. The first is the function `ftell()`, which has the prototype:

```
long ftell(FILE *pfile);
```

so it accepts a file pointer as an argument, and returns a **long** integer value which specifies the current position in the file. This could be used with the file referenced by the pointer **pfile** that we have used previously, as in the statement:

```
fpos = ftell(pfile);
```

The **long** variable **fpos** now holds the current position in the file and, as we shall see, we can use this in a function call to return to this position at any subsequent time. The value is actually the offset in bytes from the beginning of the file.

The second function providing information on the current file position is a little more complicated. The prototype of the function is:

```
int fgetpos(FILE *pfile, fpos_t *position);
```

The first parameter is our old friend the file pointer. The second parameter is a pointer to a type predefined in **stdio.h** called **fpos_t**. If you're curious about **fpos_t** then have a look at it in **stdio.h**; otherwise, don't worry too much about it.

This function is designed to be used with the positioning function **fsetpos()**, which we'll come to very shortly. The function **fgetpos()** returns zero if the operation is successful, and a non-zero integer value otherwise. Given that we've declared the variable **here** to be of type **fpos_t**, with a statement such as this:

```
fpos_t here = 0;
```

we could record the current position in the file with the statement:

```
fgetpos(pfile, &here);
```

This records the current file position in our variable **here**.

> *Note that we must declare a variable of type fpos_t. It's no good just declaring a pointer of type fpos_t* as there won't be any memory allocated to store the position data.*

Setting a Position in a File

As a complement to `ftell()` we have the function `fseek()` with the prototype:

```
int fseek(FILE *pfile, long offset, int origin);
```

The first parameter is a pointer to the file we are repositioning. The second and third parameters define where we want to go to. The second parameter is an offset from a reference point specified by the third parameter. The reference point can be one of three values that are specified by the predefined names **SEEK_SET**, which defines the beginning of the file, **SEEK_CUR**, which defines the current position in the file, and **SEEK_END**, which - as you might guess - defines the end of the file.

Of course, all three values are defined in the header file **stdio.h**. For a text mode file, the second argument must be a value returned by `ftell()` if we're to avoid getting lost. The third argument for text mode files must be **SEEK_SET**. So, for text mode files, all operations with `fseek()` are performed with reference to the beginning of the file.

For binary files, the offset argument is simply a relative byte count. We can therefore supply positive or negative values for the offset when the reference point is specified as **SEEK_CUR**.

We have `fsetpos()` to go with `fgetpos()`. This has the rather straightforward prototype:

```
int fsetpos(FILE *pfile, fpos_t *position);
```

The first parameter is a pointer to the file set up with `fopen()`, and the second is a pointer of the type you can see. We can't go far wrong with this one really. We could use it with a statement such as this:

```
fsetpos(pfile, &here);
```

where the variable **here** was previously set by a call to `fgetpos()`. As with `fgetpos()`, a non-zero value is returned on error. Since this function is designed to work with a value returned by `fgetpos()`, we can only use it to get to a place in a file that we've been to before, whereas `fseek()` allows us to go to any specific position.

Note that the verb *seek* is used to refer to operations of moving the read/write heads of a disk drive directly to a specific position in the file. This is why the function `fseek()` is so named.

With a file that we've opened for update, by specifying the mode as **"rb+"** or **"wb+"** for example, either a read or a write may be safely carried out on the file after executing either of the file positioning functions, `fsetpos()` or `fseek()`. This is regardless of what the previous operation on the file was.

Try It Out - Random File Access

To exercise our new found skills with files, we can modify a program from the previous chapter to allow us to keep a dossier on family members. In this case, we'll create a file containing data on all of them, and then process the file to output data on each of them and their parents. This example has been coded to illustrate aspects of using the C language, rather than elegance or consistency in usage. The structures used only extend to a minimum range of members in each case. You can, of course, embellish these to hold any kind of scuttlebutt you like on your relatives.

Let's look at the function **main()** first:

```
/* Example 12.5 Investigating the family.*/
#include <stdio.h>
#include <stdlib.h>
#include <string.h>

char myfile[] = "C:\\myfile.bin"; /* Physical file name    */
FILE *pfile = NULL;               /* File pointer          */

struct Date                       /* Structure for a date  */
{
   int day;
   int month;
   int year;
};

typedef struct family       /* Family structure declaration */
{
   struct Date dob;
   char name[20];
   char pa_name[20];
   char ma_name[20];
}Family;

/* Function prototypes */
int get_person(Family *pfamily);        /* Input function           */
void show_person_data(void);            /* Output function          */
void get_parent_dob(Family *pfamily);   /* Function to find pa & ma */

void main()
{
   Family member;                           /* Stores a family structure */
   Family *pmember = &member;        /* Points to the family structure */

   if((pfile = fopen(myfile, "wb")) == NULL)
   {
     printf("\nUnable to open %s for writing.\n", myfile);
     abort();
   }
```

```
      while(get_person(pmember))              /* As long as we have input */
        fwrite(pmember, sizeof member, 1, pfile);  /*    write it away */

      fclose(pfile);                    /* Close the file now its written */

      show_person_data();               /* Show what we can find out     */

      if(remove(myfile))
        printf("\nUnable to delete %s.\n", myfile);
      else
        printf("\nDeleted %s OK.\n", myfile);
    }
```

How It Works

After the **#include** statements, we have the global variables and structure definitions. We've seen all of these in previous examples. **Family** is not a variable, but has been declared as a type name for the structure **family**. This will allow us to declare **Family** type objects without having to use the keyword **struct**. Following the structure declarations, we have the prototypes for the three functions that we are using in addition to **main()**.

Since we want to use the file positioning functions as well as the basic read and write operations, the example has been designed to exercise these as well. We get the input on one person at a time in the function **get_person()**, the data being stored in the structure pointed to by **pmember**. We write each structure to the file as soon as it has been received, and the input process ceases when the function **get_person()** returns zero.

When the **while** loop ends, the input file is closed and the function **show_person_data()** is called. Within this function we use the file position getting and setting functions. Lastly, the file is deleted from the disk by the function **remove()**.

The code for the input function, **get_person()**, is as follows:

```
/* Function to input data on Family members */
int get_person( Family *temp)
{
   static char more = '\0';      /* Test value for ending input */

   printf("\nDo you want to enter details of a%s person (Y or N)? ",
                                     more != '\0'?"nother " : "" );
   scanf(" %c", &more);

   if(more == 'N' || more == 'n')
          return 0;

   printf("\nEnter the name of the person: ");
   scanf("%s", temp->name);     /* Read the Family's name       */

   printf("\nEnter %s's date of birth (day month year); ", temp->name);
   scanf("%d %d %d", &temp->dob.day, &temp->dob.month, &temp->dob.year);

   printf("\nWho is %s's father? ", temp->name);
   scanf("%s", temp->pa_name); /* Get the father's name        */
```

```
    printf("\nWho is %s's mother? ", temp->name);
    scanf("%s", temp->ma_name); /* Get the mother's name         */

    return 1;
}
```

This function is fairly self-explanatory. None of the mechanisms involved in this function are new to you. An indicator, **more**, controls whether reading data continues or not, and it is set by the input following the first prompt. It is defined as **static** so the variable and its value persists in the program from one call of **get_person()** to the next. This allows the prompt to work correctly in selecting a slightly different message for the second and subsequent iterations.

If no data input takes place, triggered when **'N'** or **'n'** has been entered in response to the initial prompt in the function, 0 is returned. If more data entry occurs, it is entered into the appropriate structure members and 1 is returned.

The next function generates the output for each person, including the date of birth of both parents, if they have been recorded. The code for this function is as follows:

```
/* Function to output data on people on file    */
void show_person_data(void)
{
   Family member;                 /* Structure to hold data from file  */
   Family *pmember = &member;  /* Pointer to Family structure        */
   fpos_t current = 0;            /* File position                     */

   pfile = fopen(myfile, "rb"); /* Open file for binary read   */

   /* Read data on person */
   while(fread(pmember, sizeof member, 1, pfile))
   {
     fgetpos(pfile, &current);   /* Save current position       */
     printf("\n\n%s's father is %s, and mother is %s.",
             pmember->name, pmember->pa_name, pmember->ma_name);
     get_parent_dob(pmember);   /* Get parent data               */
     fsetpos(pfile, &current);   /* Position file to read next */
   }
    fclose(pfile);                 /* Close the file             */
}
```

This function processes each structure in sequence from the file. At the outset, an object of type **Family** and a pointer to it are declared in the statements:

```
   Family member;                 /* Structure to hold data from file  */
   Family *pmember = &member;  /* Pointer to Family structure        */
```

The first variable declared is **member** of type **Family**, and the second is of type pointer to **Family** and is initialized with the address of the first variable declared, **member**. The variable **member** has space allocated for the structure type, and **pmember** provides a convenient working pointer.

Next, a local variable, **current**, is declared with the statement:

```
fpos_t current = 0;          /* File position            */
```

This declares **current** as type **fpos_t**. This variable will be used to remember the current position in the file. The function **get_parent_dob()** is called later in this function, which also accesses the file. It is therefore necessary to remember the file position of the next structure to be read on each iteration before calling **get_parent_dob()**.

After opening the file for binary read operations, all of the processing takes place in a loop controlled by:

```
while(fread(pmember, sizeof member, 1, pfile))
```

This uses the technique of reading the file within the loop condition, and using the value returned by the function **fread()** as the determinant of whether the loop continues or not. If the function returns 1, the loop continues, and when 0 is returned the loop is terminated.

Within the loop we have the statements:

```
fgetpos(pfile, &current);   /* Save current position    */
printf("\n\n%s's father is %s, and mother is %s.",
        pmember->name, pmember->pa_name, pmember->ma_name);
get_parent_dob(pmember);    /* Get parent data          */
fsetpos(pfile, &current);   /* Position file to read next */
```

First, the current position in the file is saved, and the parents of the current person pointed to by **pmember** are displayed. We then call the function **get_parent_dob()**, which will search the file for parent entries. On returning after the call to this function, the file position is unknown, so a call to **fsetpos()** is made to restore it to the position required for the next structure to be read. After all the structures have been processed, the **while** loop terminates and the file is closed.

The function to find the dates of birth for the parents of an individual is as follows:

```
/* Function to find parents' dates of birth. */
void get_parent_dob(Family *pmember)
{
   Family testmem;              /* Stores a relative       */
   Family *ptestmem = &testmem; /* Pointer to the relative  */
   int num_found = 0;           /* Count of relatives found */

   rewind(pfile);               /* Set file to the beginning */

   /* Get the stuff on a relative */
   while(fread(ptestmem, sizeof(Family), 1, pfile))
   {
     if(strcmp(pmember->pa_name, ptestmem->name) == 0)    /*Is it pa? */
     { /* We have found dear old dad */
       printf("\n Pa was born on %d/%d/%d.",
            ptestmem->dob.day, ptestmem->dob.month, ptestmem->dob.year);
```

```
            if(++num_found == 2)    /* Increment parent count    */
              return;               /* We got both so go home    */
       }
       else
         if(strcmp(pmember->ma_name, ptestmem->name) == 0) /*Is it ma? */
         { /* We have found dear old ma */
           printf("\n Ma was born on %d/%d/%d.",
                   ptestmem->dob.day, ptestmem->dob.month, ptestmem-
>dob.year);

            if(++num_found == 2)   /* Increment parent count    */
                return;            /* We got both so go home    */
         }
     }
  }
```

As the file has already been opened by the calling program, it's only necessary to set it back to the beginning with the **rewind()** function before beginning processing. The file is then read sequentially, searching each structure that is read for a match with either parent name. The search mechanism for the father is contained in the statements:

```
     if(strcmp(pmember->pa_name, ptestmem->name) == 0)     /*Is it pa? */
     { /* We have found dear old dad */
       printf("\n Pa was born on %d/%d/%d.",
             ptestmem->dob.day, ptestmem->dob.month, ptestmem->dob.year);

       if(++num_found == 2)     /* Increment parent count    */
         return;                /* We got both so go home    */
     }
```

The name entry for the father of the person indicated by **pmember** is compared with the name member in the structure indicated by **ptestmem**. The pointer, **ptestmem**, has the address of the family structure that was last read as a candidate parent. If the father check fails, the function continues with an identical mother check.

If a parent is found, the date of birth information is displayed. A count is kept in **num_found** of the number of parents discovered in the file, and the function is exited if both have been found. The function ends in any event after all structures have been read from the file.

To run this program you need to enter **main()** and the other functions into a single file. You can then compile and execute it. Of course, the example could have been written equally well using **ftell()** and **fseek()** as positioning functions.

As in the previous examples in this chapter, the program uses a specific file name, on the assumption that the file doesn't already exist when the program is run. There is a way in C to create temporary files that get around this.

Using Temporary Work Files

Very often we need a work file just for the duration of a program. It will only be used to store intermediate results and can be thrown away when the program is finished. Our example calculating primes in this chapter is a good example. We really only needed the file during the calculation.

We have a choice of two functions to help with temporary file usage, and they each have their advantages and disadvantages.

Creating a Temporary Work File

The first function will create a temporary file automatically. Its prototype is:

```
FILE *tmpfile(void);
```

It takes no arguments and returns a pointer to the temporary file. If the file cannot be created for any reason, for example if the disk is full, the function returns **NULL.** The file is created and opened for update, so it can be written and read, but obviously it needs to be in that order. You can only get out what you put in. The file is automatically deleted on exit from your program, so there is no need to worry about any mess left behind. You will never know what the file is called, and since it doesn't last, it doesn't matter.

The disadvantage of this function is that the file will be deleted as soon as you close it. This means you cannot close the file, having written it in one part of the program, and then reopen it in another part of the program to read the data. You must keep the file open for as long as you need access to the data. A simple illustration of creating a temporary file is provided by the statements:

```
FILE pfile;           /* File pointer                  */
pfile = tmpfile();    /* Get pointer to temporary file */
```

Creating a Unique File Name

The second possibility is to use a function that provides you with a unique file name. Whether this ends up as a temporary file or not is up to you. The prototype for this function is:

```
char *tmpnam(char *filename);
```

If the argument to the function is **NULL**, the file name is generated in an internal static object and a pointer to that object is returned. If you want the name stored in a **char** array that you declare yourself, it must be at least **L_tmpnam** characters long, where **L_tmpnam** is a constant predefined in **stdio.h**. In this case, the file name is stored in the array you specify as an argument, and a pointer to your array is also returned. So, to take the first possibility, we can create a unique file with the statements:

```
FILE *pfile = NULL;
char *filename = NULL;
pfile = fopen(filename = tmpnam(NULL), "wb+");
```

Here, we've declared our file pointer, **pfile**, and our pointer filename that will contain the address of the temporary file name. We've combined the call to **tmpnam()** with the call to open the file by putting the assignment as the first argument to **fopen()**. Because the argument to **tmpnam()** is **NULL** the file name will be generated as an internal static object whose address will be placed in our pointer **filename**.

Don't be tempted to write:

```
pfile = fopen(tmpnam(NULL), "wb+");
```

If you do, you no longer have access to the file name, so you cannot use **remove()** to delete the file.

If you want to create the array to hold the file name yourself, you could write:

```
FILE *pfile = NULL;
char filename[L_tmpnam];
pfile = fopen(tmpnam(filename), "wb+");
```

Remember - the assistance we've obtained from the library is just to provide a unique name. It is your responsibility to delete any files created.

> *You should also note that you'll be limited to a maximum number of unique names from this function in your program, but it will be at least 25, and with some implementations a great deal more.*

Designing a Program

Now we've come to the end of this chapter we can put what we have learnt into practice with our final program.

The Problem

The problem we're going to solve is to write a file viewer program. This will display any file in hexadecimal representation and as ASCII characters.

The Analysis

The program will open the file as binary read-only, then display the information in two columns, the first being the hexadecimal representation of the bytes in the file, the second being the bytes represented as ASCII characters. The file name will be supplied as either a command line argument, or, if that isn't supplied, then the program will ask for the file name.

The stages are then:

1 If not supplied, get the file name from the user

2 Open the file

3   Read and display the contents of the file

The Solution

1   We can easily check to see if the filename appears on the command line by specifying that the function **main()** has parameters. Up to now, we've chosen to ignore the possibility of parameters passed to **main()**, but when **main()** is called, two parameters are passed to it. The first parameter is an integer indicating the number of words in the command line, and the second is an array of pointers to objects of type **char**. The first of these objects is usually a string containing the name used to start the program on the command line, and the remaining objects are strings corresponding to the other words appearing on the command line. Of course, this mechanism allows an arbitrary number of values to be entered on the command line and passed to **main()**.

If the value of the first argument is only 1, then there are no words on the command line other than the program name, so we have to ask for the file name to be entered:

```
/* Example 12.6 Viewing the contents of a file */
#include <stdio.h>

int main(int argc, char *argv[])
{
   char filename[80];  /* Stores the file name */

   if(argc == 1)       /* No file name on command line? */
   {
     printf("Please enter a filename: "); /* Prompt for input        */
     gets(filename);                       /* Get the file name entered */
   }
   return 0;
}
```

Note that we also have the return type for **main()** specified as type **int**. The value returned from **main()** is passed to the operating system, and can be used as an indicator of whether the program ran successfully or not.

2   If the first argument to **main()** is not 1, then we have at least one more argument, which we assume is the file name. We therefore copy the string pointed to by **argv[1]** to the variable **filename**. Assuming that we have a valid file name, we can open the file ready to start reading in the bytes:

```
/* Example 12.6 Viewing the contents of a file */
#include <stdio.h>

int main(int argc, char *argv[])
{
   char filename[80];  /* Stores the file name */
   FILE *pfile;        /* File pointer         */

   if(argc == 1)       /* No file name on command line? */
   {
```

```
      printf("Please enter a filename: "); /* Prompt for input
*/
      gets(filename);                          /* Get the file name entered */
    }
    else
      strcpy(filename, argv[1]);   /* Get 2nd command line string   */

      /* File can be opened OK?            */
      if((pfile = fopen(filename, "rb")) == NULL)
      {
        printf("Sorry, can't open %s", filename);
        return -1;
      }
      fclose(pfile);                 /* Close the file               */
    return 0;
}
```

We've put the call to the **fclose()** function to close the file at the end of the program so that we don't forget about it later. Also, we've used a return value of -1 for the program to indicate when an error has occurred.

3   We can now output the file contents. We'll do this by reading the file one byte at a time, and saving this data in a buffer. Once the buffer is full, or the end of file has been reached, we output the buffer in the format we want. When we output the ASCII version of the data we must first check that the character is printable, otherwise strange things may start happening to the screen. We'll use the function **isprint()**, declared in **ctype.h**, for this. If the character is not printable, we'll print a period instead.

Here's the complete code for the program:

```
/* Example 12.6 Viewing the contents of a file */
#include <stdio.h>
#include <ctype.h>
#include <string.h>

#define DISPLAY 80        /* Length of display line */
#define PAGE_LENGTH 20    /* Lines per page         */

int main(int argc, char *argv[])
{
   char filename[80];  /* Stores the file name */
   FILE *pfile;            /* File pointer          */
   unsigned char buffer[DISPLAY/4 - 1];  /* File input buffer */
   int count = 0;          /* Count of characters in buffer */
   int lines = 0;          /* Number of lines displayed     */
   int i = 0;              /* Loop counter                  */

   if(argc == 1)       /* No file name on command line? */
   {
     printf("Please enter a filename: "); /* Prompt for input       */
     gets(filename);                          /* Get the file name entered */
   }
   else
     strcpy(filename, argv[1]);  /* Get 2nd command line string   */
```

```
  /* File can be opened OK?        */
  if((pfile = fopen(filename, "rb")) == NULL)
  {
    printf("Sorry, can't open %s", filename);
    return -1;
  }
while(!feof(pfile))             /* Continue until end of file */
{
  if(count < sizeof buffer) /* If the buffer is not full  */
    /* Read a character      */
    buffer[count++] = (unsigned char)fgetc(pfile);
  else
  { /* Output the buffer contents, first as hexadecimal */
    for(count = 0; count < sizeof buffer; count++)
      printf("%02X ", buffer[count]);
    printf("| ");                   /* Output separator     */

    /* Now display buffer contents as characters */
    for(count = 0; count < sizeof buffer; count++)
      printf("%c", isprint(buffer[count]) ? buffer[count]:'.');
    printf("\n");            /* End the line         */
    count = 0;              /* Reset count          */

    if(!(++lines%PAGE_LENGTH))   /* End of page?       */
      if(getchar()=='E')         /* Wait for Enter      */
        return 0;                /* E pressed           */
  }
}

/* Display the last line, first as hexadecimal */
for(i = 0; i < sizeof buffer; i++)
  if(i < count)
    printf("%02X ", buffer[i]);  /* Output hexadecimal  */
  else
    printf("   ");               /* Output spaces       */
printf("| ");                    /* Output separator    */

/* Display last line as characters */
for(i = 0; i < count; i++)
  /* Output character     */
  printf("%c",isprint(buffer[i]) ? buffer[i]:'.');
/* End the line         */
printf("\n");
fclose(pfile);                   /* Close the file        */
return 0;
}
```

The symbol **DISPLAY** specifies the width of a line on the screen for output, and the symbol **PAGE_LENGTH** specifies the number of lines per page. We'll arrange to display a page, then wait for *Enter* to be pressed before displaying the next page, thus avoiding the whole file whizzing by before you can read it.

We declare the buffer to hold input from the file as:

```
unsigned char buffer[DISPLAY/4 - 1];  /* File input buffer */
```

The expression for the array dimension arises from the fact that we'll need four characters on the screen to display each character from the file, plus one separator. Each character will be displayed as two hexadecimal digits plus a space, and as a single character, making four characters in all.

We continue reading the as long as the **while** loop condition is true:

```
while(!feof(pfile))           /* Continue until end of file */
```

The library function, **feof()**, returns true if **EOF** was read from the file specified by the argument, and false otherwise.

We fill the array **buffer[]** with characters from the file in the **if**:

```
if(count < sizeof buffer) /* If the buffer is not full  */
  /* Read a character    */
  buffer[count++] = (unsigned char)fgetc(pfile);
```

When **count** exceeds the capacity of **buffer[]**, the **else** clause will be executed to output the contents of the buffer:

```
else
{ /* Output the buffer contents, first as hexadecimal */
  for(count = 0; count < sizeof buffer; count++)
    printf("%02X ", buffer[count]);
  printf("| ");                    /* Output separator    */

  /* Now display buffer contents as characters */
  for(count = 0; count < sizeof buffer; count++)
    printf("%c", isprint(buffer[count]) ? buffer[count]:'.');
  printf("\n");          /* End the line        */
  count = 0;             /* Reset count         */

  if(!(++lines%PAGE_LENGTH))    /* End of page?        */
    if(getchar()=='E')          /* Wait for Enter      */
      return 0;                 /* E pressed           */
}
```

The first **for** loop outputs the contents of **buffer[]** as hexadecimal characters. We then output a separator character, and execute the next **for** loop to output the same data as characters. The conditional operator in the second argument to **printf()** ensures that non-printing characters are output as a period.

468

The **if** statement increments the line count, **lines**, and for every **PAGE_LENGTH** number of lines, waits for a character to be entered. If you press *Enter* the next page full will be displayed, but if you press **'E'** and then *Enter*, the program will end. This provides you with an opportunity of escaping from continuing to output the contents of a file that is larger than you thought.

The final couple of **for** loops are similar to those that we've just seen. The only difference is that spaces are output for array elements that do not contain file characters. An example of the output is shown below; it shows part of the source file for the self-same program.

```
Please enter a filename: E:\ex12_6.c
2F 2A 20 45 78 61 6D 70 6C 65 20 31 32 2E 36 20 56 69 65 | /* Example 12.6 Vie
77 69 6E 67 20 74 68 65 20 63 6F 6E 74 65 6E 74 73 20 6F | wing the contents o
66 20 61 20 66 69 6C 65 20 2A 2F 0D 0A 23 69 6E 63 6C 75 | f a file */..#inclu
64 65 20 3C 73 74 64 69 6F 2E 68 3E 0D 0A 23 69 6E 63 6C | de <stdio.h>..#incl
75 64 65 20 3C 63 74 79 70 65 2E 68 3E 20 0D 0A 23 69 6E | ude <ctype.h> ..#in
63 6C 75 64 65 20 3C 73 74 72 69 6E 67 2E 68 3E 20 0D 0A | clude <string.h> ..
23 64 65 66 69 6E 65 20 44 49 53 50 4C 41 59 20 38 30 20 | #define DISPLAY 80
20 20 20 20 20 20 20 20 20 20 20 20 20 20 20 20 20 20 20 |
20 20 20 20 20 20 20 20 20 2F 2A 20 4C 65 6E 67 74 68 20 |        /* Length
6F 66 20 64 69 73 70 6C 61 79 20 6C 69 6E 65 20 20 20 20 | of display line
20 20 20 20 2A 2F 0D 0A 0D 0A 69 6E 74 20 6D 61 69 6E 28 |     */....int main(
69 6E 74 20 61 72 67 63 2C 20 63 68 61 72 20 2A 61 72 67 | int argc, char *arg
76 5B 5D 29 0D 0A 7B 0D 0A 20 20 63 68 61 72 20 66 69 6C | v[])..{..  char fil
65 6E 61 6D 65 5B 38 30 5D 3B 20 20 20 20 20 20 20 20 20 | ename[80];
20 20 20 20 20 20 20 20 20 20 20 20 20 20 20 20 20 20 2F |                   /
2A 20 53 74 6F 72 65 73 20 74 68 65 20 66 69 6C 65 20 6E | * Stores the file n
61 6D 65 20 20 20 20 20 20 20 20 20 20 2A 2F 0D 0A 20 20 | ame         */..
46 49 4C 45 20 2A 70 66 69 6C 65 3B 20 20 20 20 20 20 20 | FILE *pfile;
20 20 20 20 20 20 20 20 20 20 20 20 20 20 20 20 20 20 20 |
20 20 20 20 20 20 20 2F 2A 20 46 69 6C 65 20 70 6F 69 6E |        /* File poin
```

Summary

Within this chapter, we have covered all of the basic tools necessary to provide you with the ability to program the complete spectrum of file functions. The degree to which these have been demonstrated in examples has been, of necessity, relatively limited. There are many ways of applying these tools to provide more sophisticated ways of managing and retrieving information in a file. For example, it's possible to write index information into the file, either as a specific index at a known place in the file, often the beginning, or as position pointers within the blocks of data, rather like the pointers in a linked list. You should experiment with file operations until you feel confident of your understanding of the mechanisms involved.

While the functions we've discussed are quite comprehensive, they are not exhaustive. You should find that the input/output library provided with your compiler provides quite a few additional functions that provide even more options in how you handle your file operations.

Supporting Facilities

At this point, you have covered the complete C language, as well as the important library functions. You should be reasonably confident in programming all aspects of the language. If you aren't, it's simply because you need more practice. Once you've learnt the elements of the language, competence is down to practice, practice, and more practice.

In this final chapter, we will drag together a few loose ends. We'll delve deeper into the capabilities you have available through the preprocessor, and we'll look at a few more library functions that you'll find useful.

In this chapter, you will learn:

- More about the preprocessor and its operation
- How to write preprocessor macros
- What logical preprocessor directives are, and how you can use them
- What conditional compilation is, and how you can apply it
- More about the debugging methods that are available to you
- How you use some of the additional library functions that are available

The Preprocessor

As you're surely aware by now, the **preprocessor** is a facility that's exercised before your C program code is compiled to machine instructions. It can execute a range of service operations specified by **preprocessor directives** that are recognized by the symbol **#**, the first character of each preprocessor directive. The preprocessor provides a means of manipulating and modifying your C source code prior to compilation. Once the preprocessor phase is completed, and all preprocessor directives have been analyzed and executed, the compiler begins the compile phase proper, which generates the machine code equivalent of your program.

We have already used preprocessor directives in all our examples, and you are familiar with both the **#include** and **#define** directives. There are a number of other directives that add considerable flexibility to the way in which you specify your programs. Keep in mind, as we proceed, that all these are preprocessor operations that occur *before* your program is compiled. They modify the set of statements that constitute your program. They aren't involved in the execution of your program at all.

Including Header Files in Your Programs

A header file is any external file, usually stored on disk, whose contents are included into your program by use of the **#include** preprocessor directive. We are completely familiar with statements such as:

```
#include <stdio.h>
```

This fetches the standard library header file supporting input/output operations into your program. This is a particular case of the general statement for including standard libraries into your program:

```
#include <standard_library_file_name>
```

Any library header file name can appear between the angled brackets. If you include a header file that you don't use, the only effect (apart from slightly confusing anyone reading the program) is to extend the compilation time.

You can include your own source files into your program with a slightly different **#include** statement. A typical example might be:

```
#include "myfile.h"
```

This statement will introduce the contents of the file named between double quotes into the program in place of the **#include** directive. The contents of any file can be included into your program by this means. You simply specify the name of the file between quotes, as I've shown in the example. With the majority of compilers, you can specify the file name with either upper- or lower-case characters. Also, you can call the file whatever name you like, and you don't have to use the extension **.h**, although it's a convention commonly adhered to by most programmers in C.

The difference between using this form and using angled brackets lies in the source assumed for the required file. The precise operation is compiler dependent and will be described in the compiler documentation, but usually the first form (with the brackets) will search the default header file directory for the required file, whereas the second will search the source directory followed by the default header file directory.

You can use this mechanism for dividing your program into several files, and of course for managing the declarations for any library functions of your own. A very common use of this facility is to create a header file containing all the function prototypes and global variables. These can then be managed as a separate unit and included at the beginning of the program. You need to avoid duplicating information if you include more than one file into your program, as duplicate code will often cause compilation errors. We shall see later in this chapter how the preprocessor provides some facilities for ensuring that any given block of code will appear only once in your program, even if you inadvertently include it several times.

> *A file introduced into your program by a **#include** statement may itself contain another **#include** statement. If so, the preprocessor will process the second **#include** in the same way as the first, and continue processing until there are no more **#include** statements in the program.*

External Variables and Functions

With a program made up of several files, you will frequently find that you want to use a global variable that's defined in another file. You can do this by declaring the variable as **external** to the current file using the **extern** keyword. For example, if we have global variables defined in another file with the statements:

```
int number = 0;
long array[20] = { 0L };
```

Then in the function where we want to access these, we can specify that they're external using the statements:

```
extern int number;
extern long array[20];
```

These statements do not create these variables – they just identify that they are defined elsewhere for the rest of this source file. The variables must be declared somewhere else in the program – usually in another source file. If you want to make these external variables accessible to all functions within the current file, then you should declare them as external at the very beginning of the file. With programs comprising several files, it's common practice to place all global variables at the beginning of one file, and all the **extern** statements in a header file. The **extern** statements can then be incorporated into any subsequent program files by using a **#include** directive.

> *Only one declaration of each global variable is allowed in a file. Of course, they may be declared as external in as many files as necessary.*

Substitutions in Your Program

The simplest kind of symbol substitution you can make is one we've already seen. For example, the preprocessor directive to substitute the specified numeric value, wherever the character string **PI** occurs, is as follows:

```
#define PI 3.14159265
```

Apart from the fact that **PI** *looks* like a variable, this has nothing to do with variables. Here, the identifier **PI** is a token, rather like a voucher, which is exchanged for the sequence of digits specified. When your program is ready to be compiled after preprocessing has been completed, the string **PI** will no longer appear, having been replaced by its definition wherever it appears by the preprocessor. The general form of this sort of preprocessor directive is:

```
#define identifier sequence_of_characters
```

Here, **identifier** conforms to the usual definition of an identifier in C, as any sequence of letters and digits, the first of which is a letter, and where the underline character counts as a letter. Note that the replacement for identifier can be *any* sequence of characters – not just digits.

A very common use of the **#define** directive is to define array dimensions by way of a substitution, to allow a number of array dimensions to be determined by a single token. Then, only one directive in the program needs to be modified in order to alter the dimensions of a number of arrays in the program. This helps considerably in minimizing errors when such changes are necessary. For example:

```
#define DIMENSION 50
int array1[DIMENSION] = { 0 };
int array2[DIMENSION] = { 0 };
int array3[DIMENSION] = { 0 };
```

The dimensions of all three arrays can be changed by modifying the single **#define** statement, and of course the array declarations affected can be anywhere in the program file. The advantages of this approach in a large program involving dozens or even hundreds of functions should be obvious. Not only is it easy to make a change, but using this approach ensures that the same value is being used throughout a program. This is especially important with large projects involving several programmers working together to produce the final end product.

I have used numerical substitution in the last two examples, but as I said, you are in no way limited to this. You could write, for example,

```
#define Black White
```

to cause any occurrence of **Black** in your program to be replaced by **White**. The sequence of characters that is to replace the token identifier can be absolutely anything at all.

Macro Substitutions

A macro is based on the ideas implicit in the **#define** directive examples we have seen so far, but provides a greater range of possible results by allowing **multiple parameterized substitutions**. This not only involves substitution of a fixed sequence of characters for a token identifier, but also allows parameters to be specified, which may themselves be replaced by argument values, wherever the parameter appears in the substitution sequence. Let's look at an example:

```
#define Print(My_var) printf("%d", My_var)
```

This directive provides for two levels of substitution. There is the substitution for **Print(My_var)** by the string immediately following it in the **#define** statement, and there is the possible substitution of alternatives for **My_var**. You could write, for example:

```
Print(ival);
```

The preprocessor would convert this to the statement:

```
printf("%d", ival);
```

You could use this directive to specify a **printf()** statement for an integer variable at various points in your program. A very common use for this kind of macro is to allow a very simple representation of a complicated function call in order to enhance the readability of a program.

Macros that Look Like Functions

The general form of the kind of substitution directive we have just discussed is:

```
#define identifier(list_of_identifiers) substitution_string
```

This shows that in the general case, multiple parameters are permitted, so we are able to define more complex substitutions.

> *You mustn't leave a space between the first identifier and the left parenthesis.*

To illustrate how you use this, we can define a macro for producing the maximum of two values with:

```
#define max(x, y) x>y ? x : y
```

We can then put this statement in our program:

```
result = max(myval, 99);
```

The preprocessor will expand it to:

```
result = myval>99 ? myval : 99;
```

It is important to be conscious of the substitution that is taking place, and not to think that this is a function. You can get some strange results otherwise, particularly if your substitution identifiers include an explicit or implicit assignment. For example, the following modest extension of our last example can produce an unexpected result:

```
result = max(myval++, 99);
```

The substitution process will generate the statement:

```
result = myval++>99 ? myval++ : 99;
```

If the value of **myval** is larger than 99, **myval** will be incremented twice. Note that it would *not* help to use parentheses in this situation. If you write the statement as:

```
result = max((myval++), 99);
```

The preprocessor will convert this to:

```
result = (myval++)>99 ? (myval++) : 99;
```

You need to be extremely cautious if you're writing macros that generate expressions of any kind. In addition to the multiple substitution trap we have just seen, precedence rules can also catch you out. A simple example will illustrate this. Suppose we write a macro for the product of two parameters:

```
#define product(m, n) m*n
```

If we then try to use this macro with the statement:

```
result = product(x, y + 1)
```

Then everything appears to work just fine, but we don't get the result we want, because the macro expands to:

```
result = x*y + 1
```

It could take a long time to discover that we aren't getting the product of the two parameters at all in this case, as there's no external indication of what's going on, but just an erroneous value propagating through our program. The solution is very simple: if you use macros to generate expressions, put parentheses around everything! We should rewrite our example as:

```
#define product(m, n) ((m)*(n))
```

Now, everything will work as it should. The inclusion of the outer parentheses may seem excessive, but since you don't know the context in which the macro expansion will be placed, it is safer to include them. If you imagine a macro that sums its parameters, you'll easily see that without the outer parentheses, there are many contexts in which you'll get a result that's different from what you expect. Even *with* parentheses, expanded expressions that repeat a parameter, such as the one we saw earlier that used the conditional operator, will still not work properly when the argument involves the increment or decrement operators.

Preprocessor Directives on Multiple Lines

A preprocessor directive must be a single logical line, but this doesn't prevent you from using the statement continuation character \, that we have already seen in the context of spreading a C language statement over several lines. We could write:

```
#define min(x, y) \
    ((x)<(y) ? (x) : (y))
```

Here, the directive definition continues on the second line with the first non-blank character found, so you can position the text on the second line wherever you feel looks best. Note that the \ must be the last character on the line, immediately before you press *Enter*.

Strings as Macro Arguments

String constants are a potential source of confusion when used with macros. The simplest string substitution is a single level definition, such as:

```
#define MYSTR "This string"
```

If you now write this statement:

```
printf("%s", MYSTR);
```

It will be converted into:

```
printf("%s", "This string");
```

Which should be what you're expecting. You couldn't use the **#define** statement without the quotes in the substitution sequence and expect to be able to put the quotes in your program text instead. For example, if you write:

```
#define MYSTR This string
...
printf("%s", "MYSTR");
```

There will be no substitution for **MYSTR** in the **printf()** function. Anything in quotes in your program is assumed to be a literal string, and so the preprocessor won't analyze it.

However, there's a special way of specifying that the substitution for a macro argument is to be implemented as a string. For example, you could specify a macro to display a string using the function **printf()** as:

```
#define PrintStr(arg) printf("%s", #arg)
```

The character **#** preceding the appearance of the parameter **arg** in the macro expansion indicates that the argument is to be surrounded by double quotes when the substitution is generated. Therefore, if you write this statement in your program:

```
PrintStr(Output);
```

The preprocessor will convert it to:

```
printf("%s", "Output");
```

You may be wondering why this apparent complication has been introduced into preprocessing. Well, without this facility you wouldn't be able to include a variable string in a macro definition at all. If you were to put double quotes around the macro parameter, the preprocessor wouldn't interpret it as a variable, but merely as a string with quotes around it. On the other hand, if you put the quotes in the macro expansion, the string between the quotes wouldn't be interpreted as a parameter variable identifier, but just as a string constant. So, what might appear to be an unnecessary complication at first sight is actually an essential tool for creating macros that allow strings between quotes to be created.

A common use of this mechanism is for converting a variable name to a string, such as in the directive:

```
#define show(var) printf("\n%s = %d", #var, var);
```

If we now write:

```
show(number);
```

This will generate the statement:

```
printf("\n%s = %d", "number", number);
```

You can also generate a substitution that would allow you to display a string with double quotes included. Assuming we have defined the macro **PrintStr** as above, and you write the statement:

```
PrintStr("Output");
```

It will be preprocessed into the statement:

```
printf("%s", "\"Output\"");
```

This is possible because the preprocessor is clever enough to recognize the need to put **\"** at each end to get a string including double quotes to be displayed correctly.

Joining Two Results of a Macro Expansion

There are times when you may wish to generate two results in a macro and join them together with no spaces between them. Suppose we try to define a macro to do this as:

```
#define join(a, b) ab
```

This can't work in the way we need it to. The definition of the expansion will be interpreted as **ab**, not as the parameter **a** followed by the parameter **b**. If we separate them with a blank, the result will be separated with a blank, which isn't what we want either. The preprocessor provides us with another operator to solve this problem. The solution is to specify the macro as:

```
#define join(a, b) a##b
```

The presence of the operator comprising the two characters **##** serves to separate the parameters, and to indicate to the preprocessor that the results of the two substitutions are to be joined. For example, writing the statement:

```
strlen(join(var, 123));
```

will result in:

```
strlen(var123);
```

This might be applied to synthesizing a variable name for some reason, or generating a format control string from two or more macro parameters.

Logical Preprocessor Directives

The last example we looked at appears to be of limited value, since it's hard to envisage when you would want simply to join **var** to **123**, since you could always use one parameter, and write **var123** as the argument. One aspect of preprocessing facilities that adds considerably more potential to the previous example is the possibility for multiple macro substitution, where the arguments for one macro are derived from substitutions defined in another. In our last example, both arguments to the **join()** macro could have been generated by other **#define** substitutions or macros. The preprocessor also supports directives that provide a logical **if** capability, which vastly expands the scope of what you can do with the preprocessor.

Conditional Compilation

The first logical directive we shall discuss allows you to test whether an identifier exists as a result of having been created in a previous **#define** statement. It takes the form:

```
#if defined identifier
```

If the specified **identifier** has been defined, then statements following the **#if** are executed until the statement

```
#endif
```

is reached. If the identifier hasn't been defined, the statements between the **#if** and the **#endif** will be skipped. This is the same logical process we use in C programming, except that here we are applying it to the generation of modified program statements.

You can also test for the absence of an identifier. In fact, this tends to be used more frequently than the form we have just seen. The general form of this directive is:

```
#if !defined identifier
```

Here, the statements following the **#if** down to the **#endif** will be executed if the identifier *hasn't* previously been defined. This provides you with a method of avoiding duplicating functions, or other blocks of code and directives, in a program consisting of several files, or to ensure bits of code that may occur repeatedly in different libraries aren't repeated when the **#include** statements in your program are processed. The mechanism is simply to top and tail the block of code you want to avoid duplicating as follows:

```
#if !defined block1
   #define block1
   /* Block of code you do not */
   /* want to be repeated.     */
#endif
```

If the identifier **block1** hasn't been defined, the block following the **#if** will be processed and **block1** will be defined. The following block of code down to the **#endif** will also be included in your program. Any subsequent occurrence of the same group of statements won't be included, since the identifier **block1** now exists.

The **#define** directive doesn't need to specify a substitution value in this case. For the conditional directives to operate, it's sufficient for **block1** to appear in a **#define** directive. You can now include this block of code anywhere where you think you might need it, with the assurance that it will never be duplicated within a program. The preprocessor directives ensure this can't happen.

> *It's a good idea to get into the habit of protecting code in your own libraries in this fashion. You'll be surprised how easy it is, once you've collected a few libraries of your own functions, to end up duplicating blocks of code accidentally.*

You aren't limited to testing just one value with the preprocessor **#if**. You can use logical operators to test whether multiple identifiers have been defined. For example, the statement

```
#if defined block1 && defined block2
```

will evaluate to true if both **block1** and **block2** have previously been defined, and so the code that follows such a directive won't be included unless this is the case.

A further extension of the flexibility in applying the preprocessor conditional directives is the ability to 'undefine' an identifier you have previously defined. This is achieved using a directive such as:

```
#undef block1
```

Now, if **block1** had previously been defined, after this directive it is no longer defined. These can all be combined to useful effect as an exercise of your ingenuity.

There are alternative, slightly briefer, ways of writing these directives. You can use whichever of the following forms you prefer. The directive

```
#ifdef block
```

is the same as

```
#if defined block
```

While

```
#ifndef block
```

is the same as

```
#if !defined block
```

Directives Testing for Specific Values

You can also use a form of the **#if** directive to test the value of a constant expression. If the value of the constant expression is non-zero, the following statements down to the next **#endif** are executed. If the constant expression evaluates to zero, the following statements down to the next **#endif** are skipped. The general form of the **#if** directive is:

```
#if constant_expression
```

This is most frequently applied to test for a specific value being assigned to an identifier by a previous preprocessor directive. For example, we might have the following sequence of statements:

```
#if CPU == Pentium
    printf("\nPerformance should be good.");
#endif
```

The **printf()** statement will only be included in the program here if the identifier **CPU** has been defined as **Pentium** in a previous **#define** directive.

Multiple Choice Selections

To complement the **#if** directives, we have the **#else** directive. This works in exactly the same way as the **else** statement does, in that it identifies a group of directives to be executed, or statements to be included, if the **#if** condition fails. For example:

```
#if CPU == Pentium
   printf("\nPerformance should be good.");
#else
   printf("\nPerformance may not be so good.");
#endif
```

In this case, one or other of the **printf()** statements will be included depending on whether **CPU** has been defined as **Pentium** or not.

The preprocessor also supports a special form of the **#if** for multiple choice selections, where only one of several choices of statements for inclusion in the program is required. This is the **#elif** directive, which has the general form:

```
#elif constant_expression
```

An example of using this would be:

```
#define US 0
#define UK 1
#define Australia 2
#define Country US
#if Country == US
   #define Greeting "Howdy, stranger."
#elif Country == UK
   #define Greeting "Wotcher, mate."
#elif Country == Australia
   #define Greeting "G'day, sport."
#endif

printf("\n%s", Greeting);
```

With this sequence of directives, the output of the **printf()** statement will depend on the value assigned to the identifier **Country**, in this case **US**.

Standard Preprocessor Macros

There are a variety of standard macros defined by the preprocessor. You'll find them described in your compiler documentation, so here I'll just mention two that are of general interest, and which are available to you.

The macro **__DATE__** provides a string representation of the date when it's invoked in your program, in the form 'Mmm dd yyyy'. Here, Mmm is the month in characters, such as Jan, Feb, and so on. The pair of characters dd is the day in the form of a pair of digits 1 to 31, where single digit days are preceded by a blank. Finally, yyyy is the year as four digits: 1997, for example.

A similar macro, **__TIME__**, provides a string containing the value of the time when it is invoked, in the form 'hh:mm:ss', which is evidently a string containing pairs of digits for hours, minutes and seconds, separated by colons. You could use this to record when your program was last compiled with a statement such as:

```
printf("\nProgram last compiled at %s on %s", __TIME__, __DATE__);
```

Note that both **__DATE__** and **__TIME__** have two underscore characters at the beginning and the end. Once the program containing this statement has been compiled, the values output by the **printf()** statement are fixed until you compile it again. On subsequent executions of the program, the then-current time and date will be output. Don't confuse these macros with the **time()** function we will discuss later in this chapter.

Debugging Methods

Most of your programs will contain errors, or bugs, when you first complete them. Removing such bugs from a program can represent a substantial proportion of the time required to write a program. The larger and more complex the program, the more bugs it's likely to contain, and the more time it will take to get it to run properly. With very large programs, typified by operating systems or complex applications such as word processing systems, or even C program development systems, they can be so complex that all the bugs can never be eliminated. You may already have experience of this in practice with some of the systems on your own computer. Usually, these kinds of residual bugs are relatively minor, with ways in the system to work around them.

Your approach to writing a program can significantly affect how difficult it will be to test. A well-structured program consisting of compact functions, each with a well-defined purpose, is much easier to test than one without these attributes. Finding bugs will also be easier with a program that has extensive comments documenting the operation and purpose of its component functions, and that has well chosen variable and function names. Good use of indentation and statement layout can also make testing and fault finding simpler.

It is beyond the scope of this book to deal with debugging comprehensively, but I will introduce the basic ideas that you need to be aware of. Then, when it comes to it, you will know which direction you are heading in and what tools should be available.

Integrated Debuggers

Many compilers are supplied with extensive debugging tools built into the program development environment. These can be very powerful facilities that can dramatically reduce the time required to get a program working. They typically provide a varied range of aids to testing a program that include:

▶ **Tracing Program Flow**
This capability allows you to execute your program one source statement at a time. It operates by pausing execution after each statement is executed, continuing with the next statement after you press a designated key. Other provisions of the debug environment will usually allow you to display information at ease, pausing to show you what's happening to the data in your program.

▶ **Setting Breakpoints**
Executing a large or complex program one statement at a time can be very tedious. It may even be impossible in a reasonable period of time - all you need is a loop that executes 10,000 times to make it a completely unrealistic proposition. Breakpoints provide an excellent alternative. Here, you define specific, selected statements in your program where a pause should occur to allow you to check what's happening. Execution continues to the next breakpoint when you press a specified key.

▶ **Setting Watches**
This sort of facility will allow you to identify variables that you want to track the value of as execution progresses. The values of the variables that you select are displayed at each breakpoint in your program. If you step through your program statement by statement, you can see whether and to what these variables' values are changed at the points you expect them to be.

▶ **Inspecting Program Elements**
It may also be possible to examine a wide variety of program components. At breakpoints, for example, inspection can show details of a function, such as its return type and its arguments. You can also see details of pointers in terms of their addresses, the addresses they contain, and the data stored at the addresses contained in the pointers. Examining the values of expressions and modifying variables may also be provided for. Modifying variables can help to bypass problem areas to allow other areas to be executed with correct data, even though an earlier part of the program may not be working properly.

The Preprocessor in Debugging

By using conditional preprocessor statements, you can arrange for blocks of code to be included in your program to assist in testing. In spite of the power of the debug facilities included with many C and C++ development systems, the addition of tracing code of your own can still be useful. You have complete control of the formatting of data to be displayed for debugging purposes, and you can even arrange for the kind of output to vary according to conditions or relationships within the program.

Try It Out - Debugging Using the Preprocessor

We can illustrate how this can be done using a slightly modified version of a previous program that calls functions through an array of function pointers:

```
/* Example 13.1 Debugging using the preprocessor */

#include <stdio.h>
#include <stdlib.h>
```

```
#define random(NumValues) ((int)(((long)rand()*(NumValues))
                                          /RAND_MAX+1))
#define test
#define testf

/* Function prototypes */
int sum(int, int);
int product(int, int);
int difference(int, int);

void main()
{
   int i = 0;                        /* Loop counter                      */
   int j = 0;                        /* Index for function selection      */
   int a = 10, b = 5;                /* Starting values                   */
   int result = 0;                   /* Storage for results               */
   int (*pfun[3])(int, int);         /* Function pointer array declaration */

   /* Initialize pointers */
   pfun[0] = sum;
   pfun[1] = product;
   pfun[2] = difference;

   /* Execute each function pointed to */
   for(i = 0 ; i < 10 ; i++)
   {
     j = random(3);                   /* Generate random index 0 to 2 */

     #ifdef test
       printf("\nRandom number = %d", j);
       if( j>2 )
       {
         printf("\nInvalid array index = %d", j);
         break;
       }
     #endif

     result = pfun[j](a, b);        /* Call random function         */
     printf("\nresult = %d", result);
   }
   result = pfun[1](pfun[0](a, b), pfun[2](a, b));
   printf("\n\nThe product of the sum and the difference = %d", result);
}

/* Definition of the function sum() */
int sum(int x, int y)
{
   #ifdef testf
     printf("\nFunction sum() called.");
   #endif
```

```
      return x + y;
   }

   /* Definition of the function product() */
   int product(int x, int y)
   {
      #ifdef testf
        printf("\nFunction product() called.");
      #endif

      return x * y;
   }

   /* Definition of the function difference() */
   int difference(int x, int y)
   {
      #ifdef testf
        printf("\nFunction difference() called.");
      #endif

      return x - y;
   }
```

How It Works

We have a macro defined at the beginning of the program:

```
#define random(NumValues) ((int)(((long)rand()*(NumValues))
                                            /(RAND_MAX+1))
```

This defines the macro **random()** in terms of a function **rand()** declared in **stdlib.h**. The function **rand()** generates random numbers in the range 0 to **RAND_MAX**, which is a constant also defined in **stdlib.h**. Our macro maps values from this range to produce values from 0 to **NumValues-1**. We cast the value returned from **rand()** to **long** to ensure that we can accommodate the result of multiplying it by **NumValues**, and cast the result overall to **int** because that is what we want in our program. It's quite likely that your **stdlib.h** will already contain a macro for **random()**. If so, you will get an error message, as the compiler will not allow two different definitions of the same macro. In this case, just delete the definition from the program.

Look at the loop in **main()**:

```
    for(i = 0 ; i < 10 ; i++)
    {
      j = random(3);                  /* Generate random index 0 to 2  */

      #ifdef test
        printf("\nRandom number = %d", j);
        if( j>2 )
        {
          printf("\nInvalid array index = %d", j);
          break;
```

```
        }
     #endif

     result = pfun[j](a, b);         /* Call random function         */
     printf("\nresult = %d", result);
  }
```

This has been modified compared to the previous version, by indexing the function pointer array using the variable **j**, which has its value generated by the macro call **random(3)**. This will generate a random value between 0 and 2. This makes the example more interesting, since we now don't know beforehand what the sequence of function calls is going to be. It depends on what sequence of random index values is generated.

Within the loop, we have two statements included if **test** is defined. The first displays the value of the index **j**. We might well want to see this value when the program is being tested. The second statement, the **if**, is just a precaution. If, by some means, we obtained a value for **j** that was outside the range of valid indexes for the array **pfun**, who knows what might happen?

If we look at one of the functions that may be called - **product()**, for example:

```
int product(int x, int y)
{
   #ifdef testf
     printf("\nFunction product() called.");
   #endif

   return x * y;
}
```

This has some code included if **testf** is defined. We can therefore control whether the statements in the **#ifdef** block are included here, independently from the block in **main()**. With the program as written above, with both **test** and **testf** defined, we will get trace output for the random index values generated, and a message from each function as it is called. We can therefore follow the sequence of calls in the program exactly.

You can have as many different symbolic constants defined as you wish. As we've seen previously in this chapter, you can combine them into logical expressions using the **#if defined** form of the conditional directive.

Using the assert() Macro

The **assert()** macro is contained in the standard ANSI C library **assert.h**. It enables you to insert tests of arbitrary logical expressions in your program, which cause the program to be terminated with a diagnostic message if a specified logical expression is false.

Try It Out - Demonstrating the assert() Macro

We can demonstrate how this works with a simple example:

```
/* Example 13.2 Demonstrating assertions */
#include <stdio.h>
#include <assert.h>
void main()
{
   int x = 0;
   int y = 5;
   for(x = 0 ; x < 20 ; x++)
   {
     printf("x = %d   y = %d\n", x, y);
     assert(x<y);
   }
}
```

Compiling and executing this code will produce output something like this (the exact wording will depend on your compiler):

```
x = 0    y = 5
x = 1    y = 5
x = 2    y = 5
x = 3    y = 5
x = 4    y = 5
x - 5    y = 5
Assertion failed: x<y, file Ex13_2.c, line 11
```

How It Works

At this point, apart from the **assert()** statement, the program shouldn't need much explanation. It simply prints the values of **x** and **y** in the **for** loop.

The program is terminated by the **assert()** macro, which calls **abort()** as soon as the condition **x<y** becomes false. As you can see from the output, this is when **x** reaches the value 5. The macro displays the output on **stderr**, which is always the display screen. Not only do you get the condition that failed displayed, but you also get the file name and line number in the file where the failure occurred. This is particularly useful with multi-file programs, where the source of the error is pinpointed exactly.

Assertions are often used for critical conditions in a program where, if certain conditions are not met, disaster will surely ensue. You would want to be sure that the program wouldn't continue if such errors arose. Example 13.1 contains exactly this kind of situation, where we are generating index values using a random number generator. With this sort of technique there is always the possibility of a bug somewhere resulting in an invalid index value. If the index is outside the limits of the array **pfun**, the result is pretty much guaranteed to be catastrophic, as we'll be trying to execute a non-existent function at a spurious address. Instead of the **#ifdef** block, we could simply have put:

```
    assert(j <= 2);
```

This is very simple and effective, and provides sufficient information to pin down where the program terminated if an error occurs. You can switch off the assertion mechanism by adding the following definition to a program:

```
#define NDEBUG
```

This will cause all assertions to be ignored. To be effective, though, it must be placed before the **#include** statement for **assert.h**. If you add this **#define** at the beginning of Example 13.2, you'll see that we get output for all the values of **x** from 0 to 19, and no diagnostic message.

Additional Library Functions

The library functions are basic to the power of the C language. While we've covered quite a range of standard library functions so far, it's impossible within the scope of this book to discuss all the standard libraries. However, we can introduce a few more of the most commonly used functions we haven't dealt with in detail up to now.

The Date and Time Function Library

Because time is an important parameter to measure, C includes a standard library of functions in **time.h,** which deal with time and the date. They provide output in various forms from the hardware timer in your PC. The simplest function has the prototype:

```
clock_t clock(void);
```

This function returns the processor time (not the elapsed time) used by the program since execution began, as a value of type **clock_t**. The type **clock_t** is defined in **time.h**, and is equivalent to **long**. The value is measured in clock ticks. To convert the value returned by **clock()** to seconds, you divide it by the constant **CLOCKS_PER_SEC**, which is also defined in **time.h**. The function returns -1 if an error occurs.

The function **time()** returns the calendar time as a value of type **time_t**. The current calendar time is the time in seconds since a fixed time and date - typically 00:00:00 GMT on 1st January 1970. The prototype of the function time is:

```
time_t time(time_t*);
```

If the argument is not **NULL**, the current calendar time is also stored in the location pointed to by the pointer to **time_t** argument. The type **time_t** is defined in the header file, and is equivalent to **long**. To calculate elapsed time in seconds between two successive **time_t** values returned by **time()**, you can use the function **difftime()**, which has the prototype:

```
double difftime(time_t T2, time_t T1);
```

The function will return the value **T2 - T1** expressed in seconds as a value of type **double**.

Try It Out - Using Time Functions

We could define a function to log the elapsed time and processor time used between successive calls, by using functions from **time.h** as follows:

```
/* Example 13.3 Test our timer function */
#include <stdio.h>
#include <time.h>
```

```
void main()
{
   long count = 100000000L,                 /* Number of loop iterations */
   i = 0;                                    /* Loop counter              */
   double x = 0.0;

   clock_t now = 0;                          /* Holds clock value         */
   time_t calendar = 0;                      /* Holds calendar time       */

   now = clock();                            /* Get current clock time    */
   calendar = time(NULL);                    /* Get current calendar time */
   printf("\nInitial clock time = %ld Initial calendar time = %ld\n",
                                                      now, calendar);

   for(i = 0 ; i<count ; i++)
     x = 3.4567 * 4.5678;                    /* Multiply 100m times       */

   printf("\nCPU time for one hundred million multiplies is %lf\n",
                                (double)(clock()- now)/CLOCKS_PER_SEC );

   printf("\nFinal clock time = %ld Final calendar time = %ld\n",
                                             clock(), time(NULL));

   printf("\nElapsed calendar time to execute the program is %lf\n",
                                    difftime(time(NULL), calendar));
}
```

How It Works

> *Depending on the speed of your machine, you may want to adjust the number of iterations in the loop to reduce the time taken to execute this program.*

This program serves to illustrate the use of the functions **clock()**, **time()**, and **difftime()**. I should warn you that the timing of the processor usage for the multiply operations won't be very precise. There are instructions other than just multiply involved in the loop and the computation, and the resolution of the timing mechanism isn't very accurate. Similarly, the elapsed time may not be very precise either. The function **time()** returns the current time in seconds, so we won't get values less than a second. It's possible to get more accurate results, but this is outside the scope of this book.

We record and display the initial values for the clock time and the calendar time with the statements:

```
   now = clock();                            /* Get current clock time    */
   calendar = time(NULL);                    /* Get current calendar time */
   printf("\nInitial clock time = %ld Initial calendar time = %ld\n",
                                                      now, calendar);
```

We then have a loop to execute the same multiply operation **count** times:

```
   for(i = 0 ; i<count ; i++)
     x = 3.4567 * 4.5678;                    /* Multiply 100m times       */
```

489

Finally, we output the values returned by **clock()** and **time()**, and calculate the clock and calendar time intervals:

```
printf("\nCPU time for one hundred million multiplies is %lf\n",
       (double)(clock()- now)/CLOCKS_PER_SEC );

printf("\nFinal clock time = %ld Final calendar time = %ld\n",
       clock(), time(NULL));

printf("\nElapsed calendar time to execute the program is %lf\n",
       difftime(time(NULL), calendar));
```

Generally, you would use **clock()** to calculate time intervals during execution of a program, as this produces a value with 1 millisecond precision.

Getting the Date

Knowing the time elapsed in seconds since a date around a quarter of a century ago is interesting, but it's often more convenient to get today's date. We can do this with the function **ctime()**, which has the prototype:

```
char* ctime(time_t*);
```

The function accepts a pointer to a **time_t** value as an argument, and returns a pointer to a 26 character string containing the day, the date, the time and the year, which is terminated by a newline and a **'\0'**. A typical string returned might be:

```
"Wed Jul 30 10:45:56 1997\n\0"
```

The argument to the **ctime()** function is the address of a value supplied by the **time()** function.

You can also get at the various components of the time and date using the library function **localtime()**. This function has the prototype:

```
struct tm* localtime(time_t*);
```

This function accepts a pointer to a **time_t** value and returns a pointer to a structure of type **tm**, which is defined in the header file. All the members of the structure are integers:

Member	Description
tm_sec	Seconds on 24 hour clock
tm_min	Minutes on 24 hour clock
tm_hour	Hours on 24 hour clock
tm_mday	Day of the month (1 to 31)
tm_mon	Month (0 to 11)
tm_year	Year (Current year minus 1900)
tm_wday	Weekday (Sunday is 0, to Saturday is 6)

Member	Description
`tm_yday`	Day of year (0 to 365)
`tm_isdst`	Daylight Saving flag (0 for daylight saving time)

This is a **static** structure, so it's overwritten with each call to the function. If you want to keep any of the member values, you need to copy them elsewhere before the next call to **localtime()**. You could create your own **tm** structure and save the whole lot if you really needed to.

Try It Out - Getting the Date

It's very easy to pick out the members you want from the structure of type **tm** returned from the function **localtime()**. We can demonstrate this with the following example:

```
/* Example 13.4        Getting date data with ease */
#include <stdio.h>
#include <time.h>
void main()
{
   char* Day[7] = {
                   "Sunday"   , "Monday", "Tuesday", "Wednesday",
                   "Thursday", "Friday", "Saturday"
                  };
   char* Month[12] = {
                    "January",   "February", "March",     "April",
                    "May",       "June",     "July",      "August",
                    "September", "October",  "November", "December"
                     };
   char* Suffix[4] = { "st", "nd", "rd", "th" };

   int i = 3;                           /* Day suffix index           */
   struct tm *OurT = NULL;              /* Pointer for the time structure */
   time_t Tval = 0;                     /* Calendar time              */

   Tval = time(NULL);                   /* Get calendar time          */
   OurT = localtime(&Tval);             /* Generate time structure    */

   switch( OurT->tm_mday )
   {
     case 1: case 21: case 31:
       i = 0;                           /* Select "st" */
       break;
     case 2: case 22:
       i = 1;                           /* Select "nd" */
       break;
     case 3: case 23:
       i = 2;                           /* Select "rd" */
       break;
```

```
      default:
        i = 3;                              /* Select "th" */
        break;
    }

    printf("\nToday is %s the %d%s %s %d", Day[OurT->tm_wday],
                OurT->tm_mday, Suffix[i], Month[OurT->tm_mon],
                                     1900 + OurT->tm_year);
    printf("\nThe time is %d : %d : %d\n",
                  OurT->tm_hour, OurT->tm_min, OurT->tm_sec );
  }
```

How It Works

In this example, the first declarations in **main()** are:

```
    char* Day[7] = {
                      "Sunday"   , "Monday", "Tuesday", "Wednesday",
                      "Thursday", "Friday", "Saturday"
                  };
    char* Month[12] = {
                      "January",    "February", "March",     "April",
                      "May",        "June",     "July",      "August",
                      "September", "October",  "November", "December"
                  };
    char* Suffix[4] = { "st", "nd", "rd", "th" };
```

These each define an array of pointers to **char**. The first holds the days of the week, the second contains the months in the year, and the third holds the suffixes to numerical values for the day in the month when representing dates. We could have left out the array dimensions and the compiler would have computed them for us, but in this case we are reasonably confident about these numbers, so this is an instance where putting them in helps to avoid an error.

We also declare a structure variable in the declaration:

```
    struct tm *OurT = NULL;              /* Pointer for the time structure */
```

This provides space to store the pointer to the structure returned by the function **localtime()**. We first obtain the current time in **Tval** using the function **time()**. We then use this to generate the values of the members of the structure returned by the function **localtime()**. If we wanted to keep the data in the structure, we would need to copy it before calling the **localtime()** function again, as it would be overwritten. Once we have the structure from **localtime()**, we execute the **switch**:

```
    switch( OurT->tm_mday )
    {
      case 1: case 21: case 31:
        i = 0;                              /* Select "st" */
        break;
      case 2: case 22:
        i = 1;                              /* Select "nd" */
        break;
```

```
       case 3: case 23:
         i = 2;                              /* Select "rd" */
         break;
       default:
         i = 3;                              /* Select "th" */
         break;
   }
```

The sole purpose of this is to select what to append to the date value. Based on the member **tm_mday**, the **switch** selects an index to the array **Suffix[]** for use when outputting the date.

The day, the date, and the time are displayed, with the day and month strings being obtained by indexing the appropriate array with the corresponding structure member value. The addition of 1900 to the value of the member **tm_year** is because this value is measured relative to the year 1900.

Variable Length Argument Lists

It can't have escaped your notice that some functions in the standard libraries accept a variable number of arguments. The functions **printf()** and **scanf()** are obvious examples. You may come up with a need to do this yourself from time to time, so the standard library **stdarg.h** provides you with routines to write some of your own.

The immediately obvious problem with writing a function with a variable number of parameters is how to specify its prototype. Suppose we are going to produce a function to calculate the average of two or more values of type **double**. Clearly, calculating the average of less than two values wouldn't make much sense. The prototype would be written:

```
double average( double v1, double v2, ...);
```

The **ellipsis** (that's the fancy name for the three periods after the second parameter type) indicates that a variable number of arguments may follow the first two fixed arguments. You must have at least one fixed argument. The remaining specifications are as you would usually find with a function prototype. The first two arguments are of type **double**, and it returns a **double** result.

The problem with variable argument lists that hits you between the eyes next is how you reference them when writing the function. Since you don't know how many there are, you can't give them names. The only possibility is an indirect method through routines supplied by the library **stdarg.h**. The library provides you with three routines that are usually implemented as macros, but they look and operate like functions, so we'll discuss them as though they were. You need to use all three when implementing your own function with a variable number of arguments.

The macros are called **va_start()**, **va_arg()**, and **va_end()**, and the first of them has the form:

```
   void va_start(va_list parg, last_fixed_arg);
```

The name of the function is obtained from variable argument start. This function accepts two arguments: a pointer **parg** of type **va_list**, and the last fixed argument specified for the function we are writing. So, using our function **average()** as an illustration, we can start to write the function as:

```
/* Function to calculate the average of a variable number of arguments */
double average( double v1, double v2, ...)
{
   va_list parg;                      /* Pointer for variable argument list */
   va_start(parg, v2);                /* Initialize argument pointer         */
}
```

We have first declared the variable **parg** of type **va_list.** We then call **va_start()** with this as the first argument, and specify our last fixed parameter **v2** as the second argument. The effect of the call to **va_start()** is to set the variable **parg** to point to the first variable argument.

We now need to know how to access the values of the variable arguments, so let's see how this is done by completing the function **average()**:

```
/* Function to calculate the average of a variable number of arguments */
double average( double v1, double v2,...)
{
   va_list parg;                      /* Pointer for variable argument list */
   double sum = v1+v2;                /* Accumulate sum of the arguments     */
   double value = 0;                  /* Argument value                      */
   int count = 2;                     /* Count of number of arguments        */

   va_start(parg,v2);                 /* Initialize argument pointer         */

   while((value = va_arg(parg, double)) != 0.0)
   {
     sum += value;
     count++;
   }
   va_end(parg);                      /* End variable argument process       */
   return sum/count;
}
```

We can work our way through this step by step. After declaring **parg**, we declare the variable **sum** as **double**, and as being initialized with the sum of the first two fixed arguments, **v1** and **v2**. We will accumulate the sum of all the argument values in **sum**. The next variable, **value**, declared as **double**, will be used to store the values of the variable arguments as we obtain them one by one. We then declare a counter, **count**, for the total number of arguments, and initialize this with the value 2 since we know we have at least that many values from the fixed arguments. After calling **va_start()** to initialize **parg**, most of the action takes place within the **while** loop. Look at the loop condition:

```
while((value = va_arg(parg, double)) != 0.0)
```

The loop condition calls **va_arg()**, another routine from **stdarg.h**. The first argument to **va_arg()** is the variable **parg**, which we initialized through the call to **va_start()**. The second argument is a specification of the type of the argument we expect to find. The function **va_arg()** returns the value of the current argument specified by **parg**, and this is stored in **value**. It also updates the pointer **parg** to point to the next argument in the list, based on the type you specified in the call. It's essential to have some means of determining the types of the variable arguments. If you don't specify the correct type, you won't be able to obtain the next argument correctly. In our case, the function is written assuming they are all **double**. Another assumption we are making is that all the arguments will be non-zero except for the last. This is reflected in the condition for continuing the loop being that **value** is not equal to zero. Within the loop we have familiar statements for accumulating the sum in **sum**, and for incrementing **count**.

When an argument value obtained is zero, the loop ends and we execute the statement:

```
    va_end(parg);                        /* End variable argument process    */
```

The call to **va_end()** is essential to tidy up loose ends that are left around by the process. If you omit this call, your program may not work properly. Once the tidying up is complete, we can return the required result with the statement:

```
    return sum/count;
```

Try It Out - Using Variable Argument Lists

Having written the function **average()**, it would be a good idea to exercise it in a little program to make sure it works:

```
/* Example 13.5 Calculating an average using variable argument lists */
#include <stdio.h>
#include <stdarg.h>

double average(double v1 , double v2, ...);        /* Function prototype */

void main()
{
   double Val1 = 10.5, Val2 = 2.5;
   int num1 = 6, num2 = 5;
   long num3 = 12, num4 = 20;

   printf("\n Average = %lf", average(Val1, 3.5, Val2, 4.5, 0.0));
   printf("\n Average = %lf", average(1.0, 2.0, 0.0));
   printf("\n Average = %lf\n", average((double)num2, Val2,
                     (double)num1, (double)num4, (double)num3, 0.0));
}

/* Function to calculate the average of a variable number of arguments */
double average( double v1, double v2,...)
{
   va_list parg;                    /* Pointer for variable argument list */
   double sum = v1+v2;              /* Accumulate sum of the arguments     */
   double value = 0;                /* Argument value                      */
   int count = 2;                   /* Count of number of arguments        */

   va_start(parg,v2);               /* Initialize argument pointer         */

   while((value = va_arg(parg, double)) != 0.0)
```

```
   {
     sum += value;
     count++;
   }
   va_end(parg);                  /* End variable argument process    */
   return sum/count;
 }
```

If you compile and run this, you should get the output:

```
Average = 5.250000
Average = 1.500000
Average = 9.100000
```

How It Works

This output is as a result of three calls to **average()** with different numbers of arguments. Remember, we need to ensure that we cast our variable arguments to the type **double**, assumed by the function **average()**.

You might be wondering how **printf()** manages to handle a mix of types. Well, remember it has a control string with format specifiers. This supplies the information necessary to determine the types of the arguments. We have seen how things don't work out right if we specify the wrong format for the type of variable we want to output.

Basic Rules for Variable Length Argument Lists

We could summarize the basic rules and requirements for writing functions to be called with a variable number of arguments:

> There needs to be at least one fixed argument in a function accepting a variable number of arguments.

> You must call **va_start()** to initialize the value of the variable argument list pointer in your function. This pointer needs to be declared as being of type **va_list**.

> There needs to be a mechanism to determine the type of each argument. Either there can be a default type assumed, or there can be a parameter that allows the argument type to be determined. For example, in our function **average()**, we could have an extra fixed argument which would have the value 0 if the variable arguments were **double**, and 1 if they were **long**. If the argument type specified in the call to **va_arg()** isn't correct for the argument value specified when your function is called, your function won't work properly.

> You have to arrange for there to be some way to determine when the list of arguments is exhausted. For example, the last argument in the variable argument list could have a fixed value that can be detected because it's different from all the others, or a fixed argument could contain a count of the number of arguments in total, or in the variable part of the argument list.

▶ There are restrictions on the types of variable arguments you are allowed to use. You can't use **char**, **unsigned char**, or **float** types with **va_arg()**. You should use **int** instead of **char** types and **double** rather than **float**. Check the documentation for your compiler for full details.

▶ You must call **va_end()** before you exit a function with a variable number of arguments. If you fail to do so, the function won't work properly.

Note that the process described for handling variable argument lists is for ANSI C. If you're using a compiler that doesn't conform to the standard exactly, you need to check your compiler's documentation for details of how to achieve this functionality.

You could try ringing the changes on Example 13.3 to understand this process better. Put some output in the function **average()**, and see what happens if you change a few things. For example, you could display **value** and **count** in the loop. You could then modify **main()** to supply an argument that isn't **double**, or to introduce a function call where the last argument is not zero.

Summary

You should now be able to count yourself as a fully-fledged C programmer. C program code will be meat and drink to you by this stage.

The header files that came with your compiler are an excellent source of examples of coding preprocessor statements, and you can view them with any text editor. Virtually all of the capabilities of the preprocessor are used in the libraries, and you'll find lots of C source code there too. It's also useful to familiarize yourself with the contents of the libraries, as many things not necessarily described in the library documentation will nevertheless be found here. If you're not sure what the type **clock_t** is, for example, just look in the library **time.h**, where you will find the definition.

To get better at programming, there is no alternative to practice. Despite the old saying, practice never *quite* makes perfect in the world of programming, and there are always ways in which you can improve. Still, whenever you get a new piece of code to work as it should, it always generates a thrill and a feeling of satisfaction. Enjoy your programming!

Computer Arithmetic

In this book, I've deliberately kept any discussion of arithmetic to a minimum. However, it is important, so we're going to quickly go over the subject in this appendix. If you feel confident at math then this chapter won't keep you long. If you find the math parts tough, on the other hand, then this section should show you how easy it really is.

Binary Numbers

First, let's consider what we mean when we write a common everyday number such as 321, or 667. Well, obviously, what we mean is three hundred and twenty one, and six hundred and sixty seven. Put more precisely we mean:

```
321 is      3 x 10 x 10   +   2 x 10   +   1
667 is      6 x 10 x 10   +   6 x 10   +   7
```

Because it's built around powers of ten we call it the decimal system (derived from the Latin *decimalis* meaning *of tithes*, which was a tax of 10% - quite good really).

Representing numbers in this way is very handy for people with ten fingers and toes, or ten of any kind of appendage for that matter. However, your PC is quite unhandy, being built mainly of switches that are either on or off - which is OK for counting up to two, but not spectacular for counting to ten. For this reason your computer represents numbers to base 2 rather than base 10. This is called the **binary** system of counting. Digits can only be 0 or 1, ideal when you only have on/off switches to represent them. In an exact analogy to our usual base 10 counting, the binary number 1101 is therefore:

```
1 x 2 x 2 x 2   +   1 x 2 x 2   +   0 x 2   +   1
```

which amounts to 13 in the decimal system. In the following figure, you can see the decimal equivalents of 8 bit binary numbers illustrated.

Binary	Decimal	Binary	Decimal
0000 0000	0	1000 0000	128
0000 0001	1	1000 0001	129
0000 0010	2	1000 0010	130
...	...	...	...
0001 0000	16	1001 0000	144
0001 0001	17	1001 0001	145
...	...	...	...
0111 1100	124	1111 1100	252
0111 1101	125	1111 1101	253
0111 1110	126	1111 1110	254
0111 1111	127	1111 1111	255

Note that using the first 7 bits we can represent numbers from 0 to 127, which is a total of 2^7 numbers, and using all 8 bits, we get 256, or 2^8 numbers. In general, if we have n bits then we can represent 2^n integers, from 0 to 2^n-1.

Hexadecimal Numbers

When we get to larger binary numbers, for example:

1111 0101 1011 1001 1110 0001

the notation starts to be a little cumbersome, particularly when you consider that if you apply the same method to work out what this is in decimal, it's only 16,103,905. You can sit more angels on a pinhead than that. Well, as it happens, we have an excellent alternative.

Arithmetic to base 16 is a very convenient option. Each digit can have values from 0 to 15 (the digits from 10 to 15 being represented by letters A to F, as shown in the next figure) and values from 0 to 15 correspond quite nicely with the range of values that four binary digits can represent.

Hexadecimal	Decimal	Binary
0	0	0000
1	1	0001
2	2	0010
...	...	...
9	9	1001
A	10	1010
B	11	1011
C	12	1100
D	13	1101
E	14	1110
F	15	1111

We can therefore represent the binary number above as a hexadecimal number, just by taking groups of four binary digits starting from the right, and writing the equivalent base 16 (also called hexadecimal) digit for each group. The binary number:

1111 0101 1011 1001 1110 0001

will therefore come out as:

F5B9E1

We have six hexadecimal digits corresponding to the six groups of four binary digits. Just to show it all works out, with no cheating, we can convert this number directly from hexadecimal to decimal by again using the analogy with the meaning of a decimal number, as follows:

F5B9E1 is $15 \times 16 \times 16 \times 16 \times 16 \times 16$ + $5 \times 16 \times 16 \times 16 \times 16$ +
$11 \times 16 \times 16 \times 16$ + $9 \times 16 \times 16$ + 14×16 +   1

This in turn turns out to be:

15,728,640   +   327,680   +   45,056   +   2304   +   224   +   1

which fortunately totals to the same number that we got when we converted the equivalent binary number to a decimal value.

Negative Binary Numbers

There is another aspect to binary arithmetic that you need to understand: negative numbers. So far, we've assumed everything is positive - the optimist's view if you will: our glass is still half full. But we can't avoid the negative side of life - the pessimist's perspective that our glass is already half empty - forever. How do we indicate a negative number? Well, we only have binary digits at our disposal and, indeed, they do contain the solution.

For numbers that we want to have the possibility of taking a negative value (referred to as **signed** numbers) we must first decide on a fixed length (in other words, the number of binary digits) and then designate the leftmost binary digit as a sign bit. We have to fix the length in order to avoid any confusion about which bit is the sign bit.

Of course, we can have some numbers with 8 bits, and some with 16 bits, or whatever, as long as we know what the length is in each case. If the sign bit is 0 the number is positive, and if it is 1 it is negative. This would seem to solve our problem, but not quite. If we add -8 in binary to +12, we would really like to get the answer +4. If we do that simplistically, by just putting the sign bit of the positive value to 1 (to make it negative) and then doing the arithmetic with conventional carries, it doesn't quite work:

        12 in binary is   0000 1100
        -8 in binary, we suppose, is 1000 1000

since +8 is 0000 1000. If we now add these together, we get:

1001 0100

This seems to be -20, which is not what we wanted at all. It's definitely not +4, which we know is 0000 0100. Ah, I hear you say, you can't treat a sign just like another digit. But that's just what we do have to do when dealing with computers because, dumb things that they are, they have trouble coping with anything else. So we really need a different representation for negative numbers. Well, we could try subtracting +12 from +4, since the result should be -8:

+4 is	0000 0100
take away +12	0000 1100
and we get	1111 1000

For each digit, from the fourth from the right onwards, we had to borrow 1 to do the sum; this is analogous to our usual decimal method for subtraction. This, supposedly, is -8, and even though it doesn't look like it - it is. Just try adding it to +12 or +15 in binary and you will see that it works. So what is it? It turns out that the answer is what is called the **two's complement** representation of negative binary numbers.

Now, here, I'm going to demand a little faith on your part and avoid getting into explanations of why it works. I'll just show you how the 2's complement form of a negative number can be constructed from a positive value; you can prove for yourself that it really works. Let's return to our previous example, where we needed the 2's complement representation of -8. We start with +8 in binary:

0000 1000

We now flip each digit - if it is one make it zero, and vice versa:

1111 0111

This is called the 1's complement form, and if we now add 1 to this we will get the 2's complement form:

	1111 0111
Add one to this	0000 0001
and we get:	1111 1000

Now this looks pretty similar to our representation of -8 we got from subtracting +12 from +4. So just to be sure, let's try the original sum of adding -8 to +12:

+12 is	0000 1100
Our version of -8 is	1111 1000
and we get:	0000 0100

So the answer is 4 - magic. It works! The carry propagates through all the left most 1's setting them back to zero. One fell off the end, but we shouldn't worry about that. It's probably the one we borrowed from off the end in the subtraction sum we did to get -8. In fact, what's happening is that we are making the assumption that the sign bit, 1 or 0, repeats forever to the left. Try a few examples of your own: you'll find it always works quite automatically. The really great thing is, it makes arithmetic very easy (and fast) for your computer.

Floating Point Numbers

We often have to deal with very large numbers: the number of protons in the universe, for example, which needs around 79 decimal digits. Clearly there are lots of situations where we need more than the 10 decimal digits we get from a 4 byte binary number. Equally, there are lots of very small numbers. For example, the amount of time in minutes that it takes the typical car salesman to accept your offer on his 1982 Ford LTD (and only covered 380,000 miles...). A mechanism for handling both these kinds of numbers is - as you will have guessed - **floating point** numbers.

A floating point representation of a number is a decimal point followed by a fixed number of digits, multiplied by a power of 10 to get the number you want. It's easier to demonstrate than explain, so let's take some examples. The number 365 in normal decimal notation would be written in floating point form as:

.365E03

where the E stands for "exponent" and is the power of ten that the .365 (the mantissa) is multiplied by to get the required value. That is:

.365 x 10 x 10 x 10

which is clearly 365.

Now we can look at a small number:

.365E-04

This is evaluated as $.365 \times 10^{-4}$, which is .0000365 - exactly the time in minutes required by the car salesman to accept your cash.

Suppose we have a large number, such as 2,134,311,179. How does this look as a floating point number? Well, it looks like this:

.2134311E10

It's not quite the same. We've lost three low order digits and we've approximated our original value as 2,134,311,000. This is a small price to pay for being able to handle such a vast range of numbers, typically from 10^{-38} to 10^{+38} either positive or negative, as well having an extended representation which goes from a minute 10^{-308} to a mighty 10^{+308}. These are called floating point numbers for the fairly obvious reason that the decimal point "floats" - depending on the exponent value.

Aside from the fixed precision limitation in terms of accuracy, there is another aspect you may need to be conscious of with floating point numbers. You need to take great care when adding or subtracting numbers of significantly different magnitudes. A simple example will demonstrate the kind of problem. We can first consider adding .365E-3 to .365E+7. We can write this as a decimal sum:

.000365 + 3,650,000

This produces the result:

3,650,000.000365

which, when converted back to floating point, becomes:

.3650000E+7

So we might as well not have bothered. The problem lies directly with the fact that we only carry 7 digits precision. The 7 digits of the larger number are not affected by any of the digits of the smaller number, because they are all further to the left. Funnily enough, you must also take care when the numbers are very nearly equal. If you compute the difference between such numbers then you may end up with a result which only has one or two digits precision. It's quite easy, in such circumstances, to end up computing with numbers that are total garbage.

ASCII Character Code Definition

The first 32 ASCII characters provide control functions. Many of these have not been referenced in this book, but are included here for completeness. In the following table, only the first 128 characters have been included. The remaining 128 characters include further special symbols and letters for national character sets.

ASCII stands for American Standard Code for Information Interchange.

Decimal	Hexadecimal	Character	Control
000	00	null	NUL
001	01	☺	SOH
002	02	●	STX
003	03	♥	ETX
004	04	♦	EOT
005	05	♣	ENQ
006	06	♠	ACK
007	07	•	BEL (Audible bell)
008	08		Backspace
009	09		HT (Horizontal tab)
010	0A		LF (Line feed)
011	0B		VT (Vertical tab)
012	0C		FF (Form feed)
013	0D		CR (Carriage return)
014	0E		SO
015	0F	¤	SI
016	10		DLE
017	11		DC1
018	12		DC2
019	13		DC3

Decimal	Hexadecimal	Character	Control
020	14		DC4
021	15		NAK
022	16		SYN
023	17		ETB
024	18		CAN
025	19		EM
026	1A	→	SUB
027	1B	←	ESC (Escape)
028	1C	∟	FS
029	1D		GS
030	1E		RS
031	1F		US
032	20		space
033	21	!	
034	22	"	
035	23	#	
036	24	$	
037	25	%	
038	26	&	
039	27	'	
040	28	(	
041	29	)	
042	2A	*	
043	2B	+	
044	2C	,	
045	2D	-	
046	2E	.	
047	2F	/	
048	30	0	
049	31	1	
050	32	2	
051	33	3	
052	34	4	
053	35	5	
054	36	6	
055	37	7	
056	38	8	

Decimal	Hexadecimal	Character	Control
057	39	9	
058	3A	:	
059	3B	;	
060	3C	<	
061	3D	=	
062	3E	>	
063	3F	?	
064	40	@	
065	41	A	
066	42	B	
067	43	C	
068	44	D	
069	45	E	
070	46	F	
071	47	G	
072	48	H	
073	49	I	
074	4A	J	
075	4B	K	
076	4C	L	
077	4D	M	
078	4E	N	
079	4F	O	
080	50	P	
081	51	Q	
082	52	R	
083	53	S	
084	54	T	
085	55	U	
086	56	V	
087	57	W	
088	58	X	
089	59	Y	
090	5A	Z	
091	5B	[	
092	5C	\	
093	5D	]	

Decimal	Hexadecimal	Character	Control
094	5E	^	
095	5F	_	
096	60	'	
097	61	a	
098	62	b	
099	63	c	
100	64	d	
101	65	e	
102	66	f	
103	67	g	
104	68	h	
105	69	i	
106	6A	j	
107	6B	k	
108	6C	l	
109	6D	m	
110	6E	n	
111	6F	o	
112	70	p	
113	71	q	
114	72	r	
115	73	s	
116	74	t	
117	75	u	
118	76	v	
119	77	w	
120	78	x	
121	79	y	
122	7A	z	
123	7B	{	
124	7C			
125	7D	}	
126	7E	~	
127	7F	delete	

Reserved Words in C

The words in the following list are **keywords** in C, so you must not use them for other purposes - such as variable names or function names.

auto	int
break	long
case	register
char	return
const	short
continue	signed
default	sizeof
do	static
double	struct
else	switch
enum	typedef
extern	union
float	unsigned
for	void
goto	volatile
if	while

Beginning

C

Beginning Java

Author: Ivor Horton
ISBN: 1861000278
Price: $36.00 C$50.40 £32.99
Available May 97

If you've enjoyed this book, you'll get a lot from Ivor's new book, Beginning Java.

Beginning Java teaches Java 1.1 from scratch, taking in all the fundamental features of the Java language, along with practical applications of Java's extensive class libraries. While it assumes some little familiarity with general programming concepts, Ivor takes time to cover the basics of the language in depth. He assumes no knowledge of object-oriented programming.

Ivor first introduces the essential bits of Java without which no program will run. Then he covers how Java handles data, and the syntax it uses to make decisions and control program flow. The essentials of object-oriented programming with Java are covered, and these concepts are reinforced throughout the book. Chapters on exceptions, threads and I/O follow, before Ivor turns to Java's graphics support and applet ability. Finally the book looks at JDBC and RMI, two additions to the Java 1.1 language which allow Java programs to communicate with databases and other Java programs.

Beginning Visual C++ 5

Author: Ivor Horton   ISBN: 1861000081
Price: $39.95 C$55.95 £36.99

Visual Basic is a great tool for generating applications quickly and easily, but if you really want to create fast, tight programs using the latest technologies, Visual C++ is the only way to go.

Ivor Horton's Beginning Visual C++ 5 is for anyone who wants to learn C++ and Windows programming with Visual C++ 5 and MFC, and the combination of the programming discipline you've learned from this book and Ivor's relaxed and informal teaching style will make it even easier for you to succeed in taming structured programming and writing real Windows applications.

The book begins with a fast-paced but comprehensive tutorial to the C++ language. You'll then go on to learn about object orientation with C++ and how this relates to Windows programming, culminating with the design and implementation of a sizable class-based C++ application. The next part of the book walks you through creating Windows applications using MFC, including sections on output to the screen and printer, how to program menus, toolbars and dialogs, and how to respond to a user's actions. The final few chapters comprise an introduction COM and examples of how to create ActiveX controls using both MFC and the Active Template Library (ATL).

Beginning Linux Programming

Authors: Neil Matthew, Richard Stones
ISBN: 187441680
Price: $36.95 C$51.95 £33.99

The book is unique in that it teaches UNIX programming in a simple and structured way, using Linux and its associated and freely available development tools as the main platform. Assuming familiarity with the UNIX environment and a basic knowledge of C, the book teaches you how to put together UNIX applications that make the most of your time, your OS and your machine's capabilities.

Having introduced the programming environment and basic tools, the authors turn their attention initially on shell programming. The chapters then concentrate on programming UNIX with C, showing you how to work with files, access the UNIX environment, input and output data using terminals and curses, and manage data. After another round with development and debugging tools, the book discusses processes and signals, pipes and other IPC mechanisms, culminating with a chapter on sockets. Programming the X-Window system is introduced with Tcl/Tk and Java. Finally, the book covers programming for the Internet using HTML and CGI.

The book aims to discuss UNIX programming as described in the relevant POSIX and X/Open specifications, so the code is tested with that in mind. All the source code from the book is available under the terms of the Gnu Public License from the Wrox web site.

Beginning Visual Basic 5

Author: Peter Wright
ISBN: 1861000081
Price: $29.95 C$41.95 £27.49

The third edition of the best selling Beginner's Guide to Visual Basic is the most comprehensive guide for the complete beginner to Visual Basic 5. Peter Wright's unique style and humour have long been a favourite with beginners and, because the book has just the one author, you can be sure that the text has a consistent voice and flow.

As with all Wrox Beginning guides, every topic is illustrated with a Try It Out, where each new concept is accompanied by a focused example and explanatory text. This way, you get to create an example program that demonstrates some theory, and then you get to examine the code behind it in detail.

Peter starts with a lightning tour of the Visual Basic 5 environment, before moving on to the creation of a Visual Basic 5 program. Critical concepts such as events, properties and methods are given the attention they deserve. You'll find yourself starting with basics, such as "What is a control and how does VB5 use them?", but you'll quickly be able to move on to more complex topics such as graphics, object-oriented programming, control creation and creating databases. By the end of the book, you'll be able to build your own application from scratch, with very impressive results.

wrox

Register Beginning C and sign up for a free subscription to The Developer's Journal.

A bi-monthly magazine for software developers, The Wrox Press Developer's Journal features in-depth articles, news and help for everyone in the software development industry. Each issue includes extracts from our latest titles and is crammed full of practical insights into coding techniques, tricks, and research.

Fill in and return the card below to receive a free subscription to the Wrox Press Developer's Journal.

Beginning C Registration Card

Name _____

Address _____

_____

_____

City_____ State/Region _____

Country_____ Postcode/Zip _____

E-mail _____

Occupation _____

How did you hear about this book?_____

☐ Book review (name) _____

☐ Advertisement (name) _____

☐ Recommendation _____

☐ Catalog_____

☐ Other _____

Where did you buy this book?_____

☐ Bookstore (name)_____ City _____

☐ Computer Store (name)_____

☐ Mail Order_____

☐ Other_____

What influenced you in the purchase of this book?

☐ Cover Design

☐ Contents

☐ Other (please specify) _____

How did you rate the overall contents of this book?

☐ Excellent   ☐ Good

☐ Average   ☐ Poor

What did you find most useful about this book? _____

What did you find least useful about this book? _____

Please add any additional comments. _____

What other subjects will you buy a computer book on soon? _____

What is the best computer book you have used this year? _____

Note: This information will only be used to keep you updated about new Wrox Press titles and will not be used for any other purpose or passed to any other third party.

wrox

NB. If you post the bounce back card below in the UK, please send it to:

Wrox Press Ltd., Arden House, 1102 Warwick Road,
Acocks Green, Birmingham. B27 6BH. UK.

Computer Book Publishers